Protestantism and Capitalism

SOCIOLOGY AND ECONOMICS
Controversy and Integration

An Aldine de Gruyter Series of Texts and Monographs

SERIES EDITORS

Paula England, *Northwestern University*
George Farkas, *Pennsylvania State University*
Kevin Lang, *Boston University*

Values in the Marketplace:
The American Stock Market under Federal Securities Law
James Burk

Equal Employment Opportunity: Labor Market Discrimination and Public Policy
Paul Burstein (ed.)

Legacies of Change: Transformations of Postcommunist Economies
John L. Campbell and Ove K. Pedersen (eds.)

Protestantism and Capitalism: The Mechanisms of Influence
Jere Cohen

Industries, Firms, and Jobs: Sociological and Economic Approaches
George Farkas and Paula England (eds.)

Beyond the Marketplace: Rethinking Economy and Society
Roger Friedland and A.F. Robertson (eds.)

Towards a Structure of Indifference: The Social Origins of Maternal Custody
Debra Friedman

The Origin of Values
Michael Hechter, Lynn Nadel, and Richard E. Michod (eds.)

Social Institutions: Their Emergence, Maintenance, and Effects
Michael Hechter, Karl-Dieter Opp, and Reinhard Wippler (eds.)

Race, Ethnicity, and Entrepreneurship in Urban America
Ivan Light and Carolyn Rosenstein

Social Capital: Theory and Research
Nan Lin, Karen Cook, and Ronald S. Burt (eds.)

Parent's Jobs and Children's Lives
Tody L. Parcel and Elizabeth G. Menaghan

Power, Norms, and Inflation: A Skeptical Treatment
Michael R. Smith

Women's Employment in a Comparative Perspective
Tanja van der Lippe and Liset van Dijk (eds.)

Protestantism and Capitalism

The Mechanisms of Influence

Jere Cohen

Aldine de Gruyter
New York

ABOUT THE AUTHOR

Jere Cohen, a sociologist at the University of Maryland Baltimore County, is the author of numerous journal articles, some of them also dealing with Weber's Protestant ethic thesis.

ALDINE DE GRUYTER
A division of Walter de Gruyter, Inc.
200 Saw Mill River Road
Hawthorne, New York 10532

This publication is printed on acid free paper ∞

Library of Congress Cataloging-in-Publication Data

Cohen, Jere, 1940-
    Protestantism and capitalism : the mechanisms of influence / Jere Cohen
        p. cm. - (Sociology and economics)
    Includes bibliographical references and index.
    ISBN 0-202-30671-2 (alk. paper) - ISBN 0-202-30672-0 (pbk. : alk. paper)
        1. Capitalism-History.   2. Protestantism-History.   3. Religion and sociology-History.
    I. Title. II. Series.

HB501. C66 2002
330.12'2–dc21

                                                                2001055316

Manufactured in the United States of America

10 9 8 7 6 5 4 3 2 1

Contents

Acknowledgments

This book was not supposed to be a life's work, but it has spanned many years. I had written a term paper on the Weber thesis for Gerhard Lenski's sociology of religion class in 1964. Then, in the late 1970s when I was teaching undergraduates about Protestant salvation anxiety, one Methodist student, Nancy Weinreich, informed me that I was wrong because they knew they were saved. Soon thereafter I resumed my research in England and America.

I would like to dedicate the book both to my wife, Joan Cohen, and my mother, Esther Cohen. I would also like to thank those who read partial drafts and/or made helpful suggestions, including Whitney Pope, Derek Gill, George Ritzer, Kurt Finsterbusch, Reeve Vanneman, and Richard Damashek. I also appreciate the encouragement of Ruth Wallace, Martin Weinberg, and George Becker. The editorial help of Joan Cohen and Peggy Marshall has been indispensable. Excellent typists at various stages of the project have been Pat Richardson, Erin Zalusky, Idesha Hardcastle, Mary Brown, Jaime Hale, Rati Sood, Jean Shryock, and Tracey Musick. Typing has been coordinated by Mary Brown and Mary Pat Armstrong. The staffs of the Library of Congress and Folger Library in Washington and Dr. Williams' Library, the British Library, and the Guildhall Library in London have provided helpful assistance for obtaining books and manuscripts. And Richard Koffler, my editor, deserves a special thanks for giving me the opportunity to publish with Aldine de Gruyter.

1
Introduction

Max Weber's *Protestant Ethic and the Spirit of Capitalism* has been an em-battled book, challenged by many, including Tawney ([1926] 1961) and Samuelsson (1961) among numerous others (see Fischoff 1944; Green 1965). Despite calls for a moratorium, debate continues over Weber's the-sis that Protestantism aided capitalist development (MacKinnon 1988a, 1988b; Zaret 1992; Hamilton 1996; Lehmann and Roth 1993). The contro-versy continues because it is still unresolved. Supporting evidence has so far been inadequate (Marshall 1982); on the other hand, decades of criti-cism have failed to discredit the idea of a religious influence on capitalist action.

However, one important theoretical issue has been more or less re-solved. Some of Weber's early critics had denied that religion could influ-ence the economy because ideational factors could not affect the material realm. But few would argue today that ideas are mere epiphenomena de-rived from the material forces of production. Indeed, neo-Marxists take pains to reassure us that Marx did not ignore the superstructure, and cul-tural Marxists like Gramsci are well-esteemed. Weberian multidimen-sionality predominates in mainstream sociology over the single-factor materialist approach. In the prevailing view, theology is only *partly* condi-tioned by its economic context; it has a developmental logic of its own. Hence, religion can and does affect economic life. The only questions re-maining are when, how, and how much.

With this theoretical principle well-accepted, it is appropriate to apply it to the case of Protestantism and capitalism. Did Protestantism have an economic effect, how strong was it, and how did it exert its influence?

Until now, answering these questions has been difficult because they have been studied primarily in the context of the *Protestant Ethic* debate. Some of Weber's defenders, including Weber himself, have conceded nothing to the critics, and have supported his thesis in its entirety. Con-versely, some opponents of the Weber thesis, such as MacKinnon (1988a, 1988b), have insisted that it is entirely wrong. Neither of these extreme

1

views is accurate. What is needed is a middle way that preserves what is correct but discards what cannot be confirmed.

This means that when Weber has exaggerated, rather than attempting to discredit him altogether, the best course is to fine-tune by scaling back the estimated magnitude of Protestantism's impact. It also means dividing Weber's thesis into component parts, testing each subhypothesis separately, and selectively retaining the ones that have been verified by the historical evidence.

If some parts of the Weber thesis are correct but others incorrect, then it must be disaggregated for testing; but that raises the question of how to divide it, and, indeed, how it *can* be divided. What are its component parts? And what is the most useful division for testing purposes?

There is a precedent for considering the Weber thesis in parts. Marshall (1980:20–27; 1982:55–64) identified "two theses," first, that the modern capitalist spirit originated in ascetic Protestantism, and second, that the spirit of capitalism was among the factors that caused modern capitalism to develop.

However, the overall thesis can be broken down even farther. Each economically relevant Protestant belief and practice can be examined separately to assess its impact. These include, for example, the duties to work, save, and profit, the salvation doctrine, the stewardship doctrine, and religious discipline.

The key to dividing the Weber thesis is found in the question of how Protestantism makes its impact. It affects capitalism in several different ways. Each of these Protestantism-capitalism links is a separate mechanism of influence, and may be assessed separately.

Weber himself stated or suggested several possible mechanisms of influence. For example, Protestantism gave the spirit of capitalism its duty to profit; Protestantism helped to legitimate capitalism; religious asceticism produced personalities well-suited for work discipline; the duty to be frugal encouraged savings and investment; and the quest to prove one's salvation, because God's favor could be shown through business success, led to a continuous, irrational drive for profit.

Some of these processes worked as Weber indicated and yet others did not, which makes a blanket assessment of his famous thesis inappropriate. Just because some religious influence occurred does not mean that the entire theory is correct; conversely, the historical absence of one hypothesized mechanism does not imply the absence of all religious influence. In fact, the Weber thesis has been difficult to disprove *in toto* because the refutation of some suggested mechanisms still leaves others viable. Only a comprehensive testing of all of Weber's subhypotheses at once can provide a proper assessment of his work.

This book aims at a broad evaluation of the Protestant ethic hypothesis.

By simultaneously examining many hypothesized mechanisms of influence, it pulls together a number both of Weber's arguments and of points of criticism. It juxtaposes historical evidence pro and con.

But critique is only part of the project. As noted earlier, the question of whether Weber was right or wrong must be subordinated to the more substantive question of Protestantism's economic impact. And that impact was not limited to the mechanisms of influence enumerated by Weber. Although he spelled out quite a few, years of criticism and debate have spawned some interesting counterhypotheses to consider. Further, there are some unstated mechanisms of influence that Weber's work implicitly suggests. Hence it is necessary to add mechanisms to Weber's list, not just to subtract his excess mechanisms that prove to be unhistorical.[1]

One unnecessary limitation in Weber's analysis is his ([1923] 1961:268–70) specification that Protestantism influenced capitalism chiefly through its religious impact on the spirit of capitalism,[2] which then provided the motive force for capitalist expansion and gave Occidental capitalism its distinctively rational character. Unfortunately, this formulation leaves out additional, direct economic effects of Protestant beliefs and practices that did not rely on the spirit of capitalism as a mediating factor. These include the work ethic, which aided production, the norm of frugality, which encouraged savings and investment, and some doctrines that helped to legitimate capitalism.

Another shortcoming of Weber's thesis is its failure to distinguish clearly between behavioral and cultural mechanisms of influence. A behavioral mechanism is one through which a Protestant's religion affects his or her economic conduct. In contrast, with a cultural mechanism, Protestant religious ideas and practices become part of mainstream culture; in turn, the culture influences economic behavior regardless of a person's religious persuasion or of any further religious influence. A cultural mechanism can continue to operate even after the religion has died out that originally supplied the economically relevant ideas or practices. An example of a behavioral mechanism is the tendency of early Protestants to work hard because it was their duty to God. An example of a cultural mechanism is the justification of capitalist inequalities on grounds that the industrious deserve more than the lazy; this belief has been bolstered by the Protestant work ethic. Weber referred to both of these types. He described behavioral mechanisms through which religion's psychological effects gave direction to practical conduct. In addition, he saw religious groups as bearers of new ideas (see Collins 1980) and stressed the impact of religious forces on "the development of modern culture" (Weber [1904–5] 1958:92, see also p. 180); ultimately, it was the "universal diffusion" of neo-Calvinist methodical qualities that made modern capitalism what it was (Weber 1946:309). The problem is that Weber did not explain that the influence on believers and on culture occurred through two distinct sets of mechanisms, which, though connected, worked somewhat independently of each other.

In sum, the analysis of Protestantism's economic effect requires some modification of Weber's original analysis. It is necessary to go beyond Weber to specify correctly the chief mechanisms through which Protestantism influenced capitalism.

Still, this study is a Weberian analysis. It relies chiefly on Weber for its theoretical framework, and derives many hypotheses from his work. Secondarily, it provides a test of his famous thesis.

WEBER'S ARGUMENT

Before we proceed to the study hypotheses, we will examine Weber's argument in detail. Most of the hypotheses are derived from Weber's work, so an explication of his ideas will illuminate the origins and rationales for these hypotheses. Moreover, since interpretations vary, it is useful to state what is meant here by the Weber thesis in order to avoid misunderstandings. Before modifying his thesis, it is important to set down how one construes the original.[3]

The Protestant Work Ethic

To begin with, Weber ([1904–5] 1958:44) associated a "spirit of hard work" with neo-Calvinist Protestants. They were urged to engage in "hard, continuous bodily or mental labour" (ibid.:158) as a religious duty (ibid.:159). Irregular work and idleness were condemned. As a result, "the Puritan wanted to work" (ibid.:181). Work became a "life purpose" (ibid.:177).

Puritan diligence led to an "increase of goods" and to superior wealth and advancement (ibid.:175). It also contributed to the accumulation of capital and to capitalist expansion (ibid.:172). Not only were entrepreneurs more diligent, but the Protestant ethic provided them with "industrious workers" (Weber [1923] 1961:269; [1904–5] 1958:177) with a "willingness to work" (Weber [1904–5] 1958:178).

Surprisingly, however, Weber placed little stress on the work ethic itself as a Protestant contribution to capitalist development. He felt that Puritanism contributed little to the content of this ethic: "the whole ascetic literature of almost all denominations is saturated with the idea that faithful labour . . . is highly pleasing to God. In this respect Protestant asceticism added in itself nothing new" (ibid.). He noted that Protestantism "deepened this idea most powerfully," but subordinated this point to his argument that neo-Calvinism's main contribution was to create "the force which was alone decisive for its effectiveness," i.e., the religious sanctions that *enforced* the work ethic. And, more importantly, he subordinated the impact of the work ethic on capitalism to the impact of another ethos, which he called the spirit of capitalism.

The Spirit of Capitalism

Weber ([1904–5]1958:64) "provisionally" defined the spirit of capitalism as "that attitude which seeks profit rationally and systematically in the manner which we have illustrated by the example of Benjamin Franklin." Franklin stressed the ability of money to "beget" money and warned that the loss of any money meant the loss of its "offspring." Good credit meant command over money that could be used to increase wealth. Moreover, time is money: idle time means lost opportunities to make money and to see that money grow. Weber (ibid.:55, 261 note 10) considered Franklin's maxims a very calculating approach to profit-making.

Beyond this, Weber (ibid.:51–53) specified that in the spirit of capitalism (1) money-making is considered a duty; (2) the earning of money is an end in itself, apart from the happiness or utility of the individual; and (3) money-making is the ultimate purpose of the person's life. He felt that this ethos was part of the sober, bourgeois lifestyle that developed in Germany and elsewhere, and part of middle-class morality in general (see ibid.:171).

Weber (ibid.:65, see also p. 72) asserted that capitalistic enterprise "has derived its most suitable motive force from the spirit of capitalism." Greed and material needs provided less impetus for sustained capitalist growth since they resulted in either irregular efforts or in a relaxation of effort once a traditional level of material comfort was achieved.

The relationship between modern capitalist institutions and the spirit of capitalism was left unclear. On the one hand, Weber (ibid.:65–67) stated that capitalist forms of organization can and do develop without the capitalist spirit; on the other hand, he considered the spirit of capitalism an important ingredient for the development of modern capitalism (see ibid.:41, 43, 72, 77, 176, 181; 1961:260; see also Marshall 1982:69–82).

Asceticism

Closely associated with both the work ethic and the spirit of capitalism is the practice of ascetic discipline and self-denial. Sustained economic activity depends on impulse control. Idleness, leisure, luxury, and pleasure need to be overcome before rational mastery of the world can be achieved. "The old leisurely and comfortable attitude toward life gave way to a hard frugality" (Weber [1904–5] 1958:68). Asceticism opposed the "spontaneous enjoyment of life" (ibid.:166) and the spontaneous expression of undisciplined impulses (ibid.:167).

Religious asceticism developed as a general approach to life and to the regulation of conduct, but it applied specifically to economic life. The work ethic is a type of ascetic conduct. Regular systematic work requires impulse control and self-discipline. Idle and unproductive activities must be curtailed. And asceticism has even further economic consequences, since it limits expenditures for enjoyment and luxury. This results in the accumulation of capital, which increases capitalist expansion. According to Weber (ibid.:172), "the limitation of consumption . . . through ascetic compulsion to save" inevitably increased wealth and made possible "the productive investment of capital."

These consequences make asceticism strongly supportive of the spirit of capitalism. If one's life goal is economic acquisition, the systematic industry and frugality provided by asceticism are important means toward the desired end.

Economic Rationality

According to Marshall (1982), Weber opposed Adam Smith's position that profit maximization was a universal human motive. He believed that the origins of the profit drive needed to be explained historically. He attributed the quest for ever-renewed profit to the development of the spirit of capitalism.

Rational economic action seeks profit systematically through repeated market operations. These operations are guided by criteria of cost-effectiveness (see Weber [1922] 1968:65–67). Proposed actions are considered in terms of their likely returns and costs, and only the most profitable are adopted.

This type of rationality presupposes that returns and costs are calculable in monetary terms (Weber [1904–5] 1958:24). Output must be made calculable through scientific knowledge of productive technology, mechanization of the production process, a fixed agenda for work, and the steady, disciplined application of labor to productive activity. Revenues may then be calculable if prices are fixed and demand is stabilized by a broad circle of purchasers in the market. Costs are calculable if wages are determined on a free labor market and the legal situation is calculable. The profitability of any operation can be calculated through rational bookkeeping, i.e., double-entry bookkeeping with frequent and regular inventories and balances; profits are determined by the difference between the initial and final balances (see Weber [1904–5] 1958:17–25; [1923] 1961:207–9).

This type of economic action, in Weber's ([1904–5] 1958:23–25) view, was not practiced equally in all societies. Rather, its dominance in the Occident alone needed to be explained, and this explanation presented a problem in cultural history. Weber believed that this type of economic action developed from the spirit of capitalism and its calculating approach to profit-seeking.

Tradition

Weber viewed tradition as a barrier to the development of economic rationality. First of all, tradition provided a mental obstacle to the quest for ever-renewed profit. Second, tradition introduced noneconomic criteria into economic decision-making.

The aim of traditional economic action is to make enough money to support one's traditional lifestyle (see Weber [1904–5] 1958:59–63). If the hourly wage is increased, the number of hours worked will be reduced to maintain this constant income level (Weber [1923] 1961:260–61). "A man does not 'by nature' wish to earn more and more money, but to live as he is accustomed to live and to earn as much as is necessary for that purpose" (Weber [1904–5] 1958:60). Traditional workers calculated "how the customary wage may be earned with a maximum of comfort and a minimum of exertion" (ibid.:61–62). In the case of the entrepreneur, the aim was to earn the "traditional rate of profit" to lead "the traditional manner of life ..." (ibid.:67). Only the "traditional amount of work" was performed (ibid.:67); hence, "the number of business hours was very moderate" (ibid.:66).

Aiming at a fixed income level is logically opposed to earning as much as possible or to the maximization of profit. As long as people thought traditionally, there was no point to striving for ever-renewed profit. Some special development was required to eliminate the traditional way of thinking in order to make room for an economically rational approach.

Tradition often interfered with the use of profitability as one's criterion for economic decisions. Often, magical and religious criteria took precedence. In China, for example, certain economic improvements were rejected because of the fear of supernatural evils (see Weber [1923] 1961:261; see also Weber 1951). In India and in Catholicism, religious ethics forbade a number of rational capitalist practices (see Weber [1923] 1961:261–62).

In addition, "the stone wall of habit" preserved customary "methods of work inherited or once learned" at the expense of "more efficient ones" (Weber [1904–5] 1958:62). And beyond this, traditional perquisites and privileges were preserved at the expense of rational practices because of the "material interests" of "officials, landholders, and merchants" (Weber [1923] 1961:261).

The employment of economically rational criteria presupposed the elimination of competing considerations that could interfere. Some special force was needed to overcome traditional barriers to economic rationality. The spirit of capitalism was that force.

The Legitimation of Capitalist Activity

Traditional religious ethics, including that of medieval Catholicism, judged the capitalist quite negatively in Weber's ([1923] 1961:262; [1904–5] 1958:73) view: the merchant "cannot be pleasing to God." Acquisition as an end was a form of turpitude that was barely tolerated (Weber [1904–5] 1958:56, 73). Capitalism could not develop fully until capitalist activity had become legitimated.

But ascetic Protestantism legitimated the pursuit of profit as follows. According to the Puritan doctrine of stewardship, "man was only an administrator" of his wealth (Weber [1923] 1961:209). He had not acquired it for himself, but was merely a trustee of what belonged to God (Weber [1904–5] 1958:170). As long as he used the money for the glory of God, and not for his own enjoyment, his gain served God rather than displeasing God. In fact, the Puritan preacher Richard Baxter considered it wrong to pass up a known opportunity for gain if, as God's steward, you were receiving wealth from God and using it "for Him when he requireth it" (quoted in ibid.:162). For Baxter, gain was justified under these conditions: "you may labour to be rich for God, though not for the flesh and sin" (quoted in ibid.:162). In fact, under these circumstances gain became a duty (see ibid.:163, 177).

Some Puritans believed that successful businessmen were "visibly blessed" by God (ibid.:177, see also p. 172). According to Weber (ibid.:163), "the providential interpretation of profit-making justified the activities of the businessman." It "legalized the exploitation" of laborers' "willingness to work" (ibid.:178). "Finally, it gave [the businessman] the comforting assurance that the unequal distribution of the goods of the world was a special dispensation of Divine Providence" (ibid.:177).

In sum, "What the great religious epoch of the seventeenth century bequeathed to its utilitarian successor was, however, above all an amazingly good, we may even say a pharisaically good, conscience in the acquisition of money, so long as it took place legally" (ibid.:176; see also [1922] 1963:252). According to Weber ([1904–5] 1958:176) "every trace" of God's displeasure toward the merchant had disappeared.

By the eighteenth century, John Wesley realized that, willy or nilly, Methodism was in a position where "we must exhort all Christians to gain all they can, and to save all they can; that is, in effect, to grow rich" (quoted in ibid.:175). Wesley (quoted in ibid.) deplored the way that riches undercut religious piety, but realized that "religion must necessarily

produce industry and frugality, and these cannot but produce riches."
Weber interpreted Wesley's words as an exhortation to gain.

Religion most strongly legitimated the businessman in nineteenth- and
twentieth-century America. Sect membership served as a badge of ethical
trustworthiness. It "guaranteed one's business honor and reliability" (Weber [1923] 1961:269). The "methodical way of life of the ascetic sects . . .
put a halo around the economic 'individualist' impulses of the modern
capitalist ethos" (Weber 1946:322).

The Calling

According to Weber ([1904–5] 1958:162–66), the Protestant concept of
the calling served both to legitimate the businessman and to help rationalize business activity. However, the Lutheran and Calvinist versions of
the calling made somewhat different contributions.

Luther's concept of the calling stressed man's duty to work at some
trade. Hence, it seems to reinforce the work ethic. It makes labor an end in
itself rather than a means of satisfying material needs (see ibid.:62). This
way of viewing work helps to justify business activity by interpreting it as
a calling (ibid.:178). In addition, Luther's concept of the calling appears
to have operated like the Calvinist version in that the "importance of a
fixed calling provided an ethical justification of the modern specialized
division of labor" (ibid.:163). This specialization of occupations has led, in
turn, "to a quantitative and qualitative improvement in production . . ."
(ibid.:161).

Despite these advantages in Luther's concept of the calling, Weber
(ibid.:162) nevertheless felt that its contribution to modern capitalism was
limited because it was too traditional and emphasized "the acceptance of
the lot which God has irretrievably assigned to man." In contrast, the
Calvinist doctrine of the calling, represented by Baxter, permitted a
change of calling for a purpose pleasing to God (ibid.). Weber inferred
that the choice of a more lucrative calling would be indicated under the
doctrine of stewardship and the injunction to become rich for God.

However, the most important advance of the Calvinist doctrine of the
calling over the Lutheran version was its emphasis on the methodical nature of work. According to Baxter (quoted in ibid.:161), "outside of a well-
marked calling, the accomplishments of a man are only casual and
irregular, and he spends more time in idleness than at work . . . and he
[the specialized worker] will carry out his work in order while another remains in constant confusion. . . ." Weber concludes that a specialized calling fosters systematic work.

Weber believed that the concept of the calling left a lasting impact on
modern culture. Despite modern secularization, "the idea of duty in the

calling prowls about in our lives like the ghost of dead religious beliefs" (ibid.:182). In Max Weber's (ibid.:69–70) words, for those "completely devoted to their business . . . business with its continuous work has become a necessary part of their lives." They sacrificed personal happiness "where a man exists for the sake of his business, instead of the reverse" (ibid.:70). Also, in conjunction with his notion of the spirit of capitalism, Weber felt that the concept of the calling bequeathed to modernity a duty to pursue wealth (see ibid.:182).

Life Organization

Besides the doctrine of the calling, which was part of the Puritan economic ethic, a more general doctrine of "precisianism" helped to systematize economic conduct indirectly. Just as the Methodists were named for their organized, methodical approach to life, the Puritans were sometimes called "precisians" because of their calculated, systematic life organization (see Weber [1904–5] 1958:117). When their methodical approach to life in general was applied to economic conduct, economic life may have acquired a more systematic character as well.

The life of the religious Puritan was systematized as a means to attain a goal. "The life of the saint was directed solely toward a transcendental end, salvation" (ibid.:118). Hence, it was important "to bring his actions under constant self-control with a careful consideration of their ethical consequences" (ibid.:119). This expedient not only reinforced Puritan asceticism and the ascetic self-control of economic conduct (mentioned earlier), but rationalized life into a purposeful means-end chain. It also systematized ethical conduct (ibid.:123) and led toward "a thoroughgoing Christianization of the whole of life" (ibid.:124).

Weber (ibid.:119) pointed out that this program of methodical self-control brought order into the conduct of its adherents. This is illustrated by their keeping track of daily transactions with God in "religious account-books. . . . The process of sanctifying life could thus almost take on the character of a business enterprise" (ibid.:124).

According to Weber , ascetic Protestantism further systematized ethical conduct by requiring "a life of good works combined into a unified system." "Single good works" could not "atone for bouts of weakness or of thoughtlessness . . . ." (ibid.:117). Weber (ibid.) contrasted Puritans' overall morality with the Catholic practices of absolution, sale of indulgences, balancing of sins with the merit of good works, and miraculous or magical means of grace such as transubstantiation (ibid.:117, 120).

The economic significance of the Puritans' rationalization of ethics is twofold. Its initial impact would be their application of systematic, methodical, and self-disciplined conduct to the business sphere, notably in the calling (ibid.:162, 163). In addition, a longer-term cultural impact would result from secularization: people would continue to lead a rational, ascetic life, only instead of salvation the unifying goal would be profit (see ibid.:53, 176).

Innerworldly Asceticism

Weber considered Puritanism innerworldly because of its regulation of mundane economic activity. Although he ([1923] 1961:262–63) also described a strong *Catholic* regulation of economic conduct, he (1958:119–21; see also Weber [1923] 1961:267) emphasized that, in contrast to Puritanism, Catholicism's highest level of regulation was applied only to the monk.

Weber contrasted Puritanism and Catholicism with regard to the directions in which they steered believers' actions. The religiously motivated Catholic seeking the highest level of morality would be driven "farther away from everyday life" and toward the monastery (this was also true of Buddhism; see Weber [1923] 1961:267). On the other hand, religious Puritans sought salvation "primarily through immersion in one's worldly vocation" (Weber [1922] 1968:630).

Mechanisms of Change

Weber described the transition from traditional economic life to the spirit of capitalism at both an individual and a cultural level. He felt that this change was often unrelated to any change in the form of economic organization (see Weber 1958:67).

At the individual level someone with the spirit of capitalism began to operate his business in a hard, calculating, and frugal way (Weber 1958:67–68). Under the "pressure of a bitter competitive struggle . . . those who would not follow suit had to go out of business" (ibid.:68). "The old leisurely and comfortable attitude toward life gave way to a hard frugality in which some participated and came to the top, because they did not wish to consume but to earn, while others who wished to keep on with the old ways were forced to curtail their consumption" (ibid.).

Once this change had been completed, and capitalism was victorious, the capitalist spirit became more commonplace than tradition. The spirit of capitalism is necessary today because "whoever does not adapt his manner of life to the conditions of capitalistic success must go under, or at least cannot rise" (ibid.:72). When the spirit of capitalism first developed, only those influenced by ascetic Protestantism displayed it. However, dominant capitalism "no longer needs the support of any religious forces" (ibid.) to give it the proper spirit. The Puritan worked in a calling for religious reasons; "we are forced to do so" for economic reasons (ibid.:181). With capitalism dominant, "men's commercial and social interests do tend to determine their opinions and attitudes" (ibid.:72). The "technical and economic conditions of machine production . . . today determine the lives of all the individuals who are born into this mechanism" (ibid.:181). At present capitalism produces and selects the personality types it needs; once in the saddle, it "can recruit its labouring force in all industrial countries with comparative ease," even though "in the past this was in every case an extremely difficult problem" (ibid.:62). Now, the attitude that labor is an end in itself is "the product of a long and arduous process of education" (ibid.).

Besides this competitive process among individuals, change occurred at the cultural level as a consequence of secularization. According to Weber (ibid.:180), "the essential elements of the . . . spirit of capitalism are the same as . . . the content of the Puritan worldly asceticism, only without the religious basis, which by Franklin's time had died away." As "the religious roots died out slowly, giving way to utilitarian worldliness . . . the search for the Kingdom of God commenced gradually to pass over into sober economic virtue" (ibid.:176). As Puritanism metamorphosed into the spirit of capitalism, its "full economic effect . . . came only after the peak of the purely religious enthusiasm was past" (ibid.).

The Enforcers

According to Weber, ascetic Protestantism could advance the spirit of capitalism, and thereby capitalism itself, because it contained a force capable of overcoming and replacing traditional attitudes. The special potency of this religion was not due to its economic ethic, which was not much different from those of other Judeo-Christian religions, but to the sanctions that enforced the economic ethic. Supernatural sanctions manifested themselves through the salvation doctrine, while interpersonal sanctions often took the form of sect discipline.

Salvation Doctrine

Weber's analysis of supernatural sanctions emphasized the impact of neo-Calvinist salvation doctrine. He was not content to understand Protestants' economic conduct in terms of their ethic alone; to the contrary, one of his chief aims (see Weber ibid.:97; see also Weber [1923] 1961:269; 1951:239–40) was "to understand the connection of that morality with the idea of the afterlife . . . ." In fact, he ([1904–5] 1958:227–28 note 3) held that the question of certainty of salvation was the "origin of all psychological drives of a purely religious character."

Weber (ibid.:121, 128) felt that neo-Calvinist salvation doctrine provided a "positive incentive" to lead an ascetic life, a "psychological sanction of systematic conduct to compel the methodical rationalization of life." Its "psychological effect was extraordinarily powerful" in Weber's (ibid.:128) view.

This was possible because "the idea of the afterlife . . . absolutely dominated the most spiritual men of that time. Without its power, overshadowing everything else, no moral awakening which seriously influenced practical life came into being in that period" (ibid.:97). In the seventeenth century "the after-life was . . . more important . . . than all the interests of life in this world" (ibid.:109–10, see also pp. 107, 118). Weber (ibid.:115, 117) postulated that this concern, in attenuated form, motivated the "average Christian," not just the most religious.

Weber (ibid.:125) "assumed the doctrine of predestination as the dogmatic background of the Puritan morality . . . ." According to this doctrine, God predestined some people for everlasting life and others for "everlasting death" (ibid.:100).

Weber (ibid.:104), noting that God's decree is fixed and immutable, concluded the following: "God's grace is . . . impossible to . . . lose" and "unattainable for those to whom He has denied it." This meant that salvation could neither be won nor lost. Weber (ibid.:115) called good works "useless . . . as a means of attaining salvation" and declared it incorrect to state that "the Calvinist . . . creates his own salvation."

Since Weber denied the possibility of *achieving* salvation, he believed that the salvation drive was entirely channeled toward achieving the *certainty* of salvation. "The question, Am I one of the elect? must sooner or later have arisen for every believer and have forced all other interests into the background" (ibid.:110). The certainty of salvation was the "highest good towards which this religion strove" (ibid.:115). It was a "duty to attain certainty of one's own election and justification" (ibid.:111). From this followed the question "how can I be sure of this state of grace?" (ibid.:110).

Weber (ibid.:113, also p. 126) considered it extremely difficult for Puritans to know their state because of God's "absolute transcendentality. . . ." Or, to be more exact, "His decrees can only be understood by or even known to us insofar as it has been his pleasure to reveal them" (ibid.:103). In short, the issue of *certitudo salutis* was "hidden in dark mystery . . . impossible to pierce" (ibid.).

Weber (ibid.:112) believed that the inherent difficulties in knowing one's state of grace led to severe "feelings of religious anxiety." The anxiety was intensified by "a feeling of unprecedented inner loneliness" since each person pursued his quest unaided (ibid.:104). "No one can help him. No priest" since his own understanding of God's word in his own heart was the crux of the matter; "no Church" since the visible church in Protestantism, a mixture of the saved and the doomed, lacked the power of the Church under Roman Catholicism; and "no sacraments" since "they are not a means to the attainment of grace" (ibid.:104). Protestants placed "no trust in effects of magical and sacramental forces on salvation" (ibid.:105); Weber ([1922] 1968:630) repeatedly stressed that ascetic Protestantism had "eliminated magic and the supernatural quest for salvation . . . ."

All these aids in the quest for certainty were available to the Roman Catholic, and none to the Protestant:

> To the Catholic the absolution of his Church was a compensation for his own imperfection. The priest was a magician who performed the miracle of transubstantiation, and who held the key to eternal life in his hand. One could turn to him in grief and penitence. He dispensed atonement, hope of grace, certainty of forgiveness, and thereby granted release from that terrible tension to which the Calvinist was doomed [and for which there was] no mitigation. (Weber [1904–5] 1958:117, see also p. 116)

Weber (ibid.:197, see also p. 128) stated that Protestants responded to religious anxiety with a sober, active systematization of life. And the greater the anxiety, the more restless and energetic the labor.

Ironically, the difficulties in ascetic Protestantism also inspired self-confidence, a virtual opposite to anxiety. According to Weber (ibid.:111–13, 118–19, 165–71), the daily struggle against sin helped develop impulse control; this self-control produced a feeling of mastery, self-confidence, and even self-righteousness. These pious Protestants considered themselves God's chosen ones; they became "self-confident saints" (ibid.:112, 121–22; [1922] 1963:259; [1922] 1968:575). The sense of confidence and mastery in turn led to hard, correct business practices and heroic capitalist action (Weber [1904–5] 1958:112, 166).

Weber (ibid.:113–14) stated that the quest for certainty could lead in either of two directions: the believer could either seek to become "the vessel of the Holy Spirit or the tool of the divine will." The former, he (ibid.:114) reasoned, led to "mysticism and emotionalism . . . the latter to ascetic action; Luther stood close to the former type; Calvinism belonged definitely to the latter."

Weber (ibid.) held that the Calvinist sought salvation by faith alone; but he (ibid.:113, 114, 121) noted that "faith had to be proved by its objective results:" by its "fruits," which included "worldly activity." Faith justified itself by the "quality of that action" (ibid.:113). In Weber's (ibid.:112) view, "intense worldly activity . . . alone disperses religious doubts and gives the certainty of grace." Worldly activities were "considered the most suitable means of counteracting feelings of religious anxiety . . ." (ibid.).

Good works were considered signs of salvation (ibid.:115, 157). In fact, neo-Calvinism became a "sort of salvation by works" (ibid.:116, see also p. 115).

Weber (ibid.:112–13) contrasted the Puritan emphasis on works with the Lutheran doctrine of justification by faith; in his view, external activity had little value in Lutheranism. Weber (ibid.:116) also contrasted Puritan and Catholic good works in that "the Catholic ethic was an ethic of intentions," whereas Puritans were judged by their results (see ibid.:141). A demand for results set a rigorous standard of conduct.

Weber (pp. 115–26) considered Puritanism especially rigorous in its regulation of conduct because it called for a "life of good works" rather than an accumulation of separate good works or a balancing of good works versus sins. Good works were not concentrated in the monasteries as in Catholicism. Nor could single good works such as a donation of money to the church balance a life of sin. It was a person's usual course of conduct that counted.

Weber (ibid.:115–21) stressed the degree of perfection demanded by a "life of good works." He wrote that the Puritan ethic required constant self-control and careful thought about the consequences of one's conduct. Grace had to be proved "at every moment and in every action" (ibid.:118). "At every moment" the Puritan "stands before the inexorable alternative, chosen or damned" (ibid.:115). In contrast, Lutheranism contained no sanction for ordering one's moral life because it permitted grace to be regained through "penitent contrition" (ibid.:126).

Hard work in one's calling was considered a good work and a sign of grace. On the other hand, "unwillingness to work is symptomatic of the lack of grace" (ibid.:159). Weber (ibid.:172) judged "restless, continuous, systematic work in a worldly calling" to be "the surest and most evident proof of rebirth and genuine faith," and described labor in a calling "as the best, often in the last analysis the only means of attaining certainty of grace."

Because of this concentration on labor, Weber (ibid.:159) claimed, "labour came to be considered in itself the end of life . . . ." This moved the Protestant ethic a step closer to the spirit of capitalism, which features economic acquisition as the end of life.

Puritanism was also linked to the spirit of capitalism insofar as wealth was considered a sign of salvation. Capitalist success, Weber (1946:322) stated, was proof of one's state of grace. He ([1904–5] 1958:164) said "that God would bless his own in this life . . . in the material sense." The attainment of wealth "as a fruit of labor in a calling was a sign of God's blessing" (ibid.:172). Therefore, material success became an important goal.

Sect Discipline

Religious organizations sometimes impose sanctions upon members whose conduct and/or beliefs do not conform to accepted codes, hoping to restore conformity. Weber (ibid.:152, 155, 178) held that this religious discipline was an important means of enforcing the economic ethic of ascetic Protestantism. In his (1946:321) view, it supplemented the impact of salvation doctrine as an enforcer.[4]

Weber wrote that discipline was strongest in the religious sects. Although the church type of religious organization "lets grace shine over the righteous and unrighteous alike" (ibid.:305), sects included "only those who . . . are religiously and morally qualified" (ibid.:306). Discipline was enforced right from the beginning. Admission to membership was "by 'ballot' after an examination and an ethical probation" (ibid.:307). "The decision was made according to whether or not the person had proved his religious qualification through conduct" (ibid.:312). After admission, there was "strict moral discipline" (ibid.:316). Sanctions could consist of a simple admonition (ibid.:317). However, they also included denial of admission to the Lord's Supper. This ceremony called for the utmost purity, and the morally impure were excluded (ibid.:314–15; [1904–5] 1958:111, 122). Even more seriously the impure could be expelled from the sect (Weber 1946:306). The judgment process was carried out by the local self-governing congregation (ibid.:315–20). Ministers and/or laypersons were responsible for making the decisions (ibid.:315–20).

Judgment was based on solid, respectable bourgeois morality (ibid.:307). The virtues desired were those of asceticism (ibid.). At one point, Weber ([1923] 1961:270) claimed that ethical fitness "was identified with business honor." "In order to hold his own in this circle," Weber (1946:320) concluded, "the member had to prove repeatedly that he was endowed with these qualities. They were constantly and continuously bred in him. . . . According to all experience there is no stronger means of building traits than through the necessity of holding one's own in the circle of one's associates." This "continuous and unobtrusive ethical discipline" bred and selected ascetic qualities (ibid.).

Comparative Religion

Weber's monumental study of the world-religions put his earlier analysis of the Protestant ethic into comparative perspective. It concluded that the economic contribution of ascetic Protestantism was distinctive and unique (Weber 1946:290; see also [1922] 1963:261). Only ascetic Protestantism, in his view, provided a positive economic ethic in which a psychological motive for worldly action derived from religion, the supreme value (see Weber 1946:289). Besides a few "small rationalist sects," only the "asceticist Protestantism" of the Occident turned the path to salvation "towards an active ascetic 'work in this world'" (ibid.:290).

The Asiatic religions were too magical, traditional, or world-rejecting. Contemplative and ecstatic religions have been "rather specifically hostile to economic life" (ibid.:289).

In Catholicism the way to salvation was endangered by attachment to money and goods (ibid.:331–32). Rejecting the possession of economic goods, ascetic Catholics fled from the world into the monasteries (ibid.:332); "the rational mode of life remained restricted to the monastic circles" (Weber [1923] 1961:268).

Weber's judgment of Lutheranism and its economic impact changed little between his early ([1904–5] 1958) and later ([1922] 1968) writings. Although Luther's concept of *Beruf* placed a positive evaluation on "ethical conduct within one's worldly calling" (Weber [1922] 1963:198–99), Weber ([1904–5] 1958:86) wrote that "the mere idea of the calling in the Lutheran sense is at best of questionable importance for the problems in which we are interested." What were important were "the lesser degree of ascetic penetration of life in Lutheranism as distinguished from Calvinism" (Weber [1904–5] 1958:127) and the fact that "Lutheranism, on account of its doctrine of grace, lacked a psychological sanction of systematic conduct" (ibid.:128). Lutheranism, to Weber (ibid.:86), meant "a step backward from the mystics" in terms of rationalization. Lutherans developed "a patient resignation toward the world's institutional structures" because assurance of salvation depended on faith and God's grace rather than good works and a methodical pattern of life (Weber [1922] 1963:198–99).

Judaism, in Weber's ([1904–5] 1958; [1923] 1961; [1922] 1968) view, contributed nothing to modern capitalism or to the spirit of capitalism directly. Jews were not engaged in manufacturing or other modern forms of capitalism until quite recently (Weber [1923] 1961:264; [1922] 1963:248–50). Their "distinctive economic achievements" were rather in retail and wholesale trade, brokerage, monetary activities, banking, credit, finance, and tax-farming, i.e., in adventure capitalism (see Weber [1904–5] 1958:166, 180, 186 note 6). One reason why modern capitalism "developed quite apart from the Jews" was due to their precarious position as a pariah people, which discouraged continuous industrial enterprise with fixed capital (Weber [1922] 1963:250). Other reasons were that Judaism was too traditional to change established practices ([1904–5] 1958:271 note 58; [1922] 1963:255; [1923] 1961:264), developed mysticism but little asceticism (Weber 1946:325; [1922] 1963:246–48,255–59), and made it impossible for the pious to prove religious merit through economic conduct (Weber [1922] 1963:251–52; see also Weber [1904–5] 1958:271 note 58).

Hence, the "notable significance" of Judaism for modern rational capitalism (Weber [1923] 1961:264; see also [1922] 1963:248) was indirect, by virtue of the historical influence of Israelite prophecy on Christianity (Weber 1946:290). Judaism "transmitted to Christianity the latter's hostility to magic" (Weber [1923] 1961:264–65; [1904–5] 1958:105, 117, 222 note 19). This was important because magic can be an obstruction to rationalization (Weber [1923] 1961:265) and can provide a means for evading the divine judgment of worldly conduct (ibid.:267).

In sum, Weber deemphasized the contributions of most branches of the Judeo-Christian tradition. Catholic and Lutheran ethics were typically antipathetic "to every capitalist tendency" (ibid.:262). And the Catholics had rationalized the world less than the Jews (Weber [1904–5] 1958:117). As for the Jews, Weber ([1922] 1963:248) denied Sombart's thesis that they had contributed distinctively to modern capitalism. In Weber's view, their chief role lay in helping ascetic Protestantism make *its* distinctive contribution.

Within ascetic Protestantism, Calvinism most strongly supported modern capitalism in Weber's view. Because of its doctrine of predestination, he ([1904–5] 1958:128) wrote that "its psychological effect was extraordinarily powerful. In comparison with it, the non-Calvinistic ascetic movements," in terms of motivating asceticism, "form an attenuation" of its power.

When Weber referred to Calvinism as an influence on modern capitalism, he was referring to neo-Calvinism (see ibid.:220 note 7), of which seventeenth century English Puritanism provided the best example (ibid.:155–56). Included among the non-Calvinist ascetic movements are Pietism, Methodism, the Baptists, and the Quakers (see ibid.:128–54).

HYPOTHESES

Since Weber's theory is multifaceted and the proposed influence of Protestantism on capitalism complex, the research to follow must translate it from an entirety into a finite set of issues to focus on and study. For this purpose a set of hypotheses has been developed as a framework for organizing the analysis. They provide a checklist of important topics that need to be examined.

Note that the hypotheses are *not* advanced because they are expected to be true in every case. Some are expected from Weber's viewpoint, but not all.

Most are taken from Weber's analysis either directly or with modifications. Others deal with issues that arose later in the debate over his thesis (see, for example, Samuelsson 1961). Each one posits a mechanism of influence through which Protestantism influenced capitalism. Hypotheses are listed below by topic in nine clusters.

HYPOTHESIS I. THE WORK ETHIC.
> Hypothesis Ia: Ascetic Protestantism led its believers to work diligently at their occupations.
> Hypothesis Ib: Ascetic Protestantism made believers think of their work as a duty.
> Hypothesis Ic: Ascetic Protestantism's innerworldly approach focused believers' attentions on economic activities.
> Hypothesis Id: Occidental culture's work ethic derived from Protestant teachings; Protestantism has helped to make work a cultural ideal.

HYPOTHESIS II. SAVING AND INVESTMENT.
> Hypothesis IIa: Ascetic Protestantism led its followers to save their money rather than spend.
> Hypothesis IIb: The money saved was often reinvested for capitalist growth.

HYPOTHESIS III. THE SPIRIT OF CAPITALISM.
> Hypothesis IIIa: Protestant teachings such as the duty to earn helped to produce the spirit of capitalism.
> Hypothesis IIIb: The spirit of capitalism appeared once the peak of religious piety had passed and the Puritan economic ethic had lost its religious component.

HYPOTHESIS IV. THE RATIONALIZATION OF LIFE.
> Hypothesis IVa: An ascetic Protestant upbringing led to a rational, methodical life and to mastery of the world.
> Hypothesis IVb: The neo-Calvinist struggle for certainty of salvation led to a rational, methodical life and to mastery of the world.
> Hypothesis IVc: Protestants' religious rationality carried over to their economic life in the form of rational business practices.
> Hypothesis IVd: The rational Protestant approach to life led Protestants to abandon traditional economic outlooks.

HYPOTHESIS V. WEALTH AND PROFIT.
> Hypothesis Va: Protestantism approved of wealth.
> Hypothesis Vb: Protestantism saw wealth as God's blessing.
> Hypothesis Vc: Protestantism approved of the acquisition of wealth.
> Hypothesis Vd: Protestantism required the acquisition of wealth as a duty.

HYPOTHESIS VI. THE LEGITIMATION OF CAPITALISM.

Hypothesis VIa: Protestantism legitimated the complex division of labor.

Hypothesis VIb: Protestantism legitimated the capitalist's role as a legal calling.

Hypothesis VIc: Protestantism legitimated profits as the fruit of an ascetic life.

Hypothesis VId: Protestantism legitimated inequalities of wealth based on different degrees of diligence.

Hypothesis VIe: Protestantism legitimated the exploitation of labor.

Hypothesis VIf: Protestantism legitimated the free market.

Hypothesis VIg: The most pious Protestants could become businessmen without religious conflict.

HYPOTHESIS VII. RELIGIOUS ANXIETY.

Hypothesis VIIa: Religious anxiety, born of the quest for certainty of salvation, was a driving force behind neo-Calvinist economic motivation.

Hypothesis VIIb: Certainty of salvation, achieved after a long struggle, provided some Protestants the confidence needed to succeed in business.

HYPOTHESIS VIII. THE QUEST FOR SALVATION.

Hypothesis VIIIa: Neo-Calvinists worked hard to prove that they were saved; industry was a sign of election and idleness of condemnation.

Hypothesis VIIIb: Neo-Calvinists sought wealth to prove that they were saved; poverty was a sign of condemnation.

Hypothesis VIIIc: The requirement of a life of good works caused the systematization of one's entire life.

HYPOTHESIS IX. RELIGIOUS PREMIA.

Hypothesis IXa: Sect discipline enforced rational economic behaviors.

Hypothesis IXb: Sect discipline demanded economic success as a condition of socioreligious acceptance.

Hypothesis IXc: Protestant economic behavior responded primarily to the possibilities for attaining religious premiums.

DATA

Most of the evidence used to test these hypotheses comes from the case of the seventeenth century English Puritans. They exemplify ascetic neo-Calvinism best. In Weber's view, they developed the Protestant ethic farthest toward an affinity with modern capitalism. The English case is especially important because England underwent the industrial revolution first, and here capitalism first dominated production. The English pioneered economic modernity; other nations could progress later by imitating or building on their advances. Many students of the Protestantism-and-capitalism thesis have concentrated on English Puritanism as the most important case. Among them have been George and George (1958), Hill (1964, 1975), Zaret (1985), Little (1969), MacKinnon (1988a, 1988b), Greaves (1981), Seaver (1980, 1985), O'Connell (1976), and Sommerville (1981).

This case provides a critical test of the Weber thesis. Since Weber claimed that the English Puritans most effectively embodied the Protestant ethic, then they, if any religious group, should exemplify his thesis in operation. But if Puritan beliefs were *not* as Weber claimed, or did not produce the hypothesized economic effects, then it seems unlikely that *other* religions would provide him better support. Failure here would be quite damaging.

One could argue that Weber himself has already conducted a study of English Puritanism to test his thesis. However, his comparative analysis, which required a wide variety of data on a number of religions, spread his overall evidence rather thinly. This needs to be balanced by an in-depth case study of the most critical case. Another shortcoming in Weber's study stemmed from his use of the ideal-type method. In *The Protestant Ethic and the Spirit of Capitalism* he set up an ideal type of ascetic Protestantism in an admittedly theoretical and unhistorical way; but then he never performed the historical study that the method requires as a second step to test the ideal type. That remaining step is performed here.

Since Weber's time, there have been a number of studies of English Puritanism that bear on the Protestantism-and-capitalism thesis; each has contributed evidence and argument, but none has resolved matters, as noted above. Sometimes the coverage of the issues has been partial; these partial treatments are drawn together here to form a more complete picture of Puritan belief and conduct. The present study combines previously gathered evidence with new for the most comprehensive possible test.

Most studies of the English Puritans have been limited to doctrines as written down and preached by ministers. However, they have lacked evidence about what the laity, particularly businesspeople, believed, and how they conducted their lives. Seaver's (1985) work has advanced beyond the other studies by analyzing the diary of Nehemiah Wallington, a Puritan merchant. The present study adds to Seaver's information on Wallington and includes data on a second Puritan merchant, Elias Pledger.

Seaver's book deals rather briefly with pastoral teachings; its chief aim is to present the Wallington data. At the opposite extreme, most other studies focus on the pastoral level without evidence on Puritan merchants. However, the present study stresses both levels at once, what the preachers taught and how this affected merchants' conduct.

Seaver's analysis is chiefly historical, describing Wallington's world without placing it into an elaborate theoretical framework. While he tested some of Weber's points on tradition and change, there was no attempt to apply the Wallington evidence in a point-by-point test of Weber's various arguments, or to test a broad model of religious effects on modern capitalism.

Perhaps because of these limitations, Seaver (ibid.:237) wrote that "the last word has not been written on Puritanism and the Weber thesis, for no one has yet attempted the kind of sophisticated theoretical and empirical study of English data that Gordon Marshall has recently done for Scotland." The present study aims to do just that by analyzing data on Wallington, Pledger, and numerous Puritan ministers within the mechanisms of influence framework. Actually, Weber's own theoretical framework is quite sophisticated, so the analysis of these data within a Weberian framework could well meet Seaver's criteria.

Levels of Analysis

In assessing a religion and its impact, Weber worked at both the theological level and the level of "practical pastoral work" (see Weber [1904–5] 1958:97, 98, 111). The former refers to the "dogmatic foundations and ethical theory" at the root of a religion, normally a written systematization of ideas (ibid.:97), while the latter takes in the "moral practice" of the religious group (see ibid.), including not only pastoral sermons and personal counsel, but also written books and tracts with pastoral advice and the application of religious principles to cases that occur in everyday life. Weber (ibid.) warned against sole reliance on theology: "We are naturally not concerned with the question of what was theoretically and officially taught in the ethical compendia of the time, however much practical significance this may have had."

The Pastoral Level

This study follows Weber's stipulation that religious beliefs be assessed at the pastoral level, not just at the theological level. It focuses on ministers' teachings directed toward the laity, rather than on scholarly analyses or the pronouncements of synods and conferences of the leading clergy. There were hundreds of Puritan clergymen in seventeenth-century England. They exerted their influence through preaching sermons, pastoral counseling, and writing directories and guides to the practice of Christianity. Popular preachers were heard and read by many.

The teachings of Puritanism survive in several forms. First, some sermons were written down, and their texts are available. Second, contemporary observers and commentators have described Puritan religion. Third, and most important, religious guides such as Richard Baxter's best-selling *The Saints' Everlasting Rest* ([1650] 1962) spell out the Puritan position point by point. Only a select portion of the record survives, as in all historical research, but a vast amount is available. (See the Appendix for a list of the Puritan divines cited or referred to in this study.)

English Puritanism produced no orthodox dogma. Although William Perkins was known as *"the* Puritan theologian" (see Breward 1970:105; see also Emerson 1968:154), much of his writing was casuistry. Puritan writings combined formal doctrine and pastoral advice. Typical is Baxter's encyclopedic *Christian Directory*, which not only taught Protestantism but applied it to the "ordinary lives of common people" (Keeble 1982:79–80).

With no single dogmatic base it is difficult to define the content of Puritanism. There was bound to be a diversity of teachings on key issues. Different preachers gave different emphases and even disagreed completely. For example, the relative importance of faith and works varied, and opposing viewpoints were found on such issues as free grace and perseverance.

Nevertheless, there was enough consistency of belief and emphasis to allow one to think about Puritanism as an identifiable belief-system (see ibid.:151). There was consensus on many key points. Treating Puritanism as an entity is not invalid as long as the disagreements and differing emphases of the individual divines are duly taken into account. No divine may be assumed typical on every point, even Baxter (see ibid.:23).

A sizeable number of clergymen are used in this study for evidence on pastoral teachings. Where possible, several clergy opinions are sampled on every point of doctrine. This sometimes reveals consensus and at other times reveals disagreements or different degrees of emphasis. If the latter, it is sometimes possible to judge which view predominated. Obtaining a range of opinion improves on the too-common practice of using a single citation or writer to represent Puritan opinion, which can wrongly focus on the atypical, and which is blind to disagreements.

Besides a range of clergy, a broad range of doctrinal teachings is studied. This permits each belief and practice to be understood and evaluated within its doctrinal context. For example, the importance of the calling as a sign of grace is evaluated within the context of all of the signs recommended for use; and the duty to become rich for God is evaluated in the context of the overall attitude toward wealth.

The impact of a doctrine must be assessed in context because the existence of a strong contradictory doctrine can negate it. The behavioral effect of the two together may be scattered. English Puritanism was often inconsistent in its teachings. As just one example, the duty to profit was inconsistent with the need to avoid wealth's temptations in order to be saved. The religion must be portrayed as self-contradictory, not as a logically consistent system. Only then can there be an analysis of how and to what degree inconsistencies got resolved, or of which of two contradictory doctrines predominated.

There are two further reasons why single tenets cannot be assessed accurately in isolation. The first is that a tenet may receive little emphasis within its doctrinal context. For example, hard work in the calling was a sign of election, but that sign was less important than many others that were mentioned and used more frequently. The second reason is that its meaning and logic may be altered out of context. For example, good works had a precise significance within covenant theology. They attested to faith, which was a condition of the covenant; the covenant, in turn, provided access to Christ, whose merit atoned for repeated sins, and who thereby justified and saved the elect.

For these reasons, this study presents each belief in the context of the broader religion. Tenets analyzed separately in prior work are recontextualized here to overcome past distortions.

Since no preacher addressed every relevant point, different writers are used here to illustrate different tenets. Hence, Puritanism is presented as a composite of numerous divines. This view accurately reflects the experience of many believers because most would hear more than one preacher. English Puritans of the seventeenth century often traveled many miles to hear preachers from neighboring parishes. Since no single preacher could cover the entire religion, each believer needed to construct a composite of teachings from various sources.

In order to treat seventeenth-century English Puritanism as a single entity, this study assumes a basic constancy between 1600 and 1675 on most relevant points.[5] And, indeed, there was more stability than change. Perkins's influence predominated at least until the Civil War (see Zaret 1985:133), and covenant theology, which developed late in the sixteenth century (see Zaret 1985:140, 148; McGee 1976:107), remained in force throughout the period of the study. English Puritanism was in a period of maturity.

Because there were differences among divines, it is difficult to prove that there were changes in Puritanism. It is easy to mistake preacher-to-preacher variation for change. For example, Puritanism would seem to have grown more concerned with good works during the seventeenth century if one compared Baxter to Ames, who came a bit before him. But Baxter differed from Ames in part because he was influenced by Richard Sibbes (see Keeble 1982:34), a close contemporary of Ames who stressed works more than Ames. A comparison between Baxter and Sibbes would reveal little difference between them despite a time gap and, hence, little change in Puritanism (see Sibbes, *Soul's Conflict*, quoted by Baxter 1653:344–47).

The Individual Level

Despite considerable evidence presented at the pastoral level in the Weber thesis debate, there were initially no data on Puritan business owners' attitudes and actions (see Marshall 1982:129–30). This has made it difficult to assess the behavioral effects of the doctrines because nobody knows whether the laity accepted and followed them. One may analyze the logic of religious ideas and infer the direction in which they would, if followed, steer lay conduct; however, this strategy assumes that pastoral teaching accurately reflects lay beliefs. That assumption is called into question by Baxter's (quoted by Keeble 1982:27) observation that each person had a subjective religion of his or her own. Clearly, individual-level data are needed to bridge the gap between pastoral and personal beliefs. Likewise, only individual-level data can bridge the gap between attitudes and action. Evidence is needed on whether and how people acted out their beliefs. For example, when conflicting doctrines make the logic of action ambiguous, only individual-level data show how believers choose and resolve the dilemma.

Furthermore, only individual-level data can adequately test some of the "unintended consequences" notions advanced by Hill (1958, 1975) and others as modifications of the Weber thesis. It has been argued that Protestant religious teachings were not received by the laity as intended by the clergy, but were filtered and selectively accepted. For example, although economic ambition was often discouraged by ministers, it may have been accepted by parishioners. The gulf hypothesized between religious teachings and personal behaviors can only be tested with evidence on personal beliefs and actions.

In short, only individual-level data can show how religious ideas affected conduct, in particular economic conduct. They alone reveal whether or not the Puritans developed the spirit of capitalism and/or economic rationality.

With data on two Puritan merchants this study provides the type of evidence that is called for. It fully utilizes their diary material by applying it to a wide range of issues and arguments concerning Protestantism and capitalism.

Until recently, there was no information on Puritan entrepreneurs' mentality and behavior. This study contributes to the task of collecting and interpreting such evidence. From now on the use of individual-level data in a multilevel study becomes the standard of evidence for judging the Protestantism-capitalism causal nexus. Empirical knowledge of Puritan entrepreneurs must confirm inferences from pastoral-level data. Wallington and Pledger represent the only available evidence of this sort on the English Puritan case, and, to a lesser extent, on the Protestantism-capitalism question in general.[6] Conclusions based on their data supplant past conclusions based on doctrinal evidence alone. In future dialogues their examples cannot be ignored or dismissed. To challenge or reverse the conclusions drawn from their lives, additional cases of Puritan businessmen will be needed.

Of course, any generalizations based on small numbers must be tentative. The conclusions of this study may not be the final conclusions on this topic. A beginning has been made in using evidence of this type, but future studies may add Puritan merchants to those now available and might confirm present conclusions or show a different picture.

There is some concern over the typicality of these merchant diarists (see Seaver 1985:13). For one thing, neither was very successful in business despite the Puritans' reputation for prosperity. It would be an even better test of the Weber thesis to study the motives and actions of some economically successful Puritan entrepreneurs. For another thing, neither of these two was an industrialist; both were merchants.[7] Perhaps economic rationality was more likely to develop in manufacturing. However, on the positive side, they do illustrate small shopkeepers' mentality; and Weber ([1904–5] 1958:65) thought that smaller capitalists best illustrated his thesis.

An additional problem is the reliance on diaries for personal data. Since they often served religious purposes, their writers tended to be more religious than the average. Among diary writers, though, the conventionality of Wallington's self-descriptions and his similarity to other writers stamp him as typical (Seaver 1985:183).

Fortunately, more clergymen can be studied than merchants. The heightened quality of their data increases confidence in the data on the laity. The diaries show a close correspondence between pastoral doctrine and lay beliefs; there is less of a gap here than some have suggested. And Seaver (ibid.:viii, 132, 138, 185, 187) reports that Puritan actions conformed closely to religious precepts. Hence, the impressions gleaned from both lay and pastoral levels confirm each other. The two provide a consistent picture of Puritan beliefs and practices. Conclusions based on a consistent combination of pastoral and lay data engender more confidence than those based on just the preachers or just the merchants.

Additional evidence comes from several nonmerchant diarists, who extend the number of laity studied. Contemporary observers, including

Baxter himself, also furnish data on lay attitudes and actions. Finally, the work of historians provides considerable information.

The English Puritans

The Puritans in England were not a distinct group, but a sixteenth- and seventeenth-century reform wing of the Anglican Church who wanted worship to become more biblical and who sought more regulation of moral conduct through parish discipline. They differed from mainstream Anglicans in doctrinal emphasis; however, despite their much heralded neo-Calvinism, their theological distinctiveness was minimal (see Bridenbaugh 1968:310).

Since a chief aim of Puritanism was to reform the Church of England from within, it is not surprising that most Puritans stayed within the established church. Few joined schismatic sects. Of the Puritan sects, the Brownists are the best known; another group called itself the Family of Love (see Hill 1964:17). However, most Puritans did not form a church organization of their own.[8] Their identification is sometimes difficult because the label "Puritan" was applied to them by others; they called their circle "godly Christians," not Puritans.

Generalizing from the Puritan Case

In order to promote thoroughness and accuracy this study examines a single religious group rather than performing a comparative analysis. Still, it may be possible to some extent to generalize the findings to other Protestant groups, and even to other Judeo-Christian groups, that have evinced to some degree, the work ethic, salvation anxiety, the rationalization of ethics, and other characteristics thought to affect modern capitalism.[9] Although English Puritanism probably provides the best example of how religion aided capitalism, these others exhibited some of the same qualities and produced some similar economic effects albeit to a lesser extent.

It is extremely important that English Puritanism's positive economic impact can be generalized to other religious groups. Because of it modern capitalism could have been and was aided by a number of Judeo-Christian religions, not just one. The cumulative effect of these groups was undoubtedly greater than that of English Puritanism alone.

METHODOLOGICAL ISSUES

Besides issues of appropriate data, there are also questions of the proper methodology for this type of study. Max Weber faced the same problems and developed some methods to deal with them. His methods can be borrowed, but they have both strengths and weaknesses.

Ideal Types

Throughout his studies of comparative religion, Weber used the method of ideal types. This means that his descriptions of these religions were purposely selective. He deliberately underscored the features that distinguished one religion from another and those he considered "decisive for the fashioning of the practical way of life" (Weber 1946:294).

Weber selected "the features that to the author are important" (ibid.); to a considerable degree these are the aspects of religious ethics that connect to "the great contrasts of the economic mentalities. Other aspects will be neglected; these presentations do not claim to offer a well-rounded picture of world religions. Those features peculiar to the individual religions . . . but which at the same time are important for our interest, must be brought out strongly" so as not to disregard "these special accents of importance" (ibid.:292). "We can of course only proceed by presenting these religious ideas in the artificial simplicity of ideal types, as they could at best but seldom be found in history" (Weber [1904–5] 1958:98).

This is all fair enough. With voluminous materials, the author must surely concentrate on the parts of present interest. In fact, the use of ideal types is unavoidable. Willy or nilly, the present study must also use this method. The composite of pastoral views that represents Puritanism here is an ideal type. The unwieldy alternative to this strategy would be to treat every clergyman as an individual and every religious statement as a discrete historical event. But in order to study Puritanism, they must be treated as an entity, and that entity is an ideal type.

Ideal types must be used, but they may be used in different ways. Weber adopted certain dangerous practices that this study seeks to avoid.

Since religions' impacts can best be understood "from an investigation of them in their most consistent and logical forms," Weber ([1904–5] 1958:98) took "the liberty of being 'unhistorical,' in the sense that the ethics of individual religions are presented systematically and essentially in greater unity than has ever been the case in the flux of their actual development. . . . the features that to the author are important must often be presented in greater logical consistency and less historical development than was actually the case" (Weber 1946:294).

On the positive side, this practice seems useful for illustrative purposes. It most clearly presents the logic of ideas that directs a religious believer toward a hypothesized course of conduct. However, on the negative side, there is a risk that this kind of simplification can lead to "historical 'falsification'" (see ibid.). For example, the construction of an ideal type may impose logical consistency when the doctrine is actually inconsistent and self-contradictory. A better strategy is to incorporate any inconsistencies into the ideal type so that they become part of the analysis.

Elective Affinities

When Weber set out to show the historical influence of ascetic Protestantism on the spirit of capitalism, he posited a causal relationship between the two (Weber [1904–5] 1958:27, 98–99; see also Marshall 1980:222–23). However, he did not attempt to *prove* causation, but employed instead the method of "elective affinities" (see Howe 1978), which attempted to show a congruence or "correlation" between ascetic Protestantism and the spirit of capitalism, i.e., to show that both aimed conduct in the same "general direction" (see Weber [1904–5] 1958:91, see also pp. 64–65, 180).

Weber (ibid.:91) explained the reason why he settled for a correlational rather than a causal analysis: "In view of the tremendous confusion of interdependent influences between the material basis, the forms of social and political organization, and the ideas current in the time of the Reformation, we can only proceed by investigating whether and at what points certain correlations between forms of religious belief and practical ethics can be worked out." In order to determine causality the temporal order of events would have needed sorting out and the material factors controlled. That would have been too difficult. Thus, the indeterminacy of causal direction explained and justified the focus on "correlations."

In the analysis to follow, Weber's own method of elective affinities will provide one approach: the congruence between religious doctrines and economic conduct will be examined. This method analyzes whether or not a doctrine's logic led to a particular course of action.

Identifying Religious Effects

Ideal versus Material Effects

It is no easy matter to prove that religion had an independent effect on the economy. Since the economy can affect religion, one must take into account the possibility that the economy has determined both religion and its effects, rendering religion an epiphenomenon. That possibility must be eliminated in order to demonstrate religious effects.

Weber ([1904–5] 1958:197) addressed this problem by arguing that salvation doctrines affected economic behavior; he viewed salvation as distinctively religious. However, the logical strategy behind his proof is flawed because even the impact of a salvation doctrine could be epiphenomenal if the doctrine had derived from the adaptation of the superstructure to the economic base. Hence, the issue of causal direction would still need to be resolved before a religious effect could be established conclusively.

Since the demonstration of salvation effects cannot by itself resolve the issue of causal direction, other logical strategies for showing a religious effect may be as good or better. For instance, it would be equally valid to show that a biblically inspired religious tenet affected economic life, or that a religious group reinforced work norms more strongly than secular influences could do. Of course, the causal direction would still need to be established to prove a truly religious effect. One method adopted here is to argue that certain beliefs entered Occidental culture through the Judeo-Christian tradition, and then fortified economic action.

Since Puritanism came to fruition only after capitalism had begun to modernize and grow, the time sequence appears to favor a materialist explanation. However, the development of ethical rationality in biblical times and the early Roman Catholic encouragement of work are religious influences that go farther back in time than the growth of modern capitalism. That suggests a mutual influence between religion and the economy.

Cultural effects are the most difficult religious effects to pin down because they develop and operate over long time spans. This study has better data on the Puritans themselves than on their cultural borrowings and influences.[10] It is likewise difficult to show that Judeo-Christian moral influence was unique. It would require a comparison of religious with nonreligious morality, and a study of how they influenced each other.

Behavioral versus Cultural Effects

Behavioral and cultural effects work differently from each other. First, behavioral effects work right away while cultural effects are felt later. It is clear that some of Puritanism's economic effects were behavioral because Puritans were economically successful in Elizabethan and early Stuart times. Conversely, by the time capitalism came to dominate production in the nineteenth century, any direct aid from Puritanism must have been cultural. A second difference between cultural and behavioral effects is that only the latter can rely on sanctions. Since those borrowing ideas from another tradition are not subject to its sanctions, the sanctions cannot sway the borrower's choice.

The effects of a salvation doctrine must be behavioral rather than cultural. Its psychological sanctions apply only in the present, but cultural effects occur later. Later generations are not bound by and do not care about premia that reinforced a moral tenet earlier; they borrow or do not borrow the tenet for present reasons.

Another difference is that cultural effects are often more selective than behavioral effects. Puritans were expected to honor all of God's commandments, but Puritan beliefs were borrowed selectively by outsiders. For example, the work ethic was borrowed by later English culture, but behavioral codes on sex, entertainment, and drinking were not. Such selectivity puts the borrowed doctrines into a new context and alters their effects. Ideas that had little effect behaviorally can have strong cultural effects. In parallel fashion, minority groups with little behavioral impact can be important as cultural models. Finally, inconsistencies of belief can be resolved when selective borrowing preserves only one of the mutually canceling doctrines.

Each age selects tenets from the past that are compatible with its own values. For example, the nineteenth century seems to have selected pro-capitalist Puritan tenets. At that time, capitalism was establishing itself as the dominant economic system.

The selection of tenets from the past, rather than from those in current use, implies a time gap between the older and the more recent usages. This suggests the occurrence of a modeling effect rather than an evolutionary development; it makes the English Puritans *models* rather than *carriers* of the work ethic. For example, the eighteenth-century Methodists, and later the Victorian puritans, took English Puritan tenets as exemplars to be followed. Puritanism's cultural effects extended both to later Christianity and to secular culture, for example, the mainstream culture of Victorian England.[11]

Unintended Consequences

Weber's doctrine of unintended consequences was advanced to explain how religious reformers who considered the goal of acquisition unethical could wind up fostering the spirit of capitalism. According to Weber ([1904–5] 1958:89–90):

> It is not to be understood that we expect to find any of the founders or representatives of these religious movements considering the promotion of what we have called the spirit of capitalism. . . . We cannot well maintain that the pursuit of worldly goods, conceived as an end in itself, was to any of them of positive ethical value. . . . We shall thus have to admit that the cultural consequences of the Reformation were to a great extent, perhaps in the particular aspects with which we are dealing predominantly, unforeseen and unwished for results of the labors of the reformers.

Weber felt that he could concede the point that Protestantism valued capitalist activity negatively, and still show that it aided capitalism positively. In his view, Protestants worked hard, saved, and rationalized life, producing wealth despite repeated clerical warnings that it distracted from the pursuit of salvation and that its temptations endangered salvation.

However, Weber was careful *not* to apply the doctrine of unintended consequences to believers' misinterpretation of religious doctrines. He never argued that individual beliefs unintended by theologians and preachers were the ones that led to rational economic conduct. On the contrary, he argued that individuals deviating from their religious teachings could have little impact. In his ([1904–5] 1958:55) view, the spirit of capitalism "had to originate somewhere, and not in isolated individuals alone, but as a way of life common to whole groups of men." In other words, a minority of believers with idiosyncratic ideas could not sustain a powerful social impact.

If rational capitalism could be supported only through the "lax interpretation of religious codes," then the religious impact upon it would have to be slight ([1922] 1963:252). Judaism exemplifies this principle. It made no direct contribution to modern capitalism partly because Jewish participation in capitalist economic transactions required "a lax interpretation of the Judaic religious code" (ibid.:242). Pious Jews were excluded from modern capitalist roles (ibid.:251–52). In contrast, Puritanism's economic impact was powerful and positive precisely because the Puritan "did not resort to any lax interpretations of religious codes" to justify and even inspire his economic activity (ibid.:252).

More recent writers like Hill (1958:230; 1975:96) and Yinger (1957:215–16) have extended the notion of unintended consequences to form hypotheses that go beyond Weber in attempting to explain the Protestantism-capitalism link. They hold that the laity interpreted religion selectively, internalizing a more procapitalist version of Protestantism than the one that was taught and preached by the clergy. Unlike Weber, they posit no reduction in religious impact due to lax interpretation.[12]

No evidence has been applied so far to any of the unintended-consequence hypotheses. But with individual-level data on merchant Puritans, it is now possible to view the gap, if any, between pastoral teachings and lay interpretation. All of these unintended consequences proposals are assessed below.

PLAN OF THE BOOK

In closing this chapter let us look ahead. Using the data and methods outlined here, each of the following chapters examines different mechanisms of religious influence. Chapter 2 examines the impact of the religion's work ethic on Puritan behavior. Chapter 3 assesses the validity of Weber's "spirit of capitalism" concept and determines the degree of congruence between Puritan ethics and the spirit of capitalism. Chapter 4 presents the Puritans' attitudes toward wealth and acquisition. Chapters 5 and 6 study the role of salvation doctrine as an enforcer of Puritans' ethical conduct. Chapter 7 tests the hypothesis that religious discipline enforced rational economic conduct. And finally, Chapter 8 traces the implications of these findings for the assessment of religion's economic impact.

NOTES

1. However, certain types of mechanism fall outside the scope of this study, notably those that are political or legal, or that eliminate institutions antithetical to capitalism or to social change (see, for example, Tawney [1926] 1961; Nelson 1949; Luthy 1960; Hill 1964, 1975; Eisenstadt 1968; Little 1969; Walzer 1965; Trevor-Roper 1972).

2. This reading departs from Collins's (1980) view that Weber had deemphasized psychological processes by the time that he expounded his "last theory of capitalism."

3. The order of presentation here is not Weber's but reflects the logic of hypothesis development in the present study. Puritan conduct norms are discussed first, and the mechanisms that enforced them afterwards.

4. Weber (1946:321) did not *replace* his certainty-of-salvation argument with his later insight on sect discipline, but held that "both aspects were mutually supplementary and operated in the same direction."

5. In support, Seaver (1985:137) found the same values expressed in two books that John Ball published, one in 1632 and the other in 1657.

6. George Boddington, the dissenting merchant cited by Grassby (1995:23 and *passim*), was probably raised a Puritan if his youthful religious intensity, attendance at sermons, and interest in powerful preaching are any indication (see Boddington diary:40). However, he switched to the Church of Christ in his early thirties (see ibid.:46).

7. Since the Puritan era preceded the industrial revolution, industrialists were uncommon.

8. Some separatists were Puritans but others were not; conversely, some Puritans were separatists but most were not. For example, the Quakers and Baptists were not Puritans. John Bunyan, though quite "puritan" in his thinking, falls outside the scope of the study because he was a Baptist. Many Independents were Puritans or Puritan sympathizers though most Puritans were not Independents; the two movements cannot be equated. The term "Nonconformist" was applied to clergymen who did not subscribe to the Uniformity Act of 1662. The nonconforming ministers varied in their persuasions and objections, but many of them were Puritans. Several thousand Puritan ministers who did not conform to the Act were legally forbidden from preaching.

9. Because Puritanism's teachings differed in content and degree of emphasis from those of Calvin himself, its economic significance cannot be generalized to Calvinism as a whole.

10. For example, present evidence is sketchy on the borrowings of later religions

and of secular culture from Puritans. It would be a monumental task to trace the influence of the leading Puritan writings and the people who read them. A number of links would have to be established. The analysis would stretch from seventeenth- to nineteenth-century England, and perhaps also to America.

11. Of course, the Puritans were not the only exemplars in the Occident. For example, modern discipline and rationality have been modeled after early business enterprises, military bureaucracies, and Catholic monks.

12. Hill's materialist formulation contradicted the more values-conscious Weber thesis in several ways even though Hill embraced Weber's notion of unintended consequences. Most fundamentally, Hill stressed the causal primacy of material interests over religious teachings. And, in addition, the selectively pious would receive the strongest economic motivation because they would be influenced by procapitalist religious teachings without the anticapitalist; the Weber thesis, in contrast, held that the most pious would receive the strongest religious impetus toward capitalist action.

2

The Puritan Work Ethic

This chapter singles out one part of Puritanism, its work ethic, to examine its impact on capitalism. Two separate mechanisms must be considered, a *behavioral mechanism*, through which Puritans' work was religiously influenced and contributed to capitalism, and a *cultural mechanism*, discussed near the end of the chapter, through which secular Occidental culture borrowed the work ethic from Puritanism. There is a persuasive case for both of these hypotheses, but with some qualifications. Puritan innerworldliness must be seen against a larger, otherworldly background.

PURITAN ECONOMIC CONDUCT

First, the Puritans did indeed follow the work ethic. Historians agree that Puritans practiced the bourgeois virtues. Marlowe (1956:45) reports that Puritanism produced sober living, hard working, and thrift. He (ibid.:42, see also p. 40) refers to their "habits of self-restraint, application and self-denial." Similarly, Hill (1964:133) and Flynn (1920:167) judged Puritans to be "the industrious sort of people." And Puritan tradesmen Elias Pledger and Nehemiah Wallington (Seaver 1985:10, 12, 13, 126–27) devoted considerable time and energy to their businesses. For instance, Wallington's diary puts him at his calling from 6 A.M. until after 7 P.M. (ibid.:112, 113). He did not lack for diligence (ibid.:125).[1] In sum, the evidence is thin but consistent on this point.

Weber's image of the Protestant as entrepreneur is a good fit to the Puritan case. Although it is impossible to identify the Puritans with any single class (Seaver 1980; Foster 1991:15–16, 20, 323 note 30; Grassby 1995:273), Greaves (1981:5) observes that "the middle class tended to prefer Puritanism." Although Puritanism "appealed to a section of the gentry," Hill (1964:133, 135; see also Grassby 1995:273) judges more of their supporters to have been "humbler" people, e.g., "yeomen, artisans and small and middling merchants." Grassby (1978:361) confirms that trade was associated with the Puritans. Puritanism flourished in London and the market towns (Emerson 1968:33). And Davies (1975:252) concurs that "the Puritans were men of the cities, merchants and masters."

According to Marlowe (1956:5), Puritanism had been associated with material success for a hundred years before the Restoration. However, popular reaction against Puritanism at that time and the operation of the penal laws drove Puritans down the social and economic scale.

Marlowe (ibid.:40, 42) argues that the Puritans' early successes were partly attributable to their ascetic work behavior. And to the extent that religion inspired their hard work and frugality, it produced economic consequences for capitalism.[2]

RELIGION AND THE WORK ETHIC

Puritanism and Hard Work

The Duty to Work

Hard work was important to the Puritans (see Emerson 1968:33), and this value was religiously based. According to Sir William Petty, a contemporary observer, Puritans believed that labor and industry were "their duty toward God" (quoted by Knappen 1933:495). They believed that one could not "stand still" when "it is God that calleth thee to labour" (see Baxter 1678:I, 232; see also Ball 1632:390). Baxter (1678:I, 376) listed a number of Bible passages commanding us to work: "six days shalt thou labour," and so forth. This gave the work ethic a religious foundation.

The Puritan calendar demanded six days of work and one of rest, hence more work than the standard Anglican calendar with all its religious holidays; and since this was by "divine prescription," there was greater religious incentive for work than the Anglican calendar provided (Davies 1975:240, 252).

Puritan ministers specially emphasized this duty to work (see Hill 1964:138). For example, Baxter (1678:I, 106) preached that God required people to work. He (ibid.:I, 376) wrote that labor was a necessary duty to "all that are Able to perform it" (see also Ball 1632:393). Similarly, Thomas Adams (quoted by Cragg 1975:147) taught "that the Father commands every son to work," so "There must be no lazy ones in God's family." And John Boyes (quoted by Davies 1975:252) declared that "Every Christian should have a sweating brow." Clearly, hard work was a Puritan norm; and the clergy pressured the laity to follow it (see also Dent [1601] 1974:192–93).

The *ability* to work implied that people *should* work in Baxter's (1678:I, 376) view. He (see also Weber [1904–5] 1958:260 note 9) wondered, "who will keep a servant that is able to work, and will not?"

Riches did not excuse anyone from work, "for he that hath most wages from God, should do him most work." "Though they have no outward want to urge them," Baxter (1678:I, 376) stated, work was still a duty. "Gentlemen" should not "think that their riches allow them to live without any profitable labor" (ibid.:I, 382; II, 130).

Neither were Puritans excused from work for a religious life of prayer and contemplation. In Baxter's (ibid.:I, 376) view, God "hath strictly commanded" labor to all. Although a religious person could cast off an "excess of worldly cares and business," such a person "may not cast off all bodily employment and mental labor" (ibid.:I, 111). Mendicants who declined to work for religious reasons burdened those from whom they received alms and defrauded those "which should have received the same" instead of themselves (Ames [1639] 1975:251, 252).

Zeal and Diligence

As a religious duty, labor was to be carried out with holy zeal, that is with earnestness, fervor, and vigor (see Baxter 1678:I, 383–85). "Zeal is much of the strength of duty," Baxter (1678:I, 384) observed. Scudder ([1673] 1813:21) instructed his flock to be "industrious." Work was to be intense.

Diligence was timely application to one's duty. It was advocated by Scudder ([1673] 1813:21), Ames ([1639] 1975:250), and Ball (1632:393–94), among others. The latter (1632:393–94) taught, "A Christian is diligently to set his hand to the worke, and through negligence to omit nothing." Thus, work was to be of high quality.

Wallington (Folger diary:413) had internalized the Puritan opposition to "Negligence and Slothfulnesse." In his view, they were to be avoided. He resolved not to stand "idle at any time nor negligent in my calling" (Seaver 1985:124). And he (quoted in ibid.:125) advised others to "Be diligent, faithful, and cheerful in the duties of thy particular calling."

Practical and Social Benefits of Work

Alongside its strictly religious supports, labor was motivated by its social benefits. For example, Baxter (1678:I, 111) felt that everyone "must employ their parts to the utmost" for the good of the Church and "the society" (ibid.:I, 377). On an interpersonal level, everyone was "bound to do all the good he can to others," and Baxter (ibid.) stressed that "this is not done by idleness, but by labour." The "good huswife" was commended because her "labour and industrie enricheth her family" (Hill [1613] 1975:45). Labor was also "commanded" both in order to "have something" to give as alms to "them that want" (Perkins [1606] 1972:III, 598) and to "neede nothing" from others (ibid.:III, 534; see also Baxter 1678:I, 377).

Another important benefit was that labor mortified the flesh, subduing pride, lust, sensuality, and luxurious inclinations; relatedly, and consistent with Weber's ([1904–5] 1958:158) assessment, diligent labor kept the mind lawfully employed, keeping out dangerous temptations, vain thoughts, and sins (Baxter 1678:I, 377; Ball 1632:298, 308). When Wallington "set up shop," he expected it to help him resist temptations (Seaver 1985:27, see also p. 126).

In conclusion, the Puritans believed that labor was ordained by and pleasing to God. Work that benefited humans or human society was God's work.

Accordingly, Wallington (ibid.:112) prayed that he would be "faithful in my calling." He (quoted in ibid.:113) "went into my shop to my employment . . . out of conscience to God's commands." He exemplifies religion's effect on economic conduct.

The Calling

The Puritan norm of hard work was reinforced and placed in an economic context by the doctrine of the calling. This doctrine required a continuous course of labor in a fixed occupation. A calling, wrote Baxter (1678:I, 111) is "a stated course of employment, in which you may be serviceable to God." It is "a stated ordinary course of labour" (ibid.:I, 377, see also p. 382; see also Perkins 1970:III, 446–47).

To avoid confusion, there should be a clear distinction between this economic usage of the term and a person's calling to Christianity. Downame ([1604] 1974:I, 47–48) and Perkins (1970:III, 451) distinguished between one's general calling as a Christian and one's economic calling with its particular duties. It is the economic, or "particular," calling that is the focus in this chapter.

The Need for a Calling

Perkins (quoted by Bridenbaugh 1968:315–16; Perkins 1970:III, 455; see also Seaver 1985:133) stated the Puritan norm when he maintained that everyone must "have some personal and particular calling to walk in"; he (Perkins [1606] 1972:I, 72) insisted that we are answerable to the duties of our calling, and cannot resign from it when we please (see also Perkins 1970:III, 472). Similarly, Scudder ([1673] 1813:21), Price ([1608] 1979:17), Ball (1632:387), Downame ([1604] 1974:I, 97), Dent ([1601] 1974:192–93), Cartwright (see Peel and Carson 1951:165), Baxter (see Keeble 1982:77), Hill ([1613] 1975:94; see also Seaver 1985:135), and Ames ([1639] 1975:248; see also Seaver 1985:133) agreed that everyone should follow a lawful calling for their own maintenance and for the benefit of all. This meant that everyone, if able, needed to be "steadily and ordinarily employed" in serviceable work; nobody must "content himself with doing some little chorres as a recreation or on the by" (Baxter 1678:I, 111). Only "they that can have no better" could "have a calling consisting of occasional uncertain works" (Baxter 1678:I, 377).

Baxter (1678:I, 377) taught that a stated calling "was needful . . . for the right performance of your labours." He (1678:I, 382) explained that "a man that is out of a stated course of labour cannot avoid idleness so well as he that hath his ordinary time and course of business to keep him still at work." Dent ([1601] 1974:199–200) concurred that "living out of a calling" caused idleness; hence, he (ibid.:192–93) judged that those who "follow no honest calling . . . live to no use" and "no body is the better for them."

Those "such as live without any calling, or such as live negligently in their calling" were considered sluggards (see Burton 1634:4). Or, worse, those without a calling were rogues, beggars, or vagabonds (see Perkins 1970:III, 455; [1606] 1972:III, 604; Peter quoted by Stearns 1954:153). Such "idle" people "burthened" the country, in Hugh Peter's (see Stearns 1954:163) view, and were "not to be suffered," according to Ames ([1639] 1975:248–49).

Diligence in the Calling

Beyond simply *having* a calling, Puritan ministers repeatedly stressed the norm of faithful application to one's calling. Baxter (1678:II, 78, 128, 216) urged people to "follow the labours of your calling painfully and diligently" (see also 1678:I, 466–69). These sentiments were echoed in chorus by Scudder ([1673] 1813:21), Dent ([1601] 1974:192–200), Ball (1632:387, 390, 391; see also Seaver 1985:137), Hill ([1613] 1975:44, 82), Perkins (quoted by Bridenbaugh 1968:315–16), and many others. The exhortation to diligence in one's calling was one of the most unanimously held and unambiguously believed principles in Puritanism. Not just the quantity but also the quality of the work was at issue.

Even the most servile tasks were to be performed with diligence (see Baxter 1678:I, 383). Perkins ([1606] 1972:I, 70) encouraged the lowly, indeed "every man, of what condition soever he be, in the diligent performance of the duties of his calling."

The doctrine of the calling emphasized that labor was a religious duty, and that work in a calling was obedience to God (see Baxter 1678:II, 78; Ball 1632:390); it came under God's commandment (Dent [1601] 1974:192–93). Furthermore, Ball (1632:390) noted that in our callings "wee doe service to the Lord Jesus." Hence, economic action became part and parcel of the practice of Christianity. With religion and economic effort fused, adherence to religious teachings made an economic impact.

Idleness

The Sins of Idleness and Sloth

The Puritans' work ethic was further intensified by their strong opposition to idleness and sloth. Preston ([1629] 1976:15; see also Baxter 1678:I, 397) considered someone idle "when he doth not that which he ought, in the time when it is required of him. He is an idle man that workes not, when he ought to work." Relatedly, "Sloth signifieth chiefly the indisposition of the mind and body . . . an averseness to labour through a carnal love of ease, or indulgence to the flesh" (Baxter 1678:I, 379). The slothful person chose "a condition of greater ease and smaller labour" (ibid.:I, 380). Sloth could cause idleness "in keeping us from our duty, and causing us to delay it or omit it" and in "making us to do it slowly and by the halves" (see also ibid.:I, 379).

Idleness and sloth were not merely vices (see Marlowe 1956:57), but sins (Perkins 1970:III, 450, 451; Baxter 1678:I, 242, 379, 386). Puritans actually confessed to wasting time (Cragg 1957:132). And Elias Pledger wrote in his diary (p. 52), "When the Lord comes let us be doing so we will not be afraid of his appearing."

Puritan ministers repeatedly condemned idleness and sloth (see Hill 1964:129–38). Baxter (1678:I, 111) directed that no man must live idly; and Dent ([1601] 1974:192) stressed that *God* allowed none to live idly (see also Cragg 1957:134; Seaver 1985:135). Richard Bernard criticized the "gentry" who "will not work" (Hill 1964:140–41), and Baxter (1678:IV, 225) complained about idle "drones" who "consume that which others labour for, but are no gatherers themselves."[3] Wallington (cited by Seaver 1985:181) faulted London for its idle. Likewise, sloth could not be tolerated (see Cragg 1975:147). Baxter (1678:I, 383) urged Puritans to "Watch against . . . slothfulness."

Puritan norms encouraged activity as they opposed idleness. For example, Sibbes (quoted by Baxter 1653:345) advised Christians to be "always Working, always Doing" rather than leading "an unimployed life." Activity was required for a pious life. Ames (see Sprunger 1972:173) declared that a righteous man is a busy man. A truly faithful person "shakes off idleness," Ball (1632:357) stated, because labor is "imposed of God."

Good Use of Time

Cragg (1975:147) presents the Puritan view that "Time must be carefully apportioned and conscientiously used." Hill ([1613] 1975:II, 84), for example, urged Christians to avoid the loss of time. And Perkins ([1606] 1972:III, 479) advised them to walk wisely, thereby "redeeming the time."

Baxter was particularly aware of the seriousness of losing time (see Nuttall 1965:115). He (1678:I, 231) directed that "Time must be redeemed from things indifferent." "To Redeem Time," he (ibid.:I, 231) taught, "is to see that we cast none of it away in vain; but use every minute of it as a most precious thing"; he (ibid.:II, 79) urged people to "Keep up a high esteem of Time; and be every day more careful that you lose none of your Time, than you are that you lose none of your Gold or Silver." Moreover, he (ibid.:I, 234, see also p. 111; see also 1653:336; see also Perkins [1606] 1972:III, 593; and cited by Emerson 1968:164) warned that "you must give account for . . . every idle hour," and therefore to "spend your Time as you would hear of it in Judgement."

In order to be "watchful redeemers of your Time," one should "make conscience of every hour and minute that you lose it not," Baxter (1678:I, 111) said. "Call your selves daily or frequently to account how you spend your Time," he (1678:I, 383) directed.

To avoid idleness, Baxter (1678:I, 111) advised people to "Watchfully and resolutely avoid entanglements and diverting occasions" which "waste your time and hinder you from your works." He (1678:II, 77) also instructed them to "Proportion the time of your sleep aright"; he judged six hours of sleep per night to be enough (see Cragg 1957:131).

Sloth was considered a great waste of time (see Baxter 1678:I, 242) since "you do no more in much time, than you might do in less, if you had a willing ready mind" (ibid.:I, 380). Baxter (ibid.:I, 231) believed that "Time must be redeemed . . . by our utmost Diligence: That we . . . put forth all our strength, and run as for our lives. . . . Our sluggish ease is an easie price to be parted with for precious Time."

The avoidance of sloth and idleness required ascetic discipline. To avoid them, "Mortifie the flesh," urged Baxter (ibid.:I, 383). Pleasure needed to be controlled because it was idle. Thus, "Time must be redeemed from the hands, and by the loss, of sinful pleasures, sports and revellings" (ibid.:I, 231; see also II, 79; Davies 1975:241).

When Baxter (1653:254) counseled avoidance of excess pleasing of one's desires, he singled out "time-wasting Recreations" as a prime danger. In Hill's ([1613] 1975:II, 79) words, "I must not then play, when I should be at worke." Perkins ([1606] 1972:III, 584) conceded that some recreations were allowable as rest from labor but they were to be moderate and sparing, and particularly sparing in time, "For we must redeem the time" (ibid.:III, 594). In short, people should "stay not long at recreation" (see Hill [1613] 1975:II, 79), and then "After exercise I must return to my calling."

One should not spend one's whole life in pleasures, sports, and gaming. Hill ([1613] 1975:II, 84) warned against intemperance and idle company. And Dent ([1601] 1974:191–93) concurred that "Both God and man" hated an "Idle life" of games and sport, drinking, dining, and gossiping.

Idleness and Sin

One religious reason why the Puritans opposed idleness was that they believed it fostered sin. Idleness was considered the "Mother and Nurse" of "many heinous sins," such as lust, fornication, drunkenness, meddling, quarreling, and theft (Baxter 1678:I, 381, 385; Dent [1601] 1974:189; Ames [1639] 1975:249). Idleness was a "course and swarm of sin" and sloth a great "nourisher of vice" (Baxter 1678:I, 383, see also p. 381).

Idleness was said to open people to temptation (see Cragg 1975:147) because "when the minde is emptie of that which is good, it is most fit to receive that which is evill" (Downame [1604] 1974:I, 116; see also Baxter 1678:I, 381; Ball 1632:308; Dent [1601] 1974:193). Ames ([1639] 1975:249; see also Baxter 1678:I, 373; [1650] 1962:111) charged that the idle "directly set themselves to . . . wickedness." To avoid sin, Cartwright (see Peel and Carson 1951:96) said to "eschue idleness and alwaies be occupied in some honest labour and busines."

Redeeming Time

Despite the religious importance of sin and its avoidance, time was not to be redeemed primarily for its own sake. Of greater importance was to find time to serve God through good works. According to Baxter (1678:I, 230), time was important primarily because it was "Mans opportunity for all those works . . . which his Creator doth expect from him." He (1653:373) pointed out that "God looks to Time for the Works sake, and not at the Work for the Time sake." So when Downame ([1604] 1974:I, 48) ordered Christians to be diligent and not "sit idlely as though wee had nothing to doe," it was because there was much to do. It was everyone's duty to be "profitably occupyed" (see Peel and Carson 1951:165). Time was not to be wasted idly (see Baxter 1678:I, 17, 242, 381; IV, 222; see also Dent [1601] 1974:190) or spent immoderately in pleasures but employed "to doe Gods will" (Perkins [1606] 1972:III, 595; Downame [1604] 1974:I, 74).

Baxter (1653:336) told each person to "Take your self for God's Steward" and lay out time for the master's use. It "must be all for God," he instructed, "either in serving him, or in preparing for his service" (see also Baxter 1678:I, 111). So "spend it in the best and most serviceable manner that you can," he (ibid.; see also II, 79) directed. If you were idle, you were said to "rob God of your service" (Baxter 1678:I, 242, see also pp. 231, 246, 380). And the greater the duty neglected, the greater the sin (ibid.:I, 379–80).

At death even "they that did most for God" were "sensible how they sinned, in losing any of their time"; they wished "that they had done much more!" (see ibid.:I, 234). Elias Pledger (diary:58) exemplifies the point: he sought to improve his time more carefully because, by past sloth, he had lost many opportunities for God's service.

THE EMPHASIS AND DEEMPHASIS OF WORK

The Direction of Puritan Norms

Since idleness was strongly and successfully opposed, Puritanism created a pool of extra time that could be devoted to other activities. But which activities? Since idleness was neglect of duty, its elimination meant more emphasis on duty (see Preston [1629] 1976:15); but not all duties were stressed equally.

To the extent that more attention to the calling was advocated, opposition to idleness encouraged economic conduct. However, to the extent that time was to be put toward more prayer, worship, contemplation, self-examination, improvement of the soul, and/or using the means of salvation, a person's energies were drawn away from the workplace. It is shown below that both tendencies occurred. Redeemed time was to be distributed between economic and spiritual activities. Pursuant to Puritan priorities, spiritual duties came first, and work in the calling was of secondary importance.

Idleness versus the Calling

Consistent with Weber, one duty to benefit from the renunciation of idleness was the calling. Work in a lawful calling was considered an antidote to idleness (Baxter 1678:I, 382) and, hence, to temptations to think or do evil (Baxter [1650] 1962:112; Downame [1604] 1974:I, 116; Dent [1601] 1974:193). Another important reason for combating idleness was to improve provision for the welfare of one's body (Baxter 1678:I, 231, 382) and one's family (ibid.:I, 231, 379). Baxter (ibid.:I, 381) and Burton (1634:259) concurred that poverty followed upon idleness. Accordingly, Baxter (1678:II, 127) ordered, "See that your poverty be not the fruit of your idleness." To combat idleness was to fight poverty. Hence, more time should be spent "in the special duties of their callings" (Downame [1604] 1974:I, 74). Baxter (1678:IV, 224; see also I, 216 and Chaderton quoted by Lake 1982:29) denounced the sinfulness, wastefulness, and prodigality of idleness and negligence "in our Callings." Thus, Puritan antipathy to idleness was economically oriented (see Davies 1975:241). It articulated with their doctrine of the calling and belief in hard work to form an overall work ethic.

Idleness versus Religious Action

However, Puritan opposition to idleness was not completely, or even predominantly aimed at economic ends. Time was to be redeemed primarily for narrowly religious purposes. Many Puritan duties were not economic but devotional. For example, Baxter ([1650] 1962:118) considered it a duty to keep one's heart in heaven and to prepare for the afterlife (1678:I, 386). And Pledger (diary:23, 48) usually meant prayer or sacraments when he referred to duty. These diverted attention from economic duties, thereby qualifying Weber's notion that religious opposition to idleness heightened economic efforts.

Christians needed to spend time not only at their particular callings but also in "the generall duties of Christianitie" (Downame [1604] 1974:I, 72–73). "The Christian in his general calling, if he will get anything by it," taught Swinnock (1663:b2; see also Price [1608] 1979:16) must be "both diligent and constant at it." She or he must be busy pursuing the business of Christianity (see Flavel 1968:V, 540).

Labor and diligence were needed in the battle against sin as well as in the workplace. Christians were to labor with "care and diligence" against Satan, said Downame ([1604] 1974:I, 30, see also p. 9).

One should not be asleep spiritually, Baxter ([1650] 1962:128, 184) warned, since "wilful laziness and slothfulness of spirit" were an impediment to the heavenly life. God will not show us his way, it was said, if we do not attend to heavenly things "but are idling away our time on earth" (see Martin 1954:154).

Of foremost urgency was salvation. This was the most important reason to struggle against idleness and sloth. Baxter ([1650] 1962:34–35, 125, 182) worried lest heaven be lost through laziness. Although a person is offered the gift of grace, he or she must labor to receive it (Perkins [1606] 1972:I, 63). Baxter (1678:I, 382 and II, 128) repeatedly warned of the need to work for one's soul since "Thou hast a pardon to procure through Jesus Christ" (ibid.:I, 233).

Baxter (ibid.:I, 232, 247, 382, 386; see also Keeble 1982:12) felt that people needed as much time as possible to save their souls. The time was short, he (1678:I, 386) warned: "How fast it flyeth away, how soon it will be at an end." He (ibid.:I, 242, see also p. 232) viewed life as a race for salvation "and therefore see that you lose no time."

Christians were supposed to be busy attending to their salvation. Toward this end, Baxter ([1650] 1962:107–8, 111, 112, 141, 144, 175–79; 1678:II, 77, 78; 1653:240, 436; 1931:113; see also Keeble 1982:100) strongly advocated heavenly contemplation, meditation, family prayer, and Bible reading.

Baxter ([1650] 1962:128–29) pointed out that the work of achieving heaven was a difficult task. It took "a great deal of labour and resolution" (ibid.:129). His list of required duties is indeed formidable: "You have all the while Gods work to do, and your souls to mind, and judgment to prepare for" (Baxter 1678:I, 219, 233):

> what abundance of Scripture truths hast thou to learn. . . . How many holy
> duties, as Prayer, Meditation, holy conference, etc., to learn . . . and to per-

form. . . . How many works of Justice and Charity. . . . to do? How many needy ones to relieve as thou art able? and the sick to visit and the naked to cloath, and the sad to comfort, and the ignorant to instruct, and the ungodly to exhort? . . . What abundance of duty hast thou to perform in thy Relations? to Parents or Children, to Husband or Wife, as a Master or a Servant, and the rest?. . . . Thou hast thy accounts to prepare, and assurance of salvation to obtain, and Death and Judgment to prepare for: what thinks thy heart of all this work! . . . it must be done in time or thou must be undone for ever!

What is striking about this list from the standpoint of assessing the Weber thesis is that most of the requirements are neither business activities nor the work of economic production. Furthermore, it was more essential to devote one's time to these noneconomic activities than to be diligent in one's calling. As Baxter (1678:I, 242, 386) put it, "Remember that thou must be zealous and diligent in this or nothing."

Other Puritans agreed with Baxter that idleness must be overcome for religious purposes. For example, Perkins ([1606] 1972:III, 582) opposed idleness because it left no time to improve the soul. He (ibid.:III, 479) advised "redeeming the time" to "lay hold of the meanes of salvation." Consistently, Elias Pledger (diary:110) wanted to be diligent and redeem his time in order to prepare for death and to be "fit and ready" for his departing hour (diary:27, see also p. 40).

Worship encompassed several important duties that required the Puritan's time. Perkins ([1606] 1972:II, 462–63), for example, commended prayer, the sacraments, and the reading and preaching of the word for the Sabbath. Fulfillment of these duties was a noneconomic reason against idleness and a purpose for which time was to be redeemed. Ames ([1639] 1975:II, 5) warned against "neglect of prayer, and other parts of worship."

Prayer in itself required a good deal of time. Puritans were not only told to pray "very often" but to pray "continually" (Preston [1629] 1976:15; Downame [1604] 1974:I, 65; Perkins 1970:III, 370, 379; [1606] 1972:II, 282, 283). By this Preston ([1629] 1976:15) meant "at the least twice a day"; Baxter ([1650] 1962:79, 147) recommended a half to a full hour of prayer daily; and Downame ([1604] 1974:I, 66; see also III, 627 and Preston [1629] 1976:15) meant that one should pray at every appropriate occasion, both publicly in church and in private. Baxter (1678:I, 232) allotted high priority to prayer; he taught that "Time must be redeemed from smaller Duties . . . when we should be at Prayer to God." Consistently, Wallington wished "to make more speed and redeem the time" for more prayer (Seaver 1985:126). And when he was vexed at oversleeping, it was because he had intended to pray (ibid.). Similarly, Elias Pledger (diary:41) wanted to redeem time so he wouldn't need to pray in haste.

Downame ([1604] 1974:II, 316) called for diligence in frequenting

"God's holy assemblies." And Sunday morning services were not enough in Baxter's (1678:II, 80) view: on the Lord's day prayer was to be resumed in the evening. Pledger (diary:55) went even farther:

> Make conscience . . . of public duty as well as private, of hearing the word preached, and meditate on what you hear. Think not that this work is done when the sermon is over, but meditate on it and pray over what you hear, not only on the Lord's day, but any week day too, as you have an opportunity.

McGee (1976:89) cites Winthrop's similar view that "A time should be set apart each weekday for further work upon the preceding Sunday's spiritual business."

Prayer was to be practiced in the family as well. Baxter (1678:II, 78) directed, "Let family-worship be performed constantly and seasonably, twice a day." After secret prayer come "the common prayers of the Family." Pledger (diary:59) tried not to neglect family prayer nor to sleep late and have no "time for my duty" to be "with God in private." Anticipating this problem, Baxter (1678:II, 128) suggested rising "earlier to get half an hour for holy duty"; and Downame ([1604] 1974:I, 68) also advised giving up some sleep to pray.

Contrary to Weber's ([1904–5] 1958:158) belief that "inactive contemplation" was considered "valueless," Baxter ([1650] 1962:140, 144, 146, 147, 149–52, 181) stressed heavenly contemplation as part of the general duty of meditation. He advised that it be practiced "constantly," or at least once a day, preferably at a "set and constant" time. "Proportion out such a part of thy time to the work," he directed. And prior preparation of the heart must have taken extra time (see ibid.:175, 179, but see also p. 140).

The Puritan call to daily prayer and contemplation belies Weber's ([1904–5] 1958:158) claim that "Sunday is provided for that." Weekday time was to be divided between the calling and contemplative prayers (but see Baxter 1678:I, 382).

Another religious duty was that of self-examination and self-judgment to know the state of the soul (see Baxter [1650] 1962:129–33 and Richard Hodges cited by Bridenbaugh 1968:274). Baxter ([1650] 1962:133) importuned his readers to "proceed in the work . . . resolutely and industriously," and to stay with it until the heart heard "its sentence. If once, or twice, or thrice will not do it, nor a few days of hearing bring it to issue, follow it on with unwearied diligence, and give not over till the work be done," he (ibid.:129–30) urged; do not let your heart be lazy or "lie down in the midst of the work."

In sum, there were important religious reasons why Puritans could not be idle or slothful. These religious causes, and not just the potential loss of capitalist labor as Weber ([1904-5] 1958:158) would have it, made the Puritans oppose idleness. When Puritans were urged to duty, it was often to religious duties rather than economic. Pastoral expectations bent their behavior in a religious direction.

These proreligious norms seem to have had an effect, judging by "the intense preoccupation of the Puritans with religion" (see Cragg 1957:182). According to Flavel (1968:V, 520), the holy frequented their prayer closets. And Cragg (1957:149) confirms the time Puritans spent contemplating things divine and examining their own hearts.

Merchant Pledger (diary:30, 33) exemplified the pattern of the devout Puritan when he devoted considerable time to hearing sermons; he attended to religious duties as well as business. Likewise, Wallington rose early for private prayer, then prayed with his wife and family before going to work (Seaver 1985:40). He felt guilty when he omitted prayer (ibid.). All day Sunday was spent in family and public prayer; then the Wallingtons tried to remember "the instructions and exhortations" all week long (ibid.:40–41). Wallington often went to lectures on weekdays, not just to Sunday services (ibid.:126; see also Folger diary:203). These religious duties "absorbed considerable time and energy" (Seaver 1985:10).

Economic versus Religious Action

Although Puritanism directed its followers toward both religious and work activities, it valued the former more. Economic duties received second priority (see Seaver 1985:125, 126). Preston ([1629] 1976:32, 89) felt that "though the businesse be great, yet that businesse, that concernes the salvation of our soules and the worship of God, is greater." Baxter (1678:I, 148), too, assigned God top priority: thus, "all your business is with him or for him."

Based on these values, Baxter (1678:I, 234; but see also p. 246 and II, 128) wrote that "If death found thee in thy honest calling, holily managed, Conscience would not trouble thee for it as a sin; And if thou rather choose to dye in prayer, it is but to choose a greater duty in its season." Consistently, religious meditation was said to keep away corruption more effectively than work (see Baxter [1650] 1962:111, 112): "If you were but busied with your lawful callings you would not be so ready to hearken to temptations; much less if you were busied above with God" (ibid.:112). This reinforced the priority of prayer over economic action.

Correspondent to Puritan priorities, diligence was stressed more for religious purposes than for economic purposes. Ames ([1639] 1975:II, 11) taught that one "ought to imploy his greatest care labour and industry" in seeking the kingdom of God. Baxter (1678:I, 380) found it "a greater sin to be slothful in the working out of our salvation . . . than to be slothful when only corporal wants or benefits are the motives" (ibid.:I, 380); and Ball (1632:383, 385) thought it shameful and "abominable" to find more diligence in "worldly businesse, than in the works of holinesse."

Not only effort but also time was channeled toward worship: the preachers advised putting time toward religion before economics. For example, in Preston's ([1629] 1976:33) judgment, "he that praies much though he be a great loofer in other things, yet he chooseth the better part." Directly deprecating business, he (ibid.:91) reflected that "he that takes lesse, he that spends more time in the things that belong to salvation, he hath made the better choise." If you "have time," he (ibid.:90) added, "to bestow in the weighty businesse of your calling, in things that belong to the good of man, much more should you in this that belongs to the worship of God."

In full accord with this was Baxter's (1678:I, 231) rating of "the Ends and Uses which Time must be redeemed for." Foremost in priority came God, either praying, meditating, or serving him. Second came "works of Publick benefit: For the Church and State: for the souls of many" (but see ibid.:I, 111). Third was work "for your own souls, and your everlasting life." And fourth, "we must Redeem Time for the souls of every particular person, that we have opportunity to do good to." Only fifth came "the wellfare of our own Bodies that they may be serviceable to our souls" and "lastly for the Bodily wellfare of others. . . . this is the order in which those works lye." Since work in the calling was identified most closely with bodily welfare, it fell into the less important categories.[4]

Since religious duties were more important than economic, Baxter (1678:II, 128) instructed that some *work* time be redeemed for religious purposes. He ([1650] 1962:144, 146–47; 1678:I, 378; see also Perkins 1970:III, 379) advised workers "to leave their labours" at set times for religious duties or, if "unable," to mix prayer and holy meditation "with your common labours in your callings"; then, "in the midst of our business we have some good thoughts of God."[5]

Consistently, the aim of diligence on the job was to eke out more time for religion: "It's they who are lazy in their Callings, that can find no Time for holy duties: Ply your business the rest of the day, and you may the better redeem some time for prayer and reading Scripture. . . . Idle persons . . . do cast themselves behind hand in their work, and then say they have no time to pray or read the Scripture" (Baxter 1678:I, 242; see also II, 78). Here the purpose of diligence on the job was not to increase production, but quite the opposite, to compress work to make way for higher religious priorities.

Contrary to Weber's ([1904–5] 1958:158) claim that contemplation was considered "reprehensible if it is at the expense of one's daily work," Puritans needed to reduce business to redeem time for religion. For example,

Baxter ([1650] 1962:147) recommended meditation at least once a day "for those that can conveniently omit other business." In his (1678:I, 231) view, "Time must be redeemed from worldly business and commodity, when matters of greater weight and commodity do require it. Trades, and Plow, and profit must stand by, when God calls us . . . to greater things."

Clearly, Puritans gave religion priority. They left shops and benches to hear weekday sermons, and returned to discuss them (McGee 1976:97); lectures were often heard on market days (Collinson 1982:260). On the other hand, any recreation meant to rest people for work was expected to come on workdays rather than the Sabbath (Perkins [1606] 1972:II, 460–61); only spiritual recreations were to be enjoyed on the Sabbath (ibid.:II, 460).

Although work time was to be lessened for religious purposes, the reverse, reducing religion for the sake of the calling, was frowned upon. Preston ([1629] 1976:20, see also pp. 32, 34) admonished readers not to omit or shorten prayer "for businesse." Likewise, Baxter (1653:296) chastised those who "cut short duties in . . . family and in secret, if not frequently omit them" in order to "be again at . . . worldly business . . . and . . . have no time to deal in earnest with Christ" or their souls. And Downame ([1604] 1974:II, 316; see also I, 120) complained about the neglect of God's word when we "spend that time in our earthly businesses." The devil said not to "neglect our busines" to hear God's word, but people should "not be hindered" from "frequenting the holy assemblies of Gods saints, with every vaine pleasure and base commoditie" (Downame [1604] 1974:II, 320).[6] Cragg (1957:130) reports that God's wrath fell on those who did business on Sundays. And Baxter (1678:I, 246 and II, 128) urged the poor, who worked long hours, to be especially careful to redeem the Lord's day for their souls.[7]

Work was not to cut into religious practice. For example, Preston ([1629] 1976:91) cautioned "that you take not too much businesse upon you" so as to spend "more time in the things that belong to salvation." And Baxter (1678:I, 245) warned that an "excess of worldly cares and business" was a "Time-wasting Thief" that could take up the greatest part of people's lives. The world "devoureth all the Time almost that God and their souls should have: It will not give them leave to Pray, or Read, or Meditate, or Discourse of Holy things" nor "to entertain . . . thoughts of the world to come, nor to do the work which all works should give place to" (Baxter 1678:I, 245; see also Keeble 1982:130). Accordingly, he (1678:I, 378) said that one's calling should not require too much labor, and "deprive you of all leisure for the holy and noble employments of the mind."

Although the calling was valued, Puritans were not urged to become grinds because that could reduce or exclude religion. Work was a duty, but the duty was not open-ended.

But just as a one-sided life based on economics would not do, neither could religious priorities be pushed too far to the neglect of the calling. When Downame ([1604] 1974:I, 65) said to pray continually, he qualified his advice to avoid neglect of "our callings." Likewise, when Baxter (1678:I, 111) gave permission to "cast off all such excess of worldly cares or business as unnecessarily hinder you in spiritual things," he reiterated that "God hath commanded you ... to labour for your daily bread" to "serve the common good" and "not to live as drones on the sweat of others only." People were to be at their callings when not with God (Baxter cited by MacKinnon 1988b:199 and by Weber [1904–5] 1958:262).

Since Baxter ([1650] 1962:175) perceived that people are naturally "backward" in both the work of meditation and work in the world, there was a danger that either could be neglected. Preston ([1629] 1976:15) said as much: "Hee is an idle man that works not when hee ought to work: So hee is sayde not to pray continually that prayes not when he ought to pray."

The ideal required a balance between religion and work. Baxter (1653:346–70) advised people not to overdo religion because God's way lies between the extremes. He (1678:IV, 223) observed that "Praying in its season is better than plowing; and plowing in its season is better than praying."

Both economic and religious callings required careful attention. In Downame's ([1604] 1974:I, 116) view, "we are continually to exercise our selves in fervent prayer ... and painfully to imploy ourselves in the workes of our callings." Baxter, too, stood for a combination of heavenly and innerworldly interests (see Keeble 1982:94). He (1678:IV, 274) felt it possible to follow one's "Trade and labour" and still "do all things right" from the standpoint of religious salvation. Nehemiah Wallington exemplifies this combination of activities. He was busy with his household, his shop, and religious worship (Seaver 1985:10).

To sum up, Puritanism rejected the monk's life as the ideal, and replaced it with a life that included the calling. However, faithfulness in one's calling was only part of a well-rounded Christian life. Work in the calling was encouraged up to a point, but not beyond that point. There was a definite minimum standard of labor and diligence (see Baxter 1678:I, 234), but economics were limited since they were never to crowd out God or religious duties. This golden mean or *via media* for work involvement tended to raise from idleness those with below-average economic motivation like Wallington but to restrain the true workaholics like Pledger. Insofar as pious Puritans put in the time their religion required for prayer, worship, self-examination, sermons, religious interaction, and so forth, long business hours were virtually precluded. The importance of religious practice set limits to work involvement. Overall, Puritan norms tended to increase work time. Nevertheless, the increase was moderate in size.

Innerworldliness and the Emphasis on Work

Puritans' emphasis on the particular calling has sometimes been attributed to their alleged "innerworldliness." According to this argument, most major religions have deemphasized the world, including work, but the Puritans considered worldly activities important, which strengthened their work ethic. However, as shown above, the Puritan commitment to work was limited, so their innerworldliness needs to be reexamined as well. Any ambivalence toward the world could contribute toward the deemphasis of work.

Partly because of the influence of *The Protestant Ethic and the Spirit of Capitalism*, it has become a truism that the Puritans were innerworldly. And quite a bit of the evidence cited earlier in the chapter is consistent with that characterization. Nevertheless, the nature of Puritan innerworldliness cannot be fully understood except against a background of seventeenth century *otherworldliness*, including a good deal of otherworldliness among the Puritans themselves.

The Otherworldly Emphasis

Although Weber never claimed much for Puritan innerworldliness, still his use of the term can be misleading since Puritanism was innerworldly in only a very limited sense. Much stronger than any innerworldly concerns was its otherworldly preoccupation with heaven and salvation. Moreover, as an obverse to the glorification of the afterlife, Puritan ministers rejected the world by criticizing and devaluing it. Although Weber adopted the commendatory term "innerworldly" as the opposite of otherworldly, the Puritans used instead the shorter "worldly," which lent negative connotations to temporal involvement.

Downame ([1604] 1974:II, 223) expressed this negativity when he associated worldliness with "prophaneness." He (ibid.:I, 19, 43) and Perkins (1970:III, 241) charged that "the world . . . bringeth men to disobedience through pleasure, profit, honour and evil examples"; and Flavel (1968:V, 539) felt that the "honours" of the world provoked and inflamed "vanity and corruption" (see also Downame [1604] 1974:III, 613). The trouble with the world, as Ball (1632:388) saw it, was that the more people "be exercised about the things of this life, the more they follow after them with greedinesse, vexation, discontent, plotting, and devising."

Disapproval of the world was expressed by dissociation from it: "we are separated from the world" when we are called to Christianity and "made members of the church," said Downame ([1604] 1974:II, 181, 183).

Likewise, Baxter (1678:I, 148; see also [1650] 1962:109 and [1696] 1931:122) set the Christian's life apart from the world: "So much of God as appeareth in our lives, so much they are . . . advanced above the rank of fleshly worldly lives" (see also Ball 1632:388, 394).

Parallel to this contrast between worldly and religious, the Puritans drew a sharp distinction between "creature" and "spirit." Some people were said to walk "after the flesh" while others walked "after the spirit" (see Downame [1604] 1974:III, 617, 642).

Those in whom the flesh predominated were called "worldlings" (see, for example, Baxter 1678:I, 221, 383; Downame [1604] 1974:II, 282, 310). The name "worldling" connoted not only a predominance of the flesh (see Baxter 1678:II, 118; 1653:273) but also of worldly concerns. Worldlings eagerly desired earthly things, and delighted in the world more than "Heavenly treasure" (Baxter 1678:I, 215–16). According to Ames ([1639] 1975:II, 5), they "wholy cleave and adhere to worldly things" rather than God; they employed their greatest care and diligence on worldly things. Similarly, Baxter (1678:I, 18) complained that their thoughts and speech were "freer and sweeter" about the world than about heaven. He ([1650] 1962:134; see also p. 131 and 1678:I, 215) reported: "If worldlings get together, they wil be talking of the world," not God or heaven. Sensual men could "talk of nothing but their worldly wealth, or business, or their reputations, or their appetites and lusts" (Baxter 1678:I, 17). Downame ([1604] 1974:II, 246) believed that "most" people were worldlings: "the children of Mammon and not the children of God," they favored "onely the things of the flesh," not "the things of the spirit." And Dent ([1601] 1974:385) concurred that "Most mens minds are wholly drowned in the love of this worlde" to religion's detriment. Even many who loved God and their Christian brethren "yet have loved house, land, credit, pleasure, and life so much more, that God hath been thrust as it were into a corner, and hath had but the worlds leavings" (see Baxter 1653:156; see also Grassby 1995:279).

In "opposition" to these "people of the world" were the "people of God" (Lake 1982:143). Whereas the wicked loved the creature as their chief good, the godly loved God as their chief good (Baxter 1653:156; see also 1678:I, 16; see also Downame [1604] 1974:II, 344). They "delight . . . in the word of God, in the works of God . . . in the ways and ordinances of God" (Preston quoted by McGee 1976:181). They "desire the company of the Heavenly Father" (Downame [1604] 1974:II, 247). For Swinnock (1663:62; see also Baxter 1678:I, 16, 45), "The right Christian is one whose conversation is in Heaven, though his habitation be on earth; he dwelleth here below, but he liveth above." The holy turned from the world, forsaking it because they preferred Heaven to earth (Baxter 1678:I, 7, 221, see also p. 170). They did not set their "minds on worldly things" (Downame

[1604] 1974:II, 229; see also Sibbes quoted by McGee 1976:139; Baxter [1650] 1962:30, 121; Ball 1632:394). They let go of all worldly hopes, pleasures, and "seeming happiness" (Baxter 1653:A5).

Puritan pastors directed Christians to be otherworldly. Baxter ([1650] 1962:180; see also p. 31 and 1678:I, 18; II, 125, 130) told them to change "from a lover of the world to a thirster after God" and "the things that are above" (Baxter 1678:I, 6; II, 128; see also I, 148; [1650] 1962:107–9, 111–12 and *passim*; Ball 1632:271). Likewise, Perkins (1970:III, 467; see also [1606] 1972:I, 84) advised everyone to "turn his heart from the pelf of this world and to seek wholly after spiritual and heavenly things." They were to subdue their love of the world (Baxter 1653:254; see also Ball 1632:395; Downame [1604] 1974:II, 229, 310, 472, 474, 475; III, 642) and "the Riches and Honours of it" (Baxter 1653:17). God had called people to "mortifie their earthly mindedness" (Baxter 1678:I, 170), and obtain "victory" over it (see Baxter 1653:Epistle Dedicatory). They were to "renounce the world, the flesh, and the devill" (Perkins 1601:103).

The Puritans believed that the world competed with God (see, for example, Baxter 1653:104). The incompatibility of heavenly and earthly interests was said to make compromise between the two impossible. Baxter (1678:I, 215) held that "unbelief prevaileth at the heart, so far as worldliness prevaileth." Conversely, those who truly believed in the "Heavenly Glory" were "carried above these present things" (Baxter 1678:I, 215, see also pp. 5, 148). "Sincere godliness" dethroned "that idol, the love of this world" (Flavel 1968:V, 577).

It was considered impossible to serve both "God and Mammon" (see Baxter 1678:I, 221; see also Dent quoted by Seaver 1985:133–34), "two masters of such contrarie disposition" (Downame [1604] 1974:I, 60). An earthly mind, for example, could not "consist with . . . heavenly duty" (Baxter [1650] 1962:124; see also Dent [1601] 1974:385). Similarly, it was deemed impossible to *love* both God and the world (see Downame [1604] 1974:I, 33; Baxter [1650] 1962:124; see also Baxter 1678:I, 221). The love of the world "keepeth out the love of God and Heaven," Baxter charged (1678:II, 125, 129; I, 221; see also 1678:I, 54; [1650] 1962:124; 1653:294). Hence "if any man love the world, the love of the father is not in him" (Downame [1604] 1974:I, 33, see also p. 36; II, 474–76; Baxter 1678:I, 215, 221; 1653:294; Perkins [1606] 1972:I, 84).[8]

Eventually, for lovers of the world, the love of God deteriorated to the point of enmity (see Dent [1601] 1974:94). Thus, the "amitie of the world is enmitie with God" (Downame [1604] 1974:I, 33). Conversely, the lovers of God grew to hate the world with its vices, irreligion, and worldly conversation (see, for example, Downame [1604] 1974:II, 475–76; Baxter [1650] 1962:296). As Hill ([1613] 1975:II, 214) maintained, "Hee that begins to thinke Christ sweet, will esteeme quickly the world as bitter."

The opposition between Christianity and the world occurred for the following reasons. First, "The world's musicke" tempted people to sin
(Downame [1604] 1974:I, 33–34). When people "taste of the world and its
vanities," lamented Downame ([1604] 1974:I, 33), they forsake the Sabbath. And Baxter (1678:I, 221) said they "save their bodies and estates,
whatever become of their souls." Furthermore, the love of the world was
a sin itself (see Downame [1604] 1974:II, 475–76; Baxter 1678:I, 215, 221);
and in cases of covetousness "it is the worldly mind . . . that is the sin at
the root" (Baxter 1678:I, 216).

Another reason for this opposition was that the world distracts from
God. When "matters in the world entangle you in transitory things . . .
your thoughts will presently be carried after them, and turned away from
God" (Baxter 1678:II, 125; see also [1650] 1962:124; Downame [1604]
1974:I, 32). To lead a heavenly life, insisted Baxter ([1650] 1962:128), one
must "separate thoughts and affections from the world"; but if, contrari-
wise, "their hearts are taken up with the world," it either displaced
prayer, holy meditation, and the reading of Scripture or, by turning "the
thoughts to worldly things," corrupted them, making them "odious to
God" (Baxter 1678:I, 221). First, it "doth cut short Religious duties, and is
preferred before them" (see ibid.:I, 215). And second, people profited very
little from hearing the word if they had "worldly cares" (see Perkins
[1606] 1972:II, 299).

As a case in point, Elias Pledger was sometimes "humbled with wan-
dering thoughts in publick prayer" (diary:27, see also p. 37); interrupted
in his duty (diary:49, see also p. 23); and unable to keep God and heaven
in his thoughts because "worldly and proud thoughts take up the room"
(diary:14, see also pp. 9, 63). He hoped that he would not "forget God" in
"the midst of all the divertisment" of men (diary:29).

Otherworldly values were constantly extolled at the expense of worldly
affairs. It was said, first of all, that the joys of heaven far exceeded the
pleasures of the world and contrasted with its miseries; and second, that
the treasures of heaven were much more worthwhile than the empty, silly
world.

Baxter (1653:239) spoke of heaven's "inconceivable joys." He (1678:I, 45)
referred to an "endless Happiness we shall have with God." By contrast,
Perkins ([1606] 1972:I, 142; see also Baxter [1650] 1962:31, 121, 158) wrote
that nothing in the world fully satisfies or contents. Even when people
strive to "enjoy the world and its labours, and what fruit they can afford,"
Baxter ([1650] 1962:92, 93; see also Ball 1632:267; Downame [1604] 1974:III,
612) contended that they never achieved the enjoyment of it, but only
wearied themselves; "our earthly cares are hard and troublesome," he
maintained ([1650] 1962:121; see also 1678:I, 219). Likewise, Ball (1632:388;

see also Baxter [1650] 1962:85) concluded that "Following after the things of this life" brought "vexation" and "discontent."

Hill ([1613] 1975:II, 213, 214) disparaged the world in even stronger terms, branding it "bitter" and "this life . . . miserable." Baxter (1678:II, 120) warned that "it is a part of hell that you are chusing upon Earth." And Pledger (diary:59), too, complained of the world's corruption. According to Dent ([1601] 1974:97), the world was "a stie of filthiness, a vale of misery" and a "river of teares."

Even when the world did afford pleasures, they were temporary. Baxter (1653:236, see also p. 239) observed, "how soon, and in how sad a case they will leave us." "Worldly and carnal men," he (1678:I, 148; see also Hill [1613] 1975:II, 213; Swinnock 1663:d2; Downame [1604] 1974:I, 35) declared, "are conscious, that their glory is a vanishing glory." Pledger (diary:27) remarked that things enjoyed were less satisfying in "consideration of the shortness of anything here below." And Wallington (Folger diary:218) set his aim toward the "indurable riches" in "God and Christ" rather than "worldly perishing things." Since Baxter (see Keeble 1982:105) found temporary mirth wanting in comparison to heaven's everlasting joy, he considered life on earth uninteresting. "Wilt thou make so much ado," he (1678:I, 218) asked, "for so short a life?" He ([1696] 1931:113; 1678:II, 128) sought happiness in heaven and called "a Christian's happiness the end of his course" (Baxter [1650] 1962:31).

Beyond the pleasure issue, life in the world was said to be of little worth. Besides salvation, Baxter ([1650] 1962:121; see also 1678:I, 386) maintained, "there is nothing else that is worth setting our hearts on." And Ball (1632:260) concurred: "It is better and more honorable to be . . . an heire apparent to Heaven, than a possessor of the whole World." Baxter (1653:239) described the world as empty and worthless, just "dung and vanity." He (ibid.:238) said to "think of all the childish Pleasures of this world . . . and what silly contemptible things they are." He (1678:I, 382) exclaimed, "To how little purpose they live in the World!" And Perkins ([1606] 1972:I, 142), Ball (1632:262, 388), and Downame ([1604] 1974:I, 35) all agreed that the world was vanity.

Ball (1632:308) and Baxter (1653:Epistle Dedicatory; see also pp. 295–96 and 1678:I, 45, 148) effectually summed up Puritan values when they said to "lightly esteeme all things here below." Baxter (1678:II, 128) said to "set as little by the world as it deserveth." "God, and Heaven and Holiness" were to be preferred before all worldly things (see Baxter 1678:I, 170, see also p. 45). In heaven were one's eternal rest (see Baxter [1650] 1962:92, 93), one's "home," one's "inheritance," one's "treasure," and one's "hopes" (see Ball 1632:271; Baxter 1678:I, 217).

Implicit in these values was a norm of disengagement from worldly affairs. Due to the "unutterable importance" (see Baxter 1678:I, 232) of eternal life, Baxter (ibid.:I, 219) counseled people to attend to matters of salvation rather than casting away "unnecessary Thoughts" on the world and losing "precious time." "Canst thou pudder here in the dust," he (1678:I, 217) asked, "and care and labour for a thing of nought, while thou hast such things as these to care for?" Consistently, Dent ([1601] 1974:95) and Downame ([1604] 1974:I, 3) said to seek heaven rather than "the things that are beneath." Hill ([1613] 1975:42; see also Perkins 1970:III, 242) reasoned: "We doe look for eternal life; therefore we should not care too much for this life." Likewise, Ball (1632:279) asked: "Why should I doate on earthly braveries, who have an eternall life that hath most excellent glory, honour, riches and happinesse?" In full conformity, Wallington (quoted by Seaver 1985:142) sought "assurance that God is my God" rather than "all the honors and profit the world could afford."

Baxter prescribed detachment from worldly employments. In his (1678:II, 78) view, one's "labor must be the labor of a Traveller, which is all for his journeys end; and all your respect or affection to any place or thing in your way, must be in respect to your attainment of the end; as a Traveller loveth a good way, a good Horse, a good Inn, a dry Cloak, or good Company; but nothing must be loved here as your end or home." Swinnock (1663:b2) agreed that although "the right Christian ... useth the creatures," s/he "enjoyeth none but Jesus Christ." And Dent ([1601] 1974:104; see also Swinnock 1663:d2) advised, "they that use this world, should be as though they used it not."[9] Baxter (1678:IV, 276), Ball (1632:271), and Perkins (1970:III, 465; [1606] 1972:I, 84) urged "the weaning of ... affection" from "all earthly vanities." And Pledger (diary:31) prayed, "Oh Lord wean me effectually from the worldly things." He (ibid.:11) begged to be "set loose to all temporal things."

Not only was detachment from the world an expression of otherworldly values, but also it was a necessary means to salvation. Participation in worldly affairs was not only lower in priority than salvation but was an impediment to it. Since, in Baxter's (1653:286–87, see also p. 310) view, the encroachment of carnal interests on Christ's rights was dangerous and damnable, people "cannot have heaven without leaving their delights and contentments on earth." He (1678:II, 121; see also Dent [1601] 1974:94) warned readers not to run so great a hazard as damnation "for some worldly gain or honor, or some fleshly pleasure." So, he (1678:I, 54; see also p. 221 and Ames [1639] 1975:II, 11) cautioned, "Promise not your selves long life, prosperity and great matters in the world, lest it entangle your hearts with transitory things and engage you in ambitious or covetous designs, and steal away your hearts from God, and destroy all your serious apprehensions of Eternity." Since "the love of this World" drew "the heart from God" (Baxter 1678:II, 129; see also I, 221), Baxter's (1678:II, 125) advice was to "keep the world from your hearts." To be of the world was to separate oneself from heaven; hence, only "those Christians shall possess it, who are not of the world" (Baxter [1650] 1962:30). So "turn the world off," urged Swinnock (1663:e, see also p. 107), "before it turn you off. . . . O get the world taken out of you . . . or ye are undone forever" (see also Baxter 1678:IV, 276; II, 128).

The Fusion of Innerworldly and Otherworldly Beliefs

Since English Puritanism was so otherworldly, as just shown, one might doubt that it could be in any way innerworldly. Yet, paradoxically, it was innerworldly at the same time (see Weber 1946:332; see also [1922] 1963:168). Any accurate analysis of Puritanism must take into account both of these contrary outlooks.

Puritanism was innerworldly in several senses. Most immediately, it was innerworldly simply because it required the performance of duties in the world (see Eisenstadt 1973:139–40). "God hath work for us to do in the world," Baxter (1678:I, 106) insisted. One could not retire into solitude since it is often "a retiring from the place and work which God hath appointed us" (Baxter quoted by Keeble 1982:77). Activity was demanded. There was presupposed before eternal rest "an actual motion" (see Baxter [1650] 1962:34). Worldly activities were to be performed in "God's Service" (Baxter 1678:I, 106, 107, 233, 382); specifically, "do all the good that you can in the world" (ibid.:II, 115; I, 233; IV, 276; see also Ball 1632:396).

Beyond this, Puritanism was innerworldly in a second sense: it added something qualitative to the performance of everyday activities. Everyday life took on meaning and significance when set in the context of eternity (Keeble 1982:77; Seaver 1985:181). First of all, since life on earth was regulated by Divine law, it became an expression of God's will. For example, Ball (1632:396) believed the work of the calling to be part of the practice of Christianity because Christians were commanded to "labour honestly in our particular vocation." Second, human deeds could glorify God if performed out of obedience to him (see Downame [1604] 1974:II, 242) or if they produced a godly, heavenly life (see Baxter 1678:I, 148; [1650] 1962:118). A third source of transcendent meaning was the relationship between worldly actions and the afterlife. Life in the world was valued as a means of preparation and trial for salvation. According to Baxter (see Keeble 1982:76), "heaven is won or lost on earth," and "none come to Heaven . . . that are not prepared by well using Earth" (see ibid.:77). As Weber ([1904–5] 1958:153) said, it was "conduct within this world, but for the sake of the world beyond."

When interpreted as religious duties, innerworldly actions that would otherwise have been despised took on sacred meaning and positive valuation. Duties were not seen as "worldly"; on the contrary, they served otherworldly values. As Weber (ibid.:154) put it, they were "in the world, but neither of nor for this world." Baxter's positive judgment of work in the world is a prime example. He (quoted by Keeble 1982:77) refuted those who "think that they should not work so hard, because it is but Worldly business." They want to "neglect their labour, that they may spend more time in serving God: as if it were no serving God to be faithful in their Masters service" (Baxter quoted by Keeble 1982:77). Work was important because it served God.

Baxter (see ibid.) considered it an error "to think that all Religion lieth in minding only the Life to come, and disregarding all things in this present life." He himself combined an interest in heaven with an interest in the social and political world. Devotion to God and salvation required the performance of innerworldly duties.

Thus, Puritanism fused otherworldly values with innerworldly action. The chief case in point is the coupling of work in the calling with the practice of Christianity (see Ball 1632:396; Perkins [1606] 1972:I, 67; 1970:III, 456–57). This transmuted religious diligence into economic effort. Paradoxically, a heavenly mind encouraged greater worldly activity. As Baxter ([1650] 1962:113) explained it, "The diligent keeping of your hearts on heaven will . . . put life into all your duties. It is the heavenly Christian that is the lively Christian." A heart in heaven made motion more vigorous in this life (see Keeble 1982:80).

The infusion of worldly activity with transcendent meaning lends support to Weber's claim that, despite Puritan otherworldliness, they were intensely innerworldly: that their otherworldliness strengthened the innerworldly aspect. But, nevertheless, the analysis cannot stop here as Weber's did. Several qualifications are in order.

To begin with, the fusion of innerworldly action and otherworldly values worked two ways, not just to strengthen but also to weaken innerworldliness. The obverse of giving the world transcendental significance was to limit interest in the world to its religious meaning. We enjoy the natural world so we can look beyond to heaven, explained Baxter (cited by Keeble 1982:108); natural objects suggest spiritual things (Baxter cited in ibid.:111). Baxter's (1678:I, 386) interest in life on earth was similarly focused on the transcendental: "Remember that thou hast thy Life and health and wit and parts, for nothing else but by thy present duty to prepare for everlasting joys." Earthly business was carried out only to serve God: in Baxter's ([1696] 1931:125) words, "I know of no other end, or trade, or business, but that I am employed in his work." Similarly, Pledger (diary:37) wrote, "I live to his glory." This approach excluded the usual creatural motives for worldly action, including for work in the world. A religious motive was provided, but other, potentially powerful motives were undercut at the same stroke. A further consequence of this limitation of interest was that not all innerworldly activity was valued. For example, not every action tended toward salvation (see Baxter [1650] 1962:34). And since only a "Holy Heavenly life" could glorify God (see Baxter 1678:IV, 275; [1650] 1962:107), earthly activities were meaningful only if they contributed to a heavenly life.

Puritanism was inconsistent about the relationship between the innerworldly and the otherworldly. Not only were these seen as fused, but, inconsistently, they were also seen as opposed, as shown at length above. Innerworldly actions were given religious meaning, yet were also opposed as worldly. Consequently, some Puritans felt ambivalent about performing worldly deeds (see Keeble 1982:77).

Insofar as the worldly and otherworldly were separable, the otherworldly took precedence. Since worldly duties were merely means to otherworldly ends, they held a lower priority than the otherworldly goals themselves. Their religious significance was less than that of the more directly transcendent parts of life. In Baxter's ([1650] 1962:121) opinion, "we must be content to mind the things below" only "so far as duty and necessity requires it."

One needed to maintain a heavenly mind though in a worldly setting (see Baxter [1650] 1962:125 and [1969] 1931:125; see also 1678:I, 148, 150; Wallington quoted by Seaver 1985:125). Though lived physically on earth, a godly life was a "conversation in heaven" (see Downame [1604] 1974:II, 474; see also Sibbes quoted by Knott 1980:54; Baxter [1650] 1962:128–29, [1696] 1931:125; 1678:I, 148, 150, 378); "then doe we not set our mindes upon worldly things" (Downame [1604] 1974:II, 229). "The godly had to live in this world" but "were not to live of it," Lake (1982:149) concluded. "They had to fulfill their secular duties with a will, but they were not to view their lives in primarily secular terms" (ibid.).

Otherworldliness and Economic Effort

This intricate combination of otherworldliness and innerworldliness applied to economic behaviors as to any other "secular duties" (see Eisenstadt 1973:139–40). Economic conduct was simultaneously praised as obedience to God and devalued as part of the world (see Baxter 1678:I, 217).

Economic behavior, despite its status as a religious duty, was by no means exempted from the Puritan condemnation of worldliness. For instance, Baxter (1678:I, 378) said that one's calling was "not to overwhelm you with cares and labour" because "many who plunge themselves into

more and greater business than they can otherwise dispatch . . . are . . .
continually alienated in their minds from God and Heaven, to get more of
the world." He (ibid.:I, 5) reminded readers that life was not only to do
their "worldly businesse"; it was wrong to "do nothing but drudge for the
world." And Downame ([1604] 1974:I, 94) warned that such drudgery was
worldly and entangled them in Satan's snares.

Downame (ibid.) reported that "the practice of most" was to "watch
and drudge night and day." However, their innerworldliness was considered a moral failing rather than an acceptable practice. For example, Elias
Pledger was contrite when he was too innerworldly. He (diary:31) wrote,
"Worldly thoughts of business take up too much room in my heart. So
that my worldly business which ought to be subordinate doth by its insin-
uation, of the devil take up too much room." Pious Puritans were aware of
their religion's ambivalence toward the work of the world. Hence, they
could not devote themselves wholeheartedly to business.

Puritan norms discouraged high levels of work involvement. Preston
([1629] 1976:91) warned that "as you must not pester your selves with too
much businesse, so likewise you must take care, that your minds be not
too much intent upon them." Ball (1632:388), too, warned against "distracting care" in our callings. The wise man, in Swinnock's (1663:d2) view,
"buyeth as one that possesseth not" and "selleth as one that hath a soul to
save." And Baxter (1678:I, 386) advised, "Drown not your hearts in worldly business. . . . If you have a necessity of labouring in your callings, you
have no necessity of loving the world, or of caring inordinately" (Baxter
1678:I, 216). They were to concentrate on economics only "as is needful to
the right doing of your work" (Baxter 1678:II, 127).[10]

Consistently, Nehemiah Wallington was critical of the businessman
who was "up early and late, very industrious and careful and painful in
use of all means, taking hold of all times, seasons and opportunities"
(Seaver 1985:126). Such a person was too worldly-wise to be a saint (ibid.).
Wallington (Folger diary:413) considered some people "over diligent."

The precedence of otherworldly values imposed a limitation on work.
Preston ([1629] 1976:92) directed Christians not to be too intent upon business because heaven is "the greater businesse" (ibid.:32). Obversely, Downame ([1604] 1974:II, 315) urged his readers not to neglect salvation,
though one may argue that "he must goe about his merchandize." And
Baxter (1653:255; see also [1650] 1962:151) noted that "we should not pre-
ferre . . . business or any vain thing before Gods Word and Worship." Religious life was to be lived fully, with attention to business reduced
correspondingly.

When thoughts of business disrupted religious worship, they were excessive and needed to be cut back. Preston ([1629] 1976:91–92) warned
that "too much intention of mind upon businesse, causeth distraction in

prayer, and . . . the soule . . . cannot loose it selfe to the performance of spirituall duties." Banish worldly business to avoid distractions in church, advised Downame ([1604] 1974:II, 365) and Baxter ([1650] 1962:151, 176, 177; see also Perkins [1606] 1972:II, 461).

In short, despite some innerworldliness, religious norms did not urge Puritans to immerse themselves in business. Economic action was to be subordinate in priority to prayer and worship, which received a heavier overall stress. Innerworldly duties were required, but they were less weighty than more otherworldly ones. This predominance of otherworldly values helps to explain the time-priorities described earlier.

FRUGALITY AND SAVINGS

The foregoing shows that Puritanism aided capitalism to a qualified extent through its work ethic. But there is more to its behavioral effect than just the boost it gave to work. Another part of the behavioral effect comes from its norm of frugality. Resources not expended on consumption could be invested in capitalist production.

The Puritans were known for frugality because of their sober living. Their "social habits made lavish spending unattractive to them" (Marlowe 1956:72). They considered extravagance a vice and waste a folly (ibid.:57, 82).

When Nehemiah Wallington was not frugal, he felt guilty about it. He (Folger diary:414) opposed "wasting such goods as God gives him in money," but spent too much on weekly news pamphlets (British diary:15; Seaver 1985:235). This made business difficult because he had "no cash reserves" (Seaver 1985:119, 122) and had trouble paying for wares to sell (ibid.:78, 120, 123, 124). His "conscience" told him that he was "remiss and unwise" in "spending" (Wallington quoted in ibid.:235, but see also p. 146). He (British diary:15) called the news books "so many thieves that had stole away my money." He wished that he could "give account . . . how I have improved and laid out every penny" (Seaver 1985:156).

The writings of the Puritan divines reveal a religious basis for these social attitudes and habits. According to Ball (1632:357, 395; see also Seaver 1985:137), it was faith that made them frugal and "carefull to preserve" what God had given. Frugality was a duty to God. Conversely, "unthrifty mispending of God's gifts" was "wrong" (see Downame [1604] 1974:I, 61).

First of all, since these gifts were "his, and not ours," prodigality was "a wasting of that which is none of our own" (see Baxter 1678:IV, 225). Baxter (ibid.:IV, 223) reminded his readers that "You are not absolute Owners of anything, but the stewards of God!" Hence, "frugality or sparing" was "an act of fidelity, obedience, and gratitude" to "the chief Owner . . . our chief Ruler"; but "Wastefulness or Prodigality" was a "sin of unfaithfulness, disobedience, and ingratitude" (see ibid.:IV, 222).

Furthermore, Baxter (ibid.:IV, 222) reasoned, "As we hold our estates under God . . . so must we devote them to him, and use them for him" (see also ibid.:223 and Seaver 1985:137). They were to be used "according to his pleasure only," Baxter (1678:IV, 223, 225) wrote; you "must expend it as he appointeth you" and "waste it not any other way." The estate had to be distributed properly, according to Baxter (ibid.:IV, 223), because "God hath appointed you several duties for your expences." You must therefore "be careful to use well what you have" (ibid.:I, 221; see also Seaver 1985:137); "it is excess when any thing is that way expended, which you are called to expend another way" (Baxter 1678:IV, 222). Furthermore, you "must see that nothing of any use, be lost through satiety, negligence or contempt: For the smallest part is of God's gifts and talents, given us not to cast away, but to use as he would have us: And there is nothing that is good so small, but someone hath need of it, or some good use or other may be made of it" (see ibid.:IV, 224; see also Ball 1632:357). Baxter (1678:IV, 222) charged that "we misspend or waste some part of our estates to the injury of God." Waste was "a robbery of God of the use or service due him in the improvement of his gifts" (see ibid.:IV, 225). It left "little or nothing to spare . . . to good uses" (ibid.:IV, 265).

A second religious reason for frugality stemmed from the identification of excessive spending, or prodigality, with sin and worldliness. Sinful desires and practices led to prodigality, which in turn supported a life of sin. Prodigality was not merely a sin in itself, but an extension of other sins. It developed as an outgrowth of fleshly desires. According to Baxter (ibid.:IV, 265, see pp. 222–25 for his list of wasteful sins and pleasures), the prodigal had an expensive "litter of Vices and Lusts to be maintained." These sinful, worldly desires were prime causes of overspending.

Conversely, frugality was a sign that the flesh had been mortified and sinful desires overcome. The frugal "laid out no more than needs upon the flesh"; they were "Mortified Christians" who therefore "need . . . little for themselves" (see ibid.:IV, 265). Since frugality grew out of mortification, Baxter (ibid.:225) said to "carefully mortify" wasteful "lusts . . . and sensuality" as the way to "escape Prodigality." Ames ([1639] 1975:255) concurred that frugality required "that wee bee not lovers of pleasures"; and Perkins ([1606] 1972:III, 537) advised "moderation of the appetite in the use of riches." So, in practice frugality dovetailed with the conquest of the flesh and sin.

In part, prodigality was opposed because it was used to support other sins. For example, Baxter (1678:IV, 225; see also I, 216) declared it a "sin" to use riches "for the provision and maintenance of fleshly lusts and

Pride"; moreover, wasting money on pleasure "feedeth a life of other vice and wickedness. It is spending Gods gifts to feed those lusts which he abhorreth."

The norm of parsimony required the employment of money in things with "necessarie uses" (see Ames [1639] 1975:254, 255; Perkins [1606] 1972:III, 536). Hill ([1613] 1975:II, 81) was scrupulous "that I buy not that which is needlesse for me." For Baxter (1678:IV, 223), "A Delight wholly needless . . . is sinful if it be purchased, but at the price of a farthing, or of a bit of bread, or of a minutes time: Because that is cast away which purchaseth it." The same held if the thing purchased was "vaine and unprofitable" (Ames [1639] 1975:254, 255; see also Baxter 1678:IV, 223).

Although the Puritan norm of parsimony is easily and amply documented, it should not be exaggerated. As with so many Puritan tenets, there is another, contrary side. Puritan frugality was not meant to be extreme, but rather a form of moderation. "Faith is . . . provident and frugall," wrote Ball (1632:357), "though not . . . pinching and niggardly." Hill ([1613] 1975:45), too, condemned "niggardly Parsimonie . . . I must not . . . spare . . . when I ought to spend" (Hill [1613] 1975:80). Ames ([1639] 1975:254, 255) recommended neither "That wee . . . envy our selves the just use of, those things we possesse . . . [n]or yet foolishly devour them," but insisted "that wee employ our money in those things, which have a reall use." Hence, the Puritan stereotype should be one of moderation rather than one of miserliness (see Poggi 1983:41).

According to Dent ([1601] 1974:76), "frugalitie, thriftinesse, and good husbandrie" were acceptable but "a pinching and niggardly keeping of our own" was a sign of covetousness (ibid.:78, see also p. 103); "not onely is he covetous which greedily desireth other mens goods: but even he also which overniggardly and pinchingly holdeth fast his owne. . . . We see the world is full of such pinchpennies that wil let nothing goe." It was "required that [frugality] doe not proceed from the love of riches; but out of conscience toward God" (see Ames [1639] 1975:255). In Ames's (ibid.:261) view, "a Covetous man sinneth . . . in retaining or keeping" riches. Downame ([1604] 1974:I, 85) warned that covetousness could masquerade as frugality. And Baxter (1678:IV, 224) insisted that "We must . . . not be sparing out of Covetousness."

Besides the danger of covetousness, another limitation on Puritan frugality was the class system and the preachers' attitude toward it. Their consensus was that expenditures be appropriate to one's station; hence, Puritanism did not reduce the expenditures of the wealthy to the level of the less fortunate. Baxter (1678:IV, 222) considered an expense excessive "when it is above the proportion of your own estate; or the ordinary use of those of your own rank." Similarly, Hill's ([1613] 1975:80; but see Seaver 1985:135) concept of frugality stipulated "That I spend not above my estate." Although Downame ([1604] 1974:I, 76) opposed the wearing of fancy attire beyond people's state and callings, neither were they to dress below their stations. According to Perkins ([1606] 1972:III, 568–69), people should dress according to their station since it was confusing if they dressed as if at a different rank. Equal and superior should not be clothed alike (ibid.:III, 582). And silk, velvet, precious stones, gold, and silver could be used if worn in meekness and humility rather than haughtiness (ibid.:III, 560–63).

Thus, Puritanism upheld traditional consumption fashions rather than undercutting them.[11] Although Puritan regulation cut excess spending by enforcing prevailing consumption norms, it did not aim to reduce the accepted standard of living to gain savings. Contrary to Weber ([1904–5] 1958:172), Puritanism did not encourage an "ascetic compulsion to save." It even fell short of Wesley's ideal, which urged Methodists to "save all they can" (quoted by Weber [1904–5] 1958:175). Consequently, its approach to frugality cannot be given primary credit for the massive savings needed for capitalist investment and expansion. Its contribution was a limited one.[12]

Even when Puritan thrift helped to generate savings, the excess funds were not available as discretionary money (Ball cited by Seaver 1985:137–38). There were religious norms regulating the disposition of these assets. One reason for frugality, according to Ames ([1639] 1975:255) was for "doing good to others." According to Perkins ([1606] 1972:III, 536, see also p. 582), "the good of others" meant especially family and kindred, "releife of the poore," maintenance of the church and true religion, and maintenance of the commonwealth. Similarly, Downame ([1604] 1974:I, 61) felt that the temptation to unthrifty misspending was wrong due to the obligation to provide for one's family, and to give more to God's ministers (see Downame [1604] 1974:II, 246). Baxter (1678:IV, 222–25; see also I, 215, 381; 1653:234; Seaver 1985:136) urged people to "forbear all needless expenses" to relieve the poor and to maintain their children, the state, and the church; other desirable expenditures were for promotion of the preaching of the Gospel, sending poor children to apprenticeships or school, and the relief of distressed families. In short, when parsimony generated surplus funds, it was required that "wee willingly bestow upon pious uses as farre, as wee are able" (see Ames [1639] 1975:255).

This norm, if followed, tended to reduce the moneys left over for business investment. Savings could not be reinvested as long as the poor and the church were in need. The norm of frugality would have raised more investment capital had it not been combined with the requirement of charitable good works.

In Wallington's case the reduction in funds was largely due to the generosity of his father (see Seaver 1985:77, 118). John Wallington, Sr., was a successful businessman, but very charitable; he had paid the debts of his son-in-law and of another poor member of his trade guild (ibid.:77, 118). Consequently, he "had given away most of what fortune he had" by the time he made out his will (ibid.:118). Also his will forgave the many debts owed him by the poor (ibid.). With only a small inheritance, Nehemiah and his brother had little capital for the continuation and extension of their family's business. Furthermore, John, Sr., could have built a larger business by reinvesting his surplus instead of giving it away.

In short, although Puritan frugality saved some money for economic investment, the amount was reduced by two factors: (1) opposition to miserliness or living beneath one's station; and (2) the duty to spend on charitable causes. Both limited the significance of frugality for Puritan business success and for English economic expansion.

THE CULTURAL EFFECT OF THE WORK ETHIC

It has been shown in this chapter that Puritanism gave a limited boost to its believers' work and savings behavior.[13] But the story does not end there. Besides its behavioral influence on the Puritans, the work ethic has significantly influenced the general *culture* of the Occident. Contrary to Weber ([1904–5] 1958:183), who exaggerated the breakdown of the Protestant ethic into pure utilitarianism in modern times, the work ethic remains with us today as a cultural value. The industrious are more respected than the lazy, for example. Activity and disdain for idleness remain general cultural values.

In fact, the work ethic's cultural influence seems to be stronger than its behavioral impact when the following reasons are considered. First of all, cultural diffusion extended this ethic from the small Puritan minority to an entire civilization, and from the Puritan era, which had ended in England by 1700, up through the industrial age and into the present. Second, these later epochs gave it a higher priority than the Puritans themselves did. As part of the Puritan faith it was subordinated to religious worship and undercut by otherworldliness; but it was borrowed culturally without many of the Puritan limitations on economic life. The devotion to work was preserved intact while the limitations on work commitment due to otherworldliness and/or religious worship were greatly diminished.

These occurrences explain Weber's observation that Puritanism's greatest influence came after its apogee had passed. First, the stronger effect, i.e. the cultural influence, occurred later, while just the weaker behavioral effect occurred during the Puritan age itself. Second, once Puritan piety had declined, the work ethic could be borrowed selectively with less reason to limit work for religious purposes.

Weber called the sixteenth- and seventeenth-century Puritans "carriers" (*Träger*) of the work ethic, but their influence worked somewhat differently than he hypothesized. Although behavioral effects increased production, profits, savings, and investment somewhat, these effects were limited for reasons detailed above. More important was the Puritans' role as a persuasive moral force on others; also they served as models of economic diligence and frugality. However, following the Restoration their influence in these capacities declined along with the Puritan movement in England, and by Victorian times they were no longer a distinguishable group; so in neither of these periods could they influence others as immediate carriers of the work ethos. It was as cultural models from the past that they were chiefly able to influence modern times.[14]

Puritanism's influence on English culture began in the sixteenth century through the influence of Puritan theologians on the Church of England,[15] and reached a peak during the reign of Cromwell, in the seventeenth century, when the Puritans briefly controlled England. After the Stuart Restoration, anti-Puritan sentiment predominated in England. Puritan preaching was silenced pursuant to the Act of Uniformity, and Puritan influence was virtually eliminated from the tenets of the Church of England.

Nevertheless, by Victorian times the cultural influence of Puritanism had resurfaced with considerable vigor. The nineteenth-century Anglican middle class insisted "on the virtue of hard work and the vice of idleness, its Sunday observance, its self-reliance, its thrift and its intolerance of the 'pleasant vices'" (Marlowe 1956:50). In Victorian England, work was part of a secular ethos, and became for many the central purpose of life. One's profession was a calling in itself, often the most important one. Linked with other principles of the secular culture by intellectuals like Tennyson, Carlyle, and Ruskin, the grip of the work ethic on people's lives was formidable. "In a business society, and one that was strongly under Puritan influence, work was an absolute necessity . . . parents and preachers, writers and lecturers, proclaimed as with a single voice that man was created to work, that everyone had his appointed calling in which he was to labor for God and man, that idleness was a moral and social sin" (Houghton 1957:189). Though too late to have inspired the industrial revolution in England, which had arrived before Victoria ascended the throne, this Victorian "cultural puritanism" undoubtedly supported England's ninteenth century economic expansion.

The growth of industry and frugality as secular English values can be traced historically by examining the handbooks of self-improvement and moral conduct that were so popular in the sixteenth and seventeenth centuries. According to Wright (1958:199), who has studied many of these books closely, the fusion of industry and thrift into a single dogma took shape in the early sixteenth century (see, for example, Elyot [1531] 1937:100) and crystallized in the seventeenth. Although the origins of this dogma predated the Puritan era, its development paralleled that of Puritanism, which suggests some Puritan influence. Wright (1958:127) found that secular seventeenth-century moralists like Braithwaite merely echoed Puritan ministers. As Puritanism developed, the volume of books stressing labor and thrift increased (ibid.:186). And as "Puritan influences became more pronounced, the emphasis on moral virtue grew stronger in the conduct books" (ibid.:126); that is, diligence and thrift were portrayed more as moral virtues and less as practical strategies. A good example of Puritan influence on a secular advice book is William Scott's seventeenth-century *Essay on Drapery*. Scott ([1635] 1953; cited by Wright 1958:166) maintained that "The Compleat Citizen" must be thrifty and industrious. He ([1635] 1953:30–33) urged diligent labor and inveighed against idleness. These values came from his "religious upbringing" (Thrupp 1953:5) and his Puritan piety (ibid.:9). Their origins are revealed by his reliance on religious sources (see ibid.:12).

The *ultimate* origin of the work ethic is somewhat clouded by its more-or-less simultaneous prominence in Puritanism and in secular culture. In fact, since industry and thrift were virtues and idleness and prodigality vices before Puritanism developed (see, for example, Clayre 1974:153), one may even suspect that these ethics are of secular provenance rather than religious. But the early roots of the work ethic were ultimately religious, stemming from parts of the Judeo-Christian tradition that antedated Puritanism.[16] The development of this tradition became the work ethic's avenue of entry into the secular mainstream of the modern Occident. Indeed, the monastic style of modern work betrays its religious roots.

As Weber pointed out, the systematization of ethics in ancient Judaism set the stage for modern Christian ethics. For example, in Puritanism the Divine command to labor is supported by a number of Old Testament sources (see Baxter 1678:I, 376). Hyma (1951), Fanfani (1935), and Samuelsson (1961:81–82) have documented that Catholicism, too, adopted an ethic of industry, sobriety, and thrift. This work ethic was preached by Bernard of Siena (Thrupp 1953:10–11), St. Benedict (in his monastic rules) and other Roman Catholic moralists. St. Bernard viewed work as a way to relate to God, not just as a punishment for the Fall (ibid.:10). This ethic applied to laypersons as well as monks. Although it lacked some of the elements and some of the intensity of the Puritan ethic, it made an earlier contribution.[17] Also, Catholicism and Lutheranism have asked people to serve God in a calling (*vocatio*).

Next came the Puritan contribution. Although Puritanism did not create the work ethic, it did, within limits, strengthen it, just as Weber ([1904–5] 1958:178) stated. Puritanism was more innerworldly than these other religions and paid more attention to the calling. George and George (1958:368) argue that the Puritans' work ethic was uniquely intense:

> the English Protestant divine can confidently be said to celebrate work in the calling . . . in a peculiarly wholesale and emphatic manner. . . . What is original in English Protestantism . . . is the intensity and frequency of the sermons on the worth of work and unhesitating application of these ideals to all social levels and all occupational groupings in English society.

In conclusion, Puritanism strengthened a work ethic that entered Western culture through the Judeo-Christian religious tradition, and then passed it on to secular culture in strengthened form. The religious factor consists in great measure of Puritanism's role in intensifying, modeling, and disseminating these economic norms.

NOTES

1. Nevertheless, "[I] neglected my Calling" for book writing "and so brought my self to some want (Folger diary: To the Christian Reader)." He attributed periodic bouts of poverty to "idleness and negligence" in his calling (Seaver 1985:130). Once he even fined himself for negligence in his calling (see ibid.:125).

2. However, religion should not be seen as the *only* cause of this conduct. Industry, frugality, and business success were also encouraged by the Puritans' middle-class status. Relatedly, in Hill's (1964:134) view, the self-employed and "small employers" occupied a marginal business position that *required* hard work and frugality as an economic expedient. Also, English Puritans were a minority (see Seaver 1985:viii), and minority groups are especially likely to attempt and to succeed at business enterprise (see Weber [1904–5] 1958:39).

3. Moreover, "a man that is paid for his labour by another . . . do rob them by their Idleness, when they withhold from them any part of that which they are paid for" (Baxter 1678:I, 380).

4. Of course, insofar as the calling served God, its importance grew; but Preston ([1629] 1976:90) stated that things of the calling "belong to the good of man." One should avoid placing the works of the calling in category 3 with the works of salvation. Contrary to Weber, it will be shown below that labor in the calling was marginal both to salvation and the certainty thereof.

5. Merchant Elias Pledger (diary:14, 55) exemplifies the acceptance of these practices.

6. But Pledger (diary:15) felt that business could justifiably reduce religious participation because "it cannot be avoided."

7. Nevertheless, John Wallington, Sr., worked on the Sabbath (Seaver 1985:203), and Nehemiah Wallington skipped a fast day service to work in his shop (ibid.:126–27).

8. This tenet was accepted by merchant Pledger, who warned against "inordinate love of the world" (Folger diary:188).

9. Pledger (diary:24) saw it as "just a passage to your rest."

10. Weber (1946:332, see also p. 291) knew that Puritanism devalued the world as "creatural and depraved." Apparently he thought that this made no ultimate difference in its impact on economic conduct. However, it did limit devotion to one's job.

11. Consistently, Trevor-Roper (1972:14) reports that the great Calvinist entrepreneurs lived "magnificently."

12. Wallington's expenditures on maids and servants (see Seaver 1985:121) may not have been considered extravagant if required by his station. Similarly, Pledger was unable to maintain his desired lifestyle. Hence, neither merchant in this study was able to save.

13. Because Puritan economic norms demanded moderation, the most pious could neither be the most economically active nor the most parsimonious. It would require a *selective* piety to strengthen the work ethic above other religious duties and to encourage extreme frugality while ignoring the duty of charity. Insofar as it did occur, selective piety must be explained by nonreligious causes related to Puritans' class position and material interests, not by Puritanism.

14. The work standards they set in the seventeenth century were partially abandoned in "Merrie England" after the Restoration and had to be reinvented later.

15. Indeed, by the seventeenth century "The Anglican apologists emphasized the dignity of labor even more than the Puritans" (Grassby 1995:290; see also Seaver 1980:19; O'Connell 1976:20).

16. Of course, as Rose (1985:31) has pointed out, the work ethic did not derive "uniquely from religious teaching."

17. Despite irrational "escape hatches" that permitted some wayward Catholics to avoid Divine sanctions, Catholicism was well able to enforce its religious norms. In fact, Durkheim's famous study of suicide found that Catholics' degree of moral adherence exceeded that of Protestants. Catholicism as well as Protestantism requires ascetic self-control to overcome sin. And the same is true in Judaism.

3

The Spirit of Capitalism

SOME LOGICAL ISSUES

The Spirit of Capitalism versus the Work Ethic

The Puritan work ethic can plausibly contribute to the explanation of Puritan economic success because it had some force and predated the Puritan prosperity of Elizabethan and early Stuart times. However, its similarity to the work ethics of other cultures makes it inappropriate as an explanation for Occidental uniqueness, and its compatibility with a variety of economic systems gives it no special affinity to capitalism. Furthermore, it can be quite traditional in outlook, as Weber knew from his study of Luther. These drawbacks undoubtedly encouraged Weber to deemphasize the work ethic in explaining the rise of rational capitalism. Instead, in describing the impact of Protestantism on modern capitalism, Weber ([1923] 1961:258–70) heavily stressed the spirit of capitalism as the prime Protestant contribution.

Since the capitalist spirit is said to have evolved out of Puritanism, achieving, in Weber's view, its definitive form only after the purely religious movement had begun its decline, this spirit apparently developed too late to account for the *early* economic success of the Puritans, which is better explained by their work ethic for reasons just stated. However, on logical grounds the spirit of capitalism seems better suited than the work ethic for explaining *later* capitalist success. As defined by Weber, it holds profit-making to be a duty and the end of life, while the work ethic produces profit only as an unintended consequence of diligence and frugality.

Nevertheless, the desire for wealth cannot in itself produce wealth when effective means are lacking; and this limits the effectiveness of the spirit of capitalism. On the other hand John Wesley (see Weber [1904–5] 1958:175) and Benjamin Franklin (see Weber ibid.:49, 53) both praised hard work as the best means to riches and Weber (ibid.:175) himself acknowledged that the accumulation of wealth can be sizeable even when wealth comes as an unanticipated consequence. So the work ethic, too, can promote profitability.[1]

It is mainly with regard to reinvestment that the suitability of the spirit of capitalism for economic growth seems greater. Where profit is sought as an end, current profits are more likely to be reinvested in future growth than where profits emerge as unintended consequences. Unintended windfalls obtained by hard work might be used for consumption or for charity as easily as for ever-renewed profit; use would depend on the entrepreneur's priorities. But the spirit of capitalism incorporates profit-making as the ultimate life-goal.

Weber (ibid.:68) used the spirit of capitalism to explain the expansion of modern capitalism. The spirit of capitalism demanded elevated levels of profit, labor discipline, and aggressive marketing which expanded the circle of purchasers (ibid.:67). Through this expansion the provision of wants became organized capitalistically to the extent that the whole epoch became capitalistic (see Weber [1923] 1961:207). Thus, the spirit of capitalism can be conceived as the part of modern capitalism that gives it its dynamic growth properties. Its role in explaining the rise of capitalism has been largely based on this characteristic.

The Aim of This Chapter

This chapter examines the effect of Puritanism on modern capitalism by virtue of its influence on the spirit of capitalism. Weber ([1904–5] 1958:78) hypothesized that the spirit of capitalism was the "intellectual child" of the Protestant ethic. However, it is argued below that there was no such influence. First of all, it is doubtful that the "spirit of capitalism" has ever existed as Weber defined it; Benjamin Franklin, Weber's only "example" of this spirit, did not embody it after all. Second, even if the spirit of capitalism did exist, it could not have developed from Puritanism in any direct fashion because of basic contradictions between the two. It would have required marked changes to transform Puritan economic norms into the spirit of capitalism; and there is no evidence that any such modifications ever occurred. Furthermore, despite some rational features, Puritan economic teachings were often quite traditional in spirit. Puritanism's traditional outlooks discouraged rational capitalism.

Who Had the Spirit of Capitalism?

To begin with, the very existence of the spirit of capitalism is problematic. Marshall (1982:68) points out that it has never been proven to exist: it remains "empirically unverified and possibly, in practice, unverifiable." Weber "provides no empirical data to substantiate his ideal type of the spirit of modern capitalism," Marshall (1980:16–17) argues; he failed "to offer any empirical evidence whatsoever as to the motivations of particular capitalists or groups of capitalists" (Marshall 1982:120, see also pp. 66–68), including "seventeenth century businessmen" (Marshall 1980:17) and "modern . . . businessmen" alike (Marshall 1982:67–68).

Moreover, Weber's (1946:309; see also [1904–5] 1958:65, 69) contention that leading capitalist figures such as Morgan, Rockefeller, and Gould did not bear "the specifically Occidental bourgeois mentality" eliminates those who would seem its most plausible exponents. It would be surprising indeed if the spirit of capitalism existed in others when it was not shared by the world's leading capitalists.

Beyond this, the absence of the spirit of capitalism among major capitalists shows that capitalistic expansion occurred without this "spirit." These business leaders, who contributed to the size and rationality of capitalism, illustrate how capitalism achieved dominance without the spirit of capitalism as a motive force.

Weber ([1904–5] 1958:55) dismissed the importance of the most heroic capitalists precisely because they were extraordinary. In contrast, he argued that capitalist expansion required the systematic generation of suitable motivation; to become dominant, the appropriate motives could not originate in "isolated individuals," but needed to be part of "a way of life common to whole groups of men." Yet, despite his intent in this passage of attributing the spirit of capitalism to the bourgeois class as a whole, his denial that large capitalists possessed it has the effect of limiting it to the class of smaller businessmen. If the capitalist spirit was no more than a mentality of small businessmen, it is doubtful that it contributed much to large-scale capitalism.

Limiting the spirit of capitalism to small businessmen has added to its evidentiary difficulties as well. While there existed some biographies of major business leaders, until recently there was scant historical record of the outlooks of small businessmen and hence no way to substantiate the spirit of capitalism's existence.

Weber's presentation of his ideal type relied too heavily on the example of Benjamin Franklin and the philosophy in his almanac. This has left the empirical grounding of the entire concept hanging by a single slender thread. Yet this example has been called into question by Samuelsson (1961:55–61) and Graham (1971:192). If Franklin himself proves not to exemplify the spirit of capitalism, it will begin to look like an empty set.[2] And it will be argued below that Franklin did not fully embody the spirit of capitalism as described by Weber ([1904–5] 1958:47–64).

FRANKLIN AND THE CAPITALIST SPIRIT

Ben Franklin and Poor Richard

For analyzing Franklin's thought, the first step is to distinguish between Benjamin Franklin and Poor Richard. Although Poor Richard was a *nom de plume* of Franklin, the viewpoint expressed through Poor Richard may not be identical to Franklin's private philosophy. It is safer to treat them separately at first and then examine their relationship later, rather than to assume a priori, as Weber did, that they represent a unity.

In the *Almanac* and related writings, Poor Richard illuminated the way to wealth. Effective means included industry, overseeing one's own business, not wasting time, and being frugal about expenditures (see Franklin 1795, 1900). In short, Poor Richard advocated the work ethic as the best means to business success.

The proffered advice was strictly utilitarian in nature. Wealth was assumed to be a goal, and the advice consisted of technically effective means to achieve that goal. The accumulation of money was not considered a higher value or ultimate end. As Poor Richard (Franklin 1900:38) said, "The use of money is all the advantage there is in having money." Weber ([1904–5] 1958:77) classified this type of orientation as "practical rationalism," not the "spirit of capitalism" (see ibid.:53).

There was no ethical content in Poor Richard's advice. Although his recommended qualities were generally regarded as virtues, they were recommended here for their technical efficacy, not for virtue's sake, as Weber (ibid.:52) well knew. Franklin referred to Poor Richard's sayings as "wisdom," not duty. They were "hints" that "if observed" could be "of service" (Franklin 1900:41). They were regarded as "proverbs" (Franklin 1795:Preface, p. 2) in the sense of truths rather than of ethical desiderata. The advice given was presented as "counsel," not "a common sermon." Poor Richard (Franklin 1900:34) wrote that his advice cost nothing, and "if you will not be angry with me for giving it, I promise you not to be offended if you do not take it." There was clearly no obligation to follow these adages. In comparison to the Puritan work ethic, Poor Richard's version represents what Weber ([1904–5] 1958:183) called a "dissolution into pure utilitarianism."

The opportunistic character of Poor Richard's maxims became even clearer when he emphasized their situational nature. Hard work and redeeming time were not advocated as lifelong principles, but as temporary stratagems for achieving their opposites! Poor Richard (Franklin 1795) counseled that leisure and pleasure would come upon those who did not pursue them. One must be diligent to gain leisure time. Like Baxter, Poor

Richard recommended diligence for redeeming time from work, but unlike Baxter, Poor Richard's aims were leisure and pleasure rather than salvation or duty to God.

In sum, Poor Richard did not expound the spirit of capitalism. Despite his colorful portrayals of rational calculation at work (see Weber [1904–5] 1958:48–50), his philosophy lacked all the ethical portions of the spirit of capitalism: acquisition as a duty, wealth as an end in itself, and money-making as the "ultimate purpose" of one's life (see ibid.:53).

Although Franklin's (1964) personal life and philosophy are much more ethically colored than Poor Richard's, they lack the same basic elements of the capitalistic spirit found wanting in Poor Richard. Franklin's attitude toward acquisition was practical rather than ethical; he viewed wealth as a means rather than an end; and moneymaking was certainly not the ultimate purpose of his life.

Unlike Poor Richard, Franklin (1981:78–91) developed a true ethos, a method of perfection through virtue. Since he (ibid.:83, for example) took God seriously, Weber ([1904–5] 1958:53) may be correct that Franklin sought a "path of righteousness" and that his philosophy was "something more than mere garnishing for egocentric motives."

Franklin (1964:79) considered order a virtue. He (1981:93) believed that life required a "good Plan," and he developed and followed a methodical plan of life (the Puritan influence in this is unmistakable). He (1964:80) felt that order gave a person more time and reduced idleness: "Let all your Things have their Places. Let each Part of your Business have its Time" (ibid.:79, see also p. 83). Hence, for him, the systematic rationalization of business grew out of the ethical rationalization of life.

However, moneymaking was not included in his ethical life plan. Rational acquisition was considered neither a virtue nor a duty. Franklin (ibid.:108) repeatedly referred to the ability of money to multiply and grow, but attributed this to its "prolific Nature." He expounded no human duty to make sure monetary growth occurred.

Like Poor Richard, he (ibid.:88) advised that industry and frugality had improved his fortune. However, also like Poor Richard, he attributed these qualities more to expediency than to duty. Due to "narrow circumstances" there was a "Necessity I was under of sticking close to my Business" (Franklin 1981:93). "My Industry in my Business continu'd as indefatigable as it was necessary. I was in debt for my Printing-house, I had a young Family coming on to be educated, and I had to contend with the competition" (ibid.:75).

Like Poor Richard, Franklin declined to consider moneymaking a lifelong principle of conduct. In 1748, while still relatively young at forty-two, he became a silent partner in the printing business, and turned it over to David Hall to manage (see Graham 1971:192). He lived forty-two more years in retirement. He (Franklin 1981:92) had long hoped that "Circumstances should afford me the necessary Leisure" to develop a new religious creed. Now, "by the sufficient tho' moderate Fortune I had acquir'd, I had secur'd Leisure during the rest of my Life for Philosophical Studies and Amusements" (Franklin 1964:119). Furthermore, "Frugality and Industry, by making my Circumstances easy, freeing me from my remaining Debt and producing Affluence and Independence would make more easy the Practice of Sincerity and Justice" (ibid.:81). In contrast to the spirit of capitalism's requirement of a duty to one's pool of capital, Franklin "was very glad to leave off making money as soon as he had a comfortable income" (ibid.:16 of Introduction). He obviously failed to regard wealth as an end in itself or as his primary purpose in life. His acceptance in later life of many jobs of public service echoed the Puritan call for a life of good deeds. However, Franklin's reputation for good living and even debauchery belie the notion that he led an ascetic life.

In sum, while Franklin's character and Poor Richard's philosophy each illustrate a few aspects of the spirit of capitalism, neither embodies it *in toto*. Neither can serve to exemplify it nor to demonstrate its existence. While Poor Richard and Franklin himself share many philosophical principles, their mentalities cannot be equated. Nor is it clear that their philosophies can be simply added together to make a "whole," as Weber ([1904–5] 1958:52–53) in effect did in his analysis of Franklin. Although Franklin's ethics add a missing dimension to Poor Richard's stark utilitarianism, they do not add the correct ethical principles needed to transform it into the spirit of capitalism. Still lacking are the key ethical ingredients: acquisition as a duty, wealth as an end in itself, and moneymaking as the ultimate purpose of life.

Franklin and the Work Ethic

It is within this context, Franklin's failure to embody the spirit of capitalism, that the Puritan influence on his work must be evaluated. As Weber ([1904–5] 1958:78) asked "whose intellectual child" the spirit of capitalism was, we may inquire whose intellectual child was Franklin's philosophy. Of course, the work ethic has developed and flourished within a number of intellectual traditions, both religious and secular, and secular wisdom certainly must have influenced a practical man of affairs like Franklin. Nevertheless, it is easy to identify a direct chain of ideational transmission that leads from Baxter to Franklin.

The figure who links these two is Cotton Mather. As a family friend of the Mathers, Franklin had considerable exposure to their worldviews. Cotton Mather, in turn, was an avid reader of Baxter, and incorporated Baxter's teachings prominently in his own work. A prime example stems from Baxter's extraordinary emphasis on doing as much good as possible (see, for example, Baxter 1653:333–36). Mather ([1710] 1966) adopted the same emphasis in one of his chief works, *An Essay Upon the Good.* "Be up and doing," urged Mather (ibid.:9). "Use all talents and opportunities to do good. Ask what good you can do each day and set a time" (ibid.:31–32). Franklin's remark that he was heavily influenced by *An Essay Upon the Good* is quite well-known. This influence is apparent in his use of the pen name "Silence Dogood" to communicate his maxims. Baxter's influence on Franklin is also evident in the latter's dedication to public service. Baxter (1678:I, 377) had advocated as many good works as possible to benefit the "Commonwealth."

Most importantly, Franklin's version of the work ethic is quite heavily influenced by the Puritan work ethic; diligence, frugality, and wise use of time were advocated by both Baxter and Mather. The chief difference is that Franklin's version was utilitarian, whereas Baxter and Mather (for example, see [1710] 1966:32) stressed salvation and duty to God.[3] This case demonstrates quite clearly what the Protestant ethic looked like after the peak of piety had passed (see Weber [1904–5] 1958:180). It looked like a secularized version of the work ethic.

Contrary to Weber, however, it did not look like the spirit of capitalism. Franklin did not advocate moneymaking as an end in life. Instead, he used his comfortable financial station as a means to pursue a life of service to the commonwealth.

It was probably *because of, not in spite of,* his Puritan roots, that Franklin could not support the capitalist spirit as Weber defined it. Mather ([1710] 1966:23) virtually echoed the otherworldliness of Baxter and the other English divines in his disparagement of "temporal business:" "Why should a soul of such high capacities . . . yet embrace a dunghill!" This strongly undercuts those who make profit an end in life. Baxter, insofar as he supported profit-making, viewed it as a means rather than an end in itself. And so did Franklin.

Hence, it is one thing to say that Baxter influenced Franklin, which he did, and quite another to say that he influenced the spirit of capitalism. The two cannot be equated because Franklin did not exemplify the spirit of capitalism. What Franklin best exemplifies is the Protestant ethic of working and saving. His example illustrates that it is quite possible to embody the work ethic without the spirit of capitalism.

THE PROBLEM OF VERIFICATION

Franklin's failure to exemplify the spirit of capitalism is quite damaging to the concept, since without Franklin there is no known example of it.[4]

Nor does Poggi's (1983:47) argument that Weber intended the Franklin example to be more expository than historical help matters; it merely concedes the point that there never was a real example.[5]

Weber has denied that capitalism's leading figures possessed it. But neither did small businessmen embody it. The data on Puritan shopkeepers yield no examples of the spirit of capitalism. The two cases differ somewhat, but neither merchant possessed the key characteristics specified by Weber.

Nehemiah Wallington endorsed only a small part of the spirit of capitalism: the duty to make money. He (Folger diary:413) considered someone guilty of negligence and slothfulness "when he doth not observe the opportunitys of his calling." However, Wallington was no exemplar himself; he (quoted by Seaver 1985:235; see also British diary:15) thought himself "very remiss" in his "getting." Nor did he consider gain an end in itself. According to Seaver (1985:126), Wallington saw wealth as a means toward religious goals. He (Folger diary:218) attributed its pursuit as a goal to the worldly. Although he tried to profit, often to pay debts and taxes, he regarded these concerns as a worry and a burden (see Seaver 1985:112, 138). Rather than seeking ever-renewed profit, his hope for his "old days" was "to sit down and rest from cares and troubles of the world and the rest of my time to employ in holy duties." Clearly, moneymaking was not his most important goal in life. His (Folger diary:218) aims were to possess God and Christ, obtain "the graces of the Spirit," and glorify God "with a holy and unblamable life." In comparison to these, "the process of getting and spending" was never a major preoccupation (Seaver 1985:112, see also p. 121). The affairs of the calling were less important than other parts of Christianity (see ibid.:125, 145).

Elias Pledger, too, lacked the spirit of capitalism. Though he was avaricious, his economic motive clearly aimed at a higher standard of living. Hence, profit was neither perceived as a duty nor as an end in itself. Although moneymaking threatened to grow into his chief life interest, his religious side fought this tendency. As noted earlier, he (quoted by Cragg 1957:131) felt guilty when he concentrated too heavily on business or when he desired more income. Far from causing his moneymaking bent, his Puritan piety opposed it. His example shows a conflict between Puritanism and the spirit of capitalism.

Weber ([1904–5] 1958:51–52) was at pains to show that famous Catholic businessmen like Jakob Fugger lacked the spirit of capitalism. However, the Puritan businessmen in this study lacked it also. The concept looks more and more like an empty category. Insofar as it lacks correspondence to the motives of early entrepreneurs, it can shed little light on the development of capitalism.

Of course, it cannot be proved conclusively that no examples of the spirit of capitalism ever existed; it is only feasible to rule out the examples that have been proposed. Therefore, the concept should be put on hold until new examples demonstrate that it did or does exist.

One trouble with the spirit of capitalism as an ideal type is that it combines so many qualities in the same person. Someone with a capitalist spirit must seek profit continuously and systematically using rational calculation; and profit-seeking must be a duty, an end, and an ultimate life-purpose. With so many defining criteria, it is no wonder that it is difficult to find examples. Of course, individual components of the spirit of capitalism have been found separately, e.g., the continuous, rational pursuit of profit (Marshall 1980:172–73, 193). What is difficult to find is the combination.

In Weber's ([1904–5] 1958:69) view modern capitalists were "men who had grown up in the hard school of life, calculating and daring at the same time, above all temperate and reliable, shrewd and completely devoted to their business, with strictly bourgeois opinions and principles." "He gets nothing out of his wealth for himself, except the irrational sense of having done his job well," wrote Weber (ibid.:71). It should not be surprising when this romanticized account of the bourgeoisie proves difficult to verify in fact.[6]

ELECTIVE AFFINITY THROUGH SIMILARITY?

The lack of examples makes the spirit of capitalism seem quite dubious, but not all of the evidence is in, so there remains a possibility that empirical grounding could be found. That possibility makes it necessary to explore a link between Puritanism and the spirit of capitalism. Could that spirit, if it did exist, have evolved from Puritanism?

Following Weber's method of elective affinities, the answer to this question may be inferred from the degree of similarity between Puritan ethics and the spirit of capitalism: to the extent that the spirit of capitalism is consistent and/or coincident with Puritan teachings, it could have developed directly out of Puritanism; on the other hand, if the two are disparate or mutually contradictory, such direct descent would seem remote.

The data below show that even if the spirit of capitalism did exist, Puritanism would not support it. It could not have emerged from Puritanism in any direct fashion because the two differed in important ways. An examination of the spirit of capitalism's chief defining characteristics, namely, gain as a duty, as an end, and as life's central goal, reveals greater differences than similarities.

Gain as a Duty

One part of Weber's definition of the spirit of capitalism finds some support in Puritanism, namely the idea of profit as a duty. Weber ([1904–5] 1958:163, 268 note 3) is correct that the Puritans made acquisition "a duty" of the calling. Baxter (1678:I, 378) preached, "If God shew you a way in which you may lawfully get more than in another way . . . if you refuse this, and choose the less gainful way, you cross one of the ends of your calling." It was "no sin, but a duty, to labour not only for labour sake . . . but for that honest increase and provision, which is the end of our labor" (Baxter 1678:IV, 225).

However, contrary to Weber, the duty was not owed to one's pool of capital but to God and to the poor, who stood to benefit from charitable good works. And not all capital accumulation was enjoined—only that intended to serve God and charity (see Chapter 4).

One line of Weberian reasoning that seems to make *all* profit a duty is actually untrue to Puritanism. Weber ([1904–5] 1958:178) noted that business activities were a calling, and all were obligated to their callings. Since the job of a capitalist is to make a profit, he reasoned, duty to that calling is by implication a duty to profit. Weber (ibid.:72) referred to it as a "devotion to the calling of making money." Though Weber's deduction is logical, its conclusion carries outside the bounds of Puritan ethics. Perkins (1970:II, 464) warned against using "the works of our calling . . . only to get wealth," so there could be no calling of making money.[7]

Profit as an End

Baxter (1678:I, 378) made it clear that wealth could not be sought as an end in itself, but only "in subordination to higher things," namely, to serve God and to do good deeds of charity or philanthropy. Riches, though "useful and profitable" as a means (Ames [1639] 1975:253), were not considered a worthy end in themselves. Hence, seeking riches for their own sake would be considered idle. Even worse, Ames (ibid.:261; see also Dent cited by Seaver 1985:134) warned that it was covetous "if riches are . . . loved for themselves." Likewise, Baxter (1678:I, 215) judged that "The love of . . . Riches . . . is the setting up of a false end. . . . It is a perverting of the very drift of a mans life, as employed in seeking a wrong end. . . . It is a perverting of Gods creatures to an End and Use clean contrary to that which they were made and given for."

Although moneymaking was a religious duty, which helped to free acquisition from the desire to consume, it was not approved as an end in itself. According to Seaver (1985:134), "the moral man must always subordinate the economic means to the larger social end." He (ibid.:133) reports that "economic activity was always properly aimed beyond itself to a social good and ultimately to the glory of God."

Weber ([1904–5] 1958:172) knew that the pursuit of riches for their own sake was condemned as covetousness and considered "highly reprehensible." Although that fact puts Puritanism at odds with the spirit of capitalism, Weber insisted on an affinity between them nonetheless. He (ibid.) argued that Puritanism encouraged the pursuit of wealth as a sign of salvation, and thereby helped to make it a life-goal. That reasoning has two major drawbacks, though. First, if certainty of salvation was the aim, then acquisition would be a means toward it, not an end in itself. Second, as will be shown below, most English Puritans of this era did not regard wealth as a sign.

Life's Central Aim

One parallel between Puritanism and the spirit of capitalism is that both organize conduct as a means to an end (see Weber [1904–5] 1958:53). In business that end has been profit and in Puritanism it was God and salvation (see ibid.:89–90). Baxter (1678:II, 78) reminded readers that "whatever you do, must be done as a means to these"; one should "do nothing in the World for any other ultimate end." All this suggests an affinity between Puritanism and the spirit of capitalism because both organized life about a single goal.

However, in the two cases life had *different* goals. Could Puritanism have been transformed into the spirit of capitalism? That would have required the substitution of economic ends for religious. But profit was rejected as life's goal by the Puritans. Baxter (ibid.:I, 378) warned "that you make not Riches your chief end." This contradicts the spirit of capitalism, which calls for profit as the chief end of life. Both Puritanism and the spirit of capitalism called for rationally organized lives, but Puritanism would judge the latter to be the *wrong* organization of life (see ibid.:I, 216). This disapproval makes unlikely the substitution of moneymaking for salvation as life's central goal.

Weber's account of how this switch of goals occurred assumes that profit-making was the central means of certifying one's elect status. A decline in religious piety would reduce interest in salvation while leaving acquisitive behaviors in place. Then moneymaking, formerly a means, would continue independently and assume the status of an end in itself. It would be central to the person's life. Thus, the spirit of capitalism would be born. As just mentioned, though, most Puritans did *not* consider profits the central sign of election. One cannot find in Puritanism the explanation for why modern businesspeople value acquisition as life's main end.[8]

In sum, Puritanism shared with the spirit of capitalism only the duty to make money, and opposed its other parts. Puritanism did not spawn the spirit of capitalism, and did not aid capitalist growth through this mechanism.

ELECTIVE AFFINITY THROUGH RATIONAL EFFECTS?

Despite these oppositions between Puritanism and the capitalist spirit, there could still be an affinity between them if both called for the rationalization of life or if Puritanism led psychologically to rational economic conduct. Each of these possibilities is examined below, beginning with psychological effects.

Pressure to Systematize Life

Despite the early Protestant Reformers' opposition to economic rationality, Weber ([1904–5] 1958:174) argued that their teachings ultimately helped to rationalize life via psychological effects on the faithful. Religion built character, and people of strong character built the modern economy. In Weber's (ibid.:176) view the chief economic consequences of the great religious movements stemmed from their ascetic influence. By fostering self-discipline they aided labor discipline among capitalist employees and toughened entrepreneurs for the rigors of striving for business success. Also, ascetic self-control produced a sense of mastery that encouraged economic boldness.

Weber was correct that the Puritans were ascetic. Their struggle against sin moved them to control bodily impulses and restrict gratification (see ibid.:118–19, 166–71).[9] This did, indeed, make the Puritans self-disciplined, according to Seaver (1985:184, 185). Wallington (Folger diary:425), for example, mortified his corruptions by denying himself sinful things. As Weber ([1904–5] 1958:118, 124–26, 153–54) argued, the need to overcome the senses led Puritans to a thoughtful, ordered life; conduct had to be methodical, systematic, organized, and calculated. Taming the flesh required constant vigilance; therefore, daily self-examination was practiced (Seaver 1985:ix, 7, 184). Since a moral life had to be a systematic life, Puritans organized their lives accordingly.

The Norm of Systematization

But beyond the psychological need for it, Puritanism *prescribed* an ordered life as a conduct norm for its followers. This norm suggests an elective affinity between Puritan teachings and the spirit of capitalism, which also requires organized action.

According to Baxter (1678:II, 78) life was to be organized around religion. Salvation was the goal, and worldly activities were to be all for this "journeys end." Life was to be an "orderly walking" with God (ibid.:IV, 234); "disorderly walking" was discouraged. Religious duties, such as "family-worship," were to be performed each "in their proper seasons"; the day's activities were to be scheduled, and time appropriately allocated, so that all duties could be accomplished daily (ibid.:II, 78). Each "work of the day" was to have its "appointed time" (Baxter [1650] 1962:147, see also p. 146). Time was to be organized, planned, and carefully accounted for. "Call your selves daily or frequently to account how you spend your time," directed Baxter (1678:I, 383), "and what work you do, and how you do it. Suffer not one hour or moment so to pass, as you cannot give your Consciences a just account of it." He (ibid.:I, 221, see also II, 131) also said to "Call your selves to a daily reckoning, how you lay out all that God committeth to your trust" so as to be "careful to use well what you have." Baxter (ibid.:IV, 226) wrote, "Keep an account of your expenses and . . . ask conscience . . . Whether such proportions are allowable before God."

A record of the internal life was to be kept as well as of the external (see Keeble 1982:139). Puritans were to record their self-judged state of grace; the record could curb complacency if necessary (see ibid.:137). Baxter recommended writing each judgment down; this facilitated annual comparisons to tell one's spiritual progress (see ibid.:138, 143). Correspondingly, Wallington (quoted by Seaver 1985:182) examined his "soul's state" by examining his conscience to find an "increase of grace." He kept a diary of the comings and goings of the Spirit (ibid.:7).

John Beadle (see Keeble 1982:140) considered it one's duty to keep a diary. Likewise, Perkins (1970:III, 474) and Baxter (1678:II, 80) advised a written record of one's sins and God's mercies. This was practiced (Seaver 1985:7–8, 11), for example, by Pledger (diary:13) and Wallington (Seaver 1985:7, 8, 118, 182), who resolved to keep his daily record in an "exact maner" as part of a "daily reconing of accounts . . . betwixt God and myself" (see ibid.:120, see also p. 112). His father had kept a similar journal (ibid.:11).

Wallington tried various schemes of self-discipline including a program of New Year's resolutions (ibid.:7, 182), an agenda of thirty-one articles for reform (ibid.:79), and a diary of his life. He (quoted in ibid.:7) exclaimed, "Oh, let not one night pass . . . in which I examined not how I spent the day." His supervision of conduct on a daily basis was a lifelong activity (ibid.:196). According to Seaver (ibid.:184) the Puritan discipline of self-examination was common by the 1620s.

Religious pressures to systematize life did make Puritan lives more organized, but Weber ([1904–5] 1958:153) exaggerated by saying that this meant "a rational planning of the whole of one's life." First, most of the recommended scheduling and record-keeping applied to prayer, sin, and other narrowly religious matters, with less attention to the rest of life. Second, prescriptions for nonreligious life were vague and general, limiting the amount of planning necessary to conform to Puritan norms. No overall plan was needed.

Effects on Economic Life

Weber's ([1904–5] 1958:124, see also p. 127) emphasis on "the Christianization of the whole of life" suggests that religious regulation went farther than the organization of religious life. It implies that religious discipline penetrated into all aspects of a Puritan's life, including the economic. For religion to make an economic impact there had to be a carryover of religious discipline into economic conduct.

This carryover could have been effectuated through several different mechanisms. First, Puritanism could have demanded the organization of economic life; second, the mental discipline developed while systematizing religious conduct could have applied itself in the economic sphere; and/or the cultural expectation for rational business organization could have been modeled after the practice of religious discipline. Each of these possibilities is examined in turn to see if it occurred and was effective.

Puritan Economic Organization

Besides its general entreaty to lead an orderly life, Puritanism specifically called for an orderly economic life. "Faith directeth wisely to order the affaires of our calling and to goe about them in good manner," preached John Ball (1632:393).

Baxter (1678:I, 382) believed that adherence to a calling *necessarily* brought about "orderly employment." Work in a calling was "more orderly," with each part done in "its time and place" (ibid.:I, 377). "Out of a Calling a mans labours are but occasional, or unconstant," Baxter (ibid.) observed. The calling gave work a continuous course. This avoided idle time and reinforced hard work. Furthermore, "A man is best skilled in that which he is used to. . . . And he will be best provided for it, with instruments and necessaries. . . . Therefore he doth it better than he could do another work" (see ibid.).

Yet, despite these pronouncements, there are few specifics about how to order one's business in a rational fashion. The teachings about an orderly economic life are thin. Puritanism provided no guidelines for scientific management. The emphasis was on systematizing individual lives rather than economic organizations.

Despite diligence in his calling, Wallington's diary reveals little systematization of business practices. For at least his first ten years in business, and probably for the bulk of his career, he had "no very precise idea" of his receipts, expenditures, or profits (Seaver 1985:118, 122, 124; Folger diary:353; British diary:144). For one thing he mingled business money with household expenses (Seaver 1985:121). For another, it seems that he kept no account books since none were catalogued among his writing volumes (ibid.:118). Only late in his career did he keep accounts (ibid.:120). For example, he knew his income for 1647 and 1648 after twenty-five years in business (ibid.:121; Folger diary:173). And Seaver (1985:121) notes that in 1647 "for once" he was "quite precise about his losses."

Wallington's imprecision is illustrated by his large losses at the hands of a journeyman who stole from the till consistently (see ibid.:119). Wallington did not know of these losses for two years, and only then through others' testimony (ibid.). He would have discovered the theft much sooner with "regular inventory and bookkeeping" (ibid.:118). Another incident exemplifies the same "lack of precision" (ibid.:120). Wallington (British diary:37) thought that he had too little to pay a creditor, but was amazed to find additional money in his pockets; then the following morning he discovered even more unsuspected cash.

His lack of planning is illustrated by his failure to set up a reserve for the payment of debts (Seaver 1985:119, 122). He was barely able to repay what he had borrowed (ibid.:123). On one occasion he was bailed out by "some unexpected customers," who brought in enough business to cover a pressing debt (ibid.). Then he was in "the like straits" again the next week (ibid., see also p. 78). Another illustration is his failure to negotiate his journeyman's rate of wages until his two-year term had ended (ibid.:118). During the two years Wallington neither paid the man anything nor set aside anything for the payment.

Wallington had no rational mastery of his affairs. He was shy and awkward in business matters (ibid.:142; Folger diary:333). Later in his career he (Folger diary:333) sensed his reason failing. He (ibid.) lamented that "I know not how to buy and sell everyone [sic] is hard for me." He (ibid.:333, 334) questioned his memory and wisdom in the affairs of his calling.

Neither did Elias Pledger engage in rational planning. He (diary:57) vowed to "let tomorrow take thought for itself" since "I am commanded to take no thought for tomorrow." This outlook can hardly provide the basis for business planning. "It is time to be troubled for these things in their course," he (ibid.) concluded, referring to his "future wants." Pledger (ibid.:78–79) felt that he should trust God "to dispose of my lot in this world." "Why should I distrust Providence?" he asked: "he has always provided." Pledger depended on God to help his trade rather than an aggressive sales campaign of the type Weber ([1904–5] 1958:67–68) associated with the spirit of capitalism. He showed no sign of the active mastery of the world attributed to the Puritans by Weber. He viewed his economic fortunes as something beyond his control. And he was likely typical in this because it conformed to the commands of Puritanism.

Although Puritanism required an accounting for time and resources, these examples suggest that some key aspects of business rationality were missing. Wallington lacked a spirit of calculation. Also, he was timid and defensive rather than bold and courageous. Neither merchant planned nor showed a sense of mastery. Although Wallington (Folger diary:413) felt a duty to pursue opportunities, he expressed no desire to improve or expand his operations. Neither merchant was the type of courageous hero required by an expanding capitalism and described by Weber ([1904–5] 1958:69).

Insofar as they were typical, Weber has stretched religious pronouncements on orderly conduct into a business rationality that just was not there. Either the norm of organizing life in the calling was ineffective or it did not go far enough. Even though Wallington reckoned his profits in later life, he was still behind many Catholic businessmen of the Italian Renaissance in the use of double-entry bookkeeping and the taking of inventory (see Cohen 1980). And there was no dream of a Wal-Mart of Wallington's furniture in every town.

There was little carryover of rationality from the religious to the economic realm. Neither Pledger nor Wallington displayed the hypothesized business rationality. Nor did either display the hypothesized character of hard, calculating boldness that could effectuate a carryover. What Wallington's example shows instead is that it was possible to organize one's religious life much more than one's work life. Puritanism helped to rationalize religious conduct, but did little to rationalize economic conduct.

It would have been difficult for a person to organize life both ways at once. The central organizing role of prayer and worship relegated economic duties to a contingent status, to be fitted into one's life piecemeal as time and energy permitted rather than as an organized whole. A life organized around religious worship rather than business practice was fully in keeping with Puritan ideals. When Puritanism attempted to impose "a new rational order on the world" (Weber [1922] 1963:259), that order was a system of moral discipline, not of modern capitalism. Similarly, Puritan world mastery aimed at mastering moral conduct, not mastering nature technologically through rational modes of production.

Cultural Modeling Effects

Since modern capitalism's rational practices were not instituted as carryovers from Puritan religious rationalization, their origins require an alternative account. Although single individuals did not transfer their methodical lifestyle from religion to business enterprise, later generations could have modeled business practice on the methodical religious lives of the Puritan devout.[10]

On the positive side, there is indeed an elective affinity between Puritan religious discipline and rational business organization. Their similarity is emphasized by the religious use of economic concepts like "debts," "contracts," and "accounts." Wallington, for example, used the metaphor of the account book to assess the state of his conscience as one would calculate one's outward estate (Seaver 1985:182, see also p. 185). Laity and clergy alike used this imagery.

However, the hypothesis of Puritan cultural influence presupposes a counterfactual time ordering, namely, that methodical Puritan religious practices preceded rational capitalism. On the contrary, many rational business techniques had already been developed by Roman Catholic entrepreneurs at the time of the Italian Renaissance (see Cohen 1980). The rise of rational economic calculation was well along by Puritan times. In fact, many rational practices were already part of the general culture and had been recorded in books of advice to young men.

Although there was an elective affinity between religious and economic rationality, one must not misjudge who was borrowing from whom. In the Puritan pastoral statements where the analogy between economic and religious discipline is most explicit, it is clear that the rational organization of Christian life was being modeled after an existing business rationality, and not vice versa. Wallington, for example, self-consciously modeled his examination of his "inward condition" after the practice of looking over one's economic account books annually (see Seaver 1985:182). Zaret (1985) was right when he argued that the Puritans borrowed their rationality from business rather than the reverse. In his view, pastoral advice to make one's calling and election sure appealed to concepts of self-interest that came from economic life. The clergy used economic imagery because it was familiar to the laity. Also, since most of the laity were more concerned about their economic than their religious accounts (see ibid.:196–97), the clergy were attempting to raise religious motivation up to the level of people's economic interest (see George and George 1958:359).

Since rationality at the time was stronger in economic than in religious action (see Smith 1599:A6), it would have been difficult for religion's weaker rationality to nurture capitalism's already strong rationality. Wallington (Folger diary:218), in support, observed that "the children of the world" were "wiser" in their getting of "outward things" than he was in getting grace. The direction of influence was for economic rationality, which was well-established, to inspire religious rationality, which was desired. Clergymen like Price ([1608] 1979:16) urged believers to pursue their salvation interests more rationally. And Wallington (Folger diary:218) reported that the rationality of the worldly "doth . . . (or should doe) stir me up in all holy dutys. . . . Striving to glorify God with holy and unblamable Life never being at rest till I have got . . . God and Christ to be mine." Clearly, economic rationality was the model for religious rationality.

The Renaissance data (see Cohen 1980) confirm Zaret's impressions and the Puritans' own statements about the direction of causal influence. These firms came too early to have used Puritan concepts to organize themselves. Rather, capitalist firms developed their own repertoire of rational practices somewhat independently. Seventeenth-century businesses borrowed mainly from their predecessors.

The Formation of the Bourgeois Class

Weber ([1904–5] 1958:174, see also p. 24) stressed Puritanism's rationalizing influence on individuals because he thought that it had created the bourgeois class, a pool of citizens with the personal qualities that modern capitalism required. He viewed class formation, including the small business class as well as the merchant aristocracy (see ibid.:279 note 93), as a prerequisite for capitalist development, and thought that any explanation of modern capitalism's rise needed to account for the capitalist class as well. Although Marx had focused on the formation of classes *for* themselves, he wrote little about the formation of classes *in* themselves, perhaps in the belief that this followed directly from a common relationship to the means of production. In contrast to Marx, Weber found it necessary to explain the existence of a class with distinctive bourgeois outlooks.

Weber ([1904–5] 1958:174) thought that the Puritan religion favored the development of a rational bourgeois life. He (ibid.:166–71) hypothesized that bourgeois sobriety and seriousness came from Puritanism. In his view, a Puritan upbringing was good socialization for the capitalist class.

Weber argued that the need for proof of religious virtue toughened Puritans into shrewd and daring capitalists. Trying to live as true Christians required discipline and rigor (see Seaver 1985:181, 194); and the resulting self-improvement made Puritans smug and self-righteous. This was reinforced in the community of saints, who felt invincible with God on their side. Furthermore, those with assurance of salvation felt like members of the elect. In Weber's ([1904–5] 1958:112, 113, 165, 166) view, these self-confident saints became self-confident businessmen.

This class-formation hypothesis suggests that Puritan believers formed personalities appropriate for the capitalist class. However, it is undercut by the examples of Pledger and Wallington, two Puritan shopkeepers who, as shown above, lacked many of the qualities that capitalism needed to grow successfully. It is true that Pledger was a convert, but Wallington was raised a Puritan; and his upbringing failed to instill the type of character needed for capitalist success. He was not well socialized for the capitalist class. Puritanism did not always produce the proper character.

ECONOMIC TRADITIONALISM

When Weber depicted Puritanism as a modernizing force that brought a decisive break with tradition, he could not have realized how traditional Puritanism was. Although Weber made much of the differences between Luther's traditionalism and the neo-Calvinists' alleged modernism, the latter were not so far ahead of Lutheranism after all. The analysis to follow reveals Puritan traditionalism in their attitudes toward obedience; the connection of economic action to basic needs; their reliance on God to provide; the choice of a calling; and dealings in the marketplace.

Obedience

One traditional aspect of Puritanism was the ideal of service in one's work. According to Ball (1632:392, see also p. 391), "the truest honor is to be God's servant." He (ibid.:391) stated that "we serve the Lord in our callings." Puritans thought of themselves as "instruments" of God (see Keeble 1982:140); Baxter, for example, considered himself "a pen in God's hand" (see ibid.:142).

People were to pursue their callings "in obedience" (see Ball 1632:393). The "meanest work," counseled Baxter (1678:II, 128), "is the more acceptable to him, by how much the more subjection and submission there is in your obedience." He (ibid.:I, 383, see also p. 126) taught that "This interest of God in your lowest and hardest and servilest labour . . . should make it sweet."

Baxter ([1650] 1962:128) wrote: "Learn to be meek and lowly"; similarly, Perkins (1601:67) advocated the "like meekness, patience, and obedience" of Christ. Elias Pledger (diary:70) apparently took these teachings to heart when he wrote "Grant that we may behave submissively." Even the rich were not to become confident or proud in their wealth but were to remain "poore in Spirit" (Perkins [1606] 1972:III, 529, 570–71, 581; Swinnock 1663:d1).

Hard work in a calling was to be performed dutifully. Dent's ([1601] 1974:197) emphasis on people fulfilling "the dueties of their places" was traditional: it was more passive than Weber's idea of rational mastery and more static than the notion of an aggressive world-transforming capitalist spirit. This Puritan attitude could provide capitalism with hard, conscientious work, but with neither rationalization nor the drive to expand.

Weber ([1904–5] 1958:58–67, 166–74) argued that Puritan diligence was more modern than the irregularity of traditional labor. And while that is true, their view of labor as service and a duty represents little beyond Luther's doctrine of the calling. And it stands opposed to the sense of rational mastery required of the heroic entrepreneur.

The Provision of Traditional Needs

In Puritanism, the end of economic activity was seen as the provision of traditional needs. Money was not valued as an end in itself, but was to be used for creature comforts. For example, merchant Elias Pledger's goal was "subsistence" (diary:28) or "a comfortable lively hood" (diary:68). This contrasts with production for purposes of acquisition (see Weber [1904–5] 1958:63–64), which disregards personal needs and is therefore not limited by them. Indeed, the Puritan approach was quite limiting.

Puritans were directed to earn only as much as necessary. According to Perkins ([1606] 1972:III, 523, 524; see also 1970:III, 466), "we crave but onely bread for our substance, that is meete to preserve us"; it was a sin to "seeke for goods more than necessarie." And Baxter (1678:I, 215, see also p. 216) wrote that desiring more than is "needful or useful" was a sign of covetousness.

Puritans were to be satisfied with the necessaries of life. Baxter (1678:I, 214–15), for example, considered it covetous to be discontent "when we have no more than our daily bread" (see ibid.:I, 215). And Perkins ([1606] 1972:III, 523) wrote, "Having foode and raiment, let us be therewith content."

Consistent with the self-limitation to natural needs was a general norm of contentment. "We ought accustome our selves to live of a little, and to be content," wrote Dent ([1601] 1974:110); "Be content with thine owne things." And Swinnock (1663:c2), Perkins (1970:III, 465; also [1606] 1972:III, 529), and Ball (quoted by Seaver 1985:137) urged "contentation with our estate, though it be mean." Similarly, Baxter (1678:I, 216; see also Dent [1601] 1974:109) considered it covetous to be "discontented with your estate" or to seek "a little more." Applying this doctrine to himself, Elias Pledger (diary:34) felt it best to emulate Christ's "contentment with his low estate." Pledger (diary:69) felt like an "unthankful wretch" because he was "frequently dissatisfied."

It was wrong to pursue wealth because contentment precluded ambition. Avoid "ambition," Perkins (1970:III, 470) advised; he (ibid.:III, 242; see also 1615:A3) said to humble ambitions and look to what God will lovingly bestow. And Downame ([1604] 1974:I, 107, see also p. 77) saw humility as the antidote "when we are tempted to ambition." Good

Christians were to "use well what you have" rather than "to get more" (Baxter 1678:I, 201), to "increase" wealth (Swinnock 1663:c2), or to "industriously seek" things that God provides (Pledger diary:26).

Puritans were warned against troubling themselves over economic success (see Ball 1632:388, 426); those who "content not themselves with their lot and condition, but desire to heape up riches . . . know no end of their cares." It was better to "moderate cares" and "confine desires of earthly things" (see Ball 1632:393), for "a godly man contented with his daily bread, hath a far sweeter and quieter life and death, than a self-troubling worldling" (see Baxter 1678:I, 219). "Happie is that man therefore," Dent ([1601] 1974:104, see also p. 108) concluded, "that is well content with his present estate whatsoever, and carrieth himselfe moderately and comfortably therein." The troubles of the ambitious could be quite serious. In fact, Dent (ibid.:94) maintained that the "unsatiable desire of having" was "a most daungerous thing." Similarly, Hill ([1613] 1975:43) warned that "Adam not contented with his own estate, brought himselfe and his posterity to destruction."

But earthly misery was not the chief danger in discontentment. Perkins ([1606] 1972:III, 523) warned that "seeking abundance is a hazard to the salvation of the soule" since "They that . . . desire to be rich, and content not themselves with things necessarie, fall into the snare of the Devill." And Dent ([1601] 1974:406) asked, "What shall it profit a man to winne all the worlde and loose his soule?" In contrast, "contentation" was mentioned as a sign of salvation (see ibid.:257). A person showed true faith, in Ball's (1632:358) view, if he or she "sees riches in God, and is content in His love."

The Doctrine of Providence

God's Provision for Human Wants

The doctrine of God's providence also worked to discourage ambition. This was the belief that "The Lord our God . . . hath . . . promised to make competent provision for his children" (see Ball 1632:347). This doctrine balanced and qualified some of the more activist strands in Puritanism.

First of all, it was asserted that God "knows our wants:" "that yee have need of . . . food and raiment," "that earthly blessings be so necessary for the maintenance of this life," and "that we cannot be without them" (see Ball 1632:347, 394). Second, it was believed that "The Lord will . . . showre his blessings plentifully on them that put their trust in him" (see ibid.:351). He had promised to "feede them in a good pasture and upon the high mountains of Israel" (see ibid.:354). Baxter ([1650] 1962:128) wrote that God would not forget the humble, and Ball (1632:347) agreed that "The meeke shall eate and be satisfied"; and Perkins (1615:A3) warned against a person "doubting but he will be given all things necessarie."

Since God would provide, the necessity of human effort was called into question, for "you shall want nothing that is good for you." Baxter (1678:I, 220) asked, "cannot you trust his promise? If you truly believe that he is God, and that he is true . . . you will sure trust him rather than trust to your own forecast and industry. Do you think his provision is not better for you than your own?" The effect was to discourage self-reliance (see also Ball 1632:354).

Ball (ibid.:350–51) criticized those who, wanting "earthly blessings . . . never cease, with excessive care, diligence, and vexation to hunt after them." They felt that they had "none but my selfe to trust to." But they could cast their burden of care and toil "upon the Lord, whose eye is over us for good." Ball (ibid.:259) praised those with faith, who "resteth upon his grace to receive from him whatsoever may be good and profitable for them."

Perkins (1615:A2–A3; see also Ball 1632:388, 397) complained when people cared for the "successe of their labours," and pointed out that "this care belongs to God alone." When we "have done the workes of our callings," he (1615:A3) taught, "faith . . . maketh us commend to God the blessing, successe, and event thereof." Similarly, Baxter (1678:II, 127) advised a person, "Take care how to discharge your own duties, but be not too careful about the event, which belongs to God." Likewise, Ball (1632:393–94) exhorted them to leave the "successe. . . . of their endevours to the good will and pleasure of God."

Although, as Weber ([1904–5] 1958:163) argued, Puritanism promoted capitalism by making profit a duty, the divines in this context commanded the contrary, to take no care whatever for the profitability of one's work. Far from stressing profit as a duty, Perkins ([1606] 1972:III, 524) declared that the "seeking of abundance is a fruite of diffidence in the providence of God" and "must be cut off." Ball (1632:353) described an opposing duty *not* to strive for profit: "Now seeing the Lord hath . . . assured us all needful blessings, it is our duty by faith to . . . rest quietly upon his word, to find reliefe at such time, and in such measure, as he knows to be expedient."

Conflicting Signals

Puritanism gave conflicting signals about the role of humans and of God in determining profits. On the one hand, it stressed, "The hand of the diligent maketh rich" (Ball 1632:387), and "Hee that gathereth by labour shall encrease" (ibid.). Swinnock (1663:b2) wrote, "The Tradesman in his particular calling, who intendeth to make any thing of it, spendeth most of his time at it . . . furthering his calling. It is not the Picture of . . . the Master standing with his hands in his Pocket that will preserve his family."

Yet, on the other hand, Ball (1632:399, see also p. 348) wrote that faith "waiteth upon God for good success." One should not rest upon his own skill, but upon the Lord (ibid.:390). Baxter (1678:I, 220) was even more emphatic: "if you are not content with his provisions, nor submit your selves to the disposals of his love and wisdom, you disoblige God, and provoke him to leave you to the fruits of your own care and diligence: And then you will find that it had been your wisest way to have trusted God."

The Co-action of Humans and God

The resolution of this dilemma combined both extremes into a complex whole that involved the co-action of humans and God. But the preachers were inconsistent about the nature of the co-action.

In one approach God provided the means of success and humans used them. According to Ball (1632:397–98), "To provide meanes is the work of God: it onely belongs to us, to use them." Once God gave the opportunities, Ball (ibid.:357) wrote, the human contribution came into play: "He that is silent, expecting Gods helpe when means faile, cannot sit still when meanes be at hand." This view denied any contradiction between action and trust in God. According to Ball (ibid.:398), "Faith layeth hold upon the promises of aide and provision with one hand, worketh with the other." Moreover, "He that rests most confident upon Gods blessing for all good things of this life, will be most diligent to seeke them by lawfull meanes."

Another way of reconciling the apparent dilemma between passivity and action distinguished between duty and responsibility. In Ball's (ibid.:394) view, "A Christian is diligently to set his hand to the worke, and through negligence omit nothing that is of moment to effect and bring it to passe. But having . . . laboured painefully, he must . . . roll his burthen upon the Lord, who has promised that all things shall be well regarded." This gave the Christian the same duties as if humans were responsible for the outcomes, while simultaneously attributing to God the actual responsibility.

According to George and George (1958:364), the Puritan who diligently followed a calling was taught that God would provide a "sufficiency to meet his worldly needs," or "aboundance" in Dod's view. If the Christian was dutiful, God furnished the reward. Owen Stockton (diary:3), for example, believed that God had promised to bless his work in his calling so he should not labor in vain.

The Puritans gave God credit for all good success while acknowledging human inaction as a possible cause of failure. People could make their conditions worse but could not augment profits. One's works were really the works of God to whom praise and thanks were due (Keeble 1982:141, 142). In Swinnock's (1663:d2) words, the right Christian "giveth God the prayse of all his plenty, believing that not his own diligence, so much as Gods gracious providence is the origin of his prosperity."

All in all, Puritanism was clearer about the duty toward diligent labor than about human responsibility for success or failure. On the one hand, Puritans could not ethically slacken their efforts in response to the doctrine of providence, but on the other, responsibility for the outcome was believed to be divided between themselves and God. Since such diffusion of responsibility can lead psychologically to inaction, these doctrines induced Puritans to passivity concerning business success. By fostering inattention to profitability, they weakened goal rationality.

Elias Pledger's Traditional Outlook

Since Elias Pledger was a Puritan businessman, his example illustrates how these doctrines played out when applied to business life. His diary provides good evidence about the doctrine of God's providence and its effects since it constitutes a major theme of that book.

First of all, it is clear that Pledger (diary:57) accepted the providence doctrine since he wrote that "we . . . are clothed by the providence of God, who will not starve his children, either with hunger or cold"; "Your father knows you have need of these things and will certainly provide them for you." He (ibid.:31, 57, see also pp. 14, 26, 45, 67) considered it best to trust God's providence and "an argument of little faith to distrust the providence of God."

Yet, despite these beliefs, he (ibid.:45) confessed that "Want of trade much discomposes me and makes me frequently distrust the providence of God." He (ibid.:14, 28, 40, 41, 45, 57, 67, 69, 70, 71) mentioned "distrustful thoughts of the providence of God" repeatedly. Pledger (ibid.:69) felt guilty when he had such thoughts. He (ibid.:79) prayed, "Help me against distrust of the providence of God"; "I pray frequently against it," he (ibid.:45) wrote. Clearly, there was a conflict within Pledger's mind. He was torn between sticking to the doctrine and responding actively to his economic situation. Pledger's mental turmoil reflected frequent dissatisfaction with his family's level of worldly comfort (ibid.:41, 42, 57, 69, 70). But since these feelings were incompatible with the norm of contentment, he (ibid.:36–37) professed that "I desire to be content" and asked God to "mortify me to the things here below, that having food and raiment I may be there with content" (ibid.:69, see also pp. 36–37).

Devotion to the doctrine tended to keep Pledger's economic goals modest. He (ibid.:28) was only concerned about obtaining "a supply of those necessaries which thou has promised to thy children"; he (ibid.:57) mentioned "meat and bodily raiment" specifically. He was neither seeking limitless profits nor profit for its own sake, abstractly separated from human wants.

The second issue concerns the control of economic outcomes. Consistent with the doctrine of providence, Pledger believed that economic provision should be left to God. He (ibid.:36) resolved to entrust his success to God, expressing both a "desire to commit myself and all my affairs of a serious nature" into God's hands, and a "desire to acquiesce in his dispensation of providence" (see also ibid.:26, 28, 40, 41). He (ibid.:36, see also pp. 23, 42, 68, 78) determined to "let him appoint my lot and portion what he will"; and he (ibid.:68) "cast the burden and care of all my temporal concerns upon he who has promised to care for me."

These resolutions by no means renounced the duty of hard work. One was expected to use "all the lawful means" (see ibid.:28) in order not to make business worse through neglect of duty. Accordingly, Pledger (ibid.:68) prayed, "Lord let me not by any imprudence or negligence of mine" forgo a good living by "not using the power thou has given." Rather than inaction, Pledger was aiming at a division of labor with God. "Let us mind our duty in our place," he (ibid.:72) specified, but "leave the fruit of our diligent labor to God. . . ." He (diary:57) made it clear that God was to be responsible for the results when he wrote "Let me not trouble myself about anything but my duty."

Pledger's division of responsibility with God restrained him from focusing on the attainment of profit goals. Since economic rewards were to be provided by God, Pledger (ibid.:57) reasoned that "you need not be so careful about them." This attitude reduced the rationality and planning in his work, and engendered pessimism about his mastery of the situation. "We cannot add anything to our condition by our taking thought," he (ibid.) declared; "We may and do make it worse but cannot make it better."

In conclusion, Pledger showed considerable economic traditionalism. He worked to obtain traditional wants rather than to increase a pool of capital; and although he was diligent, his efforts were dutiful rather than rational because he doubted that they could bring about his goals. Since both he and God were in part responsible for economic success, he did not feel in complete control of his fortunes. Moreover, when he tried to contemplate better results, he felt guilty because he lacked the appropriate dependence. In short, the doctrine of providence discouraged some of his impetus to success, which had been inspired by secular causes.

Nehemiah Wallington's Traditionalism

Pledger's traditional outlook was shared by Wallington. He felt no drive to accumulate money for its own sake or for business expansion.[11] Since he was continuously in debt (Seaver 1985:123), he was "moved . . . to be more diligent" by a "grat want of money" (British diary:6; see also Seaver 1985:126).

Wallington (Folger diary:415, 231, 351; letters:176) thought that he should be content "though I be never so poore" because happiness lay in Christ rather than money. Discontent and grumbling were sins (Wallington cited by Seaver 1985:129). Yet he (letters:175, 176; Folger diary:156, 403; Seaver 1985:196) was sometimes discontent. He (quoted by Seaver 1985:124) thought that this "murmuring and discontent" was a "great project of the devil to bring me to misery." He wrote down some "Remedies against Discontent" (see ibid.:4), and prayed for God "to give me patience and not to murmur in any hard conditions whatsoever" (British diary:144). He was displeased with himself when his shop took in little money but he was still "somewhat contented" (ibid.) and "did not murmur" (ibid.:148). He (Folger diary:425, 426) wrote that he glorified God "in being content with any Portion that God hath given me."

Like Pledger, Wallington (ibid.:414) sought to "avoid distrust of Gods providence." To distrust his providence was to doubt his omnipotence (see Seaver 1985:153). Even though he had "littel," Wallington (British diary:26) believed that he should trust in God. He (ibid.:112) resolved to "rely on my Father's promise that none that trust in him shall want." When he (Folger diary:403, see also p. 156) found "many distrustful . . . thoughts," he prayed for God to "cause me to trust in his mercys."

Like Pledger, Wallington depended greatly on God to send prosperity (Folger diary:351). In his (ibid.; British diary:37) view, it was easy for God to make people rich or poor. He (British diary:26, 144, 170; Seaver 1985:120) prayed for God to send him customers and profits; then he (Folger diary:491; British diary:26, 144, 170) considered good trade the answer to his prayers. He (British diary:12, 26, 29, 144; Folger diary:353, 403, 491; Seaver 1985:122, 123) repeatedly credited God for sending in customers and revenues; and he likewise thanked God for the ability to borrow and pay debts (British diary:115, 144; Folger diary:491; Seaver 1985:123).

Wallington (cited by Seaver 1985:108) never saw prayer as a substitute for the means of self-help. He (Folger diary:413) agreed with the preachers that "the hand of the deligent maketh rich" and "a slothfull hand maketh poor." As Seaver (1985:174) points out, reliance on God was not incompatible with human responsibility and agency. Christians had to labor for their daily bread as well as pray for it (ibid.:137). Still, the diffusion of responsibility could only discourage active planning, a sense of mastery, and as Weber ([1904–5] 1958:179) put it, "individualistic motives of rational legal acquisition by virtue of one's own ability and initiative."

Rather than acting independently, Wallington (Folger diary:94; Seaver 1985:17–18, see also pp. 185–86) sought to conform to Christian teachings. As a "servant" of God (see Wallington Folger diary:234), he (British diary:144) sought "to submit my will" unto the will of his "Master." This attitude is closer to Weber's account of Lutheran traditionalism (see Chapter 1 above) than to the neo-Calvinist rationality that he ([1904–5] 1958:170) hypothesized.

Tradition and the Doctrine of the Calling

The concept of the calling was also viewed traditionally by the Puritans. Baxter (1678:I, 376) discussed it under the heading "Directions for the Government of the Body" since its aim was to maintain the body to serve God. Besides one's own body, the "maintenance of Wife and Children" was part of one's duty (ibid.:I, 110). Labor in the calling was also meant to help and serve others (see Perkins [1606] 1972:III, 526; Ames [1639] 1975:248). It was valued for its social contribution (see Seaver 1985:133, 134; Dent [1601] 1974:193).

Even more important than these traditional duties was the duty to serve God through one's calling (see Baxter 1678:I, 379; II, 128; [1650] 1962:126; Ball 1632:391, 392, 393). The emphasis was clearly on the duty component, which makes the Puritan concept of the calling quite comparable to Luther's and even to the Hindu notion of *dharma*.

The Puritan doctrine of the calling stressed staying in one's place, which was quite traditional. Ball (1632:387) urged, "Let every man abide in the same calling wherein he was called." Likewise, Perkins ([1606] 1972:III, 473) warned that "by the law of God, every man is to range himselfe within the limits of his calling, and not to dare, once to get out of it"; one should "continue and abide in his calling without change or alteration" (see Perkins 1970:II, 470, see also p. 449) and "keepe his own standing" (see Bridenbaugh 1968:315–16; see also Downame [1604] 1974:I, 48 and Dent quoted by Seaver 1985:134).

The Puritans viewed society as an interdependent whole "with each person given a finite social role to which he ought assiduously to keep" (see Lake 1982:28). "In the temporal regiment," wrote Perkins (1970:III, 382), "thou must do according to thine office." Downame ([1604] 1974:I, 47, see also p. 48) put it similarly: Christian soldiers each had their stations in camp, "their vocations whereunto they are called of God within the limits whereof they are to containe themselves." And Baxter (1678:I, 380; see also IV, 221) agreed "that every man must labour in the works of his own Calling, and do his own business ... and take that for the best employment for him, which God doth call him to, and not presume to step out of his place, and take the work of other mens Callings out of their hands."

These highly traditional teachings stand in contrast to Weber's interpretation. He ([1904–5] 1958:162) wrote that "In the Puritan concept of the calling the emphasis is always placed on [its] methodical character . . . not, as with Luther, on the acceptance of the lot which God has irretrievably assigned to man." But acceptance of one's lot was clearly emphasized in the Puritan doctrine of the calling.

A change of calling was not totally barred if made "upon urgent and weighty causes . . . especially private necessity and the common good" (Perkins 1970:II, 472). As Baxter (1678:I, 110) saw it, "The Apostle . . . bids every man abide with God in the place he is called to, but forbids them not to change their state when they are called to change it." In short, "No man must take up or change any calling without sufficient cause to call him to it: But when he hath such cause, he sinneth if he change it not" (see ibid.:I, 111).

Nonetheless, Perkins (1970:II, 472) warned that we cannot resign from our callings when we please. Baxter (1678:I, 110; see also George and George 1958:363) elaborated further: "Either you are already engaged in your Calling or not: If you are, you must have greater reasons to desert it, than such as might require you at first not to choose it." And one could make "no unnecessary change as if it were necessary" (Baxter 1678:I, 110).

Consistent with its inhibition of any change in calling, Puritanism discouraged attempts to rise above one's station (see George and George 1958:360, 362, 363, 369). Downame ([1604] 1974:I, 48) complained that "there is nothing more pernitous to an armie as . . . when some intrude themselves into others place, as when the common soldier will be an officer, the Lieutenant Captaine, and the Captaine, Generall of the armie." Likewise, in Perkins's (1970:II, 456) view, a person should "keep his own standing" rather than "think other men's callings better for us than our own" (see also Perkins [1606] 1972:III, 568–69, 582). And Baxter's (1678:I, 110, see also pp. 70, 379) advice was consistent: "If God have called you to serve him in a low and mean imployment, he will better accept you in that work, than if you undertook the work of another mans place, to do him greater service." These teachings reinforced the traditional status order.

The lowly were encouraged to remain in their callings as Samuelsson (1961:37) has argued. According to Ashton (see Lake 1982:139), "We must not be ashamed of our calling or condition of life, how base soever it be but stay therein, lowly without all pride and not seek to intrude . . . into another." And Ball (1632:392) agreed that "Faith permits us" to persist at "work looked down upon in the world." Baxter (1678:I, 379) advised those "called to the poorest laborious Calling" not to complain because

God "hath chosen this for thy good," and "valueth thy obedience to him the more, by how much the meaner work thou stoopest to at his Command." Conversely, Chaderton (see Lake 1982:139, 146), considered it a sin to be dissatisfied with one's estate.

One should not, in general, seek a more rewarding calling. This mitigated against the application of economic rationality in changing jobs or trades.

Yet, consistent with the possibility of changing one's calling with sufficient reason, it was sometimes permissible to improve one's economic situation since "God no where forbids men to change their employment for the better, upon a sufficient cause or call" (see Baxter 1678:I, 111). Although economic advancement was discouraged, it was not completely banned.

As Weber ([1904–5] 1958:162, 163, 177) pointed out, citing Baxter, a more profitable occupation sometimes served God best. Baxter (1678:IV, 225) wrote that it was "no sin but a duty . . . to choose a gainful Calling rather than another, that we may be able to do good, and relieve the poor."

However, contrary to Baxter, Perkins ([1606] 1972:III, 473) considered magnanimity a vice because it could "make men to attempt high and great matters above their reach, and so to goe beyond their callings." One could conclude that the Puritans were divided on this point. Alternatively, Baxter's statement may be considered a later development than Perkins's.

Note that Baxter qualified the duty to choose a gainful calling very carefully, requiring it only when the end was to become rich for God and the poor, not otherwise.[12] Furthermore, it was only approved for the one end. Hence, this duty is properly seen as an exception to the general prohibition against changing to a more lucrative occupation, rather than as an overall prescription for career mobility.[13]

Since one's end had to be charity or public service, advancement to a more gainful calling under Puritan doctrine was still traditional, albeit not so traditional as staying immutably in one's place. Hence, Baxter's (1678:I, 378) directive concerning a gainful calling was not much of a break with tradition nor much of a step toward modern economic rationality.

The desirability of gainful callings with great potential for charitable deeds was balanced by the Puritans against other criteria for choosing a calling. For example, Perkins (1970:II, 462) and Ball (1632:389, 391) concurred that a calling must be "serviceable to the church, Common-wealth, or private family." And according to Baxter (1678:I, 378), "The Trade or Calling" most conducive to "the service of God, and the publick good . . . is to be preferred."

Surprisingly, Baxter did not consider the most gainful callings the most conducive to the public good despite their potential for philanthropy:

"The Callings most useful to the publick good, are the magistrates, the Pastors and Teachers of the Church, Schoolmasters, Physicions, Lawyers, and c., Husbandmen, (Plowmen, Grasiers, and Shepards): next to them are Mariners, Clothiers, Booksellers, Taylors, and such other that are employed about things most necessary to mankind" (see Baxter 1678:I, 378). Perkins's (1970:II, 460) top choices were similar: for example, he regarded the preaching vocation "above any other."

Baxter (1678:I, 378; see also Perkins 1970:II, 449) gave the public good a higher priority than riches since it was "a prison and constant calamity" to do "little good . . . though he should grow rich by it himself." For example, "a Schoolmasters Calling . . . is of so great use to the common good . . . that it is fitter to be chosen . . . than richer and more honoured employment" (Baxter 1678:I, 378).

Merchants and manufacturers were judged more by their product than by their incomes. For example, "some callings are employed about matters of so little use (as Tobacco-sellers, Lace-sellers, Feather-makers, Periwig-makers, and many more such)" that one "may choose better" (Baxter 1678:I, 378; see also Ames [1639] 1975:249). Perkins (1970:II, 462) charged that "the tradesman that getteth his living by making . . . fashions . . . which serve for no use but to be displayed flags and banners either of folly, or pride, or wantoness" was "much to be blamed."

Baxter (1678:I, 377, 378; see also Ames [1639] 1975:249–50 and Hill [1613] 1975:II, 80) recommended avoiding businesses where the work is sinful or where "gaine dependeth so much upon mens sin." For example, "The calling of a Vintner and Ale-seller" was "so very dangerous that . . . a man that loveth his soul should be loth to meddle with it . . . the work of your calling" must "be safe, and not very dangerous to your souls" (see Baxter 1678:I, 378).

The soul's advantage took priority over an occupation's earnings potential (see Hudson 1949:13). According to Baxter (1678:I, 378), "when two callings equally conduce to the publick good, and one of them hath the advantage of riches, and the other is more advantageous to your souls, the latter must be preferred"; "next to the publick good, the souls advantage must guide your choice." A leisurely calling was best for religious purposes: "if it be possible," Baxter (1678:I, 378) advised, "choose a Calling" that will "allow you to commixed thoughts of greater things" and "convenient intermissions for them." Clothiers and tailors, though poor, could talk and think of "heavenly things" as they worked (see above).

This evidence refutes Weber's ([1904–5] 1958:162) view of how a calling was judged in usefulness and "in the sight of God." Instead, it supports his critic Samuelsson (1961:37). Weber ([1904–5] 1958:162) claimed that "the most important criterion is found in private profitableness." But public service, the avoidance of sin, and time for religion were considered more important by the Puritans.[14]

Nehemiah Wallington accepted these teachings and tried to live by them. Rather than making haste to be rich, he believed people were to glorify God "in whatsoever state and condition we are in" (Wallington Folger diary:414–15; see also letters:32, 103 and Seaver 1985:126, 127). He agreed with Richard Greenham's mandate not to "vary" one's calling because it was God's work (see Seaver 1985:129). People needed "good grounds" and "good warrant" for changing from their "first calling wherein the Lord your God had set you." When Wallington (Folger diary:327) considered leaving his nonlucrative trade as a turner (see Seaver 1985:113–15, 118), he had to wrestle with the problem of "how shall I know that I have a call from God to . . . give over my calling. . . . The Apostle Saith Let every man abide in the same vocation wherein he was called." After searching God's will and the Bible, Wallington stayed at his calling (see ibid.:142).

Market Ethics

Another traditional part of Puritanism was its system of business ethics. According to Seaver (1985:126) the Puritans' "ethic of getting and spending" was not far from that of the medieval moralists. This kept the devout from following the most rational business strategies (see ibid.:127–42; Samuelsson 1961:38–39).

Puritanism limited and regulated economic action, and required a balance between profit and other aims. These other values included honesty, fairness, and merciful dealing with the poor (see Seaver 1985:107, 131, 136). These ethical constraints limited rationality in two ways. First, calculability is virtually impossible if people's individual needs must be taken into account. For example, labor costs are most easily calculable when labor is treated as a commodity. Second, rational self-interest cannot be optimized if the personal needs of employees and customers must be taken into account and satisfied as well.

Although rational capitalism required single-minded dedication to profit, there was no way for profit to become one's sole consideration without contradicting important maxims of Puritan economic ethics. Profit maximization was unethical in Puritanism. Dent (cited by Seaver 1985:124) opposed the desire to gain riches "in all haste by hook or by crook." Instead (for reasons explained below in Chapter 4), Baxter (1678:IV, 103) wrote of "proportionable moderate gain" to maintain a family and Ames ([1639] 1975:250) of "moderation in the desire of gaine."

Rather than duty to one's pool of capital, Baxter (1678:IV, 97) stressed "The true love of your neighbor, and the denial of your self." The profit principle had to be weighed against those ethical concerns (see Hudson 1949:10–11). Rather than "think only of your own commodity and gain," Baxter (1678:IV, 97) instructed, "remember how much more you will lose by sin, than your gain can . . . amount to"; so, "Regard the publick good above your own commodity." For example, it was "not lawful to take up . . . any oppressing Monopoly or Trade, which tendeth to enrich you by the loss . . . of many" (see Baxter 1678:IV, 97).

Ames (cited by Sprunger 1972:174) and Baxter (1678:IV, 97) urged sellers' attention to the good of the buyer, and said to "meditate on his wants and interests," which may be "as great as yours." Each was to endeavor that "he whom I deal with may be a gainer by the bargain as well as I," according to Baxter (1678:IV, 103);[15] and if he was the poorer of the two, the bargain had to be "more to his commodity than to yours."

One needed to be sure that labor in one's calling "wrongeth not others" (Baxter 1678:I, 377). "Do as you would be done by," Baxter (ibid.:IV, 206, see also p. 209) exhorted, "and oppress not your poor brethren." Any commodity had to be gained "without the hurt of our brethren" (Downame [1604] 1974:I, 78). It was considered dishonest for people "to raise their owne profit, by the dammage of others" (see Ames [1639] 1975:250; see also Baxter 1678:IV, 205 and Hill cited by Seaver 1985:136). One was not to oppress others out of "covetousnesse," wrote Dent ([1601] 1974:219, see also p. 203), nor rack and pinch (ibid.:215); a landlord sinned by "getting money from his poor tenants by racking of his rents" (Smith quoted by Emerson 1968:129).

One should not, in Baxter's (1653:296) view, be "hard to those you buy and sell with." One must not be "cruelly exacting" in collecting "all our Rights and Debts of the poor," and must refrain from "squeezing the purses of subjects or tenants, or those that we bargain with" (Baxter 1653:253). Hill (cited by Seaver 1985:136) also advocated mercy and friendly dealing with the poor in buying and selling.

In Ames's (quoted by Sprunger 1972:174) opinion, "to bee willing to buy cheape, and sell deare, is . . . common, but yet a common sinne, except it is bounded within . . . certain . . . limits"; he advocated just prices in business affairs. Likewise, Perkins (1970:III, 385) warned, "loath be you to sell . . . too dear for undoing your neighbor." In answer to the question, "May I desire or take more than my labour or goods are worth, if I can get it?" Baxter (1678:IV, 103) replied that it was "false" to take as "much as any one will give" if that was "above what its reasonable to take."[16] To those who assumed "that every man will get as much as he can have," he (ibid.:IV, 104) retorted that "It is not so among Christians." Baxter (ibid.:IV, 104) likewise dealt with the question, "May I buy as cheap as I can get it, or give less than the thing is worth?" and his (ibid.) answer was also negative.[17]

Borrowing money to make more money, so central to Franklin's calculus of acquisition, was approved by Baxter (ibid.:IV, 206) as long as certain ethical conditions were met; and lending money was also permissible. However, the debt was not to be exacted rigorously (ibid.:IV, 209; Ames [1639] 1975:241). Pledges, pawns, or mortgages could be taken as security;

however, one could "take not that from a poor man for a pledge, which is necessary to his livelihood and maintenance," nor "keep a pledge he cannot spare, but to his ruine and misery (as . . . his tools, his house, & c.)" (see Baxter 1678:IV, 207).[18]

Usury, the collection of interest for taking a loan, received a mixed reception from the Puritans. On the one hand, Nathaniel Holmes (see Sprunger 1972:175) opposed it; Henry Smith (see Emerson 1968:123, 129) preached against it; Arthur Dent ([1601] 1974:203) considered it a potential source of oppression; and Price ([1608] 1979:31) considered it uncharitable, anti-Christian, and damnable. On the other hand, Perkins, Ames, and Baxter all found usury acceptable in certain circumstances (see Sprunger 1972:174; Baxter 1678:IV, 207–8; Ames [1639] 1975:141, 241, 242, 250); it was lawful when it was "charitable," e.g., when it gave the borrower a profit (see Baxter 1678: IV, 207–9). Nevertheless, it was sinful "when it is against either Justice or Charity" (see Baxter 1678:IV, 207, see also p. 209; see also Ames [1639] 1975:240, 241, 243, 250).

In dealing with the poor, Baxter (1678:IV, 210) argued that contracting "for a certain sum of gain" makes usury "unlawful."[19] Then "whether the borrower gain or lose . . . I will have so much gain: that is, Whether it prove merciful or unmerciful, I will have it"; but "no contract may absolutely require that which may prove uncharitable" (see ibid.:IV, 210).

In sum, Puritan ethics required that each transaction be judged in terms of its benefits to all parties affected. Calculating gain in money terms alone was sinful if people's needs were not taken into account. Gain could not lawfully be one's sole end, nor could the growth of an abstract pool of capital.

Modern capitalism, where decisions are based on rigorous calculations rather than the human equation, where contracts are fixed and absolute regardless of unpleasant consequences, and where there is generally a single price regardless of the wealth of one's trading partner, is irreconcilable with Puritan ethics. It seems most unlikely that Puritanism could have nurtured the "peculiarly calculating sort of profit-seeking" that Weber ([1904–5] 1958:55) was trying to explain, or that Puritan ethics could have combined with this spirit of calculation to provide an ethos for capitalism.

Wallington's Business Ethics

The Wallington case illustrates these market ethics in actual operation. It shows that they were taken seriously and did conflict with capitalist practice.

Seaver (1985:132, see also p. 185) reports that Wallington tried to practice the morality of the marketplace as taught from Puritan pulpits. He opposed oppression and cruelty or unmercifulness toward the poor (ibid.:107). He (quoted in ibid.:124–25) resolved not to "take any more for my ware than it is worth." And he (British diary:15) prayed that in "every thing I either buy or sell . . . that I may deal . . . with an upright heart . . . not seekeing my owne ends only, but as the good of them I deal with." As examples, he destroyed some counterfeit coins rather than pass them (see Seaver 1985:141–42) and returned the purchase price of aspen trenchers that his apprentice had misrepresented as maple (ibid.:132). In Seaver's (ibid.:131) view, being a Puritan inhibited sharp practices and profiteering. Of course, besides his moral self-image, Wallington's reputation was also an important consideration: he desired to be and was "taken to be . . . a very honest plain dealing man" (British diary:5; see also Seaver 1985:130, 132).

Wallington resolved to deal justly, uprightly, and truthfully, but often down in his shop "all this is forgot" (Seaver 1985:126). Still, when he acted unethically, he felt guilty (British diary:9; Seaver 1985:140). When he lost a customer that he lied to, he attributed it to God's punishment (British diary:29–30), which he considered just (Seaver 1985:131). He worried about whether he had robbed others by lying and deceit (ibid.:120). And he had bad dreams about his dishonesty; in the dreams he lacked peace of mind or envisioned hell (British diary:9; Seaver 1985:140, 186). This shows how Puritan market ethics worked to restrain pure self-interest.

Yet Seaver (1985:129–30) reports that success in business "seemed all too often to depend on," as Wallington put it, "lying deceit, oppression, bribery, usery, false weights, false measures, or . . . like iniquity." Riches were "all too often . . . a consequence of sharp practice," of "lying and oppression" and/or "cruelty and unmercifulness to the poor" (see Wallington quoted in ibid.:128).

Because of Puritan market ethics, there was a conflict between religion and the pursuit of material self-interest (see Seaver 1985:138, 142). The higher Wallington's economic status had been, he (Folger diary:426) essayed, "the worse my soule had bine." Wallington saw the godly as "sheep in the midst of wolves" (Wallington quoted by Seaver 1985:159); still, he (Folger diary:292) advised doing justice in trading, even at the loss of considerable money.

It is clear that Puritan business ethics restricted the practice of free-market capitalism. Like certain Asian religions analyzed by Weber, Puritanism erected traditional restraints that impeded capitalist pursuits. Wallington, like the Catholic merchants described by Weber ([1904–5] 1958:73), could hardly please God unless he ran his business in a traditional manner. Puritan traditions were incompatible with modern economic rationality.

Wallington's attribution of unbridled acquisition to the worldly, rather than the godly, places the unregulated pursuit of gain outside of Puritanism, rather than within it. According to Seaver (1985:135, 137), seventeenth-century gains in the market economy grew up around people like Wallington and not because of them. He (ibid.:128, see also p. 126) writes that declines in traditional economic obligations were "not owing to Puritan individualism."[20]

Conclusion

Puritanism was not an external force that broke down tradition; it was traditional in itself. It emphasized God's power, not humans' mastery over nature. People were to serve obediently as God's instruments, not to act independently according to their own visions. These teachings encouraged passivity and discouraged rational striving. Combined with norms of contentment and staying in one's place, they also discouraged business expansion. Neither merchant in this study sought to break with tradition and transform the economy, and neither planned nor achieved business growth.

Puritanism did not contain the ethos for capitalist expansion. It was more compatible with a static economy than with change and growth. It did little to instill nontraditional attitudes. As Seaver (1985:129) put it, Puritan values and attitudes did not "aid and abet the entrepreneurial spirit."

The pious Puritan's work discipline depended more on duty and obedience than on achieving economic success goals. Hence, it was more traditional than rational, closer to Luther than to the calculating spirit that Weber associated with the rise of capitalism. The Puritan emphasis on duty above gain also contrasted with the spirit of capitalism because in the latter the pursuit of gain was life's central value.

In sum, the Puritan ethic was quite different from the spirit of capitalism. Despite a few similarities, there were sharp differences and even direct oppositions between them. There was no strong elective affinity between them, but at best a partial affinity.

NOTES

1. Both the work ethic and the spirit of capitalism provide a moral component to help assure continuous application to economic pursuits. In that regard both are more effective motives than pure greed. The difference is that in the work ethic duty is to one's calling and in the spirit of capitalism toward one's pool of capital.

2. Even conceding Weber's ([1904–5] 1958:200 note 28) point that entrepreneurs with the spirit of capitalism were "not any empirical average type," there should be at least one reasonable example of it to warrant its scientific consideration.

3. Franklin's utilitarianism was not encouraged by Puritanism. Utilitarianism has its own history of developmental influences.

4. In an early book, Marshall (1980:259) claimed that the spirit of capitalism existed in Scotland, but in fact uncovered no duty to increase capital (see, for example, ibid.:172–73, 193).

5. Weber ([1904–5] 1958:200 note 25) explicitly stated that his ideal type of *traditionalism* was "for the purposes of illustration." From this precedent it is reasonable to infer that his *spirit of capitalism* discussion was also illustrative. But if so, he could have easily stated so explicitly, as he did with traditionalism. In fairness to Weber, he (ibid.:48, 64) had regarded the Franklin example as "provisional." However, he never developed any others to replace it.

6. Beetham (1985) has criticized Weber for whitewashing the character of the bourgeoisie. Although Weber ([1904–5] 1958:200 note 28) knew that this type of entrepreneur was not "any empirical average type," he apparently assumed that this type of entrepreneur existed since he (ibid.) declared them "the object of our study."

7. Devotion to the calling was required, but to making money forbidden. Only in later ages, when secularization had eroded ethical constraints against covetousness, could it be virtuous to follow a calling of making money (see Chapter 4).

8. Even if Puritans had made moneymaking a central goal, as they grew irreligious their motive would die with them, and the spirit of capitalism would die out once the supply of apostate Puritans had been exhausted. Relatedly, on the institutional level, the Protestant ethic cannot explain how business firms adopted the abstract goal of profit as their chief end. This began prior to the Reformation.

9. Jews and Catholics needed to control sin, too, but Weber considered their standards to be relatively lax. He thought that Puritan standards were closer to those of Catholic monks than to those of the average Catholic.

10. Of course, insofar as Wallington was typical, modern business practices could not have been modeled on Puritan *business* conduct since it was not very rational. But Puritan discipline could have added more discipline to economic life by becoming a general feature of Western culture.

11. Although he knew it was slothful if one "doth not observe the opportunitys of his calling" (Wallington Folger diary:413).

12. Moreover, it will be shown in the next chapter that Baxter warned against that upward course for most people. His reservations restricted the applicability of and thus further limited the duty to choose a gainful calling (see also Hudson 1949:11–12).

13. Moreover, the preachers were on guard against the potential misuse of this loophole by hypocrites for personal advancement. Baxter (1678:I, 110) warned them, "take not other mens work upon you, without a call, under any pretence of doing good." Ball (1632:389), too, insisted that we must "bee assured our calling is of God, and that hee will accept of our service in that estate and condition of life." And in Perkins's (1970:III, 461) words, "every man must so enter that he may truly in conscience say, God hath placed me in this calling."

14. Although Weber ([1904–5] 1958:162) conceded that "the judgment of a calling, and thus its favour in the sight of God," was "measured primarily in moral terms," he maintained that "private profitableness" was the most important criterion "in practice." Regarding "practice," two objections arise: (1) since Weber had no information on actual practice, his assertion about it was sheer speculation; and (2) to the extent that practice differed from preaching, its causes are to be found *outside* the Protestant ethic, not within it.

15. Unless "he be rich" (Baxter 1678:IV, 103). Or "if it be taken for granted beforehand, that both buyer and seller will stand to the bargain whatever it prove," then the buyer of underpriced merchandise "may enjoy his gain" (see ibid.:IV, 205).

16. However "in dealing with the rich . . . it is lawful to take as much as they will give you" if they "understand what they do" (Baxter 1678:IV, 97, see also p. 103).

17. Baxter (1678:IV, 104, 205) further specified that one may not "make advantage of anothers ignorance or error" or necessity in bargaining. It was considered covetous to "consider not their loss or want" (ibid.:I, 215).

18. One could "take the forfeiture and keep a pledge or Mortgage" only if it was an "act of Merchandize" among "Merchants and Rich men" (see Baxter 1678:IV, 207).

19. Baxter (1678:IV, 210) limited these scruples to the poor; but "in cases of Merchandize, where mens poverty forbiddeth not such bargains, I see not but it is lawful to sell a greater uncertain gain, for a smaller certain gain; and to make the contracts absolute" (similar is Ames [1639] 1975:241–42).

20. Nor, in his (1985:137) view, did traditions change much or break down during the period of English Puritanism. Guild regulations, for example, changed little.

4

Wealth and Its Acquisition

Religion can provide institutional support for the economy by fostering positive attitudes toward wealth. Thus, Puritanism could have enhanced capitalist growth if it encouraged acquisition (see Weber [1904–5] 1958:172, 177), which is critical to capitalism. Two different mechanisms might have produced that effect: (1) Puritanism could have stimulated the profit drive in its believers, and (2) Puritanism could have legitimated capitalism through approval of acquisition and related capitalistic practices. These possibilities may be evaluated in the light of Puritan teachings about wealth.

THE PURITAN POSITION ON WEALTH

Wealth in Itself

The Puritans regarded wealth, in and of itself, as neutral. For example, Ames ([1639] 1975:253; see also Perkins [1606] 1972:III, 527, 528) declared that "Riches . . . in themselves, are morally neither good nor bad, but things indifferent which men may use for either well or ill."

This moral neutrality worked both positively and negatively. On the positive side, it was unnecessary to repudiate wealth a priori. Baxter (1678:IV, 225) pronounced it "no sin . . . to labour . . . for that honest increase . . . which is the end of our labour." And "If God give abundance," Perkins ([1606] 1972:III, 526) declared, "we may take it, hold and use it as Gods stewards." Likewise, Hill ([1613] 1975:45–46) approved of riches honestly gained and properly used.

Material benefits could be considered "good" (see Baxter 1678:II, 127). For example, Ball (1632:349–55, 357) and Pledger (diary:11, 46) called an abundance of food, drink, clothing and shelter "good things" for "our good and comfort." They flowed from the providence of God (Ball 1632:347, 353–54; Pledger diary:14, 45, 52, 59, 85) and were regarded as "mercies" of God (Baxter 1678:I, 220; Pledger diary:11, 52). Perkins ([1606] 1972:III, 524, 534, see also p. 526; 1615:A3; Cragg 1975:153), too, judged wealth to be "a good thing," and said that "it is the blessing of God to be rich."

In Baxter's (1678:I, 220; see also I, 214; II, 127) view these expressions of "our Fathers care and love" should attune our hearts to "Gratitude and Praise." Similarly, according to Swinnock (1663:B10; see also Ball 1632:395 and Hieron quoted by Emerson 1968:180–81), the right Christian "when he aboundeth in goods . . . aboundeth in thankfulness to the Giver."

Insofar as riches were good things, "they may be loved," Baxter (1678:I, 214) allowed. "All love of . . . riches is not sin," he argued. Downame's ([1604] 1974:I, 34 and II, 477; see also George and George 1958:357–58) view was similar: "We may love them" as long as "our love be subordinate to the love of God, our brethren and spirituall things."

But despite these positives there were at the same time important negatives that undercut capitalism. To begin with, Puritanism's neutrality toward wealth implied that it possessed no intrinsic value; it was an idle vanity. Baxter (1678:IV, 263) advised "that we know the vanity of worldly riches," and Downame ([1604] 1974:I, 32), too, called riches vanities. Dent ([1601] 1974:86, see also pp. 119, 397) said not to be "knit to the clod, and the penny," which were "but dung and drosse." Likewise, Baxter (1678:I, 217) compared riches to "dust and chaff." "Value not Wealth and Honor above that rate which the wisest and most experienced have put upon them," Baxter (1653:Epistle Dedicatory) cautioned; "allow them no more of your affections than they deserve."

This devaluation of wealth stemmed in part from the shortness of life. "Dost thou make so great a matter of it, whether thou have much or little for so short a time?" Baxter (1678:I, 218) challenged; for "how little do the wealth and honours of the world concern a soul that is going into another world." You "need not these things," he (ibid.:I, 222) advised; for "is it any great matter whether thou be Rich or Poor, thou art going so fast into another world where these are of no signification" (ibid.:I, 218). Perkins's ([1606] 1972:III, 478) view was similar: riches were "vaine and transitorie" because we bring nothing into the world and carry nothing out (see ibid.:III, 532).

Because the afterlife was so important, "riches temporall" were not considered to be "the true riches"; true wealth was what made people "rich before God" (see ibid.:III, 531). For example, the "least dramme of faith" was said to be "more precious than gold" (see Ball 1632:147). Swinnock (1663:110, see also d2) said to "Value thy self, not by thy estate in this, but by thy inheritance in the other world." Similarly, Baxter's (1678:IV, 263) advice was to "regard the interest of God and our souls, above all the treasures of the world." Heavenly "joyes" were superior because they were more lasting, "an eternal weight of glory" compared to gold, a "fading possession" that "perisheth" (see Ball 1632:147, 386, 394). Typically, Swinnock (1663:338, see also p. 346) considered "the redemption of my soul" to be "more precious" because "earthly favours" could not be carried into the afterlife. Similarly, Preston ([1629] 1976:32; see also Pledger diary:46) judged that wealth "comes not into any comparison with grace" and Perkins ([1606] 1972:III, 531; see also p. 478 and Downame [1604] 1974:I, 61) maintained that riches were "dross and dung compared to the winning of Christ."

These value judgments had direct implications for conduct. Since godliness was "the great gaine," Perkins ([1606] 1972:III, 482) directed, "all gaine must give place to godlines." Similarly, Baxter (1653:Epistle Dedicatory; see also 1678:I, 218) advised his flock to "Be more solicitous for the securing of your Consciences and Salvation, then of your honors or estates." Rather than "tiring and vexing your selves" for "unnecessary things," he (ibid.:I, 217, 219; see also Ball 1632:347) advised minding "greater things than Riches," which concerned people's "everlasting state."

Given religion's greater importance, wealth was viewed as a pointless distraction from the true goal of life. According to Perkins (1615:A2–A3), concern over success led to "many needlesse and superfluous businesses." And Baxter (1678:I, 222) saw wealth as "a trouble, and burden, and interruption of your better work." Rather than thinking about God, glory, Christ, and the angels and saints, Baxter (1650:124; see also 1678:I, 17) complained, some spent their time "in looking over thy bills and bonds, in viewing thy money, thy goods, thy cattle, thy buildings or large possessions." The "baites of prosperitie" drew people out of the right way, Downame ([1604] 1974:I, 4) lamented. And Baxter (1650:124) warned, "if thou . . . beginnest to taste a sweetness in gain, and to aspire after a fuller and higher estate, and hast hatched some thriving projects in thy brain, and are driving on thy rising design, believe it, thou art marching with thy back upon Christ, and are posting apace from this heavenly life."

Nehemiah Wallington, though a merchant, accepted his religion's devaluations of wealth. He (Folger diary:218) thought of worldly riches as "perishing things" as opposed to "durable riches." Since "making hast to be rich" was worldly, it was something to "avoid" (ibid.:414). Wallington sought the "assurance that God is my God" rather than "all the honor and profit the world could afford" (see Seaver 1985:142). Not money, but Christ, "Answers all things"; with Christ, "though I be never so poore I ought to be content; for all my happinesse lies in this one precious jewell" (Folger diary:231). Elias Pledger, too, sought, for religious reasons, to reduce his drive for pecuniary gain. His focus on acquisition was much stronger than Wallington's, and he tried to bring it under control.

The Puritan devaluation of wealth was more consequential than one would expect from the Weber thesis. Ironically, Weber ([1904–5] 1958:156–57) knew that Puritanism favored the pursuit of salvation over the pursuit of wealth. And he (ibid.:157) also was aware that acquisition was considered a "distortion from the pursuit of a righteous life." Yet, he did not qualify his thesis accordingly; he felt that certain "unintended consequences" could override these values.

Wealth as a Cause of Sin

Even worse than its distracting qualities was the power of wealth to lead to sin. For instance, Adams (quoted by George and George 1958:358) taught that "prosperitie encreaseth iniquitie." Downame ([1604] 1974:I, 19, see also p. 95) warned that Satan used the baits of honor and commodity to tempt people to sin. And Perkins ([1606] 1972:III, 524; see also Ames [1639] 1975:254) observed that riches were "(in some men) occasions of sinne."

These sins were taken more seriously than Weber thought. He minimized their import. Although Weber ([1904–5] 1958:156–57), like his critic Samuelsson (1961:37), knew that wealth was considered dangerous, and wrote that "Examples of the condemnation of the pursuit of money and goods may be gathered without end from Puritan writings," he (Weber [1904–5] 1958:163) believed that in Puritanism "Wealth is . . . bad ethically only in so far as it is a temptation to idleness and sinful enjoyment of life, and its acquisition is bad only when it is with the purpose of living merrily and without care." "The real moral objection," he (ibid.:157) argued, "is to relaxation in security of possession, the enjoyment of wealth with the consequence of idleness and the temptations of the flesh."

Although these sins were indeed attributed to wealth by the Puritans, they were far from the only sins or the most serious ones that wealth could cause. As relatively minor sins, they make the wealth-leads-to-sin connection seem unimportant in shaping the overall Puritan attitude toward wealth. Also, Weber (ibid.:69) makes them seem atypical of the successful capitalist. Consequently, his short list of sins minimizes the perceived sinful consequences of riches and understates Puritans' serious reservations about them.

Weber is correct that wealth was seen as a cause of idleness. For example, Baxter (1678:I, 382; II, 130) blamed much idleness on wealth. He (ibid.:I, 382) wrote that "Those that abound in wealth, and have no need to labour for any bodily provisions, should be especially watchful against this sin. . . . The Rich and Proud are under a continual temptation to live idly. For they need not rise early to labour for their bread."

Closely related was the sin of time-wasting (see ibid.:II, 130–31): "They think their wealth alloweth them to play, and Court, and complement away that precious time, which no men have more need to redeem" (ibid.:II, 130); they "are wasting their lives in a multitude of little, ceremonious, unprofitable things," including pleasures, entertainment, clothes, food, and the decoration of house and garden (ibid.:II, 131).

Weber is also correct that wealth was thought to encourage people's enjoyment of the flesh. For example, Flavel (1968:V, 539–41) claimed that prosperity leads to sensuality and earthly pleasure. And among the "Temptations of Prosperity" Baxter (1678:II, 130–31) included gluttony, drunkenness, lust, and wantonness.

Weber's treatment of this point is informative as far as it goes. But wealth was said to encourage other major sins as well. Foremost among them was covetousness.

Covetousness

Wealth could be esteemed to a moderate degree (see Ames [1639] 1975:260–61; Hill cited by Seaver 1985:136; this rebuts Samuelsson 1961:37), but no greater (see Dent quoted by Seaver 1985:134). If "our love passe these limits it is corrupt and carnall" (Downame [1604] 1974:II, 477; see also Baxter 1678:I, 216). Also, wealth could be sought for use in God's service, but not for worldly ends (Baxter 1678:I, 214, 216). To violate these norms was to covet. "Covetousness," explained Perkins (1970:III, 464), "is a notorious vice whereby all men, almost, apply their callings and their works whereof to the gathering of wealth and riches. This is one of the head and master sins of the world."

"Covetousness is a most grievous sinne," declared Hill ([1613] 1975:44; see also Ames [1639] 1975:261). And Downame ([1604] 1974:Epistle Dedicatory; I, 74–75; see also I, 61 and Smith 1599:A3) warned that "the toyling way of insatiable covetousnesse" leads to sin, hell and destruction. Covetousness "would destroy" because it was "Idolatry" (Baxter 1653:297; Downame [1604] 1974:I, 78; Hill [1613] 1975:89; see also McGee 1976:180). Baxter (1678:I, 215) wrote of the "Malignity or Greatness of this sin"; he (1653:299) considered it one of the three great heart sins, and judged that "all men" have too much of this sin (see ibid.:297). "It would do much to cure the love of money," Baxter (1678:I, 221, see also p. 215) predicted, "if you knew how pernicious a sin it is"; "be afraid," he (1653:295; see also pp. 287, 294; 1678:I, 245, 383; II, 127; IV, 97, 205, 221) warned, "lest you should be guilty of this sin."

The proper desire of riches was for "that proportion which may sustain us as passengers to Heaven" and satisfy "the service of God" (see Baxter 1678:I, 214). But since the flesh demanded more, it was a sign of covetousness to desire "more than is needed or useful to further us in our duty" (ibid.:I, 215, see also p. 216). It was "Covetousnesse . . . if any shall so give himself over to the heaping up of riches that hee neglects his duty towards God and his Neighbour" or turns from them (see Ames [1639] 1975:261). And it was covetous when the love of worldly prosperity and its pleasures overtopped "the pleasures of holiness, the favor of God, and our everlasting Happiness" (Baxter 1678:II, 119; I, 215; see also I, 221; II, 130; 1653:156).

Wealth as a Cause of Covetousness

Wealth itself was not condemned, only the desire for wealth. Downame ([1604] 1974:I, 78; see also Baxter 1678:I, 217; Dent [1601] 1974:103; Joseph Hall quoted by George and George 1958:357) wrote that it was not the rich who were covetous, but "such as set their hearts upon riches." Nevertheless, the rich were especially *inclined* to love of the world (see Downame [1604] 1974:I, 78). Dent ([1601] 1974:95) warned, "The love of money encreaseth as money it selfe encreaseth." Flavel (1968:V, 539) wrote that the "honours of the world . . . provoke and inflame" ambition. And Ball (1632:352) charged that the rich man "rejoyceth in his riches." While wealth did not inevitably produce covetousness, it tended in that direction (see Baxter 1653:98).

Wealth as a Cause of Other Sins

Besides the sins already mentioned, wealth was said to lead to a variety of others. These additional sins were also important.

Closely related to covetousness was the sin of worldliness. Ames ([1639] 1975:254) said that "love of the World was a special temptation of riches," and Downame ([1604] 1974:I, 78), too, accused the rich of loving the world. Similarly, Swinnock (1663:d2, see also pp. 99–106) thought that "Prosperous men are most prone to prophaneness." And Chaderton (see Lake 1982:142) believed that "a rich man shall not enter into the kingdom of God" because "the kingdom of heaven is not of this world but they are of this world." Heaven was seen as "a spiritual kingdom, not a carnal one"; so it was hard for the rich man to reach heaven because of "the carnal disposition of his soul" (Chaderton quoted by Lake 1982:142).

"Riches and honours," in Flavel's (1968:V, 538) view, also encouraged vanity and corruption. Baxter (1653:164) hypothesized that if he had greater abundance, vanities might carry him away as others.

It was agreed by Downame ([1604] 1974:I, 78, 94), Flavel (1968:V, 539), Swinnock (1663:104), Ames ([1639] 1975:254), Chaderton (see Lake 1982:142), and Baxter (1678:II, 130) that the rich were especially inclined to pride. "Prosperity breedeth pride," said Ashton (see Lake 1982:142), and Swinnock (1663:105) declared that it was difficult for the rich to remain humble. "The foolish heart of man is apt to swell upon the accession of . . . wealth," Baxter (1678:II, 130) observed, "and men think they are got above their neighbors, and more honor and obedience is their due, if they be but richer." This could lead to "Tyranny and Oppression" of others (Baxter 1678:II, 131), since they had contempt for the poor (Downame [1604] 1974:I, 78) and did not sympathize with people's poverty (Swinnock 1663:109). And it could also lead to "disobedience" (Ashton quoted by Lake 1982:142; see also Perkins 1970:III, 241). Chaderton considered pride particularly dangerous because "humiliation" was needed for heaven (see Lake 1982:142).

Furthermore, as Samuelsson (1961:37) has pointed out, prosperity was said to lead to "oblivion of God" and neglect of religion (see Flavel 1968:V, 539–41; Swinnock 1663:97, 100). Many professed Christ in their want and adversity, complained Downame ([1604] 1974:I, 32), but cast off this profession when they became prosperous. In his (ibid.:I, 78; see also Ball 1632:360) opinion, the rich were inclined to coldness in religion and forgetfulness of God. Hill ([1613] 1975:80) summarized matters, pointing out "that it is hard to be rich and religious."[1] Meanwhile, Nehemiah Wallington (British diary:175) prayed against riches "Lest I be full and deney thee."[2]

Conclusion: Wealth, Sin, and Salvation

Though riches were not inherently bad, they were considered "dangerous" (see Ball 1632:361; see also George and George 1958:358; Samuelsson 1961:37, 39, 41). They were "thornes" that could prick, in Perkins's ([1606] 1972:III, 524) opinion, like a "knife in the hand of a child, likely to hurt, if it be not taken away." And Dent ([1601] 1974:93; see also Dent quoted by Seaver 1985:134) warned that whoever sucked the breast of "profit . . . he shall be poysoned."

Ames ([1639] 1975:253; see also Swinnock 1663:d1, 91; Perkins [1606] 1972:III, 524, 536; Dent [1601] 1974:85; Hill [1613] 1975:44, 89; Ball 1632:360; George and George 1958:357) explained that wealth was dangerous because "it containes the evill of great and desperate temptations." And Baxter (1678:II, 129; see also p. 127; I, 218; 1653:112, 164; see also Baxter cited by Hudson 1949:10; Downame [1604] 1974:I, 94; Pledger diary:32) agreed that "riches . . . may destroy" because they are "plentiful provision for tempting corruptible flesh." He (1678:II, 78; see also Hudson 1949:13–14; Dent [1601] 1974:285; George and George 1958:358) noted that "very few escape."

Wealth exceeded poverty in its temptations. Compared to the poor the rich were said to "live in greater temptations and dangers" (see Baxter 1678:II, 130; see also p. 126 and 1653:111, 164, 457).

Wallington (Folger diary:158) agreed with the divines that "worldly wealth" was "unrighteous Mamon" and riches were "snairs ... from heaven." He (British diary:175; see also Seaver 1985:99–100, 129) feared that there were "farr many more temptations in riches" than in poverty. These came not only from "the sins of his Calling" but "from the Comforts of his Calling" (Folger diary:414). They included pride, earthly-mindedness, misgetting, miskeeping, and misspending (Seaver 1985:129; British diary:175).

Hence, according to Baxter (1678:II, 130; also cited by Samuelsson 1961:41), "the rich, if ever they will be saved, must watch more constantly, and set a far more resolute guard upon the flesh, and live more in fear of sensuality than the poor." It was necessary for them to "be most diligent in fortifying" their hearts and minds "against those more dangerous temptations of riches" (see Baxter 1678:II, 78; Ames [1639] 1975:254; see also Baxter 1653:112; Flavel 1968:V, 528; Swinnock 1663:d1, 91). It was considered difficult for the wealthy to stick to the straight and narrow. The "high places of the world are slippery places," Hieron (quoted by Emerson 1968:182) commented, "in which it is hard to go with the right foot."

This made "the way to Heaven much harder, and salvation of the rich to be more difficult ... than of other men" (Baxter 1678:I, 219; see also Hudson 1949:13–14). Like Baxter (1678:II, 126; 1653:98), Ames ([1639] 1975:253) maintained "that it is very difficult for a rich man to enter into the Kingdome of Heaven." Baxter (1678:II, 126) declared riches to be a "hindrance to mens salvation." Similarly, in Downame's ([1604] 1974:I, 19, see also pp. 32, 99) view, "the golden apples of riches ... by stooping down to gather them, we may be hindered in running the Christian race" (see also Ames [1639] 1975:253–54).

Baxter (1678:I, 219) considered salvation of the wealthy to be "rare, proportionately." "How hardly," he (1678:II, 126; see also I, 219; 1653:98; Burton 1634:271) asked, "shall they that have Riches enter into the Kingdom of God?" And Hill ([1613] 1975:89) agreed that "rich men come hardly to heaven."

The reason was, in Downame's ([1604] 1974:II, 337) words, that riches "make us unfit to enter God's kingdom." They "defile the owner," Ames ([1639] 1975:253–54) wrote. And Hill ([1613] 1975:44, 89) lamented that "by riches I am most subject to be spoiled." Baxter (1678:II, 126) questioned, "how few of the Rich and Rulers of the earth are holy, heavenly, self-denying, mortified men?" Rather, in Chaderton's view, the rich tended to be unrighteous (see Lake 1982:142). And Swinnock (1663:91) agreed that prosperity will "often prove prejudicial to holiness."

Although riches were not intrinsically sinful, they tended to become so in practice. The godly man could have wealth without being corrupted (see, for example, Ball 1632:395; Swinnock 1663:d1; Dent cited by Seaver

1985:134; see also Hall cited by George and George 1958:357), but "Riches and other temporall blessings to sinfull men that have not the gift to use them wel, are dangerous . . . and choake the grace of God" (Perkins [1606] 1972:III, 536). Although "in their own nature they are good," Baxter (1678:II, 127) wrote, "it is . . . through your own corruption, that they become so dangerous" (see also Ames [1639] 1975:253).

In sum, although there was nothing inherently bad about wealth, the Puritans were leery of it. In Ames's (ibid.:254, see also p. 250) words, "Riches are not absolutely to be desired."

Although a wealthy person could be saved if fortified by strong piety, and then could benefit from wealth, its temptations were considered likely to lead the average person into sin. Not only idleness and sensuality, as Weber well recognized, but covetousness, worldliness, pride, vanity, and irreligion were among the sins common to the wealthy. Thus were their souls endangered.

Wealth as a Sign of God's Favor

A further dimension of the Puritan position on wealth concerns its value as a sign from God. Despite its dangers, it could have still been valued if it showed God's favor.

Wealth as a Blessing

Weber ([1904–5] 1958:164, 172; see also Little 1970) did think that wealth showed God's favor; economic success demonstrated "God's blessing" more than in any other religion, he (Weber [1922] 1968:575) insisted. In complete opposition, however, Samuelsson (1961:47) has claimed that there was "no hint" that riches signified "Divine Love." In fact, the most accurate view lies between these two extremes. Since wealth was a mixed blessing, opinion was divided over whether God had done a favor to the rich. Some Puritans considered wealth a sign of God's favor while others did not.

On the positive side, Marlowe (1956:72, see also p. 5) has referred to the Puritan "belief that material prosperity was an outward and visible sign of Divine approval." As an example, Hugh Peter and his followers "interpreted all their worldly successes as proofs of God's favor" (see Stearns 1954:424).[3]

Success could attest to a person's closeness to God because whoever followed God would prosper (see Lake 1982:151). "Belief in God brings good successe," Ball (1632:351; see also p. 399; Miller 1963:481; Perkins 1970:III, 242) wrote; indeed, "The Lord" showered "his blessings plentifully upon them, that put their trust in him." Consistently, Pledger (diary:11) believed that anyone who feared God "shall want no good thing."

Conversely, the unfaithful were punished (see Lake 1982:152). When un-scrupulous merchants lost God's blessing, they labored in vain and could go bankrupt (see Downame [1604] 1974:I, 75).

Yet, despite this support, the preponderance of Puritan thought coun-tered Weber's argument. Greaves (1981:550–51) writes that though "sev-eral" Puritans considered prosperity "a reward of godliness" and hence a sign of God's favor, this "theme received modest mention in comparison with the idea that godliness and prosperity are *not* directly associated." First of all, wealth was generally not considered a reward for obedience because it was given out of God's "free mercie and goodnesse" rather than earned (see Downame [1604] 1974:I, 79; Preston [1629] 1976:125; see also Emerson 1968:22). Second, those who received wealth now were not necessarily blessed later, either with future riches (Downame [1604] 1974:I, 80) or salvation (see Samuelsson 1961:37 and Chapter 6 below). Hi-eron (quoted by Emerson 1968:181) told of "some who have their portion only in this life, and yet have no part in Heaven."

People's wealth was no proof that they were pleasing to God; New (1964:100) has found that it was "not *prima facie* evidence of godliness." Smith (1599:B; see also Burton 1634:271) observed that many of the wealthiest were wicked. And according to Wallington (quoted by Seaver 1985:128), "it is no argument that God loves a wicked man because he is rich." Ashton (quoted by Lake 1982:136; see also Bolton and Downame quoted by George and George 1958:358; Downame [1604] 1974:II, 172) ob-served that "wicked men are not always plagued but sometimes have prosperity"; but eventually they would be punished (see, for example, Price [1608] 1979:36–37). Similarly, Hieron (see Emerson 1968:181) taught that "a man may prosper outwardly and yet still be hateful and abom-inable before God." In Sodom "their wealth was great" (Swinnock 1663:98); and though Tyrus was "honored for Merchants and Merchan-dise . . . the Lord threatneth this feareful desolation to Tyrus for her abom-inable sinnes" (Price [1608] 1979:37).

To explain God's apparent inconsistency in rewarding the wicked, Bax-ter (1653:298) reasoned that God will "very often . . . let hypocrites . . . prosper . . . because they have their portion in this life, and the reckoning is to come." Burton (1634:270) taught a different variation on this theme: "oftentimes worldly riches are meanes to the wicked to make them worse and worse, having wealth to corrupt themselves." This exposed the wick-edness of those God planned to condemn.

Baxter (1678:II, 126; see also 1653:181–83; Hudson 1949:9–10) cautioned, "take heed that you judge not of God's Love . . . by your Riches or Pov-erty, Prosperity or Adversity, as knowing that they come alike to all, and love or hatred is not to be discerned by them"; Hieron taught that "outward prosperity" was no evidence of God's favor (see Emerson

1968:180–81); and Downame ([1604] 1974:II, 173, see also pp. 171A, 172), held that "no man can have assurance of Gods love and favour by these outward benefits bestowed both upon the godly and wicked."[4] To the contrary, Hieron (quoted by Emerson 1968:181) considered it faulty "to conclude I am highly in Thy favor, because Thou hast enriched me." And Baxter (1678:II, 126) judged such a conclusion to be the product of a worldly mind.[5]

In sum, economic success may well have demonstrated God's blessing more closely in Puritanism than in other religions. Still, for most Puritans that association was not very close.

Poverty and Affliction

Downame ([1604] 1974:I, 80; II, 141–43, 257; see also II, 173) and Ball (1632:336, see also p. 183) denied that worldly afflictions, such as poverty, were signs of God's hatred. Poverty did not provide conclusive evidence of God's disfavor (see Burton 1634: 269, 273). According to Wallington, "poverty is no token of God's displeasure . . ." (quoted by Seaver 1985:128). Consequently, Baxter (1678:II, 126) said to "judge not of God's Love . . . by your . . . Poverty."

It is true that poverty *could* be a punishment for sin, as Baxter (1678:II, 127) noted: "Slothfulness and idleness is a sin that naturally tendeth to want, and God hath cursed it be punished with poverty." He (ibid.) directed his readers to "See that your poverty be not the fruit of your idleness, gluttony, drunkenness, pride, or any other flesh-pleasing sin." However, poverty did not always indicate sinfulness, as Samuelsson (1961:38) has written. For example, Burton (1634:270) observed that "dishonesty and wickednesse" did not always "goe by poverty and want." Thus, "good and honest men may be poore and yet good and honest still" (ibid.:269–70; see also Peel 1937:14 and Seaver 1985:134).

Economic adversity was not only used to punish sin: God also used it (1) as a means of correction to benefit his chosen by making them better (Downame [1604] 1974:I, 132; II, 157–58; Burton 1634:270; Ball 1632:183, 395), weaning them from the world (Baxter 1678:II, 128; see also Pledger diary:23), and protecting them from the temptations of wealth (Dent [1601] 1974:125–26); and (2) as a test of character or faith (Downame [1604] 1974:II, 257; Wallington British diary:34, 112). These several possibilities rendered its significance indeterminate. There were a number of explanations of why someone loved by God remained poor. It was difficult when interpreting poverty to distinguish between chastisements to the godly and punishments to the wicked. Although poverty could indicate the presence of sin and the need for reform, it need not; it was often considered a sign of God's love instead (see Perkins 1970:III, 374). Conversely, wealth was not considered necessary as an indication of God's favor, nor was acquisition sought as a means of obtaining such a sign. Elias Pledger, for example, in his diary, never linked his desire for greater wealth to a need for a favorable sign from God.

Wealth as a Duty

In his attempt to demonstrate Puritan encouragement of wealth and profit, one of Weber's strongest supports is the Puritan belief that profit was a duty. He ([1904–5] 1958:162) wrote that "if . . . God . . . shows one of His elect a chance of profit, he must do it . . . the faithful Christian must follow the call by taking advantage of the opportunity." And this characterization is basically accurate.

Some writers have arrived at negative assessments of the Weber thesis without ever considering this Puritan teaching. This has been unfair; it must be given full consideration. Nevertheless, when set into the overall context of Puritan beliefs, the duty to profit is revealed as a minor duty, not one of great consequence. It is argued here that Weber, while correct in reporting it, has exaggerated its importance for Puritanism, and hence its direct behavioral impact on the seventeenth-century English economy.

Growing Rich for God

Wealth, despite other religious drawbacks, had one chief spiritual advantage over poverty: as Swinnock (1663:d2) said, a person "hath opportunity thereby of being rich in good works." The wealth could pay for the works. This combination of wealth and good works was valued. In Dent's ([1601] 1974:197) view, "it is a worthie thing to be a good rich man, which doth much good with his riches." Baxter (1678:I, 220; see also II, 127) pointed out that God's monetary gifts "are the Tools by which we must do much of our Masters work." Riches could "enable us to relieve our needy brethren," and to "help mens souls and the Church of Christ" (Baxter 1653:336–38; 1678:I, 214; IV, 225–26).

Not only was such charity desirable, but it was a duty. Ames ([1639] 1975:255) said that it was "required . . . that wee willingly bestow upon pious uses." "Give alms," directed Perkins ([1606] 1972:III, 596–97, see also pp. 598, 606–7). And Baxter (1653:101; see also 1678:I, 215, 217), too, considered "shewing mercy to the poor" a duty. Nehemiah Wallington accepted these teachings. He saw an obligation to relieve one's "poor brethren," especially in times of dearth (cited by Seaver 1985:129).

In order to fulfill this duty, Perkins ([1606] 1972:III, 598) taught, a person "is commanded to labor in his calling that he might have something to give them that want." And Baxter (1678:IV, 266; see also pp. 222, 225 and 1653:101) agreed. By contrast, the slothful "have nothing to do good with"

(Baxter 1678:II, 78). "Idleness disableth you from doing good to others" (ibid.:I, 381). Even the rich were bound "to live Laboriously . . . that they may have the more to do good with" (ibid.:IV, 263).

Industry made charity all the more virtuous. "He is the best servant for God, that will be laborious . . . that he may be able to do good," declared Baxter (ibid.:I, 217). He "frugally getteth and saveth as much as he can . . . that he may have the more to give to pious and charitable uses" (ibid.:IV, 224).

Besides industry, Baxter (ibid.:IV, 225) encouraged *profit* for charity's sake. He (ibid.:I, 378; see also IV, 225) explained that "You may labour to be Rich for God . . . ." and "in that manner as tendeth most to your success and lawful gain." In fact, when charity was the aim, no effort was to be spared and no opportunity overlooked in the quest for profit (see Ames [1639] 1975:250; see also Cragg 1957:131). Otherwise, "you refuse to be Gods Steward, and accept his gifts, and use them for him when he requireth it" (Baxter 1678:I, 378). These teachings indicate a duty to obtain profits for God's service.

However, this should not be construed as a general exhortation to pursue economic gain (see Hudson 1949:11–13). The rightness of gain depended on the motive. Baxter (1678:I, 378; see also IV, 263) made it clear that gain was approved only for one purpose: "But then your end must be, that you may be the better provided to do God's service, and may do the more good with what you have." For those who did not direct their profits toward good deeds, gain was disapproved: "Riches for our fleshly ends must not ultimately be intended or sought" (ibid.:I, 378; see also IV, 222 and Taylor cited by Hill 1975:96). That was "a sin" (Baxter 1678:IV, 225).

Closely related to, and indicative of, the motive was the question of "How they use that which they labour for" (ibid.:I, 217). "If they use it for God, and charitable uses," Baxter (ibid.:I, 217; see also Perkins [1606] 1972:III, 627) commented, "there is no man taketh a righter course." However, riches had to be used to further "the duties of piety" (Ball 1632:393); if used improperly, their acquisition was wrong.

The Puritans never prescribed profit-making in an unqualified manner. It depended on one's ends, and the acceptable ends were quite restrictive. Profit-making for other purposes was no duty at all. Contrary to the impression left by Weber, there emerged no generalized duty to make money.

The Dangers of Stewardship

Besides the spiritual dangers of wealth itself, enumerated above, Puritans faced special perils when they endeavored to be rich for God. As

God's stewards, they faced complete accountability and additional responsibilities that accompanied additional riches. People were "to give an account unto him, both for the having and using of those riches" (Perkins [1606] 1972:III, 528–29; see also 1970:III, 472). The issue of having riches included the ethics of how money was obtained. At judgment, Smith (quoted by Emerson 1968:131) declared, "he that hath money must answer how he came by it." Ball (quoted by Seaver 1985:137) not only stipulated that things both had to be "well and honestly gotten" but also "wisely and justly used." Similarly, Perkins ([1606] 1972:III, 535) warned that "We must so use and possesse the goods that we have" as to "tend to Gods glorie, and the salvation of our soules." Each of God's stewards would ultimately have to "give account of how you laid out your . . . riches to your master's use" (Baxter 1653:336). Baxter (1678:I, 111, see also p. 221) entreated, "Ask your selves seriously how you would wish at death and judgment that you had used all your . . . wealth; and resolve accordingly to use [it] now." Wallington (British diary:15; see also Seaver 1985:129) accepted these responsibilities. He wrote that "I must one day give a Count before the grat God as how I have gott my mony: So I must give an account how I have improved and laid out every penny I have gott."

The proper use of riches not only revealed the propriety of the *motivation* for obtaining them, as discussed above, but also indicated how effectively God was *served* by their aggregation. The steward was responsible for advancing God's work.

It was difficult to determine and follow the best allocation of expenditures because "all must be wisely proportioned" (see Baxter 1678:IV, 223 and Perkins [1606] 1972:III, 536). The "good effects" of each choice had to be weighed (see Baxter 1678:IV, 223). When "two goods come together to our choice, the greater is to be chosen, or else we sin," Baxter (ibid.:IV, 222) warned; "So doth God require that his Servants labour to be skilful in his Service, as to be able to compare their businesses together and to know which at every season to prefer."

Of course, riches had to be devoted to necessary uses: nothing was to be wasted, spent carelessly, or squandered prodigally on proud or sensual living as seen above in Chapter 2 (see also ibid.:I, 216 and IV, 224, 225, 265). Not only would that rob God, as stated earlier, but also "the poor:" it was "an inhumane vice, to waste that on pleasures, pride, and other needless things, which so many distressed persons stand in need of" (ibid.:IV, 225). Therefore, Baxter (ibid.) urged that "every man should . . . not only forebear all needless expences but those also that are needful but to . . . conveniencies." The rich, in particular, were "bound" to "retrench all unnecessary expences" (ibid.:IV, 263, see also p. 224).

The stewardship doctrine prescribed stringent requirements for charitable contributions, intensifying the general duty to give charity. Since the steward owned nothing, his entire fortune had to be used for God's purposes (Perkins [1606] 1972:III, 528, 532; Swinnock 1663:342; Baxter 1678: II, 130; IV, 222, 225; Ball quoted by Seaver 1985:137–38). "And if you let the poor lye languishing in necessities," Baxter (1678:IV, 223) warned, "you must answer it as an unfaithful Servant" (see also Perkins [1606] 1972:III, 607).

Charity needed to be substantial to be acceptable. God would not take just the scraps that the flesh could spare, but needed to be first served; otherwise he would "take them for no servants of his," Baxter (1653:340) warned. Giving "now and then an alms" would just "deceive your Consciences" (Baxter 1678:I, 216); nor would God "be put off with your Tithes or Scraps" (ibid.:II, 130).[6] But "to save the lives of people in want," Baxter (ibid.:IV, 225; see also I, 215–16) directed, "we must spare any thing from our selves, which our own lives can spare. And to relieve them in their deep poverty, we must abate much more than our superfluities." The rich were therefore "bound not only to give all that the flesh can spare . . . but deny themselves, and mortifie the flesh" (see ibid.:IV, 263; see also I, 381 and 1653:254). Baxter (1678:IV, 209) taught that one "must not say, I cannot spare it, when your necessity may spare it, though not your pleasure" (see ibid.:IV, 209; see also I, 216).

The rich had a special responsibility to feed and clothe the poor and do other good works (Baxter 1653:338; see also Swinnock 1663:342). All were to give "according to our ability," said Baxter (1678:IV, 261); hence, "he that hath a full stock of mony . . . must give proportionably out of his stock" (ibid.:IV, 263; see also II, 131 and 1653:110; see also Perkins [1606] 1972:III, 535, 615). In short, the greater the wealth, the greater the responsibility; and the greater the danger of failing to live up to one's responsibility.

For Puritans who sought profits, it was all too easy for the duty to earn, diligently undertaken, to become covetousness inadvertently when charity proved insufficient. Then it gained only God's disfavor rather than credit for good works.

The Puritan doctrine of stewardship cut two ways. Not only could one find God's favor by being a good servant, but one could arouse God's anger by erring. According to Baxter (1678:I, 219), if

> you desired Riches but for the service of your Lord, and have used them for him, and can truly give this account, that you laid them not out for needless pleasure or pride of the flesh, but to furnish your selves, and families, and others for his service, and as near as you could employ them according to his will, and for his use, then you may expect the reward of good and faithful servants: But if you desired and used them for the pride and pleasure of your selves while you lived, and your posterity or kindred when you are dead, dropping some inconsiderable crums for God you will then find that Mammon was an unprofitable Master.

Because it could bring punishment as well as reward, this doctrine not only encouraged the accumulation of riches to serve God, but it discouraged riches on account of the additional responsibilities and dangers. According to Baxter (1678:I, 221; or see Hudson 1949:14), if one believed in the doctrine and "the judgement of God, it would make you more careful to use well what you have, than to get more: And it would quench your thirst after plenty and prosperity, when you perceived you must give so strict an account of it."

Downame ([1604] 1974:I, 79) reasoned that when "called to an account" as stewards, "the greater our receipts be, the greater will be our reckoning." "Remember," warned Baxter (1678:I, 219; see also p. 211 and 1653:338; see also Hudson 1949:13), "that the more you have, the more you have to give account for. And if the day of judgement be dreadful to you, you should not make it more dreadful, by greatning your own accounts." "Make me to remember," Hieron (see Emerson 1968:182) wrote into a Puritan prayer, "that, the more I have, the greater shall be mine account and the harder for me to be saved."

These teachings were not lost on the merchant class. Wallington (British diary:175) drew the same conclusion as the preachers: "where much is given, much is required for account must be given how we have gott our riches. . . . And how we have layd out our means" (see Seaver 1985:128, 129).

Baxter's Pastoral Advice

Although it was a duty to grow rich for God, fulfillment of the duty could endanger salvation. Paradoxically, one could further salvation through performance of duty only at the cost of seriously hindering salvation. Hence, duty and danger to the soul had to be weighed against each other before endeavoring to grow rich.

Baxter's advice was to avoid wealth. He (1678:II, 127) judged that "it is more rational ordinarily to pray against Riches than for them, and to be rather troubled when God maketh us Rich, than when he maketh us poor." This was true "in respect to our selves . . . though to do good to others Riches are more desirable" (Baxter 1678:II, 127). In other words growing rich for God helped others but was not the best course for one's own soul.[7]

According to Baxter (1678:II, 127), "no wise man will long for the hinderance of his salvation or pray to God to make it as hard a thing for him to be saved, as for a Camel to go through a Needles eye." He (ibid.:I, 219) asked,

Would you have your salvation more difficult, and doubtful, and impossible with men? You had rather choose to live where few dye young, than where most dye young? and where sicknesses are rare, than where they are common? If you were sick, you had rather have the Physicion, and Medicines, and Dyet which cure most, than those which few are cured by? if the Countrey were beset with Thieves, you had rather go the way that most scape in, than that few scape in?

His (ibid.) answer was to "Believe Christ heartily, and it will quench your Love of Riches."

Baxter (1653:316–17) counseled against deliberately enduring hazards; he advised Christians not to do more than their duty required: "if God put Riches into your hand . . . you must not cast away your Masters talents . . . by a holy improvement of them, you may further his service and your salvation. But this is no reason why you should . . . desire or seek so great a danger" (Baxter 1678:I, 219). As Hudson (1949:13–14) put it, "riches were not so much to be sought as to be regretfully accepted."

In deciding on a course of service to God, as in choosing a calling (see Baxter 1678:I, 378), care was to be taken for the safety of one's soul.[8] "Take heed what you thrust yourselves upon," Baxter (ibid.:I, 110) cautioned. He (ibid.:II, 127) considered riches a mistake for most: "our folly in spiritual matters is so great, that we have little cause to be too eager for that which we are inclined so dangerously to abuse, and which proves the bane of most that have it."[9]

A Minor Duty

When Baxter's teaching is viewed in its entirety, it becomes apparent that he has misled Weber ([1904–5] 1958:162) with his oft-quoted warning that "you cross one of the ends of your calling" when you refuse an opportunity for gain. Ironically, in the passages cited above, he advised Christians to "choose the less gainful way" and hence to "refuse to be God's steward," i.e., to cross one end of their callings because of the need to make election sure. What the passage quoted by Weber (ibid.) failed to tell was that the end to be crossed was a lesser one that could be preempted by the ultimate end of salvation. The end of donating to relieve the poor was a material good, which was lesser than the spiritual good of saving one's soul. Growing rich for the poor was not even the chief *material* end of the calling. Perkins ([1606] 1972:III, 526; also cited by MacKinnon 1988b:196–97) taught that "the end of a man's calling, is not to gather riches . . . for the poore; but to serve God in servicing of man." In other words, when Puritans worked at their callings, their chief duty was to serve God through their labors, not by raising money for charitable purposes (see Ball 1632:391 and Ames [1639] 1975:248; see also Walzer 1965:215).

In short, Weber was correct that Puritans felt a duty to become rich for God. But it was a lesser duty, which needed to be weighed and balanced against other, greater duties. Although it generated pressure toward gain, the spiritual dangers in it generated even stronger counterpressures against. These, along with the temptations of wealth and the evils of Mammon, were repeated more often and stressed more emphatically than the duty itself.

Hence, the duty to grow rich for God failed to reverse the negative-leaning Puritan attitude toward wealth. Despite this duty, the Puritans remained quite mixed about wealth. Inconsistently, Puritanism both made wealth a duty and devalued it.

The Behavioral Impact of the Duty to Grow Rich

Actual practice seems consistent with these teachings and their emphasis. Apparently, the duty option was rarely chosen: Baxter observed few who dedicated themselves to becoming rich for God. Few sought gain for this purpose, he (1653:337–38) alleged: rich men had opportunities to do good "if they had hearts. . . . But I hear but of few that do ever the more in it." They should do good "more faithfully than they now do," he (ibid.:339) complained.[10] This indicates that Puritan economic conduct was not driven by the need to obtain more money for the poor.

Merchant Elias Pledger serves as an example. When he was successful in his business, he (diary:52) confessed that "God has been wonderful good to me in his outward providence to me" but "I have wretchedly never been more negligent and careless to my duty towards Him. . . . He has heapt a multitude of outward mercies upon me but I have woefully abused them." This passage reinforces Baxter's impression that few Puritans devoted their lives and fortunes to becoming rich for God.

Pledger's pronouncements about his economic motives were mixed. He (ibid.:27, 28, 42, 68, 76) purportedly sought gain both to serve God and his "generation" and to earn a "comfortable" living. He (ibid.:76) said that he desired an "increase" in "substance" for "the glory of God and the good for others as well as my self." However, he (ibid.) questioned the "sincerity" of his charitable motives and, as noted above, neglected these duties as business improved. Hence, it is doubtful that Pledger's acquisition motive derived primarily from charitable objectives. More likely, his resolutions of service to God and his generation were rationalizations for economic motives of a secular nature.

There is no indication that Pledger intensified his acquisitive behavior for charitable purposes since (1) he was already doing his economic best for strictly materialistic ends as he stated in his diary (see above); and (2) his stated means of increasing wealth for greater service was to ask it as a mercy from God. He said nothing about modifying his economic conduct to become rich for God.

Neither did Wallington attempt to become rich for God. Though "remiss" in the "getting" of wealth (see Chapter 3 above), he was not very concerned about God's disapproval. He wrote in his diary, "I hope and trust the Lord hath forgiven me this and all of my other sins" (Seaver 1985:235). There is no sign of an urge to profit for charity. According to Seaver (ibid.:118), he showed an "apparent lack of interest in money matters."

In sum, Pledger and Wallington did not conform to the duty to engage in enterprise to raise money, feed the poor, and support the church. From the available evidence Puritan business was not typically driven by the need to amass charitable funds.

The Economic Impact of This Duty

Insofar as the Puritan merchants in this study were typical, and Baxter's observations on the matter correct, those economically motivated by the duty to grow rich for charity were atypical, and too few to aid capitalism substantially. Probably much more common as economic motivators were the usual secular desires for wealth and success (see Grassby 1995:197–99 and Rose 1985:31, 36) along with the work ethic, which was advocated much more strenuously by the divines than the duty to grow rich for God and the poor.

If the duty to grow rich for God was of any economic significance, it must have been longer-term. However, even the cultural influence of this norm seems slight. Occidental culture never emphasized a duty to increase one's possessions. Weber distinguished between foolishness and neglect of duty if one's possessions did not increase; he saw the latter (more dutiful) attitude as critical for the growth of capitalism. However, such a duty never became important in secular culture nor was its fulfillment a force for capitalist expansion.

Wealth as an Unanticipated Consequence

Profit could have been generated as an unintended consequence of Puritan doctrine if the laity believed in the obligation to accumulate wealth while selectively rejecting or ignoring teachings about the dangers of wealth and the low priority assigned to the norm of increasing God's talents. Moreover, they could have reinvested the capital they earned so dutifully if they also selectively ignored the charitable purposes of the duty to earn. This selective piety would presumably flow from their material interests, which favored the acceptance of doctrines that encouraged gain and rejection of those that opposed it.

But despite the plausibility of this version of "unanticipated consequences," particularly to the historical materialists, there are reasons to doubt its empirical validity. First of all, the divines had expressly countermanded selective obedience. The Puritan quest for perfection demanded that "all God's commandments" be respected and obeyed (Flavel 1968:V,

597). Sibbes (quoted by McGee 1976:69) insisted that "partial obedience is indeed no obedience at all." It was regarded as hypocrisy. You could not just select what you liked from the Gospel, or retain a few pleasurable or profitable sins. Ball (1632:396), referring both to the calling and the practice of Christianity, affirmed the need for "respect to one duty commanded as well as another." To keep any commandment, it was necessary to make "conscience" of them all. In short, Puritanism specifically addressed the possibility of selective piety. It was forcefully exposed and opposed. The loopholes of an economically liberal interpretation had been closed (see Downame [1604] 1974:II, 232, 234, 241, 408, 507–8; Perkins [1606] 1972:I, 64, 65; Flavel 1968:V, 600). Under the circumstances, selective practices would have been quite difficult.

A second reason to doubt the selective piety thesis is based on actual behavior. Wallington did *not* overemphasize the duty to profit; in fact, he (quoted by Seaver 1985:235; also see above) neglected it and then did not take his neglect very seriously. This contradicts the hypothesis that Puritan merchants selectively overemphasized the religious doctrines that most favored capitalist activity.[11] A third reason to doubt the selective piety approach is attitudinal. Its assumption that lay beliefs wandered from pastoral teachings is not supported by present evidence. The Puritan merchants in this study adhered closely to the preachings of the clergy. Indeed, the correspondence between the beliefs of preachers and diarists is striking. Even Pledger, whose materialistic drive was powerful, and whose economic conduct exceeded the Puritan ideal, correctly recognized and often regretted his deviation from the religious norm (see Chapter 2 above). In short, the evidence indicates that pastoral teachings were the norms actually in use, and does not support the notion of systematic distortion or filtering of clerical teachings by the laity. Nor did these businessmen conform to Hill's image of the morally comfortable bourgeois, lightly and thoughtlessly dismissing any religious rules at odds with their material interests.

THE LEGITIMATION OF CAPITALISM

Max Weber's interest in the legitimation of institutions extended to his work on the Protestantism-and-capitalism question. He concluded that Protestantism helped to justify the modern capitalist system. Since legitimation was not complete without justification in terms of a society's highest values, he considered religious legitimation a crucial supplement to purely secular legitimations.

The issue of legitimation differs from other issues considered here so far. It is not so much a matter of whether ascetic Protestantism fostered or enhanced modern capitalism or its spirit as of whether these religions *approved* of modern capitalism and capitalist activities.

As with many of the mechanisms discussed above, it becomes clear that both behavioral and cultural effects must be considered. In this case, behavioral effects justify the capitalistic behaviors of Puritans while cultural effects reflect the impact of Puritan beliefs and patterns of conduct on the societywide legitimation of modern capitalism. For some of the same reasons discussed above, cultural effects were stronger than behavioral effects.

In order to legitimate capitalism, several elements of the system have needed justification. The division of labor, wealth, profit, inequality, and what Marxists call the exploitation of labor stand prominent among these. For each of these elements the degree of Puritan approval is assessed. Puritanism helped to legitimate capitalism insofar as it approved of these capitalist practices.

The Division of Labor

For the first of these elements, the division of labor, the Protestant influence on legitimation seems minimal. It has been claimed (see Weber [1904–5] 1958:161) that the doctrine of the calling helped to legitimate the complex division of modern labor, but the complex division of labor was well established and legitimated centuries prior to the Reformation. Since it has required little additional justification as it expanded thereafter, any further legitimation would have been superfluous.

More specifically, the Puritan doctrine of the calling provided little justification for adding the role of capitalist to the division of labor. As shown in Chapter 3, Puritans could not approve of "the calling of making money" because moneymaking was not an acceptable end.

The Legitimation of Wealth

The Puritans, like most other Judeo-Christian religions, gave some approval to wealth. Perkins ([1606] 1972:III, 527) wrote that "if we have possessions and abundance, we may with good conscience injoy them as blessings and gifts of God." One did not need to give away one's superfluity, but could keep more than just what was necessary (see Perkins [1606] 1972:III, 608). The fact that Pledger could pray for wealth (see above) shows its legitimacy before God.

However, the Puritans did not endorse all wealth. Nor was the use of lawful means to attain it enough (see Baxter 1678:I, 216). In addition, the rich needed a "religious right to riches," not just civil title (see Hill [1613] 1975:40).

And religious approval was conditional. Wealth was only a good thing if God added his blessing to it (see Ball 1632:360 and Pledger diary:26), and God's blessing was not automatic. Zaret (1985:189–90) has pointed out that it was people's faith that entitled them to material possessions. And Smith (1599:c) specified that the godly rich were the ones with "the blessing of the Lord." However, the rich were not to be honored if they were ungodly or preferred riches to piety (Perkins [1606] 1972:III, 627–28). The wealth of the godly was justified, but the wealth of the ungodly was not.

Puritan approval of wealth was conditional in other ways as well. According to Hill ([1613] 1975:45–46), Puritanism "warranteth the possession of riches" if (1) they are gotten "by honest labour"; (2) "I put no trust in them"; (3) "I spare not, when I ought to spend them on others"; and (4) I am not "a niggard to mine own state and person."

The first of these conditions placed stipulations on the means of acquisition. Wealth could only be legitimate if the means of obtaining it were virtuous. Since the means of choice was hard work, the Puritan work ethic helped to justify wealth. As Weber ([1904–5] 1958:172) put it, when wealth was obtained as a "fruit of labor in a calling," it was an indication of God's blessing. Later, in the eighteenth century, John Wesley approved of riches that were produced by diligence (see ibid.:175).

Since the English Puritans predated Wesley, their beliefs on this point were nuanced a bit differently. Although they believed that "the hand of the diligent maketh rich" (Ball 1632:387), they did not think that human labor created the wealth directly. Also required was the co-action of God to bless their labor. They did not preach the labor theory of value; their doctrine did not simply justify keeping the quantity of wealth that one's labor had produced. Rather, industry helped to justify wealth because it was a virtuous means.

The second condition was commonly stated by the divines, including Perkins ([1606] 1972:III, 529), who felt that the rich man could only be justified if "he bestoweth not his love and confidence upon his wealth." At issue here was one's attitude toward riches.

The third and fourth conditions tied the approval of wealth to its proper use. People were to be honored for their riches only if they were used rightly as instruments to uphold and maintain virtue (ibid.:III, 627–28).

The third condition reaffirmed Dent's point (see above) that someone could be "a good rich man" by doing "good with his riches." Consistently, Pledger (diary:76) felt justified in praying for wealth on the grounds that he could use it to do good for others. Clearly, philanthropy provided an important justification of capitalism and the capitalist class. Philanthropy helped to justify the accumulation of wealth.

The fourth criterion required that a person live up to his or her station in life rather than being a miser. Miserliness would undercut the religious justification of wealth because it was a sign of covetousness. Beyond these four, Perkins ([1606] 1972:III, 530–33) made moderation and contentment additional conditions for the acceptability of wealth; discontent would be another sign of covetousness.

Despite the possibility that these conditions could be satisfied and wealth justified, the Puritans by no means legitimated every wealthy person. In fact, it was considered difficult for the rich to meet the criteria because wealth's snares and temptations often drew people away from godliness; at the very least, a strong effort was required to resist these temptations (see above). Recall also that Baxter felt the rich did too little good with their wealth; this violates condition 3 above. In short, there was no blanket approval of the whole capitalist class. Wealth was often suspect.

The Legitimation of Inequality

A common feature of capitalistic systems is economic inequality. The legitimation of these inequalities has been an enduring problem for capitalism. But ascetic Protestantism has helped with a solution.

As Weber ([1904–5] 1958:177) stated, Puritanism rationalized the presence of economic inequalities in terms of God's will. According to Baxter (1678:I, 217), "God giveth not to all alike: He putteth ten talents into the hands of one servant, and but one into anothers . . . to be entrusted with more than others, is no sin." Because inequalities were created by God, they were therefore legitimate.

Beyond this, the godly deserved wealth, but the wicked did not; God's elect deserved more materially than did reprobates (see Marlowe 1956:54). This justified inequalities during periods of Puritan ascendancy; the material success of the Puritans showed God's special favor. But after the Restoration, when Puritan fortunes declined (see ibid.:5), the same justification no longer applied; a theodicy of poverty seems more appropriate to the Puritans' new situation.

A more durable idea stemmed from the belief that diligence justified wealth. The wealthy were said to be industrious and the poor lazy. Actually, this principle could be applied more readily to the poor than the rich because, as noted above, wealth was caused by the co-action of people and God, not just by the quality of human effort. Puritans tended to credit God for the mercy of wealth rather than claim that they had created it or deserved it.

The Legitimation of Exploitation

On the other hand, and contrary to Weber ([1904–5] 1958:78; [1923] 1961:269), Puritanism never did legitimate the exploitation of workers.

Although the work ethic required wage-earners to labor diligently, and although "every servant" had to "serve the Lord in serving their Masters, and from God expect their chief reward" (Baxter 1678:I, 379; this supports Weber [1923] 1961:269), nonetheless, Puritan teachings repeatedly and forcefully opposed the oppression of the poor (see Dent [1601] 1974:219; Baxter 1653:253; 1678:IV, 206, 209). Baxter (1653:254) urged compassion "to our servants and labourers" rather than hardness (Baxter 1653:296). And Hill ([1613] 1975:80; see also Seaver 1985:136) said to be certain "That I enriche not my selfe by the labour of the poore." Wallington's example shows that this belief was held by merchants, not just the clergy. He wanted the ministers to speak out even more against oppression of the poor (Seaver 1985:107). Contrary to Weber ([1923] 1961:269), God did not, by rewarding good workers with salvation, relieve employers of the duty to pay a fair wage.

The Legitimation of Profit

Weber attached considerable importance to the legitimation of profits because profit-seeking and profit-making were central to capitalist action. Hence, their legitimation was critical to the legitimation of the capitalist system.

The main problem was that the pursuit of profits was self-interested and akin to greed. Both Durkheim and Weber puzzled over how it could have become regarded as a moral good. Yet, this had to happen in order to put capitalism on an ethical basis.

Weber believed that ascetic Protestantism contributed to the justification of profits. "The inner-worldly asceticism of Protestantism first produced a capitalistic ethics," he ([1922] 1968:587–88) declared. "Above all, Protestantism interpreted success in business as the fruit of a rational mode of life" (ibid.:588). Likewise, profit was justified as the fruit of an ascetic life (Weber [1922] 1963:220).[12]

Although the nineteenth and twentieth centuries have justified profits in that way, owing in part, ironically, to Puritan influence, the Puritans themselves could not use the same reasoning. Because God codetermined profits, and sent them for various purposes, sometimes as snares rather than rewards for a job well done, the link between work and profit remained more indeterminate, so profits could not be legitimated indiscriminately by the presumption of diligence. Furthermore, since industry alone could not produce profits without God, they were not seen simply as the fruit of asceticism no matter how much labor had been expended. Hard work could neither fully explain nor fully justify profit.

Nevertheless, when God's blessing converted labor into profit, the profit was justifiable because the work that went into the equation was motivated by the duty to labor rather than covetousness. Thus could unsought profits be justified by the work ethic. On the other hand, sought-after profits could not be justified so easily because approval depended on the motive for seeking them. For example, profits earned for covetous or worldly purposes were sinful no matter how much work had been put in.

The justification of profits depended more upon motive than on how much work went into one's business. Profits were legitimate if unsought or sought to serve God; but they were not approved when desired for their own sake (see Perkins 1970:II, 464), to rise in rank or status (see Baxter 1650:124), or for immoderate material benefits (see Ames [1639] 1975:250).

Most acquisition was devalued because it was considered worldly activity; only that which furthered religious aims was legitimate (see, for example, Baxter 1678:I, 378). It needed to be part of God's service and to further charitable good works (Downame [1604] 1974:II, 477).

The Puritan emphasis on charitable good works helped to legitimate monies used for philanthropy. Not only were business profits viewed as a source of philanthropic benefit, but the softening of self-interest by motives of charity and duty made profit-seeking more acceptable morally. Thus, Puritanism, though its approval was selective, put what money-making it did countenance on a firmer moral basis.

The selective legitimation of profit was also based on its amount. Puritans saw no moral problem with earning a modest profit to derive one's living from business enterprise. For example, neither Pledger nor Wallington questioned the rectitude of profit-making itself. They were far from the Marxist position that all profits are unfair. However, income was to be commensurate with one's social standing, not so great as to permit a rapid rise (see Ball cited by Seaver 1985:137). Puritanism did not condone unlimited profit-making.

Any immoderate desire for profit was considered greedy, covetous, sinful, and un-Christian (see Ames [1639] 1975:250). Likewise, too much attention to earnings was considered temporal and carnal (see, for example, Downame [1604] 1974:II, 477 and Pledger diary:11, 42). And rational profit maximization was ethically unacceptable as noted above in Chapter 3. In short, Puritanism did not unleash limitless capitalist activity.

Nor did the doctrine of the calling serve to legitimate profits. Although it could be argued that the conduct of worldly business was no more than the use of diligence in one's calling (see, for example, Dent [1601] 1974:76), nevertheless a Christian was not supposed to devote his or her calling to the gathering of riches (Perkins 1970:II, 464); its chief aim was service. In short, profit-making was not justified simply on grounds that it was part of one's calling.

Weber ([1904–5] 1958:176) was wrong to state that Puritanism approved all acquisition as long "as it took place legally." Its approval was selective; it did not justify profit-making in general (see New 1964:100). As with the possession of wealth, discussed above, Puritan ethics went far beyond the law in placing moral strictures on gain. Contrary to Weber ([1904–5] 1958:177), "formal correctness" in business did not always bring the "fulness of God's grace."

Puritanism did not act as Weber (ibid.:172) thought: as a "release of acquisitive activity." Rather than treating acquisition permissively, the clergy sought to subordinate it to religious control. They did not relax the early Christian critique of wealth, but tried to wean people away from Mammon. For example, the intent of the stewardship doctrine was not to invest business-as-usual with religious meaning by making it a duty, but, by encouraging a sense of stewardship, to make wealth more accountable for serving good ends. Rather than accepting economic materialism as an end, this doctrine subordinated it even more to religion.[13]

Neither merchant diarist felt that the unrestrained pursuit of profits was justified. Recall that Pledger, a man with a powerful thirst for material gain, tried to restrict his concentration on business matters for religious reasons; he felt that he should let God take care of profitability. Similarly, Wallington (see Chapter 2 above) considered it worldly to utilize all means and opportunities for business success. He (see Seaver 1985:127, 142) eschewed the unethical and "crafty" means often required for prosperity because they were incompatible with being a good Christian. In short, Puritanism did not condone unbridled acquisition, but proscribed it. The irreligious were perceived to practice it, but the pious could not.

Weber judged that Puritanism gave profit-making an ethical basis by making it a duty. He ([1904–5] 1958:177) wrote that with good moral conduct a businessman "could follow his pecuniary interests as he would, and feel that he was fulfilling a duty in doing so." However, economic gain did not necessarily fulfill one's duty. For one thing, acquisition alone without disbursement for religious causes was unacceptable (see Baxter 1678:IV, 266). There was no duty to accumulate wealth in isolation from its use in achieving God's ends. Indeed, there was no ethic of accumulation at all because greater revenues were to be combined with higher levels of charitable expenditure.

Furthermore, it was shown above that the duty to profit could not be performed acceptably without a proper motive, and that a failure to distribute would cast doubt on whether charity was the sincere motive for acquiring one's wealth. Successful acquisition could be a sign of covetousness and worldliness as easily as a sign of performing one's duty. An improper motive could make it covetous despite its outward propriety (Ames [1639] 1975:260–61; Baxter 1678:I, 216; see also 1653:295; Downame [1604] 1974:II, 349; Perkins [1606] 1972:III, 529; Preston [1629] 1976:51).

Weber ([1904–5] 1958:177) oversimplified the Puritan's situation when he judged God's blessing to descend "as long as . . . the use to which he put his wealth was not objectionable." Not only did the charitable requirements on God's stewards make it rather difficult to use the money unobjectionably, but, in addition, the intent of its acquisition needed to be that the owner "have the more to do good with" (Baxter 1678:IV, 263). Profit was only legitimate if the motive for seeking it was charitable as well as its uses.

Piety and Laxity

In Weber's ([1922] 1968:587–88; see also [1922] 1963:251–53) view, ascetic Protestantism provided a better religious legitimation of capitalism than Catholicism did. Devout Catholics could not go into trade because "the inevitabilities of economic life" were too far from "the Christian ideal." Only Catholics "who were lax in their ethical thinking" could take up a business career. And the same, he ([1922] 1963:251–61) said, was true of traditional Jews, as noted above in Chapter 1. In contrast, the Protestant ethic "opened the way for a career in business, especially for the most devout and ethically rigorous people."

However, the data on Pledger and Wallington presented above in Chapters 2 and 3 belie the latter claim. Both merchants perceived a conflict between rational capitalist practice and their religion's ideal. The materialistic Pledger felt guilty about exceeding Puritan economic limits, and the guilt-ridden Wallington felt out of place in a business career (see Seaver 1985:142). Neither felt justified in pursuing rational business activities. Their feelings and actions more closely resembled those Weber associated with lax and pious Catholics, respectively, than the ones that he attributed to ascetic Protestants.

Clearly, devout Puritans could not find capitalist individualism legitimate. The pious were most aware of the sins associated with it and the pastoral warnings against it. They would have been most sensitive to its incompatibility with the godly life. Furthermore, they would have been most likely to curtail practices that were religiously disapproved.

Yet, an alternative possibility remains, namely, that Puritanism helped to legitimate capitalism to the morally lax. Going beyond Weber, Hill and Yinger (see Chapter 1 above) have hypothesized that entrepreneurs with a secular desire for gain employed Puritan teachings in a self-serving way to justify their profit-making activities. According to this hypothesis beliefs were applied in ways that the preachers had not anticipated to justify activities that they had set out to condemn. In other words, the legitimation of capitalist individualism was strengthened as an "unanticipated consequence" of Puritan teachings.

If their hypothesis is correct, one likely distortion would have been the legitimation of all acquisition under the guise of philanthropy. Since any monetary gains tend to encourage philanthropy by adding to the surplus funds available, all profits could have been seen as potentially beneficial. When economic aims were unclear or undefined, as they frequently were, potential donors could have easily received the benefit of the doubt. Since, as Baxter (1678:II, 130) noted, virtually everyone gave *some* charitable donations, nearly all gains could have been rationalized in charitable terms; then at the same time charity could have been minimized in favor of a career of profit, reinvestment, and business growth. This practice may have inadvertently legitimated some profits Puritanism had not meant to condone; it had not intended to legitimize any that were not accumulated in God's service.

The less devout could have subscribed to such lax interpretations. Some could have been hypocritical and others simply insensitive to the maxims the preachers taught. In either case "a godly motive could become a cloak for economic calculation" (Hill 1975:97–98).

The divines knew that some of this was taking place. For example, Baxter (1653:297) was aware that many covetous people "finde excuses and fair names and titles to cloak" this sin.

However, since the aim of the stewardship doctrine was not to justify profit, but to make the rich more accountable for serving good ends, Puritanism worked to close any loopholes through which the forbidden behaviors could become justifiable. Weighty requirements of charitable giving and purity of motive closed the moral loopholes for hypocrites who hoped to pursue utilitarian aims while posing as God's servants. The doctrine of stewardship was not so easily misused as a pretext for feeling pious about economic accumulation. The preachers distinguished between those who followed the teachings and those who invoked them as flimsy excuses for the unauthorized pursuit of gain.

First of all, as noted earlier, Puritans were suspicious of the desire for gain. Rather than fulfillment of religious duty, it was often interpreted as a sign of covetousness.

Second, despite the subjective nature of covetousness, the Puritans had ways of telling who was covetous (see Ames [1639] 1975:261).[14] It was not so easy to practice this sin and simply deny it to one's self and one's cobelievers.

Baxter (1678:I, 216–17) was able to expose some pretenses, or "counterfeits of . . . freedom from covetousness which deceive the worldling." A person sometimes thought that "he is not Covetous" because "he hath a necessity of doing what he doth for more . . . he . . . scarcely hath whereon to live"; because of a "necessity of labouring in your callings"; "because he useth no unlawful means, but the labour of his calling, to grow rich";

because he "wrongeth no man"; and "because it is but for his children that he provideth." But Baxter (ibid.) replied that lovers of the world were "covetous for all these," refuting each pretense in turn. He let none of these lax interpretations stand. None justified a strong drive for gain.

In sum, general awareness and anticipation of lax interpretations and hypocritical justifications limited the degree to which the duty to grow rich for God could be selectively interpreted in favor of utilitarian acquisition. Puritanism gave economic gain a positive religious meaning only under limited and stringent conditions.

The Capitalist Conscience

Weber exaggerated the Puritan legitimation of profit-making when he wrote that seventeenth-century religion bequeathed to modern times "an amazingly good, we may even say a pharisaically good, conscience in the acquisition of money" (see Chapter 1 above). In fact, the Puritans had no clean consciences to bequeath to modern times (see Tawney [1926] 1961:305).

As indicated above, the difficulties in making business conduct conform to religious ideals could make the pious feel guilty and anxious. Even if every attempt was made to follow pastoral teachings, comfort was elusive. Several familiar features of the religion contributed to this.

First of all was Puritanism's suspicion of the motives underlying acquisition. Baxter (1653:297; but see also 1678:I, 217) wrote that "all men" were covetous. Without the proper religious aims, acquisition would be religiously unacceptable; so whether or not one's motives were pure was a source of worry (see, for example, Swinnock 1663:d1, 91). Pledger (diary:26) observed that without God's blessing "riches will but aggravate our guilt here and increase our misery hereafter."

Another source of worry stemmed from the need for God's stewards to account for the way wealth was used (see above). According to Baxter (1653:340), no part of people's wealth "will then be comfortable to them, but that which was laid out for God."

Moreover, Puritans *deliberately* worried about their economic conduct because of the general admonition to avoid security over sin (see Downame [1604] 1974:I, 3, 5–7, 11, 110, 113 and Baxter 1653:134, 226). To feel at ease was not only presumptuous (Perkins [1606] 1972:I, 42; Baxter 1653:274) but a sign of a carnal man or reprobate (see, for example, Lockyer quoted by McGee 1976:137 and Downame [1604] 1974:II, 142). It was Satan who gave people "a pharisaicall conceite" (Downame [1604] 1974:I, 92; see also Frontispiece and Baxter 1653:283). This was considered most dangerous to the soul (Flavel 1968:V, 517, 594; Downame [1604] 1974:I, 7, 30, 48; II, 249, 541; Baxter 1678:II, 124; 1653:235, 393).

Puritanism stressed critical self-examination as a means of detecting and overcoming sin (see Baxter 1653:146, 331 and cited by Knott 1980:11, 70 and Keeble 1982:137; Sibbes cited by Knott 1980:58; Ambrose quoted by Keeble 1982:138; Perkins 1970:III, 357 and Perkins quoted by Porter 1971:281). It aimed to prick people's consciences, not just reassure them. Fear and trembling was the norm among Puritans (see Baxter 1653:201, 204; see also Hill [1613] 1975:172 and Stannard 1977:79). One could not have a clear conscience and still be a good Puritan.

Elias Pledger provides a prime example of the conscience of a Puritan businessman. He often felt guilty due to overconcern with his business fortunes. Similarly, Nehemiah Wallington frequently felt conflict in his conscience over his business practices (see Seaver 1985:142). He (Folger diary:327; see also Seaver 1985:142) worried that his business hindered him from being a good Christian. According to Seaver (1985:138, 142), his scrupulosity made trading "a constant moral battle." The resulting tension was difficult for him to live with (ibid.:142).

Cultural Effects On Legitimacy

The previous sections have examined the rightness of capitalism to the English Puritans. However, in addition, Puritanism influenced attitudes toward capitalism in the general culture of the Occident, furnishing and reinforcing maxims that served to justify it to the broader populace. These cultural mechanisms must be taken into account, too.

In fact, Puritan beliefs aided legitimation more effectively through cultural mechanisms than they did behaviorally, largely due to the transformation of religious ideas during the cultural borrowing process. They were not only removed from their original doctrinal context, which changed their meaning, but also they were borrowed selectively. The general culture tended to appropriate the procapitalist tenets of Puritanism without the anticapitalist parts. This process extended from the seventeenth to the nineteenth century.

Cultural effects were also enhanced by the demise of English Puritanism in the late seventeenth century. The associated decline in Puritan piety reduced the obligation to rely on God for profits, the influence of strictures against covetousness, warnings against endangering one's salvation through prosperity, and denunciations of Mammon. All this lowered disapproval of profit-seeking and the "calling of making money" in the succeeding centuries.

A decline in the belief that God controlled profits permitted post-Puritan generations to legitimate wealth, profits, and inequalities in a new way. Having strengthened their work ethic by borrowing from the Puritans, they applied it to the legitimation issue differently from the Puritans.

The belief that God codetermined profits gave way to the idea that labor had created them. Then the entrepreneur was entitled to profits insofar as his or her hard work had gone into producing them.[15] They constituted a fair reward for labor contributed. Intended as well as unintended profits could be justified by this logic. That was important because capitalist growth depends on profit-seeking, not just upon unsought profits.

Today, gain is still justified in terms of the work ethic. We value not just prosperity, but earning the money. For example, heirs are respected less than the founders of the family fortune. We respect self-made men and women most. This sentiment is strengthened by the belief that work created the wealth.

Even when profits are of unknown provenance, they are nevertheless deemed legitimate. They are presumed to stem from hard work whenever it could have been a significant means.

According to the work ethic, not only do hard workers deserve the fruit of their labor, but just as in Puritan times (see above) poverty is said to be deserved as the fruit of laziness. This notion has become part of the general culture, and as such has legitimated capitalistic inequalities quite effectively for three centuries (see, for example, Grassby 1995:301).

Besides the decline of certain religious doctrines, a second factor that has strengthened the legitimating role of the work ethic has been an increase in the value of work itself. In English Puritan times work was subordinated to other religious priorities such as salvation and worship (see Chapter 2). This limited its capacity to bestow respectability upon its fruits. Once appropriated as part of the general culture, however, and removed from the Puritan religious context, it took on new importance. By the Victorian age it was receiving top priority, and many people, both religious and secular (contrast to Weber [1904–5] 1958:177), lived to work rather than the reverse. By then it could lend considerable prestige to the profits it produced.

In sum, the work ethic was a portion of Puritanism that was selected for incorporation into general Western culture. It was taken out of its religious context when many other Puritan tenets were not adopted. It justified profits better in its later, cultural form than in its earlier, religious form.

Note that Puritanism did not give profits a positive cultural valuation of their own. They could be highly valued only when linked with work. Since Puritanism devalued most forms of profit-seeking and profit-making, it failed to legitimate them directly through religious approval. Instead, it legitimated them indirectly through their association with work. Puritanism made work a religious duty, and work legitimated profits. Thus, the legitimation of profit became an unintended consequence of Puritanism, and later of Methodism.

Puritanism did little to change cultural attitudes toward profit-in-itself because its duty to profit never became important in the general culture. Therefore, this exception to the Puritan condemnation of profit-seeking could not have served as the critical opening for the later cultural approval of profit in general (see, for example, Merton 1968) nor been generalized into a wholesale legitimation of profit-seeking.

More positive in its influence was the Puritan ideal of charitable good works. Carrying forward the earlier Jewish and Catholic teachings on charity, it reinforced philanthropy as a value in the Occident, enhancing the latter's ability to legitimate profits in the general culture. Then, acquisition became legitimate because it served philanthropic ends. Moreover, the Puritan stewardship doctrine with its ethic of civic service has strengthened the image of the businessman as philanthropist, which helps to make business a commendable profession.

In conclusion, Puritanism was mixed on acquisition and suspicious of it; the Puritans did not give it full religious approval. They aided in its legitimation chiefly by strengthening the values of work and philanthropy in the general culture. These ideals then helped to legitimate capitalist activity in society-at-large.

The English Puritans did not help with capitalist legitimation directly so much as they furnished some ideational materials out of which justifications were constructed by future generations. The justifications were not part of the religion. Puritanism itself could not fully approve of modern capitalism; although it accepted some aspects of capitalism, its doctrines were mutually inconsistent and its appraisal consequently mixed. However, in seeming adherence to the principle that ideas follow material interests, the general culture selected primarily those Puritan beliefs that were consistent with its own values. Taken alone, without many of the old allegations of sin, they contributed to a highly positive assessment of capitalist activity. This is consistent with Weber's contention that the Puritan impact came after its peak of religious enthusiasm had passed.

The Legitimation of Capitalism in Historical Perspective

It may be concluded that Puritanism helped to legitimate capitalism through both behavioral and cultural mechanisms, but primarily the latter. Two Puritan doctrines were involved, most importantly the work ethic, but also the duty to profit in order to perform charitable good works for the poor.

However, the significance of this benefit must be qualified in two ways. First of all, religious legitimations of capitalism were not the only ones; their necessity was reduced to the extent that legitimations of a secular nature sufficed. Second, Puritanism's contributions, and especially its cultural effects, came quite late in the history of capitalist development; they were not around to legitimate modern capitalism in its early stages.

There should be no mistake about it: business was well-established by Puritan times. Unlike the Weberian image of Protestantism opening the door for fledgling capitalism, one finds instead a powerful merchant class to be legitimated. "O London," wrote Price ([1608] 1979:36), "thou . . . sittest like a Queene, al thy citizens being as so manie Merchants, thy Merchants as so many Princes."

Furthermore, business was already well-legitimated, primarily on secular grounds. A quotation from Price (ibid.:37) makes it clear that wealthy business classes had been highly respected since Biblical times: "I find no Citty more honored for Merchants and Merchandise then Tyrus in the prophesie of Ezekiel." Wealthy merchants were likewise honored in the Renaissance cities of Italy as revealed by funeral orations of the fifteenth and sixteenth centuries, as well as by their dominant social and political positions. By the turn of the seventeenth century Price (ibid.:13) wrote, "Many acknowledge the necessitie, dignitie, and excellencie of marchants, and they have approved the marchant of al men, to be the most diligent for his life, the most assiduous for his labor, the most adventurous on the sea, the most beneficiall to the land, the glorie of his countrie, and the best piller of his commonwealth." And Grassby (1995:52, 390–91, see also p. 378) writes of the same period that businessmen, though disliked, were respected for their "importance" and society's dependence on them.

It had been well understood for centuries that businesses served the community, providing employment and enhancing local wealth (see Baron 1969 and Herlihy 1969). Hence, by Puritan times, capitalist behavior had long been regarded as a civic good.

The Puritans reinforced this judgment through their belief that the good of the community was God's will (see Weber [1904–5] 1958:265–66). The work of their callings served the poor, the church, and the commonwealth, and, as noted, some profit-making was justified by its philanthropic uses. This approach put some capitalist activity on a positive moral basis by dissociating it from self-interest, but it was not to be the decisive capitalist ethic. Much more important for the legitimation of capitalism was the secular philosophy of utilitarianism.

A century after English Puritanism's decline, Jeremy Bentham, Adam Smith, and the Mills found a new way to justify capitalism in terms of the public good. Capitalism was said to be a productive system, and in productivity lay the wealth of nations. Furthermore, since community benefit consisted in the happiness of individual citizens, it was often advanced best by each individual pursuing his or her own happiness. This philosophy gave profit-making a positive moral basis not by disassociating it from self-interest but by tending to equate self-interest with the good of everyone (compare Grassby 1995:297). This solved both capitalism's need for legitimation and the puzzle posed by Weber and Durkheim over how a selfish activity like private profit-making could be made into a moral good. Over the next two centuries, during which modern capitalism grew to dominate production, it was justified primarily in this secular way.

Puritanism contributed less to this utilitarian philosophy than Weber ([1904–5] 1958:265–66) thought. Since civic prosperity was considered a good centuries before Puritanism emerged, as just noted, the notion of community benefit did not hinge on the religious or impersonal nature of Puritan charity, and in fact had helped to legitimate capitalist activity for centuries before the Puritan movement. Even more important, the Puritans rejected the equation of self- and social interest (Seaver 1985:138). Unrestrained appetite and ego were not thought conducive to the common good (ibid.). They favored altruistic service over rational self-interest. Ultimately, their approach could only justify some profit-making while, as we have seen, most remained suspicious.

In sum, capitalism over the centuries has been legitimated primarily by its ability to produce civic wealth (see, for example, Marshall 1980:147–48). This justification has been chiefly secular in nature. Puritanism contributed little to it.[16]

Philanthropic legitimation also has a utilitarian side because philanthropy underscores the benefits of capitalism to the community. Although Puritanism strengthened this value (see above), its contribution here, too, must be judged in historical perspective. The philanthropic ideal antedates the Puritans, and it hardly needed the extra significance given it by their doctrines of stewardship and growing rich for God. Puritanism's contribution was minor.

Perhaps the secular legitimations of capitalism would have been sufficient without religious legitimation contributing as well. Despite criticisms, capitalism tended to be accepted for bringing prosperity. It did not suffer an outcast status or need religion to make it respectable. Religion never raised capitalism from disreputability to legitimacy. Weber assumed that religious legitimation was important to the health of modern capitalism. However, it may not have played a crucial role. Since the wealthy were respected in civil society since time immemorial, we do not need Puritanism to see why successful businessmen are looked up to.

First of all, since religious and civic ideals can differ, civic legitimacy is possible without religious legitimacy. And second, not every institution needs to be legitimated in terms of religious values. If approved by some social values, an institution can be viable without the blessing of the very highest values. Moreover, in modern times religious values are not truly dominant. Consequently, it is not clear that capitalism needed God's approval to expand, or that it needed religious businessmen.

Businessmen were more legitimate in the secular world than in the religious. In the former, utilitarian grounds were usually decisive. The Christian world, in contrast, could be quite anticapitalist. Not only Roman Catholics characterized "the desire for gain as *turpitudo*" and rejected "activity directed to acquisition for its own sake," as Weber ([1904–5] 1958:73) has noted, but, as seen above, the Puritans, too, condemned acquisition for its own sake and, in most cases, regarded the desire for gain as sinful covetousness. And, like the Catholics, the Puritans opposed capitalist practices that violated traditional Christian market ethics. Hence, there was little difference between Puritans and Catholics on these points. Reservations about business and capitalism were characteristic of the Christian tradition. Criticisms of profit-seeking as greed and covetousness were drawn from the Bible.

As time went on religion grew more favorable to business.[17] The Catholic position just described softened (see deRoover 1963); and Protestantism accepted the businessman's calling. New (1964:49) points out that the bourgeoisie have found justification under both Catholicism and Lutheranism.[18] As early as 1528, Puritan William Tyndale argued that "the merchant is a better Christian than a monk" (see Porter 1971:269). This was faint praise because Puritans opposed monks; but later Price ([1608] 1979:5, see also p. 19) asked, "What trade more honorable than the marchant?" Such blanket approval was qualified by Baxter (1678:I, 378) and Perkins (1970:II, 462), who enumerated which merchants served useful purposes and which were idle or sinful (see Chapter 3). But by the nineteenth century Protestant church membership put a halo around many businessmen; it enhanced respectability and gave the presumption of fair dealing in accord with Christian business ethics (see Weber 1946:312, 322 and [1923] 1961:269–70).

Grassby (1978:361–62) reports that attitudes toward business values changed along a broad front beginning in the seventeenth century. Intellectuals, economic writers, journalists, essayists, satirists, poets, and antiquarians, as well as divines, had written that profit was exploitative, middlemen were parasitic, and private interests injured the public good; however, "as the English economy grew, the anti-acquisitive attitudes . . . declined." Trade became more widely regarded as useful and merchants proud and self-confident. Writers stressed the productiveness of trade. The participation of the gentry in trade elevated its status (see ibid.:363). Fees and salaries enjoyed no moral superiority over profits (see ibid.:375). There emerged "no dominant system of anti-business values" (ibid.).

As business became more dominant, it established beliefs that legitimated itself.[19] Weber (1946:271) has called such beliefs a "theodicy of good fortune." It was into this belief system that culturally borrowed Puritan teachings were introduced, for example beliefs that God favors the wealthy and that hard work and philanthropy justify material acquisition.[20] Capitalism selectively appropriated these tenets, removed them from their sacred context, and hung them onto its new framework of beliefs. As Weber observed, this reformulation could only occur outside the context of true religious piety.

Although religious beliefs provided some of the content for the new ideology, it was not primarily religious in its nature or inspiration.[21] Puritan teachings neither required nor encouraged such an ethos; indeed, they could have supported a critique of capitalism as easily as a justification of it.[22] Religion was not out front leading the material forces. Rather, the dynamic of legitimation was one in which a dominant class constructed its own justification. Puritanism itself, which stems from the Tudor period, came too soon to have been a "superstructure" that grew out of the capitalist system after it had come to dominate. Nevertheless, some Puritan ideas, available in the society as options within its cultural heritage, became part of the ethos that arose as capitalism achieved full domination.[23]

Because much of Puritanism's contribution to legitimation was cultural, its impact came later, despite Weber's emphasis on justification during the infancy of the new system, when participation was optional. Although Puritanism aided the legitimacy of mature capitalism, Weber ([1904–5] 1958:72) found such late assistance unnecessary because dominant capitalism could select and compel the supportive behaviors it required. People had to work hard at their callings once modern capitalism was in command.[24] Hence, the actual timing of Puritanism's impact on legitimacy would be highly ineffective.

However, Weber's analysis here is faulty because it is inconsistent with another of his theoretical principles, one that is more general and that he stressed more continuously throughout his work. Those who dominate, despite their power, do need legitimation. It promotes stability and enhances the likelihood of survival. Thus, eighteenth- and nineteenth-century capitalism did need legitimacy, and Puritanism contributed to it through its cultural impact. Through this mechanism Puritanism helped to stabilize and preserve mature capitalism.

Puritanism's cultural contribution to capitalist legitimation, though not of critical importance, was probably timed effectively. According to Homans (1961), new practices typically spread because they are more rewarding than old; that would make legitimation unnecessary for growth during capitalism's early phase. But a dominant economic system needs legitimation to stabilize its institutional character and preserve itself as the status quo. Puritanism's help was appropriately timed because there are difficulties in remaining dominant, not just in becoming dominant.

NOTES

1. On the incompatibility of God and Mammon, see Chapter 2 above.

2. Marlowe (1956:40) and Seaver (1985:194) report that a number of Puritan saints who prospered actually did become less devout.

3. Peter seems atypical. According to Stearns (1954:380), his concern for the material welfare of his people was "unusual in a Puritan divine." Still, he represents the minority who believed that wealth showed God's favor. Michaelsen (1953) considers this belief part of a Puritanism "gone to seed," but Peter's adherence to it belies the notion that it was accepted only by the marginally devout or that it developed later as English Puritanism was dying out.

4. Baxter (1653:393) maintained that interpretations of prosperity and success deluded even the godly. He (1678:I, 217) considered it impossible to understand why God puts more "talents into the hands of one servant" than another.

5. Those Puritans who considered wealth a sign of God's favor may, indeed, have done so out of their own self-interest as members of the wealthy classes, and not because of pastoral teachings.

6. Baxter (1678:II, 130) noted that "There are few rich men of all that go to Hell, that . . . give nothing at all to the Poor."

7. Of course, a person still needed "to do good to others" rather than live entirely for "his own soul" (Baxter 1678:I, 376).

8. Hence, the decision was to take into account the greatness of the sins one would be tempted by; whether or not people usually overcome those sins; one's ability to withstand temptations; and the number of others whose contributions could substitute for one's own (Baxter 1678:I, 110). The greater the danger of sin, the greater the warrant "to avoid doing good" (ibid.).

9. Baxter's (1678:II, 127) judgment that "our strength is so small, and the difficulties so many and great already," implies an insufficient margin of safety for adding to the risks of salvation, even for the pious. Similarly, Ball (1632:360) lamented that "we have no power to wield a good estate well."

10. Perhaps the charitable actions of John Wallington, Sr., were exceptional. According to Seaver (1985:118), he gave away most of his fortune during his life, and even more in his will.

11. However, in one instance Wallington (British diary:37) skipped a sermon because he "must & ought" to attend his shop. Only later did he feel guilty about missing the sermon.

12. Since Weber ([1904–5] 1958:157, see also p. 174) also states that Puritanism condemned profit-seeking, he seems inconsistent.

13. If people seek wealth as a duty or to glorify God, this subordinates gain to religion.

14. Its signs included: "When we make too much ado in the world for riches, taking too much upon us" (Baxter 1678:I, 215); "an eager . . . desire of getting" (Dent [1601] 1974:77) or "after earthly things" (Baxter 1678:I, 215; see also Ames [1639] 1975:5, 261–62); "When we are . . . pleased if we do but prosper, and have plenty in the world" (Baxter 1678:I, 215); or if our "joy and sadnesse" depend on "successe in those externall affaires" (Ames [1639] 1975:5, 261–62).

15. The new doctrine also undercut the legitimation of profit insofar as capital-

ists do not do much work. Since the capitalist did not work, Marx argued, neither should he eat.

16. Weber ([1904–5] 1958:74–75) equated legitimation with ethical approval, and ethical approval with religious approval. In doing so, he (ibid.:177) may have underestimated the importance of utilitarian bases of legitimacy. Also he may not have distinguished between utilitarian thinking, which had regarded civic prosperity as a good for centuries, and the philosophy of utilitarianism, which formalized utilitarian thinking at the end of the eighteenth and into the nineteenth century.

17. In Hill's (1975:100) view, Protestantism was "moulded by those who dominated in that society." Ministers had to "tag along behind what seemed right to the consciences of the leading laymen in their congregations" (see ibid.:91). While this hypothesis sounds plausible, it should not be exaggerated. Preachers remained quite faithful to reformed Protestant theology; agreed among themselves rather than reflecting diverse local pressures; and often disturbed their congregations with calls for moral reform and threats of damnation.

18. The Catholic church still expresses reservations about capitalism, however. When the capitalist nations emerged victorious in their cold war against Soviet communism, Pope Paul warned them of their moral shortcomings.

19. According to Grassby (1995:394), seventeenth-century businessmen had no ideology; so it developed later.

20. Although most Puritans did not interpret successful acquisition as a sign of God's favor, as indicated previously, some did. The beliefs of the minority were later borrowed by mainstream culture.

21. Likewise, any selective choice of certain teachings to ignore, while following others, by Puritan businessmen must be explained by nonreligious forces, most likely material forces related to the nature of the businessman's situation.

22. According to Grassby (1995:389–90) seventeenth-century Protestantism could not have served as the ideology of business because it was too antibusiness. It denounced profiteers and charged that individualism undermined community ideals.

23. To the extent that these justifications arose after the fact and supported the material interests of the profit-making class, they illustrate Marx's base-superstructure model of society rather than Weber's hypothesis that ideas can causally influence the way the economy develops.

24. Weber was inconsistent here. He ([1904–5] 1958:176–77) stressed the legitimacy attained by mature capitalism while at the same time insisting that there was little need for legitimacy.

5

Religious Anxiety

One reason, in Weber's ([1904–5] 1958; [1923] 1961) view, why Puritan doctrine was such a powerful influence was that it was a *religious* doctrine. For him, the essence of religion was its concern with salvation; and Puritan religion, he said, channeled this concern into restless, driving economic conduct. Moreover, as noted earlier, this factor was intensified by the extreme importance of salvation in the sixteenth and seventeenth centuries. Great intensity was said to stem from the tremendous salvation anxiety generated by the neo-Calvinist doctrine accepted by most Puritans. Weber ([1904–5] 1958:108) argued that, under this doctrine, salvation uncertainties produced extreme anxiety that gave life a restless, active quality. This was just what capitalism needed for continuous operation and steady growth.

Moreover, in his view this anxiety fueled a drive for certainty of salvation, which sought to overcome fears by proving election. Since good Christians would be the ones saved, it was necessary to conform to the religion's behavioral requirements to demonstrate one's elect status. So, in effect, this drive enforced Puritan norms. On the other hand, if religious anxiety was actually minor in its strength or effects, then the hypothesized enforcement mechanism could not operate as depicted.

This chapter assesses the strength of Puritans' salvation anxiety. The aim is to gauge the effectiveness of their salvation doctrine as a source of motive energy for economic conduct and as an enforcement mechanism for their behavioral standards. It will be shown that Weber's ([1904–5] 1958) analysis of Puritan anxiety was quite one-sided. Although Puritanism could and indeed did induce anxiety, it was also able to comfort the anxious, to some extent alleviating their doubts and fears; its self-contradictory array of teachings produced a mixed effect rather than enduring anxiety.

KNOWLEDGE OF ONE'S ESTATE

Weber thought that salvation anxiety was maximized by the doctrine of predestination, which, as neo-Calvinists, the Puritans adhered to. Under this doctrine, he ([1904–5] 1958:103) wrote, God's eternal decree of salvation or damnation was inscrutable, and anxiety stemmed from its unknowability and, hence, the impossibility of knowing whether or not one was saved. Citing the Westminster Confession of 1647, he (ibid.:100) referred to God's "secret counsel" concerning the decree that predestined some to eternal life and others to everlasting death.

But by the seventeenth century, contrary to Weber (ibid.:100, 103), predominant pastoral thought had gone far beyond Calvin, and held that one's state of grace, i.e., salvation or condemnation, was quite ascertainable. By 1600, according to Miller (1963:50), hundreds of Protestants had written to oppose "that Popish doctrine that thinks it impossible to know that he is in an estate of grace" (see, for example, Downame [1604] 1974:II, 186–87; Dent [1601] 1974:261, 273; Baxter 1653:150; Whitaker quoted by Lake 1982:207 and cited by Coolidge 1970:122; Flavel 1968:V, 525; and Chaderton quoted by Lake 1982:166–67).

Perkins (see Miller 1963:86; see also Porter 1971:227 and Reilly 1948:12) and Downame ([1604] 1974:II, 582) considered it erroneous to believe that nobody can be certain of being saved; and Flavel (1968:V, 583–84, see also pp. 524, 525) agreed that "we are not to think assurance of our sincerity impossible." Perkins (quoted by Reilly 1948:12; see also Perkins [1606] 1972:I, 87; 1970:III, 257, 369), Ames ([1639] 1975:A2; see also p. 9, which contradicts Miller's 1963:194 interpretation), Dent ([1601] 1974:260), Ball (1632:256–57), and Downame ([1604] 1974:II, 188) all held that "men may attaine to a certaine knowledge of their own election." And Downame (ibid.; see also Perkins cited by Reilly 1948:12) specified that the knowledge could be obtained "without any special revelation after an ordinarie manner."

Sources of Information

Since God's decrees were secret, they could only be known indirectly. Downame ([1604] 1974:II, 189) cautioned that people could not search into God's decrees, but deemed it possible to gather assurance out of God's revealed word. Similarly, Perkins (1970:III, 250; see also Dent [1601] 1974:308 and Whitaker quoted by Lake 1982:203) proclaimed that since "the decree . . . is secret," it was not known "but by that which is after it, namely by the effects thereof" (see also Dent [1601] 1974:319–20 and Cartwright quoted by Lake 1982:80–81). Nevertheless, these roundabout means of knowing could provide adequate evidence of one's state of grace. Perkins (1970:III, 257) went on to say, "They have not this knowledge from the first causes of election, but rather from the last effects thereof." They did not see God's secret decree, Downame ([1604] 1974:II, 226) allowed, but could "attain evident knowledge of it."[1]

One source of information stemmed from God's revelations to humankind. In Puritanism, God was "much less remote and unpredictable" than in the time of Calvin (Zaret 1985:128, see also pp. 160–61). God "communicated unto us," Downame ([1604] 1974:II, 226; see also Baxter [1650] 1962:119) pointed out; he revealed his will in the Gospel (see Downame [1604] 1974:II, 270; see also pp. 172, 174 and Ball 1632:214; see also Eusden 1958:25), which set forth the conditions for salvation. To know one's estate, Baxter recommended comparing the soul's qualifications with these known criteria (see Knott 1980:72). Likewise, Downame ([1604] 1974:II, 533) recommended God's word for judging a person's estate.

Among the revelations of the Bible had been the covenant of grace, which spelled out what people needed to do to be saved (Zaret 1985:152). According to Zaret (ibid.:157–58), the known conditions of the covenant informed the search for evidence of one's estate. They told what criteria to use for self-assessment. These criteria "described and pointed out the persons to be saved" (Miller 1963:389–90).

Since in the covenant God had promised salvation in return for man's faithfulness (see Eusden 1958:28; see also Zaret 1985:152), evidence of faith in Christ could provide knowledge of one's election. Therefore, "whosoever is certaine that he hath faith . . . may be certaine also of his election, though he never presumptuously search into Gods secret counsaile" (Downame [1604] 1974: II, 271). Likewise, according to Dent ([1601] 1974:262), "in Christ Jesus we doo already sit together in the heavenly places . . . we are as sure of it, as if we were there already."

A second type of information to identify the saved came from observing the salvation process at work. This process was not considered mysterious by the divines; they felt they knew a lot about it. In their view, there was a "golden chain" of events proceeding from election and leading to salvation, which was neither instantaneous, automatic, nor invisible. Those who had been elected had to be justified (i.e., absolved before God) and to be sanctified (made more righteous) by the holy Spirit before they could be saved.

It was possible to witness the steps leading up to salvation; one could see the process working in the elect. According to Blake (quoted by Coolidge 1970:126–27),

> though we do not directly and immediately know God's election, predestination, and decreeing that we shall be saved, yet we may plainly see . . . impressions hereof in ourselves, lively resembling that which is secret in God's

hidden counsel . . . so we not seeing God's secret decree . . . may notwith-
standing attain to the evident knowledge thereof by that impression which
it maketh in us.

According to Perkins (1970:III, 257; see also [1606] 1972:I, 75 and Reilly
1948:25) and Downame ([1604] 1974:II, 515), the effects of election included "the testimony of God's Spirit," which could serve as evidence (see
also Chaderton quoted by Lake 1982:167). Perkins ([1606] 1972:I, 75)
taught that with the testimony of the "holy Ghost" one "need not ascend
into heaven to search the secret counsel of God, but rather descend into
his own heart to search whether he be sanctified or not" (Perkins 1970:III,
159; see also Reilly 1948:9). Similarly, Downame ([1604] 1974:II, 211–12,
222) wrote that the Spirit of God, knowing God's "counsels," testifies to
the faithful to assure them that they are saved. According to Dent ([1601]
1974:319–20),

when once we feele the work of grace within us . . . by the Holy Ghost . . .
then are we sure and out of all doubt, that we are predestinate to life. And it
is even as much as if God had personally appeared unto us, and whispered
us in the eare, and tolde us that our names are taken, and written in the
booke of life.

Puritans believed that the effects of the Spirit's presence or absence
were discernible (see Baxter 1653:141; McGee 1976:241). Saltmarsh ([1647]
1847:175) was convinced that "pure spiritual assurance" was known to
those who have it; likewise, Dent ([1601] 1974:265) wrote that "he that
hath the spirit of God, knoweth certainely he hath it" or *could* know it
with "a due triall."

The very same was said about faith: because it was effected by the holy
Spirit (see Zaret 1985:157), it was considered one of the effects of election
(see, for example, Ball 1632:85; see also Downame [1604] 1974:II, 270–71).
Accordingly, it could inform "the true Believer" of "his owne estate" (Ball
1632:219, see also p. 90).

This was deemed possible because faith was readily perceptible. As
Dent ([1601] 1974:265) put it, "he that hath faith, knoweth that he hath
faith." Perkins (quoted by Reilly 1948:12–13; see also Baxter 1678:IV, 275)
and Ames ([1639] 1975:5; see also II, 14 and Baxter [1650] 1962:28) concurred. And Downame ([1604] 1974:II, 193, 272) reasoned that it was easy
to tell faith from no faith just as when you saw fire you knew you were
seeing it. Furthermore, people could know whether or not they believed
in the Gospel (ibid.:II, 195). They could know whether or not they believed "God's gracious promises," Downame (ibid.:II, 195, see also

p. 264) argued. Likewise, Ball (1632:219) held that a person who "believeth the promises by faith . . . knoweth himselfe a believer."

Another effect of election was sanctification (see Ball 1632:85; Perkins 1970:III, 257; Dent [1601] 1974:319–20). Since it was effected by the holy Spirit, it was evidence of salvation taking place. Downame ([1604] 1974:II, 221, see also p. 187) held that "those who are . . . in some measure sanctified, may ordinarily attaine unto the assurance of their election." He (ibid.:II, 272) considered it easy to tell righteousness from unrighteousness. And Perkins (1970:III, 235–36), too, said that with sanctification people could know God's will.

These "effects of God's election" provided knowledge of salvation inasmuch as they "worked as signs" (see Downame quoted by Coolidge 1970:127 and Downame [1604] 1974:II, 192, 587). For example, Dent ([1601] 1974:33) wrote of "certaine signes and tokens . . . whereby al men may certainly know that they are sanctified, regenerate, and shall be saved." The divines taught their followers to apply the signs to determine their own state of grace (see Reilly 1948:10–13). This provided an indirect route around the secrecy of God's counsel. One could not know God's decree, but could know "those posterior signs which are sure attestations of it" (see Perkins 1970:III, 94–95).

Scripture added confidence to the feasibility of sound determinations. Since St. Peter had exhorted Christians to "Give all diligence to make your election sure," Perkins (quoted by Reilly 1948:12–13) reasoned "Now in vaine were it to use diligence if the assurance of election could not bee any waies compassed." Dent ([1601] 1974:262) used the same reasoning (see also Downame [1604] 1974:II, 197).

Consistent with their belief that valid judgments were feasible, the Puritans encouraged "self-trial and thorough examination" (Flavel 1968:V, 588, see also pp. 536, 581). Ball (1632:100) preached that "by examination it is to be discerned and knowne whether we believe." And Baxter ([1650] 1962:85; see also pp. 156–57 and 1653:118) considered it profitable "to take an account of your own estates" (see also Chaderton quoted by Lake 1982:167).

There were prescriptions about how to proceed to receive a correct testimony. One method (described by Baxter [1650] 1962:133) was to "set the conditions of the Gospel and qualifications of the saints on one side, and thy performance of those conditions and the qualifications of thy soul on the other side, and then judge how near they resemble." This approach was deemed accurate because "Thou hast the same word before thee to judge thyself by now, by which thou must be judged at the great day" (ibid.:133; but see also 1653:146). Another method employed descriptions of the process of regeneration, which "enabled the reader to determine whether he had experienced it" (Keeble 1982:133, see also p. 134). Marks and signs of the sanctified soul were based on "character and conduct" (ibid.:133). A person was to "follow the search of his heart . . . till he were assured" (Baxter quoted in ibid.; see also Baxter [1650] 1962:133).

Defects in the Evidence

Still, despite the possibility of making election sure, Puritans believed that certain obstacles hampered judgment. Saltmarsh ([1647] 1847:178) held that the evidences of salvation were viewed "darkly as in a glass; and as these are shadowed and clouded, so is the assurance." Baxter (1653:161), too, reported that people "do not alwaies know" who shall be saved: lacking perfect knowledge of their election, they had "but a defective, interrupted assurance of it" (ibid.:214), which was "mixt with imperfection, and oft clouded" (ibid.:208).

Baxter cited several detriments to knowledge. First of all, since there were different degrees of grace, no vast chasm separated saints and reprobates, making it difficult at times to tell them apart (see Keeble 1982:136; see also Baxter 1653:119–21, 125). Weak Christians with the smallest degree of grace were borderline cases difficult to appraise with certainty (see Baxter 1653:124, 125, see also p. 131). Second, there were different degrees of sin and of sinning, with no clear boundaries between. Baxter (1653:123) asked, "can any man on earth tell us just how great or how often sinning will stand with true Grace, and how much will not? who can find those punctual bounds in the Word of God?" A third difficulty was that people's minds were a jumble, which made it difficult to see what was in them; this made it hard to tell sincerity from deceitfulness "and false pretenses" (Baxter 1653:126–27, 129). Also, people's minds were changeable; resolution for Christ fluctuated daily (Baxter 1653:127–28). Fourth, and finally, was the problem of perseverance. "If a man have the fullest Certainty in the world that he is God's child," explained Baxter (1653:161; see also p. 160 and [1650] 1962:93, 106, 107, 108; see also Chaderton quoted by Lake 1982:159), yet "if he be uncertain whether he shall so continue to the end, it is impossible that he should have a Certainty of his Salvation. For it's he only that endureth to the end that shall be saved."

Although in principle the signs of salvation were explicit, in practice they were less clear (see, for example, Reilly 1948:24). In McGee's (1976:65) judgment, the assessment of a Puritan's estate was "tricky and deceptive" because it was subjective. Another problem was the large number of signs: with so many there were bound to be conflicting indications. Also, the variation from preacher to preacher as to what the signs were, which signs to stress, and what constituted an adequate performance sent conflicting signals. These residual ambiguities in the signs of election led to imperfect knowledge of God's decree. One could practice self-examination for many years and possibly still be unresolved, left in doubt, or mistaken (see Baxter 1653:146; see also Seaver 1985:196).

In view of these limitations, the goal of *certitudo salutis* was often unattainable. However, it appears that a good likelihood of salvation was adequate to bring comfort (see Baxter 1653:166–67, 173–74; see also below). Puritan religion frequently provided enough knowledge to meet this lesser standard.

Not only was it deemed possible in principle to judge one's estate, but the preachers had laid out the path to the relevant information. Salvation anxiety arose, but not from the doctrinal impossibility of knowing one's state, i.e., not from the predestination doctrine per se. This differs from the situation described by Weber ([1922] 1968:100), who emphasized the secrecy of God's counsel. Knowledge was not limited by God, whose signs and revelations were cognized in abundance. Rather, the individual's own weakness was the chief source of ambiguity (see, for example, Seaver 1985:7, 31, 181; see also Downame [1604] 1974:II, 171, 188 and Ball 1632:111). Imperfections made it difficult to display the signs (see Baxter 1678:IV, 276 and also Flavel 1968:V, 537); there could be no definitive evidence of salvation as long as faith and obedience were imperfect (see Baxter 1653:208, 209; Dent [1601] 1974:270; Lake 1982:158–59).

Since a person's sins decreased obedience (see Baxter 1653:270, 271, 275–77), sin was one of the strongest causes of Puritan anxiety (see Downame [1604] 1974:II, 141, 256; Baxter 1653:A5, 273, 284, 405; 1678:II, 115, 122; [1650] 1962:123; Perkins [1606] 1972:I, 88–90; Saltmarsh 1649:171–74; Ball 1632:111; Dent [1601] 1974:272; Pledger diary:4–6, 17; Seaver 1985:14, 15, 42, 124, 128, 186, 195, 196). Yet it was a factor largely overlooked by Weber. Sin probably caused more doubts than the inscrutability of God under the predestination doctrine (see Downame [1604] 1974:II, 188). More fear was caused by specific negative evidence than by the difficulty of obtaining evidence.

Since uncertainty and anxiety over salvation did not hinge on the mysteries of predestination, similar salvation worries have occurred among nonpredestinarian Protestants as well. For instance, though Baxter (e.g., 1678:II, 116) was no predestinarian, there is no hint that uncertainty and anxiety in his flock were any the less for it.[2] Nor did the absence of predestinarianism among the Baptists guarantee them freedom from uncertainty. Rather, it is likely that wherever Christians have believed in salvation and damnation, anxiety has developed over their fates, and its degree has depended on various other factors aside from predestination.

THE TWO FACES OF PURITANISM

Not only did Weber overestimate the anxiety caused by belief in predestination but he exaggerated Puritan anxiety levels overall. Puritanism
had two faces, both a disturbing and comforting side, and Weber stressed
the former.

A Norm of Anxiety

Consistent with Weber's scenario, Puritanism did encourage fear. A certain amount of anxiety was expected and even demanded. "Work out
your salvation with fear and trembling," directed Baxter (1653:204; see
also Hill [1613] 1975:172 and Stannard 1977:79). In Downame's ([1604]
1974:I, 42) view, people were supposed to fear the Lord. They were to fear
God's wrath and threatened judgments (Baxter 1653:204, see also p. 207),
and "to feare punishment and hell" (Perkins [1606] 1972:I, 51; see also
Downame [1604] 1974:II, 416, 504; III, 618); Baxter's *Saints Everlasting Rest*
and Dent's *Plaine Man's Pathway to Heaven* painted the horrors and tor-
ments of hell severely in many stern passages (see Dent [1601]
1974:399–407; Keeble 1982:104).

God was angry when people sinned, Downame ([1604] 1974:II, 301) explained; whoever lived unrighteously, he (ibid.:II, 273, see also p. 416)
warned, would die and burn in fire and brimstone. And Ames ([1639]
1975:18; see also Lake 1982:163) admonished that even the "faithfull ought
to feare, to tremble at . . . the wrath of God and damnation, as due unto
them for their sinnes."

Since humans were imperfect and could not fulfill God's law (see Downame [1604] 1974:I, 122; II, 300; see also Seaver 1985:43), guilt, shame, and
self-blame became the norm (see Downame [1604] 1974:II, 506 and also
Perkins [1606] 1972:I, 55; see also Chapter 4 above). After judgment by the
law, Ames ([1639] 1975:8) ordered that "there must follow . . . griefe and
feare because of sin" (see also Baxter 1653:432; Lake 1982:163; Flavel
1968:V, 597; Perkins [1606] 1972:I, 181; Downame [1604] 1974:I, 123; II, 490,
509; III, 635, 639).

A Norm of Assurance

Opposed to this norm of anxiety was a norm of assurance, which encouraged Puritans to find themselves among the elect (see Keeble
1982:133). "The faithful . . . are called to confidence," Ames ([1639]
1975:18) insisted; "There is not only a possibility for the believer to come
to this certainty, but it is his duty also, never to rest contented till he have
obtained it" (ibid.:II, 33). Christians were commanded to believe and "to
know that they were sincere" (Baxter 1678:III, 150; but see also 1653:189,

190). Puritans were "directed to seek and follow after Christ, till we come to be assured, that he dwelleth in us as the fountaine of life" (see Ball 1632:425–26). Dent ([1601] 1974:264, see also pp. 268, 272, 273) wrote, "we must . . . grow to some certaintie." Similarly, Baxter ([1650] 1962:132–33) said to "rest not till you can call this Rest your own; sit not down without assurance." Consistent with the norm of assurance, Puritans were opposed to doubts (see, for example, Downame [1604] 1974:II, 186, 187; Ames [1639] 1975:18; Chaderton quoted by Lake 1982:166–67). Puritans were expected "to resist them, to fight against them, and so much as it is possible to expell them, and drive them out" (Ball 1632:92; see also Perkins 1970:III, 259 and Lake 1982:99).

Although Weber ([1904–5] 1958:111) knew about this duty to attain certainty, he did not connect it to the development of comforting doctrines and practices that reduced anxieties. Yet that was one of its effects, as will be seen below. These doctrines and practices helped Puritans grow more confident of election, thereby satisfying the norm.

Two Pastoral Messages

The norms of assurance and anxiety complemented each other. Each was invoked by the divines for a separate purpose, based on the two sorts of people who received pastoral attention (see Breward 1970:III, 389). As Downame ([1604] 1974:II, 366) described it, "he who findeth his heart hard and secure, must feede upon the threatnings of the law, to the end he may be humbled . . . and resolved into teares of unfained repentance; he that is of a broken heart and contrite spirit, must feede upon the sweete and gracious promises of the Gospell."

The norm of anxiety was targeted at the security of the average English Protestant (see Lake 1982:163). It was used (*inter alia*) as an antidote to presumption (see, for example, Downame [1604] 1974:II, 249, 251). According to Breward (1970:III, 389), "it was pastorally necessary . . . to prod those who were tempted to rest content." Baxter (1653:132–33) felt that weak Christians needed to be chastised so they would improve. And if true faith and repentance were lacking, Perkins's ([1606] 1972:I, 197) prescription was to stir up sorrow for sins (see, for example, Foster 1991:86). The purpose was to encourage repentance and further the redemptive process (see Perkins [1606] 1972:I, 172, 178, see also p. 93).

Another target of this message was the hard-hearted sinner (see Downame [1604] 1974:II, 249). The Puritans wanted to crack down on sin (see Emerson 1968:56). To these people, Baxter (1653:397) disclosed, "we preach swords." Dent exemplifies this: after enumerating their sins, he ([1601] 1974:274, see also p. 276) asked "what hope can you have to be saved?" Similarly, Downame ([1604] 1974:II, 140) and Perkins ([1606]

1972:I, 96) warned that those who lived in sin could have no assurance but should fear themselves among the rejected if they so continued. The ultimate aim was their repentance and recovery (see, for example, Perkins [1606] 1972:I, 196; Baxter 1653:224).

The divines were censorious because they wanted people to have "true assurance," not just comfort (see Downame [1604] 1974:II, 249). They offered less comfort than many rival ministers (see Baxter 1653:153 and *passim*; also Seaver 1985:107 and McGee 1976:59).

Although their emphasis on finding sins was far from comforting, the Puritan preachers could also be very consoling (see Reilly 1948:10). Richard Rogers, for example, presented divinity so that people were neither "cast down with needless fear" nor "destitute of encouragement" (see Pettit 1966:51; see also Ball 1632:181, 184). Although in Dent's (quoted by Emerson 1968:169–70; see also Chaderton quoted by Lake 1982:128; see also Bridenbaugh 1968:293) view, sermons were to rebuke not soothe, Sibbes (quoted by Knott 1980:61) also tried to assure in his sermons, offering "guidance through storms of doubt" to quiet the soul and settle fears. Furthermore, the pastors conducted personal visitations to comfort people with fears and troubled consciences. Hence, the norm of assurance was not just part of the "formal doctrine" but was applied at the pastoral level.

The preaching of the Gospel was by its nature reassuring because acceptance of the word implied that the promises of salvation through Christ pertained specifically to the believer. The ministers encouraged this conclusion, trying to persuade believers that they were God's children (see Downame [1604] 1974:II, 221).

According to Reilly (1948:10; see also Breward 1970:III, 389; Holifield 1974:44), the preacher's "chief work was to furnish guides whereby a man might assure himself of his own personal election." Giles Firmin, for example, tried to "ease troubled souls" (see Stannard 1977; see also Pettit 1966:188 and Keeble 1982:74); Arthur Dent had "consoled many bruised and tender consciences" (see Davies 1975:119); and Thomas Goodwin had encouraged those with doubts (see Haller [1938] 1972:149). Arthur Hildersam's "contemporaries praised him for his capacity to satisfy the doubtful" (see Holifield 1974:51).

Perkins ([1606] 1972:I, 93, see also pp. 103, 172) specifically advocated "the ministring and convaying of comfort" to one "that hath confessed his sinnes, and is truly humbled for them." He (ibid.:I, 103, 112, 196) also recommended that a melancholy person be treated by searching for his or her signs of grace and by applying "such promises of God . . . as are most large and comfortable." Baxter (e.g., 1678:II, 114), too, gave directions to help remove the causes of doubts. He (1653:270, see also pp. 220, 281) noted that comfort was used on "those that are troubled more than needs."

To sum up, the two messages of Puritanism were comfort and fear. As Baxter (1653:400) put it, the divines preached both God's love and the dangers of refusing it. Through these messages the divines manipulated people's anxiety levels, each time using the appropriate doctrine either to upset or to reassure. Coolidge (1970:125) has stated that a pastor could either "reassure the souls under his tutelage" or "use the good old anxieties for all that they are worth." Reaffirming the latter possibility, Lake (1982:158) observes that there was "exploitation of . . . doubt by puritan preachers." That could raise anxieties considerably. As evidence, converts' comfort levels rose once they had switched away from Puritan divines (see Baxter 1653:153). Indeed, Baxter (ibid.:396–97) confessed that in trying to reach ignorant sinners, his sermons overbruised fear-troubled consciences. Puritan ministers sometimes worked against themselves, and later needed to undo the consequences of their handiwork. According to Holifield (1974:44), they worked to "allay anxieties that they themselves had helped arouse."

Although the two messages could be targeted to two separate audiences, the entire congregation often received a mixture of both. Baxter (1653:155, see also p. 205) argued for a balanced presentation because the Gospel had "precepts and threatnings as well as Promises." Downame ([1604] 1974:II, 250) and Perkins ([1606] 1972:I, 103, 173) concurred. The balance between comforting and unsettling messages led toward an intermediate level of anxiety because the conflicting indications in the two messages produced a mixed result. This intermediate pull served to make the insecure more secure and the secure less secure.

THE CASUISTRY OF COMFORT

It should be clear from the comforting side of Puritanism that uncontrolled anxiety was not the norm, nor were fears allowed to go unchecked. Great fears were an unintended consequence in Puritanism and were treated as deviant; there were pastoral efforts to conquer them, which tended to diminish the high anxiety levels that Weber expected.

Linked to the norm of assurance was a comforting message which encouraged belief in a favorable outcome (see, for example, Downame [1604] 1974:II, 250). Regrettably, Weber's writings offer little hint of this comforting casuistry.

Weber and others have presented the uncertainties in Puritanism. Now their view must be balanced by detailing the comforting side of the religion. It will be seen that its comforting beliefs were known, accepted, and internalized by the laity. Their feelings of assurance were commonly based on or rationalized in terms of these beliefs.

The General Consolations

God's Mercy

Hopes of glory were raised by God's mercy. Baxter (1678:II, 115) considered the "mercifulness of God" one of "the general grounds of comfort." People could "trust God with our souls, and . . . our salvation" (Baxter 1678:I, 53; see also [1650] 1962:84 and 1653:175, 190). Baxter (1653:248, 250), Dent ([1601] 1974:419), and Ball (1632:176, 227) taught that none should "doubt the mercy of the Lord." Sins were pardoned by God's mercy (Downame [1604] 1974:II, 437, 467, 515), which outweighed the magnitude of human sins (Downame [1604] 1974:II, 542–43, see also pp. 428, 467; see also Hill [1613] 1975:165). According to Stearns (1954:50), "by exhibiting . . . mercy . . . God had tempered his justice."

Christ as Savior

It was in mercy that God had sacrificed his Son to redeem and save humankind (Dent [1601] 1974:421; Ball 1632:210, 420; Downame [1604] 1974:II, 142–44, 163, 174, 176, 566; Baxter 1678:II, 116). Christ, in turn, "provided the ground for . . . individual . . . assurance," hope, comfort, and safety (Lake 1982:166, see also p. 165; Baxter 1653:220; Downame [1604] 1974:II, 189; Hill [1613] 1975:160). He came and died to save (Baxter [1650] 1962:52; Downame [1604] 1974:II, 420; Hill [1613] 1975:332).

"Why should I not confidently and comfortably hope," Baxter ([1650] 1962:159–60; see also 1653:222 and Perkins [1606] 1972:II, 345) asked, "when my soul is in the hands of so compassionate a Saviour?" Since the judge would be their Savior, Downame ([1604] 1974:II, 247) pointed out, they could go boldly to judgment without fear of condemnation. Assurance was based in part on Christ's intercession with God (see Flavel 1968:V, 585; see also Chaderton quoted by Lake 1982:166). As the mediator for humankind (see Dent [1601] 1974:414 and Downame [1604] 1974:II,177), he would present people perfectly just before God (Baxter [1650] 1962:85). This protected them from God's wrath; though guilty, they were acquitted and obtained God's "everlasting blessing" (Downame [1604] 1974:I, 56, 114; see also II, 422–23 and Pledger diary:7 of reverse pagination). Dent ([1601] 1974:267–68, 414–15; see also Pledger diary:7 of reverse pagination and p. 19; see also Ball 1632:288) and Baxter ([1650] 1962:84) assured that he was able to save all those he brought before God.

Christ had lived and died to save sinners (see Baxter 1678:I, 53; Perkins [1606] 1972:II, 345; see also Downame [1604] 1974:I, 114; Ball 1632:227; Pledger diary:19). He had "endured the punishment due to the sin of man" (Scudder [1673] 1813:194; see also Saltmarsh 1649:177; Downame

[1604] 1974:II, 564; Wallington quoted by Seaver 1985:128), so God's justice was satisfied and people's sins forgiven (Scudder [1673] 1813:194; Saltmarsh 1649:177; Hill [1613] 1975:166; Dent [1601] 1974:421; Downame [1604] 1974:I, 114; II, 163, 434–36, 564–65). They were "saved by his life" (Dent [1601] 1974:421). The "causes of fear" were now removed (Seller [1679] 1803:188).

The Covenant of Grace

God's mercy was further extended through the "covenant of grace" (see Scudder [1673] 1813:194; Downame [1604] 1974:II, 143; Zaret 1985:137, 156), a contract between God and humanity that offered redemption by Christ "with all the benefits of his death" (Ball 1632:420; Baxter 1678:II, 116; see also Scudder [1673] 1813:194). Under the "New Covenant," sin could not condemn, for "Ye are not under the Law, but under Grace" (Saltmarsh 1649:177; see also Downame [1604] 1974:I, 114; III, 635), which was "freely given" to the "unworthy."

God had promised salvation and eternal life (see Perkins [1606] 1972:I, 51; Flavel 1968:V, 584–85), and was "engaged by covenant to receive us" (Seller [1679] 1803:191; see also Downame [1604] 1974:II, 145, 190 and Baxter 1678:II, 115). So Christians could "now plead . . . the great charter of the gospel"; they held a "title of grace" (Seller [1679] 1803:185; see also Zaret 1985:156).

In exchange, the condition "required on man's part is, that man accept of and enter into this covenant, believing in Christ, in whom it is established" (Scudder [1673] 1813:194; see also Downame [1604] 1974:II, 145, 198, 434; Ball 1632:211, 252; Seller [1679] 1803:191). Faith in Christ "answers the promise, and receives the pardon" (Ball 1632:211, 219; Hill [1613] 1975:II, 52, 217; Downame [1604] 1974:II, 145, 207, 564; see also Baxter 1653:66).[3] Fulfilling this condition entitled people to Christ's performance of the covenant (Seller [1679] 1803:191–92). Christ became theirs along with his merits (Downame [1604] 1974:I, 56, 114; II, 271, 436, 553, 563, 585), which caused their justification (ibid.:II, 201, 563, 564; see also I, 114).

Baxter (1678:II, 115–16) and Downame ([1604] 1974:II, 541) emphasized the universality of the covenant promises; they were offered to all who did not exclude themselves through unbelief or impenitence. "He hath excepted from the conditional covenant no man in the world," Baxter ([1650] 1962:157) taught, "nor will exclude any from heaven who will accept his offer"; "They may all have Christ and Life if they will" (Baxter 1653:45, 47–48; see also pp. 42, 117 and Ball 1632: 210, 219, 420; see also Pledger diary:7 of reverse pagination and Mrs. Stockton diary:2).

Clearly, the elitist doctrine of predestination was softened by the teaching that the covenant of grace was offered to everybody (see Stearns 1954:49).[4] Through the covenant, Stearns (1954:50, see also p. 49) has written, "the rigors of absolute predestination were amelioriated."

Eusden (1958:30) reports that "covenant thought was . . . a doctrine of comfort and assurance" (see also Breward 1970:III, 84, 93 and Zaret 1985:150, 151, 153). According to Cragg (1975:152), Ames's version of the covenant was immune from doubt. Divines like Preston (quoted by Stannard 1977:75) and Bulkeley (quoted by Coolidge 1970:123) considered the covenant of grace a "comfortable doctrine" that "doth settle the soul in peace." And Ball (1632:419) and Downame ([1604] 1974:I, 54; II, 142, 174, 190, 261, 505; see also Mrs. Stockton diary:5) felt that anyone "resigned . . . unto Jesus Christ" and hearing God's "merciful promises" could be assured of salvation.[5] When preachers wanted to reassure, they repeated the covenant promises (see Perkins [1606] 1972:I, 196). People's fear, Ball (1632:181) advised, was "to be removed, by calling to Minde the promises of God . . . in the word of grace."

God's Pardon of Sin

God's mercy also expressed itself through the forgiveness of sin (see Pledger diary:6 of reverse pagination; Mrs. Stockton diary:2, 6, 21; Wallington cited by Seaver 1985:43). So when sin caused doubt and fear, Perkins ([1606] 1972:I, 197; see also pp. 173, 176 and Ball 1632:180) taught "God's mercy for pardon." Ball (1632:176; see also p. 171 and Downame [1604] 1974:II, 428; III, 646) considered his mercies endless, and Ball (1632:170) and Baxter (1653:190) said that he was "ready to forgive" (see also Pledger diary:18–19 and Mrs. Stockton diary:10). He had a long history of pardoning repentant sinners, Downame ([1604] 1974:II, 464; see also Baxter 1653:183–85 and Ball 1632:176) pointed out; so, according to Hill ([1613] 1975:II, 168–69; see also Dent [1601] 1974:419 and Downame [1604] 1974:II, 424, 467), "if you can sue to him for mercie, hee will forgive them all." Then "can you . . . feare eternall damnation?" (Hill [1613] 1975:II, 161–62; see also Dent [1601] 1974:263 and Downame [1604] 1974:II, 208).

Repentance and Pardon

Sins could be cleansed away through repentance (Downame [1604] 1974:II, 289; see also pp. 415–16 and Perkins [1606] 1972:III, 613). Downame ([1604] 1974:II, 424; see also p. 437 and Dent [1601] 1974:419) maintained that "all those who truly repent . . . may have full assurance that their sinnes are forgiven them." Repeated sins were believed to be pardoned many times if repented truly each time (Downame [1604] 1974:III, 645–46, 652; see also Ball 1632:176; Perkins [1606] 1972:I, 176; Lake 1982:164).

God received people back after they had strayed (Downame [1604] 1974:II, 242, 440–41; III, 673–74), as long as they renewed their repentance for their "severall slips and falls" (Perkins quoted by Reilly 1948:35; see also Downame [1604] 1974:II, 300 and Cartwright quoted by Peel and Carson 1951:80; see also Pledger diary:17, 19 and Mrs. Stockton diary:10). This assured them once more of salvation (Reilly 1948:38).

This doctrine, which permits many sins without losing salvation, contradicts Weber's ([1904–5] 1958:115, 117, 118) image of Puritans afraid of a single slip.[6] It also contradicts Weber's (ibid.:117) erroneous statement that Puritanism contained no "cycle of sin, repentance, atonement, release" and "renewed sin"; he sought through this argument to differentiate it from Catholicism and Lutheranism, which he considered less rigorous.[7]

God would accept repentance at any time (Downame [1604] 1974:II, 398, 462, 463; Ball 1632:176, 229). Furthermore, it could be "in small measure" as long as it was true (Downame [1604] 1974:II, 271, 511).

Beyond this, most Puritans (e.g., Perkins 1615:21 and [1606] 1972:I, 97) believed that the *desire* for repentance counted as effectually as "repentance it selfe"; even sorrow for sin counted because it was "the beginning of repentance" (Perkins [1606] 1972:I, 98–99). Consequently, Perkins (ibid.:I, 102–3; see also pp. 98, 112–13, 175, 176 and 1615:34, 42) wrote, "He that hath an unfained desire to repent and beleeve, hath remission of sinnes and life everlasting." Likewise, Downame ([1604] 1974:I, 120; see also pp. 119, 126 and II, 208, 496, 516–17; see also Dent [1601] 1974:413) taught that "he that would repent, doth repent."

In sum, this was a merciful God indeed. His gracious promises reassured the Puritans that they could qualify for salvation. The rigorous side of Puritanism was countered by these comforting doctrines.

Applying the Consolations

Although the Gospel was comforting, it was unsound to rest one's assurance on its general comforts (see Baxter 1653:66): a person would not be saved just because God was merciful or Christ died for sinners (see Baxter 1653:67). On the contrary, Christ's ransom applied not to all, but to just a minority (see Downame [1604] 1974:II, 298; see also Dent [1601] 1974:292). Although no sin was too great for Christ's merit, Perkins ([1606] 1972:I, 174, see also p. 195) noted a problem as to whether or not one "can applie the merit of Christ unto himselfe." He (ibid.:I, 94) stated that "the promises of the Gospel . . . were indefinite in regard of whole mankind"; they applied only to people who had been effectually called (see Downame [1604] 1974:II, 471, 473). Consequently, Gospel assurances were balanced by doubts about whether or not one had been elected (see Dent [1601] 1974:270). As Ball (1632:110, see also p. 93) stated, "though the salvation of the Beleever be as certaine as the word of promise . . . yet it is not so infallibly knowne to the believer himselfe, it being farre more easie to conceive, that a beleever shall be saved, than to assure the conscience, that he is a true Believer."

To apply the doctrine and dispel those doubts it was necessary to find in oneself the "undoubted . . . markes" which showed to whom the general consolations pertained (see Downame [1604] 1974:Epistle Dedicatory). But on the comforting side, "if a man have these . . . evidences of his salvation, sure it is, his Title and interest to Heaven, is good" (see Dent [1601] 1974:260, 278).

Faith

Christ was applied to one's particular case through faith (see Downame [1604] 1974:I, 114, 117; II, 221, 563–64; Dent [1601] 1974:415). Faith "layeth hold upon the generall promises made to Believers. . . . Hee that believeth shall be saved" (Ball 1632:219; see also pp. 90, 98; Flavel 1968:V, 530; Downame [1604] 1974:I, 119; II, 192–93, 198–99, 588).

The standards for passing the test of faith were, for the most part, easy and consoling. This lessened doubts and reduced anxiety.

First and foremost, only the smallest measure of faith was needed to prove one's salvation (see Zaret 1985:159). The weakest faith could be true (Downame [1604] 1974:II, 549, 550–51; Ball 1632:140, 168, 172, 189; Perkins 1615:31; Ames [1639] 1975:14; see also Wallington quoted by Seaver 1985:43), and any true faith could apprehend Christ and his benefits (Perkins 1970:III, 258; Downame [1604] 1974:II, 271, 553, 588; Ball 1632:143, 146) and confer eternal life (Downame [1604] 1974:II, 198, 202, 264–65, 271, 549, 552; Ball 1632:146, 167; Perkins [1606] 1972:I, 51; 1615:3; Perkins quoted by Pettit 1966:63). Hence, "even the smallest impulse toward true belief could be interpreted as a sign of elect status" (Lake 1982:157, see also pp. 158–59).

Imperfect faith was no grounds for doubt either. It could still apprehend Christ (Ball 1632:101, 167; Downame [1604] 1974:II, 264–65, 552; Perkins [1606] 1972:II, 347). Even when shaken with doubts and incredulity, it lived and retained its nature (Downame [1604] 1974:II, 264–67; see also Dent [1601] 1974:269–70; Ball 1632:84, 109–10, 257; Saltmarsh 1649:172; but see also Downame [1604] 1974:II, 513–15 and Whitaker quoted by Lake 1982:99).

Beyond this, Zaret (1985:159) has pointed out that even the *will* to believe was enough to save by faith (see Perkins [1606] 1972:I, 51; 1615:31–33; Perkins quoted by Pettit 1966:63). As Perkins (1615:21–23, see also p. 31) put it, "the desire to beleeve, is faith" even "in the want of faith" (see also Perkins [1606] 1972:I, 51; II, 346; Downame [1604] 1974:II, 516). Hence, wanting Christ was having him (Baxter 1653:241–42).

These comfortable pronouncements were complicated by some additional requirements to prove election. However, even these extra demands were softened.

One complication was that faith, to be true, had to grow (Flavel 1968:V, 572; Downame [1604] 1974:II, 538; III, 638; Perkins 1970:III, 230; [1606] 1972:I, 101; 1615:48; see also Zaret 1985:160 and Lake 1982:159). Growing faith was necessary for assurance (Downame [1604] 1974:II, 537–38, 551–52). Yet, to soften this extra requirement Downame (ibid.:II, 552, 561, 562–63) reassured that God would not condemn anyone with the least measure of true faith. Rather, to a person who had any, more would be given (ibid.:II, 552–53, 562–63). Hence, anyone with a small amount of faith could be assured of future growth (Reilly 1948:44; see also Ball 1632:189). Furthermore, according to Ames ([1639] 1975:II, 17; see also Downame [1604] 1974:II, 525), "the increase of Faith is not to be expected at every moment, and at all seasons of our life."

A second complication was the need to confirm a lively faith by observing its fruits (see Downame [1604] 1974:II, 143, 272, second page 272, 540, 550–52, 569). These "fruits" were the virtues believed to derive from and accompany faith, and to be symptomatic of its presence. But those who did not see the signs and fruits in themselves were comforted as follows. First of all, according to Downame ([1604] 1974:II, 195–96, 530; see also pp. 493, 525 and Perkins 1615:32), fruits might not appear soon after conversion but might take months or years. Second, according to Downame ([1604] 1974:II, 196, 525–27) and Ball (1632:187–88), faith could not be known by its fruits in times of affliction, sorrow, illness, temptation, or corruption for "in winter" even "the most fruitfull tree" would "be taken for barren." Third, according to Ames ([1639] 1975:II, 17), "the want of many fruits may argue Faith to be languishing, or weake, but it cannot argue that there is no Faith." He (ibid.:II, 16) maintained that fruits "belong to the well being of Faith, not absolutely to the being of it." Consequently, Baxter (see Keeble 1982:135) argued that one could be certain of salvation even if the fruits and consequents of faith were withheld.

In sum, the pastors frequently softened the requirements of faith, its growth, and its fruits. Sometimes, as Lake (1982:158–59) has put it, "the merest impulse toward God could be seen as a sign of true belief."[8] That could increase assurance and reduce anxiety.

Sin and Salvation

Sinning questioned a person's inclusion in the covenant because the most frequent sinners were "farthest from . . . obedience," and obedience was a condition of the covenant (Baxter 1653:274, see also pp. 270, 273, 276; see also Dent [1601] 1974:270 and Seaver 1985:43). However, sinners were reassured that they were saved anyway. True Christians could still fall into committing sins (see Downame [1604] 1974:III, 625–26, 650, 652; see also Dent [1601] 1974:296–97), but were considered righteous because they were justified by Christ (see Dent [1601] 1974:297; see Downame [1604] 1974:II, 581–82, 589; see also Wallington quoted by Seaver 1985:44). Thus were sinners saved.

The preachers consoled that sin was common to both saved and damned (see Downame [1604] 1974:I, 130, 131; see also III, 599, 607–8 and Perkins [1606] 1972:I, 178–79). Ames (quoted by Mosse 1968:75), Flavel (1968:V, 596), and Baxter (1653:102, 114–15, 404; see also Keeble 1982:72, 125) denied that occasional sin was cause for doubting (see also Saltmarsh 1649:176). In fact, one could fall into sin "often" without condemnation (Downame [1604] 1974:III, 643).

Furthermore, any victories over temptation were a sign of regeneration (ibid.:II, 153, see also pp. 133–34, 136–37). Resistance to Satan must come from the holy Spirit, which "assured that in the end we shall obtaine victorie" (ibid.:II, 521).[9]

Even in the absence of righteous *behavior*, proper *attitudes* toward it could provide assurance (see, for example, ibid.:I, 122, 128–29 and Wallington cited by Seaver 1985:43). Displeasure at failing to overcome sin, sorrow for sin, hatred of corruption, and the desire for sanctification and holiness of life placed them among the saved no matter "how weakly soever" they actually fought sin (Downame [1604] 1974:I, 119–20, 129; II, 522; III, 637, 655; Perkins [1606] 1972:I, 183, 184; see also Dent [1601] 1974:268).

The "desire to forsake . . . sinnes" was a sign of regeneration because it was a work of God (Downame [1604] 1974:I, 126; II, 153, 523). It could substitute for the deed itself, according to Downame (ibid.:I, 120) and Perkins ([1606] 1972:I, 183; see also p. 97, but see Baxter 1653:273 for an exception), as long as "there be . . . an endeavour to performe the purpose of the minde. . . ."

The Relaxation of Behavior Standards

Just as the desires to believe and to overcome sin could substitute for actual faith and sanctification, desires could also count for repentance, obedience, and the other graces (see Downame [1604] 1974:I, 120, 122; II, 511, 516–17; III, 599; Perkins [1606] 1972:I, 97, 98, 183; 1615:42; but Baxter 1653:155 is more qualified). This tended to shift the proofs of election from outward actions to inward affections (see Downame [1604] 1974:I, 120; III, 630; see also Baxter 1678:I, 107; II, 144). It was not so different from the Roman Catholic ethic of intentions (see Weber [1904–5] 1958:116 and Chapter 1 above; see also Mosse 1968:74, 89, 114).

Additionally, one could feel the holy Spirit internally (see Downame

[1604] 1974:II, 519, 520, 588). And since it witnessed to one's salvation, it brought comfort and assurance (Downame [1604] 1974:II, 174, 211–14, 519, 520, 588 and *passim*; Perkins [1606] 1972:I, 75; 1615:33; Dent [1601] 1974:261, 265).

It was easier for Puritans to display these internal, psychological characteristics than to meet objective behavioral standards. For example, it was easier to desire to be holy than to systematically follow a holy life. Therefore, it was comforting to know that the desire could be substituted for the deed. Surely this softening of standards mitigated anxiety.

Perseverance

An important obstacle to salvation was the need to persevere to the end, abiding in Christ with continued consent and obedience (Baxter [1650] 1962:28, 35, 93; Baxter 1653:161; Baxter 1678:II, 125; III, 14; Perkins [1606] 1972:I, 81, 101; Downame [1604] 1974:I, 110, 111; II, 240). According to Ball (1632:277; see also Downame [1604] 1974:II, 248), many good Christians feared "they shall never hold out" [but] "should fall away." And any evidence of actual backsliding was even more disturbing (see Saltmarsh 1649:53–54).

In opposition to these doubts stood the Puritan "Doctrine of Perseverance" (see, for example, Baxter 1678:II, 116), which guaranteed the faithful that they would persevere, thereby eliminating the problem of backsliding and overcoming doubts about the future. According to this doctrine it was impossible for "they which once truely believe" to fall away and be condemned (Downame [1604] 1974:II, 559; see also Ball 1632:146, 286, 288; but for a conflicting view see Whitaker cited by Lake 1982:224). So a faithful Christian could "be assured on good grounds, of a victory" even before facing "his remaining trials" (Flavel 1968:V, 584).[10]

Downame ([1604] 1974:III, 674) explained that faith was constant and permanent by nature, not temporary. As a gift of God, it "is never taken away" (ibid.:II, 559; see also II, 552, 560, 562–63 and III, 662–63). The "sentence of pardon granted shall never be reversed . . . even after some grievous fall" (Ball 1632:119, see also pp. 104, 120; but for Baxter's opposing view see 1678:II, 124, 125 and Keeble 1982:71–72). Under predestination, God's decree was unchangeable (Downame [1604] 1974:II, 177, 190, 559 and III, 659–60, 665–67; Perkins 1970:III, 259; Dent [1601] 1974:321; Ball 1632:229, 280). Those that he had saved, he would not forsake later (Ball 1632:163, 177, 258, 277).

This doctrine softened the requirement of perseverance. Although Weber ([1904–5] 1958:117) thought that assurance required an entire "life of good works," comforting beliefs countered the rigorous demand for lifelong persistence and the anxiety it spawned.

In fact, this "Doctrine of Perseverance" held out a double comfort. Not only could those presently in God's favor feel confident about their futures, but also those with present doubts could take comfort from favorable past judgments. Anyone who now felt no faith or "weake declining faith" could "stay and settle his minde" by recalling former times (Ball 1632:163, 175; Perkins [1606] 1972:I, 113); past integrity, holiness, and righteousness were "not . . . taken away" (Ball 1632:175; see also Downame [1604] 1974:II, 481, 503, 504, 529, 531). Or "if at any time we have had assurance that the spirit of God hath dwelled in us . . . we may assure our selves that it hath not forsaken us" (ibid.:II, 497 and also III, 665, 668, 671–73; see in support Baxter [1650] 1962:157; 1653:376; Keeble 1982:137, 139; but see also Baxter 1678:IV, 275 and 1653:379, 385–86). This reassured Christians that they had not fallen away even if present self-judgments were unclear or unsettling.

The Probability of Salvation

As argued earlier, despite considerable information about people's state of grace, it was difficult to attain complete certainty (see, for example, Baxter 1678:IV, 276 and 1653:146, 155, 208; see also Downame [1604] 1974:II, 246). This was particularly true for weak Christians, whose imperfections often led to conflicting signals (Downame [1604] 1974:II, 195; Saltmarsh 1649:172–73; see also Lake 1982:158), but even strong Christians could be uncertain (see, for example, Baxter 1653:145). According to Baxter (1678:III, 150), "few of the best attain to a full certainty of their own sincerity."

However, as noted above, Baxter (1653:158) considered it unnecessary to be anxious just because one lacked complete certainty. One could lead a comfortable life without it, in which true peace could be attained (ibid.:159, see also pp. 151, 169). In lieu of certainty, Baxter (ibid.:175) advised, "take the Comfort of your Probabilities of . . . Salvation." Those with more probability of sincerity could have more peace of mind (ibid.:177). A strong probability was a great comfort and delight (ibid.:178), and "A settled calm and peace of soul" was "not to be undervalued" (ibid.:228; see also pp. 174, 227 and 1678:II, 116).

Baxter (1653:173–74) used this probability concept to comfort the doubtful. If a person wanted to reform, be obedient, and get rid of sin, Baxter (ibid.:176) asked, "may not you . . . see a strong Probability that it shall go well with you?" He (ibid.:489) counseled the fearful to keep in mind the probability of special grace, and he ([1650] 1962:159–60) said to judge "from the Word, and from the mercies" the probability that the general promises applied personally.

It will be shown below that the probabilities distinctly favored the Puritans. Hence, this approach provided effective comfort.

At first glance their odds may have seemed slim. For example, Baxter ([1650] 1962:84; but see also 1653:171–72) saw the chosen as "a small part of lost mankind . . . fewer they are than the world imagines." Likewise, Dent ([1601] 1974:287 and *passim*; see also Flavel 1968:V, 593; Downame [1604] 1974:II, 179, 246; and Lake 1982:158–59) held that "the number of Gods elect on the face of the earth, are very fewe."

Yet, upon closer inspection the Puritans' chances improved dramatically. First of all, as Dent ([1601] 1974:287) put it, "let there be taken away from amounst us, all Papists, Atheists, and heretickes." Similarly, Downame ([1604] 1974:II, 283) considered all pagans and Turks to be outside the covenant. Since salvation depended on being called by hearing the word preached correctly in a true church, it was obvious which parts of the world's population must comprise the bulk of the reprobates (see, for example, Perkins 1970:III, 369–70).

Since the chosen were to be redeemed by Christ (see Baxter [1650] 1962:35, 84; Hill [1613] 1975:152, 154, 160, 165; see also Owen Stockton diary:2), non-Christians could not qualify. Downame ([1604] 1974:II, 199) insisted that it was the Christians and only the Christians who were "saved and redeemed by Christ" and "who are elected to salvation in God's eternall decree."

Puritans were further convinced of their elect status because they were English. Downame (ibid.:II, 151) believed that God had "chosen us amongst all nations to be his Church." Earlier John Foxe had taught that England was God's "elect nation"; and Cromwell, too, considered it the "new Israel" (see Stannard 1977:40; see also Seaver 1985:180).

Most Puritans belonged to the Church of England and, though they thought it needed further reformation, considered it a true church (see Collinson 1967:25; see also Foster 1991:51, 62). Baxter (cited by Weber [1904–5] 1958:166) exemplifies that attitude toward it. Membership in a true church was thought to improve one's chances of salvation; thus, Downame ([1604] 1974:II, 516; see also Sibbes quoted by Holifield 1974:43) stated that the hope of pardon was "nourished and increased" because "the Lord hath placed us in his church." The first reason was that a sound understanding of Christian doctrine was necessary for an accurate judgment of one's estate (see Baxter 1653:155); and proper self-assessment was a critical tool in the process of becoming saved. Second, a true church gave people "the outward meanes" for achieving faith and repentance, namely "the ministerie of the word and administration of the sacraments" (Downame [1604] 1974:II, 516; see also Coolidge 1970:147). Downame ([1604] 1974:II, 516, see also pp. 479, 564; see also Wallington Folger diary:202–3 and Foster 1991:39) considered these necessary conditions for salvation. He ([1604] 1974:II, 283, see also p. 144) declared without qualification that the saved were in the church, and Dent ([1601] 1974:423) insisted that "not one without the Church should be saved."

Max Weber misrepresented Puritanism when he ([1904–5] 1958:104–5) wrote that no church could help Protestants confront salvation because of their "complete elimination of salvation through the Church and the sacraments." As just shown, the church did play a role in the Puritan salvation process.[11]

Furthermore, Weber overestimated the level of interdeterminacy caused by the belief that "the membership of the external Church included the doomed" (see ibid.:104). Although church membership was no guarantee of salvation (see Collinson 1967:25, 26 and 1988:26), it did enhance assurance when Puritans examined their "Probabilities of Grace."

Weber ([1904–5] 1958:110) argued that God's elect were an "invisible Church," not the visible, or institutional, church. Invisibility meant that their identities could not be learned; it was denied "that one can learn from the conduct of others whether they are chosen or damned" (ibid.). In principle, this made it impossible to tell whether or not the complement of the chosen few had already been filled by others, and, inversely, how much room remained in heaven for oneself.

However, in practice, the Puritans felt confident that they could guess who were the elect. Most of the world's population seemed obviously unqualified for salvation, including the non-Christians, non-English, and non-Protestants. As Baxter (1653:172) pointed out, there were few Protestants. Furthermore, Dent ([1601] 1974:287, see also p. 290) reasoned, "let there be shoaled out all . . . notorious evil livers; as swearers, drunkards, whoremongers, worldlings, deceivers, coseners, proud men, rioters, gamesters, and al the prophane multitude . . . all hypocrites, carnall protestants, vaine professors, back-sliders, decliners, and cold Christians." And Baxter (1653:172) concurred that even most Protestants were grossly ignorant, profane, erroneous, schismatic, or scandalous. This left the Puritans themselves among the small remnant of the saved. Many considered themselves among the "probable elect" (see Stannard 1977:73 and Preston cited by Davies 1975:168).

They regarded themselves as the people of God, the "godly" among the "vulgar" (Foster 1991:11, see also p. 50), the "chosen few" among the carnal multitude (ibid.:8, 11, see also pp. 6, 46, 109). William Perkins saw the bulk of Englishmen as an ungodly multitude and the saving remnant as but a "few corns of wheat" in "a heap of chaff" (Collinson 1988:23–27); Baxter (quoted by Keeble 1982:149–51, see also pp. 116, 121) gauged that the Puritans included "the greatest number of the godly" in England; and Hugh Peter and his followers imagined themselves separated out from the common herd of sinners (see Stearns 1954:424). Contemporary Anglicans complained that the Puritans considered themselves "holier than the rest" (see McGee 1976:233). Marlowe (1956:40, 42, 49, 57) calls them arrogant, self-righteous, and self-justifying; and McGee (1976:189), too, labels them smug.

Identification of the saints was facilitated by the existence of loosely connected networks "by which the godly associated themselves with each other" (Foster 1991:16). The Puritans' distinctiveness was known and recognized (Seaver 1985:190). They self-consciously separated themselves from their more profane neighbors (ibid.:187, 188–89; see also Lake 1982:282). McGee (1976:181–82, 184) writes that those who sanctified the Sabbath and delighted in the word sought out each other's company. They recognized each other, and accepted the godly into their community (see Lake 1982:282; see also Seaver 1985:98, 189–90 and Foster 1991:14–15).[12]

Knots of Puritans met separately from official parish functions for purposes of discussing sermons and Scripture, fasting, and prayer; their gatherings were called "conventicles" (see Foster 1991:13, 19, 50, 96–97). According to McGee (1976:189, see also p. 185), their "godly brotherhood" was quite exclusive. Members of Puritan networks were aware, then, of who the visible saints were: "though by a great distance of place they be severed . . . they know by reports one another" (see Foster 1991:50–51; see also Seaver 1985:190–91).

Since the identity of the most godly Christians was obvious, one could be fairly certain who would be saved. In fact, Baxter (quoted by Keeble 1982:152) once said of the Puritans, "If God love them not, I have not yet met with the people whom I may say he loveth." Conversely, Downame ([1604] 1974:II, 280) maintained that God did not save those with "no fellowship in the communion of saints."

This Puritan elitism was reassuring in the face of the belief that God's elect were few in number and that few would be saved (see Downame [1604] 1974:II, 179; Flavel 1968:V, 593; Dent [1601] 1974:283–93; Baxter 1653:324). The door of the church was considered much wider than the door of heaven (see Keeble 1982:27 and Collinson 1967:25). But the Puritans, according to Reilly (1948:9), "though they might accept and preach the condemnation of the majority of mankind . . . assumed for the most part that they themselves were among the few fortunately favored by God."

Nehemiah Wallington saw himself as one of the "people of the Lord" (see Seaver 1985:143). According to Seaver (ibid.:34, 104, 187, see also pp. 16, 95, 101–2, 130, 191), he knew that he had been born into a special community of God's children, and "Almost all of Wallington's connections . . . have taken place within the godly community." Wallington (cited in ibid.:104, see also p. 145) felt it necessary to keep company with the godly in order to be converted. He "doubted whether salvation was possible outside the community of saints" (ibid.:103). He saw his own affection for the saints as a mark of God's child (ibid.:189; see also Wallington Folger diary:286), and he (cited by Seaver 1985:130, see also p. 170) was confident that God would not forsake his own.[13]

Anxiety and the Religious Climate

Weber's ([1904–5] 1958:101–9, 117) exaggeration of Puritan anxiety was partly based on his judgment of the harshness and "extreme inhumanity" of the predestination doctrine. The "icy" climate an individual faced when confronting the problem of salvation created, in his (ibid.:104, 107, 108) opinion, a feeling of isolation. According to Weber (ibid.:104–5), the individual remained solitary because God, Christ, the clergy, the church, and the sacraments were all "of no use to salvation"; with predestination each person's destiny had been decreed "from eternity." Although there is a good deal of truth to this assessment, it is inconsistent with the bulk of his analysis and, when made consistent, becomes inaccurate. The problem is that, as Weber (ibid.:115) himself recognized, it is "more correct" to say that the Puritan created "the conviction" of his or her salvation, not the salvation itself. So the important issue is not whether God, Christ, the sacraments, the clergy, and the church could effectuate salvation, but, rather, whether they could enhance the assurance of it. Putting the question that way, the answer is that all of these agents contributed to the Puritan's reassurance. In the quest for assurance they tended to be warm, soft, and human rather than icy, harsh, and inhumane.

An Icy God?

Weber ([1904–5] 1958:103–5) portrayed the Calvinist God as "a transcendental being" who was separated from humanity by "an unbridgeable gulf." His majestic decrees were unquestionable and "quite incomprehensible" in this view. "The Father in heaven of the New Testament, so human and understanding, who rejoices over the repentance of a sinner . . . is gone," Weber (ibid.:103) averred.

But Downame ([1604] 1974:II, 142–46 and *passim*; see also Ball 1632:183) considered God a gracious and loving father, who had promised good to his children, and whose actions proceeded from love and tender care. His love and goodness were grounds for hope (Downame [1604] 1974:II, 135–36, 142). Similarly, Baxter ([1650] 1962:138) considered God a friend, and one whose love was infinite. He (ibid.:157 and 1678:II, 115) pointed out the Lord's goodness, and advised readers that God's heart was upon them (Baxter [1650] 1962:119). Dent ([1601] 1974:323, 419), too, pointed out God's "kindnesse" and "love." These pastoral teachings may have influenced Wallington. He saw God as kind and loving, not a hard master (see Seaver 1985:75).

God punished only "as a father" to correct; his wrath was a "semblance" (see Downame [1604] 1974:II, 301). He would spare them in his love (ibid.:I, 127; see also II, 226, 227) for he was "very loath we should perish" (Dent [1601] 1974:292–93, 420, 426, 427).

According to Downame ([1604] 1974:II, 445, 566 and III, 611) and Baxter (1678:II, 116), God showed his love for humankind by giving his Son to die for people's sins. Christ, in turn, was definitely loving and on the side of his faithful (see Downame [1604] 1974:II, 450, 453, 454, 456–57, 560, 562). Puritans expected all good from Christ (see ibid.:II, 295, 562). Weber makes the religion seem more impersonal by deemphasizing Christ.

Reciprocally, Puritans felt affection for God (see Baxter 1653:71 and Downame [1604] 1974:II, 227). Wallington (quoted by Seaver 1985:43) considered it "sweet and comfortable" to know God. Also, Puritans loved and trusted in Christ (see Downame [1604] 1974:II, 295). Baxter ([1650] 1962:120, see also p. 126) and Pledger (diary:54) both looked forward to enjoying the presence of God and Christ in heaven.

Weber's position does receive some support. Ball (1632:214) allowed that "it is a difficult thing to looke beyond the cloud of iustice, and . . . to believe, that there is forgivenesse with God." Similarly, Downame ([1604] 1974:II, 268) conceded that the flesh saw God as an angry, severe judge; only the spirit saw God as a merciful father. Baxter (1653:243–44) observed that many people imagined negative or fearful things about God; likewise, Mrs. Stockton (diary:2) heard that hard thoughts of God were a common "faileing" among "the peopel of God." It is difficult to know how common this harsh image of God was; but clearly, and contrary to Weber, a loving image predominated at the pastoral level and among the merchants in this study.

Baxter (1653:183–85, 446 and [1650] 1962:143) held that communication with God was possible through prayer and heavenly meditation, which allowed people to enjoy God and develop affection and delight in him. The more people meditated, the less their "strangeness" with God and the greater their closeness and affection toward him (Baxter [1650] 1962:113, 114, 147). Downame ([1604] 1974:II, 395, 474) concurred that with repeated prayer people began to direct their conversations and affections toward heaven. For example, Elias Pledger was able to converse with God (diary:58, 59) and to enjoy communion with him (ibid.:49).

This evidence supports Eusden's (1958:28) contention that later Puritan doctrine "canceled out the austerity and remoteness of Calvin's supreme being and made God more approachable." Also confirmed is Zaret's (1985:160–61) conclusion that the remote, unfathomable God of Calvin had been revised into a being more familiar and intelligible.

According to Eusden (1958:25), "The warm devotionalism of the Puritans . . . was a full step removed from the stony piety of John Calvin. John Preston and others preached again and again that God revealed himself to men as not only perfect, unchangeable, almighty, and eternal but also kind, patient and abundant in mercy. . . . Here was a God who could be known intimately in the personal experience of believers." Or as Stearns (1954:50) put it, "God was no longer terrible, but comforting." Typically, Downame ([1604] 1974:III, 612) preached that Christ had reconciled his people to God.

The Sacraments

Weber ([1904–5] 1958:104–5) argued that the sacraments were no help to the religious pilgrim's salvation; and, moreover, there were "no magical means of attaining the grace of God." Nevertheless, it should be kept in mind that the Puritans did practice baptism and communion; and these "seals of the covenant" helped to assure them that they were saved.

Perkins ([1606] 1972:II, 403, 455) saw both baptism and communion as signs of the covenant and seals of the promises of God. As signs they represented the mercies offered in the covenant (Perkins 1970:III, 162) and as seals they confirmed "God's mind and will in the communication of his grace" (Ames quoted by Holifield 1974:61). Downame ([1604] 1974:II, 142–43, 438), Ball (1632:402, 419), and Cotton (cited by Holifield 1974:139–40) are only a few of the divines who considered the sacraments covenant seals.

Baptism received people into the church (Downame [1604] 1974:II, 208, 439) and admitted them to the covenant (Ball 1632:409). It reminded them that a person with true faith would not be judged by the law (Downame [1604] 1974:II:439, see also p. 208). Cotton (quoted by Holifield 1974:139–40) considered it "a pledge of salvation." To Ball (1632:409, 414), it was a "seale of . . . remission of sinnes" and "immortal life." Having God's word "confirmed . . . by seale in Baptisme, they have great cause to rest assured" (ibid.:414; see also Holifield 1974:44).

Puritan preachers also "spoke of the Lord's Supper . . . as a covenant seal" (see Holifield 1974:51; Downame [1604] 1974:II, 439; Ball 1632:419, 421; Perkins quoted by Davies 1975:314; Hill [1613] 1975:43). It confirmed the truth of God's promises (see Downame [1604] 1974:II, 208, 225), and was "as if he should say, I have promised to forgive you your sins" (Preston quoted by Holifield 1974:51; see also Perkins 1970:III, 375 and [1606] 1972:II, 346).

Taking communion also confirmed the communicant's receipt of God's promises (Downame [1604] 1974:II, 208, 225) and helped to assure "that receiving the outward signe as he ought, hee shall be partaker of the thing signified," namely, "Christ himselfe, and all his benefits" (Ball 1632:402). When the minister sealed God's offer of Christ to the faithful, the communicant testified to his or her own "application" of Christ by faith (see Holifield 1974:54).

Holifield (ibid.:53) states that "The sacrament . . . worked by evoking a subjective sense of assurance in the mind of the communicant." Cotton (quoted in ibid.:139–40) considered the Lord's Supper "plentiful nourishment" to the worthy receiver; Downame ([1604] 1974:II, 142–43, see also p. 438) felt that it "may assure us of his love and favour"; and Preston "seemed to suggest that no anxiety could survive heartfelt participation in the sacrament" (quoted by Holifield 1974:51, see also pp. 40, 42). Of course, as Holifield (ibid.:51, see also p. 47) reminds us, "the seal obliged God only to save the truly faithful, the elect." Nevertheless, "that did not hinder the merely presumed faithful from finding in the Lord's Supper a sense of assurance" (ibid.:51).

Nehemiah Wallington (Folger diary:273–76) came to the Lord's table "to renew my Covenant"; it was a "drawing nigh" to God and a dedication of oneself to him. There was an expectation of spiritual joy and thankfulness (ibid.:276), and, indeed, Seaver (1985:125) reports that such spiritual exercises brought him a sense of satisfaction and emotional peace. To Elias Pledger (diary:12–13) the sacrament commemorated Christ's bloody suffering. He (ibid.:33, 37, 38, 40, 41, 42, 45, 49, 55, 64, 66, 67) was frequently comforted, quickened, or "enlarged" at the Lord's Supper.

Sometimes, of course, the sacraments failed to deliver their expected psychological lift (see, for example, Pledger diary:23, 42, 51, 69). Sometimes conscientious communicants feared the punishment for unworthy communion more than they were comforted by the sacrament (Baxter cited by Holifield 1974:28; see also Hill [1613] 1975:57). Further, the sacraments alone were insufficient evidence of salvation (see Downame [1604] 1974:II, 141; Cotton cited by Holifield 1974:139–40; Sibbes quoted by Holifield 1974:48). Yet, despite these drawbacks, Perkins (1970:III, 240; see also Holifield 1974:44) judged them "very effectual to enforce particular assurance," and so did Downame ([1604] 1974:II, 222). This counters Weber's insinuations to the contrary.

Even more directly counter to Weber's argument that the sacraments were of no effect were those Puritans who believed that the sacraments could affect one's salvation (see Holifield 1974:76, 99–100, 103, 107–10, 119). For example, Downame ([1604] 1974:II, 222, 271) held that the sacraments were made effectual by the holy Spirit. Such teachings disconfirm

Weber's (1958:105) claim that there were "no magical means of attaining . . . grace."[14]

Downname ([1604] 1974:II, 516) considered the sacraments part of the "outward meanes" of salvation. Since the Gospel promises were offered by the right use of the sacraments (see ibid.:II, 206, 564; Hill [1613] 1975:50; Baxter 1678:IV, 273), they could help save people (see Perkins 1970:III, 217; Holifield 1974:53). For example, Perkins ([1606] 1972:II, 308), Bradshaw (quoted by Holifield 1974:59), and Downname ([1604] 1974:II, 207) held that they applied Christ and his benefits to their intended receivers; and Elias Pledger (diary:13) agreed. Of course, Weber was correct that prevailing Puritan doctrine denied that the sacraments could save reprobates (see Holifield 1974:46, 47, 70, 96–97, 102–3, 119, 120; see also Downname [1604] 1974:III, 596; Perkins [1606] 1972:II, 315, 320, 330–31, 344, 345; 1970:III, 218). However, many Puritans presumed themselves to be a probable elect. For them, the sacraments were a means to salvation as well as a source of comfort.

Alone or Together?

Weber ([1904–5] 1958:104) reinforced his emphasis on the psychological loneliness of the individual by suggesting that the neo-Calvinist pilgrim was physically and literally "forced to follow his path alone." However, that image of loneliness is factually undercut by the company and support actually received from fellow Puritans.

There is, to be sure, some truth in Weber's depiction of the pilgrim's quest as solitary. According to Baxter ([1650] 1962:149–50) people mostly experienced God in private. Zaret (1985:150) and Seaver (1985:19) cite the introspective nature of the search for evidence of election, faith, and grace. During self-examination, Baxter ([1650] 1962:149–50; see also Keeble 1982:103) recommended solitude for meditation because a crowd distracts. He ([1650] 1962:133) said to "get alone and question with thyself."

However, self-examination did not need to be solitary. If one were not able to do it well, Baxter (1678:IV, 276; see also II, 116, [1650] 1962:133 and 1653:182) recommended, "get the help of some able friend or Pastor and do it in a way of conference with him." In fact, at one point Baxter ([1650] 1962:181) advocated solitary meditation only "when all means are denied thee," for example when a minister was unavailable.[15]

In like fashion, Perkins ([1606] 1972:I, 104; see also Breward 1970:III, 389 and Holifield 1974:44) prescribed assistance for those distressed by religious melancholy: "the partie in distresse must be taught, not to rest upon his owne judgement, but alwaies to submit himselfe . . . to be advised by others that are men of wisdome, judgment, and discretion." The person could then be treated by others looking for signs of grace (Perkins [1606]

1972:I, 196). In extreme cases, "If the distressed partie, be much possessed with griefe . . . he must not be left alone, but alwaies attended with good companie" (ibid.:I, 104, see also p. 167).

In general, Perkins (ibid.:I, 169) considered it wise in "the keeping of the heart . . . to establish our thoughts by counsell" rather than trusting to oneself. Similarly, Baxter (1653:326–27) recommended the confession of sins to a minister or friend. In cases of conscience he (1653:Epistle Dedicatory) insisted that "Pastors must guide you." The pastor confirmed you "by his judgment of your case" or could "confute your mistakes" (Baxter 1678:IV, 276).

Ball (1632:301–2) saw a different advantage: others may see a person's graces, both faith and fruits, when the person cannot. Hence, as Baxter (1678:IV, 274) put it, "a faithful friend or Pastor may do that, which may much support you, and relieve you against inordinate doubts and fears, and shew you that your sincerity is very probable."

Downame ([1604] 1974:II, 461) was also optimistic about the pastors' ability to reassure: "the afflicted soule . . . may receive no small assurance by the testimonie of Gods faithfull ministers." If diverse ministers, after due examination, declared a person saved, this should have been, in his (ibid.:II, 462) view, an immensely forcible argument. They were "appointed of God to this function" and were "inabled to discerne and iudge of mens estates better than they themselves" (ibid.:II, 461, see also p. 462).

Nevertheless, Baxter (1678:II, 116) cautioned that "their judgment cannot be infallible of you." One could obtain "a very strong conjecture," but not certainty (ibid.).

In practice, the use of a guide was common. The business of salvation was "more often than not pursued in company" (Foster 1991:24). Pledger gave his minister an account of his soul so that his religious fitness could be judged. Likewise, Nehemiah Wallington looked to the preachers all his life for counsel and guidance (Seaver 1985:187, see also pp. 30, 37, 105, but see also p. 110). He (see ibid.:105) asked his parish curate, Henry Roborough, whose judgment he trusted, to examine him and tell him the true state of his soul. And he also consulted with other ministers (see ibid.:81, 87).

It must be conceded that some evidence shows only a minority seeking pastoral guidance. Indeed, Downame ([1604] 1974:II, 246) lamented "how few the number is in these daies, who receive the Lords ambassage to their spiritual comfort." However, he clearly chalked this up to indifference rather than to the intrinsically solitary nature of the Puritan salvation process. Actually, the indifferent majority who made the divines "shepherds to the few" tended not to be Puritans at all but, according to Foster (1991:19), non-Puritan parish Anglicans. Furthermore, Downame's report is contradicted by Whately's observation that many required pastoral help with their problems (see Haller [1938] 1972:27).

For their part, Puritan ministers extended guidance to the uncertain (Breward 1970:III, 389). Richard Baxter well exemplifies the divines who counseled religious pilgrims. According to Martin (1954:150; see also Keeble 1982:82), he "supplemented his preaching by much visitation of people in their homes and by personal dealing with individuals." Much of his work was one on one; and he also instructed families (see Keeble 1982:82, 86). He had, in Keeble's (ibid.:17) words, "intense pastoral concern" for the struggling believer. Likewise, other preachers went house to house to advise (see Baxter [1696] 1931:176).

According to Reilly (1948:25, see also p. 10), "It was the principal work of the Puritan preacher to suggest ways of scrutiny into the process of conversion and to supply tests for . . . doubtful souls." Consequently, it was unnecessary for each pilgrim to work out his or her salvation separately. The path to self-assessment and to assurance was spelled out by the clergy.

Even when no clergyman was present, believers were not left to confront their fates alone, since pastoral care could be extended in writing. Ministerial handbooks told what needed to be done to assess one's state and to gain in assurance (see Knott 1980:69; Holifield 1974:40, 44–45). For example, Richard Rogers (quoted by Reilly 1948:10) set out in *Seven Treatises* "to shew who are true believers, and the children of God, and how men . . . may know that they are so." Baxter wrote voluminously to console the saints (see Keeble 1982:14). In his *Christian Directory* and other works he stressed the everyday application of doctrine and the resolution of cases of conscience (ibid.:72–73). This aided the "babes in Christ," lapsed and backsliding Christians, doubters, and the fearful and troubled (see ibid.:73; see also Baxter 1678:II, 114). Baxter (quoted by Keeble 1982:75) told how to achieve a "confirmed state of grace." Perkins, Ames, Dent, and many others wrote similar guides (see Watkins 1972:11).

The clergy were not the only counselors. For instance, Zaret (1985:145–46; see also Seaver 1985:33–34, 184, 188) has pointed to the household unit. Wallington had received religious counsel in his family as a youth; his father had offered him spiritual comfort (see Seaver 1985:76, 110). Later, he was comforted by his brother-in-law (ibid.:81).

Spiritual guidance extended beyond the household as well (see, for example, Pledger diary:13). Puritan conventicles "thrust personal spiritual experience out of the privacy of individual meditation" and "into the public arena" (Foster 1991:96). "The life of faith," writes Cragg (1957:156), "might begin in the lonely anguish" of a sinful soul. "But it always ended in membership in some society of like-minded persons." In these meetings, Foster (1991:96) notes, the godly would "probe into one another's spiritual affairs." The Puritans looked "to each other for comfort, support, and encouragement" (see McGee 1976:203). McGee (ibid.:207–8, see also pp. 183, 188–89) states that their groupings could give a "comforting reas-surance that all will be well . . . The godly brethren . . . helped to breed in each other . . . confidence." Hence, participation "was a means of growth in assurance of salvation" (ibid.:206, see also p. 203).

For example, Nehemiah Wallington, in his older years, served as an ad-visor to saints who were spiritually troubled (Seaver 1985:109–10, 190, see also p. 8). He was a sympathetic listener (ibid.:110), and people sought him out (ibid.:190). He tried to comfort the anxious; this was sometimes successful though not always (ibid.:109–10).

In conclusion, Coolidge (1970:147) was correct that Puritans were not characteristically single individuals alone and apart wrestling with their sins. Rather, in Foster's (1991:288) words, they "pursued their individual destinies in a collective context." They were generally informed by "min-ister, treatise, or experienced friend" (ibid.:72). "The pilgrim bound for the heavenly city had companions on the way," states Cragg (1957:156). "It was no solitary quest to which he had been called . . . and even when he seemed most completely alone he was encouraged by the voices of those who journeyed with him."

ANXIETY AND ASSURANCE

The comforting side of Puritanism gave it the *potential* to breed assur-ance as well as anxiety, but following are the actual results. The individual data below contain direct information on people's levels of security and anxiety.

Since Puritanism was a religion of contradictions, both able to terrify and reassure, it should come as no surprise when historians (e.g., Davies 1975:168, 246 vs. 115; Cragg 1957:156 vs. 151; Marlowe 1956:49, 81, 131–32 vs. 134, 137–38) report both that Puritans were confident and that they were fearful. Some writers have emphasized the positive side (e.g., Walzer 1965:218, 317; Simpson 1955:2–5, 100, 115; Knappen 1933:14–15; 1965:394; Walker 1970:212; New 1964:104; Mackinnon 1988a; Grassby 1995:275) and some the negative (e.g., Stannard 1977:41, 75; McGee 1976:207; Briden-baugh 1968:276; Holifield 1974:40, 41), but both sides were present. Even Max Weber, who stressed Puritans' anxiety (see, for example, [1904–5] 1958:108), referred to them sometimes as "self-confident saints" (see Chap-ter 1 above and Weber [1904-5] 1958:113, 166).

The Feasibility of Assurance

Some Puritans became quite sure of their election. For example, John Winthrop (quoted by McGee 1976:16, 45; see also Seaver 1985:19) delighted "in the comfort of my salvation." Hugh Peter (quoted by Stearns 1954:424) believed he would be with Christ "in glory"; and he also persuaded his followers of their sainthood. Richard Baxter gained assurance of his sincerity (see Keeble 1982:134), and his wife, too, was certain of her salvation (see Nuttall 1965:95). Richard Sibbes and John Davenport believed in their conversions (see McGee 1976:60). Dorothy Stockton (diary:2) was "convinsed that I . . . had gone to Christ," and Oliver Cromwell died happy, believing himself in a state of grace (see Hill 1970:221). Likewise, certain Puritans in Cromwell's government were confident in their faith and grace (see Walker 1970:210–12). Among the Puritan merchant diarists, Pledger (diary:56) considered himself a child of God, one "that is not slain but returns to their king." He (diary:62) believed that God would save "his elect. . . . Hopefully our deliverance is near." Wallington, too, concluded that he was among the elect (see Seaver 1985:43, 44, 110, 124), "a child of God and not a hypocrite." He (quoted in ibid.:17; see also pp. 8, 195 and Folger diary:308) believed "that I am out of Hell, not roaring with the damned."[16]

In short, as Downame ([1604] 1974:II, 549) put it, some "are most certainly perswaded of their salvation in Christ." Although Weber ([1904–5] 1958:110) implied that under predestination only Calvin himself could be certain of salvation, the evidence shows that comfort was far from impossible for the Puritans.

Doctrinal Causes of Assurance

Puritans' assurance frequently rested on their acceptance of the comforting doctrines described above. Salvation by Christ was named most frequently. Hugh Peter (quoted by Stearns 1954:424) felt freed by Christ from "the law of sin and death." Likewise, Owen Stockton (diary:2) was comforted because Christ had come to save sinners from "hel." Similarly, his wife Dorothy (diary:4, see also p. 21) thought that Christ's blood "clenseth from all sin" and that Christ's righteousness could "make me acceptable with the." She (diary:5, see also p. 17) believed that this was a "sure way for the recovery and salvation of fallen man." Similarly, Nehemiah Wallington (quoted by Seaver 1985:43, see also pp. 7, 8) based his feeling of election partly (see additional reasons in ibid.:44) on Christ's mercy: "he will spare me and take pity on me." He (cited in ibid.:85, see also p. 195) said that God's greatest mercy was giving him Christ.

Dorothy Stockton (diary:21) named another comforting doctrine when she (diary:15, see also p. 21) grounded her "hope of eternall Life upon . . . the covenant of grace." Similarly, Cromwell was "confident" in part because "Lord . . . I am in covenant with thee" (quoted by McGee 1976:54–55).

The idea of conversion also fostered assurance. According to Simpson

(1955:2), "The essence of Puritanism . . . is an experience of conversion which separates the Puritan from the mass of mankind and endows him with the privileges . . . of the elect. The root of the matter is always a new birth, which brings with it a conviction of salvation." Similarly, Seaver (1985:15) reports that when Puritans had religious crises, "Conversions . . . brought these crises to a happy conclusion." And Grassby (1995:275–76) attributes the *certitudo salutis* of Puritan merchants to youthful conversions. In support, Elias Pledger expressed no doubts or anxiety about salvation since his conversion as a youth; as stated earlier, his troubles ended with his conversion (diary:8).

Also comforting was the doctrine of perseverance. Cromwell felt assured because he believed that "grace once known could never be lost" and that "once he had been in a state of grace" (Hill 1970:221). Finally, in Lake's (1982:19) view, the doctrine of justification by faith engendered a "sense of election."

The Relative Frequency of Anxiety and Assurance

As indicated earlier, Baxter (1653:169, see also pp. 151, 152–53, 155, 157; see also Keeble 1982:72) thought that certainty of salvation was "not so common a thing." He (1678:II, 116) remarked, "how few do we find, that can say, they are certain of their . . . salvation. Alass, not one of very many." However, the numbers of the secure were swollen by those with "false assurance" (see Hildersam quoted by Stannard 1977:74), including the presumptuous (Downame [1604] 1974:Epistle Dedicatory), the hypocritical (see Baxter 1653:164), and those "content with religious and moral appearances" (Breward 1970:III, 389). Although they lacked positive assurance, they were untroubled because they were carnally secure (Baxter 1653:164, see also pp. 152, 281–83; see also Downame [1604] 1974:II, 223). According to Baxter (1653:396–97), there were many of these ignorant sinners. He (cited by Keeble 1982:121) perceived that the church was filled with easy consciences. He (1653:152) considered "most too secure." Similarly, Perkins (1970:III, 84) declared that "most men nowadays are secure . . . in the . . . gospel. . . . Tell him what you will, his song is this, God is merciful. . . . By this means it cometh to pass that he leadeth a secure life."

Then there were those between the extremes of security and anxiety. This middle ground was produced by norms that opposed both despair and overconfidence, by a mixture of demanding and comforting doctrines, and by preachers who both consoled the fearful and stirred up anxiety over sin. These opposing forces pushed in an intermediate direction, countering the extremes of both upset and arrogance. Because Puritanism was self-contradictory it produced some mixed effects.

Those in the middle were buoyed up by hope (see Baxter 1653:173; see also Stannard 1977:39). Baxter (1653:152, see also p. 174) reported "some in so good hopes . . . as calmeth their spirits." He (1678:II, 116) testified that "many Thousands of these do live in some peace of Conscience, and quietness, and comfort, in the hopefulness and probabilities to which they have attained." Flavel (1968:V, 525) concurred. In fact, "Experience tels us that the greatest part of Christians on earth do enjoy that Peace and Comfort" (Baxter 1653:174).

At the high-anxiety end of the scale Baxter (1653:152) reported "some in great doubts and fears," and Downame ([1604] 1974:Epistle Dedicatory; see also II, 186) referred to some who were inconsolable. Ball (1632:181, 183) reported that "Sundry Christians . . . be unsetled with feares"; some even considered themselves "utter reprobates." And Saltmarsh ([1647] 1847:178) confirmed that "many are cast down and afflicted as to this thing of assurance, and pine and consume." Their distress had "two degrees," according to Perkins ([1606] 1972:I, 88–89), the lesser being fear and the greater "Despaire." Some were "Melancholy," Baxter (1678:II, 114) noted.

Wallington is a prime example. Before becoming convinced of his election, he was "wracked by religious anxieties" (Seaver 1985:110, 195); he was troubled by doubts and temptations (ibid.:43). In his youth he went through an acute crisis (ibid.:15–16). He was "troubled in my mind and melancholy" (quoted in ibid.:16, see also p. 105); he felt "many sorrows" (see ibid.:16). He had suicidal despair (ibid., see also p. 195); he attempted suicide more than once (see ibid.:22–25). He ran away from home more than once (ibid.:21–22, 29). His depression lasted about a year (ibid.:24). After that, periods of melancholic despair remained a recurring problem until his 40s (ibid.:25, see also pp. 12, 42, 195, 196; see also Folger diary:116).

Wallington (see Seaver 1985:109) advised one gentlewoman who lamented her religious inadequacies by weeping, some days eating nothing, and crying out "Oh Lord, forgive her." Similarly, Elias Pledger's diary (see p. 53) documents his sister Mary's fear of hell.

Of course, the effects of religious anxiety were softened and mitigated by the comforts of pastoral reassurance. Nevertheless, Perkins ([1606] 1972:I, 105) reported that "usually it is long before comfort can be received"; and it may be "small." Similarly, Pledger (diary:17) wrote that many dejected Christians ignored consolation. During periods of religious melancholy Wallington would accept no comfort from his father or minister (see Seaver 1985:76, 110; see also Downame [1604] 1974:Epistle Dedicatory).[17]

Still, the number of the anxious should not be exaggerated. Although Sibbes (cited by Knott 1980:52) lamented that spiritual calm was unlikely in this life, Baxter (1653:396–97), writing somewhat later, observed few troubled consciences; "how few," he (1653:397) exclaimed, "have been pricked at the heart." In fact, he (1653:397) judged that "we have seldom past one, or two, or three troubled Consciences in an Auditory."[18] Similarly, Hildersam (quoted by Stannard 1977:74) judged that for every one who was desperate, there were twenty with "false assurance."

In sum, there were various degrees of peace and comfort. Despite the lack of true certainty, there was considerable security; probably only a minority were highly anxious. A number believed themselves to be among the probable elect (see above). This supports Weber's ([1904–5] 1958:112) notion that Puritanism bred self-confident saints.

The assessment of Puritan anxiety is complicated because the anxious and the secure were to some extent the same people. For one thing, certainty and doubt could be mixed together simultaneously. Ball (1632:111, see also p. 257) declared that people had "a measure of true and comfortable assurance ... mixed with many feares and doubts"; and Baxter (1653:208) said that assurance was "but mixt with imperfection."

For another thing, people changed over time, often cycling through an early period of anxiety followed by a stage of newfound assurance (see, for example, Ball 1632:257 and Cragg 1957:156). Mrs. Stockton (diary:2) exemplifies this phenomenon since "after a long time of walking in darknes and seeing no light it hath pleased God ... to scatter those clouds which did so darken my mind." Likewise, Wallington experienced joy and comfort later in life, after years of struggling (Seaver 1985:21, see also pp. 43, 44, 105, 195).

One may ask how many years of trouble were typical, and how many years of calm in a Puritan life. As Downame ([1604] 1974:II, 395) pointed out, the earlier one's repentance, the longer the peace of it could be enjoyed, and the fewer the years of fear. The few known biographies display an enormous range. At one extreme, Pledger's period of trouble was short; he evinced little fear of reprobation after his youthful conversion. At the opposite extreme was Nehemiah Wallington, who struggled in uncertainty for thirty years before his religious crises ended (see Seaver 1985:15, 21, 42, 43–44, 105, 195; see also Folger diary:187). Intermediate was Richard Baxter (1653:162–63, 293), whose doubts and "trouble of minde" lasted for seven years. And, not unlike Baxter, there is some evidence that Oliver Cromwell's melancholy was present in his late twenties while his conversion did not occur until his late thirties (see Hill 1970:46).

Besides this patterned movement from stage to stage Lake (1982:165) has referred to a more short-term "oscillation between anxiety and assurance." According to Wallington (see Seaver 1985:21), the Christian's pilgrimage had both gloomy and sunshine days, risings and fallings. Likewise, Baxter (1653:383, see also p. 152) reported that people's self-judgment fluctuated; they sometimes thought two contrary things in an hour. He (1653:230) said that those with the most violent joys had, when fears arose, the most terrible sorrows. Most people were mutable in their apprehensions, he (1653:148) wrote, soon losing whatever assurance they had attained.

Saltmarsh (1649:173) and Baxter (1653:A5, 270, see also pp. 246, 271, 273, 275–77) thought that comfort and assurance rose and fell with obedience or sin, so there was "inconstancy and unevenness" in the average person's peace. Even godly people, through neglect, sins, and uneven walking, lost the evidence for their assurance (Baxter 1653:148, 149). The inconstancy of the evidence caused fluctuations in judgment.

Amidst this variability Baxter addressed people's *usual* degree of comfort. He (1653:227, 228, 231) denied that joy was a Christian's ordinary state; rather, "Peace of conscience" was "your ordinary diet." Oscillations occurred about that baseline as Puritans fluctuated between joy and doubt. It is evident that doubts, fears, and even crises were common (see Ball 1632:111; Seaver 1985:15); still, these could be mastered and overcome "that they may not much interrupt thy peace" (Baxter [1650] 1962:133; Dent [1601] 1974:269). They took the form of lingering doubts rather than of total uncertainty, of constant insecurity, or of raging anxiety.

On the negative side, assurance was not constant, but "many times is . . . shaken with many difficulties, feares, and doubts" (Ball 1632:92, 257; see also Dent [1601] 1974:269, 270; Baxter 1653:208). The interruption of assurance was proved "by the daily complaints . . . of Gods people" (Baxter 1653:209). Even the best had storms and interruptions (see ibid.:211). Even after Wallington's reformation, he suffered periods of melancholy and despair (see above).

However, on the positive side, "the Lord in great mercy doth recover them"; they were only upset "for a time" (Dent [1601] 1974:270). They only lacked assurance *occasionally* (Baxter 1653:285). This contradicts the impression left by Weber ([1904–5] 1958:108) that religious anxiety provided an enduring stimulus to economic action.

In conclusion, religious anxiety was present, but not normally rampant. It had neither the constancy nor degree of intensity conveyed by the Weber thesis and by some religious historians. It was tempered through pastoral counseling and the development of softer, more comforting doctrines, which diluted its strength. Since Puritanism both fostered and reduced salvation anxiety, its effect was mixed. Moreover, since anxieties arose but intermittently, its elective affinity with the need of capitalism for continuous, restless action was only partial.[19]

EFFECTS OF ANXIETY AND ASSURANCE

After documenting a certain level of Puritan salvation anxiety, the next logical step is to assess its consequences as a motivator of economic action. The Weber thesis presupposes that Puritans typically reacted to anxiety with restless, systematic, rational activity. But there is little in the historical record or in the principles of psychology to support that supposition.

It is true that one response to anxiety is a heightened arousal level; this could increase restless activity. However, because doubt fluctuated and worries were periodic, heightened arousal and restless activity could only be maintained for a limited time, just as long as the conscience flared up. They were generally not permanent states. Since salvation anxiety was not as constant or lifelong as Weber implied, it could not produce a continuous, driving motive, an "ever-renewed" quest for profit, or continuous business enterprise. Moreover, anxiety often reduces performance. Overanxiety is unlikely to produce a systematic, rational approach.

In fact, the history of Puritanism reveals that the usual consequence of uncertainty was melancholy, not rational action. Baxter (1678:II, 114) wrote that "fearful troubled Christians that are perplexed with doubts" needed treatment "against Melancholy and Despair." Despair was accompanied by sorrow and sad discomfort (see Baxter 1653:284). He ([1650] 1962:123) also said that these worries indisposed people. Similarly, Downame ([1604] 1974:II, 146, 185) said that doubting produced torment, desperation, and infirmities. In short, uncertainty of salvation led not to activism, but to dejection and distress. Some were too broken up to function. Nehemiah Wallington (see Seaver 1985:16, 21–25, 43, 76, 81) exemplifies this pattern: as noted above, he was troubled and melancholy, suffered deep despair, and remained in a depression for about a year; indeed, he often experienced "paralyzing depression."

Another psychological reaction to anxiety is flight, and Puritan anxiety could lead to flight from the world rather than innerworldly action. Prime examples of this are Wallington's suicide attempts and his running away from home (see Seaver 1985:21–25). Doubtful, melancholy Puritans sometimes retreated to their homes, and could remain inside for days. There they examined their hearts and wept because of their fears (see Flavel 1968:V, 581, see also pp. 592–93). They were not "up and doing"; their anxiety reduced their action.

It is exactly the *contrary* thesis that finds support: it was Puritan *assurance* that fostered action. That thesis is confirmed both by the observations of contemporaries and by historians.

First of all, assurance implied hope, which was encouraging. In Baxter's ([1650] 1962:160) view, it led to courage, boldness, resolution, and action: "Cannot I do all things through him that strengtheneth me?" Hope led people to "adventure upon the greatest difficulties" (ibid.:159). Similarly, Downame ([1604] 1974:II, 273, see also p. 222) claimed that assurance made people serve God better. Thomas Taylor (quoted by Hill 1970:220) declared, "Nothing is more industrious than saving faith." And Richard Sibbes (quoted by Cragg 1975:153) observed, "As soon as God's grace has seized on us, presently it puts us on doing."

Historians of Puritanism have recognized the validity of this principle.

For instance, Hill (1970:220; 1975:89) claims that assurance, not fear, produced the Puritans' "exuberant efforts." He (1970:222) quotes Professor Haller's statement, "Men who have assurance that they are to inherit heaven, have a way of presently taking possession of the earth." Their courage and confidence extended to the economic as well as the political sphere, Hill (ibid.) asserts. New (1964:23) concurs that "God's assurance . . . inspired Puritan activism." Lake (1982:19) states that the "sense of election" lay behind the Puritan drive for reformation. Marlowe (1956:49, 131–32), too, writes, "This conviction of being one of the Elect had . . . given to English Puritanism its . . . self reliance, its endurance . . . its concentration on self-improvement" and "self-confidence."

Marlowe (ibid.:53, 57, 134) sees a "sense of responsibility" as one link between elect status and innerworldly activism. The Puritan God expected more of the elect than of others (McGee 1976:27; see also Stearns 1954:50; Baxter 1653:339; 1678:I, 107; IV, 259). In addition, their earthly labors served not to discover whether or not they had been elected, but to demonstrate that they had (see Marlowe 1956:57). As Stannard (1977:9) puts it, they were "proving to themselves and to others that they were of the elect; their method of life was that of the predestined to glory." In Lake's (1982:282) words, the Puritan tried "to externalise his sense of his own election through a campaign of works."

In short, although this religion pushed both toward anxiety and toward assurance, it was those who became assured who were impelled toward innerworldly action. It is doubtful that religious anxiety produced lives of strenuous activity, but quite probable that assurance did. Through this means, Puritanism could have produced some of the heroic merchants with "clarity of vision and ability to act" of whom Weber ([1904–5] 1958:69, 112) has written.

Nevertheless, it must be cautioned that none of the Puritan merchants analyzed in this study, neither Elias Pledger, who was basically assured, nor Nehemiah Wallington, who worried about salvation for much of his life, fit the description of the entrepreneur in Weber's ideal-type. Nor did Nehemiah's economic conduct change much when he gained assurance of his salvation (Seaver 1985:194–95).[20] The only Puritan business success found in these diaries was John Wallington, Sr., Nehemiah's father.

It remains an open question how many heroic Puritan businessmen were produced in this way. Since the Puritans were a minority faction, and since their anxiety levels ranged considerably, they may have generated too few self-confident saints to serve as the foundation for England's capitalist class. It is also unclear whether or not their confident activism was, to any substantial degree, efficacious in transforming the economy.

NOTES

1. Some Puritans, for example a friend of Pledger's (diary:6 of reverse pagination), maintained that election was unknowable. Nevertheless, it is counterfactual to regard their beliefs as the predominant Puritan position as some scholars have (e.g., Stannard 1977:41, 42, 44, 72–73; McGee 1976:52–53; Lake 1982:151).

2. Since religious anxiety did not hinge primarily on the doctrine of predestination with its secrecy, Weber's misleading use of Baxter as an example of neo-Calvinism is not a very serious error despite MacKinnon's (1988b:189–94) blistering critique.

3. The condition was alternately stated as faith and repentance (see, for example, Perkins [1606] 1972:I, 94, 102–3; see also Scudder [1673] 1813:195 and Pledger diary:7 of reverse pagination); this added one additional requirement. Faith put people into the covenant, but in order to use it to claim their pardon, they needed to repent their sins. Baxter ([1650] 1962:28, see also p. 85) also stressed the additional stipulation of enduring to the end. And according to Hill ([1613] 1975:53) faith, charity, obedience, and holiness of life were all required by covenant (see also Baxter 1653:274 and Preston cited by Pettit 1966:14).

4. Weber ([1904–5] 1958:111) gave this possibility short shift.

5. The condition of the new covenant was considered easier to meet than that of the Law, which people "could not perfourme" (see Downame [1604] 1974:II, 190, 240; see also p. 577 and Baxter 1678:II, 144).

6. Weber ([1904–5] 1958:117) was correct that Puritans felt judged on their lives as a whole, but that life did not have to be perfect. According to Baxter (1678:I, 108), "every carnal act will not prove you servants to the flesh"; or as Dent ([1601] 1974:427) put it, "some fewe infirmities, do not argue a wicked man." The grain of truth in Weber's viewpoint is that a single unrepented sin could endanger salvation. However, the practice of daily repentance produced an expectation of pardon.

7. Weber ([1904–5] 1958:117) was wrong that a Puritan "could not hope to atone for hours of weakness or of thoughtlessness by increased good will at other times, as the Catholic or even the Lutheran could."

8. Perkins ([1606] 1972:II, 347; see also I, 78, 98 and 1615:10) and Downame ([1604] 1974:III, 638; see also I, 122) comforted that "never so little measure of Gods grace in us" was a sign of the holy Spirit and hence of regeneration.

9. Since the effects of sanctification were typically small at first, a small degree of sanctification gave good hopes of true regeneration (see Downame [1604] 1974:III, 601–2).

10. Not every Puritan believed in this doctrine. In particular, Baxter (1653:166) would "not say, that I am Certain of this, that all are elect to salvation, and shall never fall away totally and finally, who sincerely Believe and are Justified." Nevertheless, he (quoted by Nuttall 1965:120) wrote, "My strong opinion is for perseverance."

11. Weber ([1904–5] 1958:104) was more correct when he conceded that *"extra ecclesiam nulla salus. "*

12. New (1964:32–33, 40, 43; compare Weber [1904–5] 1958:113) said that they acquired a "holy community" character, a fellowship of visible saints. According

to Seaver (1985:103) this community of saints was more extensive but more exclusive than the parish or precinct. It came into existence in the 1580s (ibid.:187–88), and Foster (1991:97) reports that the Puritans' "sense of solidarity" increased in the 1620s.

13. Yet Wallington was uncertain of his election for years after he knew that he was part of a special community (see Seaver 1985:34). Not all in the godly community were necessarily saved (see ibid.:144).

14. Besides the sanctifying effects of the holy Spirit, other means of escaping systematic ethical justice were Christ's assumption of human sins; people's ability to become part of Christ and take on his righteousness; and the justification of sinners by making the faithful appear righteous to God. Also, Weber ([1904–5] 1958:116–17) was only partly right that ministers lacked the magical power of absolution to aid salvation. Some believed that the ministry's power to remit sins was binding in heaven (see Downame [1604] 1974:II, 205, 461 and Baxter 1678:IV, 273).

15. Most puzzling is Weber's ([1904–5] 1958:106) statement alleging Puritan "warnings against any trust in the aid of friendship of men." "Even the amiable Baxter," he (ibid.) continues, "counsels deep distrust of even one's closest friend." Actually, Baxter (1678:II, 116) advised "choose such a man to help you, as is . . . Well acquainted with you; And undervalue not his judgment."

16. Wallington's friend James Cole was sure of his salvation, too (see Seaver 1985:95).

17. Baxter (1653:285, see also pp. 160–61) found that lack of assurance could come to the holiest believers. Many of the godliest Christians had complaints, doubts, and troubles, though they "walk uprightly with God" (Baxter 1653:183; see also pp. 209, 211, 405 and Baxter quoted by Keeble 1982:105–6). For example, in Seaver's (1985:105) judgment, Wallington's worries came from being overly conscientious (see also Dent [1601] 1974:268; Flavel 1968:V, 599; and Baxter 1678:II, 115).

18. Whately (quoted by Haller [1938] 1972:27), in contrast, reports many "spirituall weepers"; some, at least, were worried about the hereafter, although, according to Haller (ibid.), others were worried about "their future here" in an "age of perplexing change."

19. Contrary to Weber, it is by no means clear that Puritanism caused more salvation anxiety than Roman Catholicism despite the sacramental "escape hatches" of the latter (see, for example, Downame [1604] 1974:II, 187). Still, Puritans tended toward doubting salvation more than Methodists, Baptists, Lutherans, and/or most Anglicans. Because Puritanism stressed the need for faith to be proved by its fruits, it made salvation seem more difficult than some of these other religions (see McGee 1976:59).

20. He did not become a confident entrepreneur (see Seaver 1985:142); however, he may have begun to keep business accounts (see ibid.:120).

6

The Signs of Salvation

According to Weber, a major portion of Puritanism's economic influence derived from its salvation doctrine. The followers of this doctrine, he argued, were pulled in an economic direction. To be sure of election, it was necessary to search for the signs of salvation in oneself; and anyone lacking these qualities sought to modify his or her conduct in order to demonstrate the signs more clearly. This process impelled behavior toward more intense capitalist actions because they could serve as signs of election. The purpose of this chapter is to test this important part of Weber's thesis by assessing the direction(s) in which Puritans' salvation quest actually pulled.

Before proceeding to the evidence, though, it should be made clear that the pull of the salvation doctrine is not necessarily the same as the pull of Puritan conduct norms. Weber ([1904–5] 1958:155–57), for example, believed that the "maxims of everyday economic conduct" condemned "the pursuit of money and goods," while at the same time profit-making, as a sign of God's blessing (see ibid.:163–64), indicated a state of grace and enhanced one's certainty of salvation. Moreover, he (ibid.:197, see also p. 97) considered the pull of the salvation doctrine stronger than that of everyday conduct norms because the former was backed by "the sanctions of salvation and damnation."[1]

Weber was correct to distinguish between these two separate pulls, even when he misjudged the nature of the pulls themselves. For example, profit-making for charitable purposes was advocated as a conduct norm, but it raised dangers that could threaten salvation (Baxter 1678:I, 219). Consequently, the pull of the salvation doctrine upon profit-making was negative (ibid.), countering the positive pull of the norm of stewardship. As a second example, conduct norms opposed idleness and demanded hard work in one's calling; yet (contrary to Weber [1904–5] 1958:121, 172, 178), it will be seen that these behaviors were rarely mentioned among the signs of salvation and, hence, received little impetus from the salvation doctrine.

In general, conformity to everyday conduct norms could not always guarantee one's election. Hence, assessment of the salvation doctrine's pull requires more than a recital of Puritan conduct norms. It is necessary to consider the signs of salvation.

Up until this point the signs of salvation have been summarized briefly or detailed in a piecemeal fashion. The aim now is to create a more complete catalog of signs, which can evidence their great range and number in order to view those emphasized by Weber within the larger context that surrounded them.

A broad variety of signs, chiefly noneconomic, were cited as the marks of a regenerate soul. The sheer number mentioned, and the importance of many noneconomic signs, belie Weber's ([1904–5] 1958:172, see also pp. 112, 178) claim that the work of the calling was the surest proof of election. Moreover, Puritans were mixed over whether or not wealth was a sign of grace. It becomes clear that economic conduct was not central to the Puritan quest for certainty when the economic signs are viewed in their context within the whole salvation doctrine.

One obvious point that can be overlooked when assessing the signs of salvation is that the elect were those who were the most religious Christians. Hence, the best signs of being elected were a person's religious beliefs and practices. In that regard the Puritans differed little from other Christian groups. Though distinctive in other ways, their criteria for recognizing a saved soul generally resembled those used throughout Christianity.

FAITH

As shown earlier, faith was an important sign of salvation (Dent [1601] 1974:258, 259, 265; Baxter 1653:76, 86; Ames [1639] 1975:II, 9, 34 and quoted by Sprunger 1972:171; Flavel 1968:V, 530). Indeed, Perkins (quoted by Reilly 1948:13; see also Perkins [1606] 1972:I, 82, 97) considered saving faith "an infallible marke of election." Ball (1632:108, see also pp. 90, 248–50, 256, 257) said that "every Believer that knoweth himselfe to be a Believer may be certaine of his salvation," and Downame ([1604] 1974:II, 588, see also pp. 145, 174 and *passim*) stressed that anyone who believed "needeth no other arguments to assure him." Conversely, without faith, "wee cannot have any assurance," Downame (ibid.:II, 319, see also pp. 140, 209–10, 228, 320, 409, 414) stated. Baxter (1653:76) and Ball (1632:89) concurred.

Application of this sign required an understanding that true faith was more than just assent to the theology (Downame [1604] 1974:II, 533; Perkins [1606] 1972:I, 60). It had to be a "lively" faith (see, for example,

Ball 1632:114, 278; Downame [1604] 1974:II, 207, 209, 272, 288, 512; see also Keeble 1982:71). According to Baxter ([1650] 1962:125; see also Downame [1604] 1974:II, 512), "when a man's religion lies only in his opinions," it was "a sure sign of an unsanctified soul." Rather, Baxter (1653:87) referred to faith as an "Act," and spoke of a life of faith (1678:I, 58; see also Ball 1632:428).

True faith could be known by its inward feelings and its outward acts (see Ball 1632:186–87; Ames [1639] 1975:6; Downame [1604] 1974:II, 525, 587); the latter were needed to make it a lively faith. Examples include avoiding sin and performing holy duties (Perkins [1606] 1972:I, 61 and II, 346; Downame [1604] 1974:II, 523–24). Yet activity was not always necessary to assure election. Baxter (1653:53, 239) considered willingness or acceptance an "Adequate act of faith."

THE FRUITS OF FAITH

According to Perkins (quoted by Porter 1971:282; see also Breward 1970:III, 359), a lively faith, like a live tree, showed itself by "certain fruits which it brings forth." These "fruits," actually the Christian virtues, could confirm one's faith (see Downame [1604] 1974:II, 195, 587; Perkins 1970:III, 371; Chaderton quoted by Lake 1982:285; Baxter cited by Keeble 1982:69). Since they were "inseparable" from faith (Downame [1604] 1974:I, 83; II, 288, 578, 587), they provided "outward signs and marks by which a true profession of faith could be known" (McGee 1976:65, see also p. 64). Ames ([1639] 1975:6; see also Ball 1632:93 and Dering cited by Lake 1982:18) referred to "a certainty of Faith which ariseth from the proper acts of it distinctly perceived." As Weber ([1904–5] 1958:114; see also McGee 1976:64, 67) said, faith was known by conduct. However, if the fruits were lacking, it could mean that faith itself was lacking. Nobody could be assured but those "who bring foorth the fruites of their faith" (Downame [1604] 1974:II, second pp. 271–72; see also pp. 218, 525–26 and Ball 1632:93). Because faith was never severed from its fruits, a person's state of grace could be judged by the fruits (see Perkins 1970:III, 371). For example, Dent ([1601] 1974:295) stated, "I judge you . . . by your fruites, which is lawfull."

Repentance

One important fruit of faith was repentance (Downame [1604] 1974:II, 482, 509 and *passim*; see also Ball 1632:223, 339; Ames [1639] 1975:II, 15; and Perkins [1606] 1972:I, 54–55). Penitence stemmed from faith and faith showed itself through repentance (Downame [1604] 1974:II, 210, 272, 588;

see also Perkins [1606] 1972:I, 52, 54–55). Hence, Christ's promise to save the faithful applied only to those "who approve their faith by the lively fruite thereof unfained repentance" (Downame [1604] 1974:III, 617). Those without repentance were destitute of faith and unqualified for salvation (ibid.; Baxter 1653:54, 59; Ball 1632:100). Hence, repentance was a sign of salvation (Downame [1604] 1974:II, 258 and *passim*; Dent [1601] 1974:306; Baxter 1653:86–87, 91, 234–35; Perkins [1606] 1972:I, 102–3, 112–13; Ames cited by Sprunger 1972:171; Saltmarsh [1647] 1847:176–77). Indeed, Lake (1982:164; see also Downame [1604] 1974:II, 414) assures us that it was a "central sign."

One reason for its importance was its inclusion as a condition of the covenant; consent to the covenant was the most critical sign of the elect (Downame [1604] 1974:II, 411, 444, 504; see also Coolidge 1970:126 and Baxter 1678:II, 116). Also, since the way to salvation was to gain forgiveness from sin through repentance (Downame [1604] 1974:II, 282, 289, 436, 444; III, 652; Baxter 1678:II, 144; IV, 272; Perkins [1606] 1972:I, 102–3; III, 478), they were, in effect, judged on whether or not they had repented.[2]

Sanctification

Sanctification, or purification (see Chapter 5), was another fruit of faith (Perkins 1970: III, 234; Downame [1604] 1974:II, 198, 523–24; see also Peter quoted by Stearns 1954:59 and Ball 1632:273, 275). Hence, it assured one of belief (Downame [1604] 1974:II, 195, 198, 522–24; Perkins [1606] 1972:I, 84; Baxter [1696] 1931:125 and cited by Keeble 1982:14); but if a person lacked sanctification, true belief was "none of his" (Baxter [1696] 1931:110; see also 1653:54, 59 and Downame [1604] 1974:II, 272).

Since sanctification stimulated righteousness and reduced sin, the sanctified led a holy life, and were ultimately "unblameable before him" (Dent [1601] 1974:319). Therefore, evidence of sanctification assured salvation (Perkins [1606] 1972:I, 73–74, 76–77; 1970:III, 257–58; Baxter [1650] 1962: 29, 54, 138; 1678:II, 144; Dent [1601] 1974:319–20; Downame [1604] 1974:II, 230, 231 and *passim*, but see also Cotton quoted by Coolidge 1970:131–32 for a more qualified version). Conversely, the unsanctified could have no assurance (Downame [1604] 1974:II, 140, 230, 231, 273, 293; see also Baxter cited by Keeble 1982:69).

The sanctified could be known by their relative freedom from sin (Downame [1604] 1974: II, 230, 273–74, 289–91, 293; Baxter 1653:88, 118). Unlike the unregenerate, they hated sin, resisted it, and were troubled when they committed sins (Downame [1604] 1974:II, 230 and III, 643–44, 649; Perkins [1606] 1972:I, 76–77; Baxter 1653:91, 117, 118, 444; Flavel 1968:V, 541–43, 561–63).

Good Works

Good works, too, were fruits of faith (Ball 1632:57, 383; Downame [1604] 1974:I, 83; Baxter 1678:IV, 263), and as fruits of faith, they were signs of election (Downame [1604] 1974:II, 278–79, 540; see also Reilly 1948:47 and McGee 1976:181). These acts, even when external (McGee 1976:65–66), could show internal faith (Chaderton cited by Lake 1982:285; Baxter 1678:IV, 259), and they were signs of a lively faith (Downame [1604] 1974:I, 83, II, 144, 540, and III, 578–79; see also McGee 1976:64–66). Conversely, belief was only considered true if it led to good works (Ball 1632:114; Smith [1599] 1976:D6; Baxter 1678:IV, 266; [1650] 1962:30; Downame [1604] 1974:I, 83, 84, 143–44; Whitaker, Chaderton, and Ashton quoted by Lake 1982:99, 160). "Shew me thy faith by thy works," quoted Perkins (1601:89–90).

There is support for Weber's ([1904–5] 1958:115) view that good works were needed "as a sign of election." Although a person was justified by faith, Perkins (1601:89) declared, "the justification of the faith . . . whereby faith is declared to be true faith . . . is by workes." Since a justifying faith was only one of the effects of election, it was normally not found alone but joined with all the other religious virtues, including good works (Downame [1604] 1974:I, 83; II, 192, 288, 578–79; Perkins [1606] 1972:II, 361; Ball 1632:56–57, 100, 114; Smith [1599] 1976:D6; Baxter 1653:116). Hence, according to Downame ([1604] 1974:II, 578; see also I, 83 and Ball 1632:114), "wee necessarily require [works] in the subject or person iustified." Faith without works was insufficient for salvation (Downame [1604] 1974:I, 84, 89). Perkins ([1606] 1972:II, 361; see also Hill [1613] 1975:53 and Baxter 1678:IV, 268) held that faith "alone saveth not, but hope, love, repentance, good works, and all divine virtues."[3]

On the one hand, good works could serve as positive signs (McGee 1976:64, 66; Reilly 1948:44, 47; Marlowe 1956:57; Eusden 1958:31). According to Perkins (quoted by Porter 1971:290 and Perkins [1606] 1972:III, 615; see also I, 86–87), they assured "life everlasting." Conversely, the absence of works was a negative indication (see McGee 1976:193–94), since the elect were zealous of good works (Dent [1601] 1974:278). The Saints' Rest was not the estate of those who denied Christ in their works (Baxter [1650] 1962:29–30; see also pp. 34, 93 and 1653:146).

Good works could serve as a basis for salvation or damnation (Downame [1604] 1974:I, 83; see also II, 235, 278–80 and III, 598; Dent [1601] 1974:277–78; Perkins [1606] 1972:III, 535). Dent ([1601] 1974:391) and Baxter (1653:81, see also pp. 275, 332–33; see also 1678:I, 107, 234; II, 144) stressed that "We shall be Judged according to our Works." Likewise, merchant Elias Pledger (diary:51) wrote that "every man's work will be judged . . . in order to the final determination of his sentence."[4] For this reason, Baxter (1653:81–82) taught, "we must judge our selves according to our Works." For assessing someone's estate "his workes shall declare him and testifie of him" (Dent [1601] 1974:391; see also Perkins [1606] 1972:II, 362 and Smith [1599] 1976:D6).

The Importance of Good Works

Good works are especially pertinent to the Weber thesis because they could be economic works. Insofar as election was proved by works, Puritans could have been encouraged to reassure themselves through economic action. Therefore it is vital to know not only that good works were a sign, but to assess how important a sign they were.

In view of the evidence above, one may agree with Weber ([1904–5] 1958:228 note 41) that faith was proved through works and with Lake (1982:163) that good works were "demanded." Weber's ([1904–5] 1958:115) judgment that works were "indispensable as a sign" also seems valid inasmuch as the divines sometimes declared them necessary (see, for example, Ball 1632:114). Nevertheless, their importance must be qualified for a number of reasons.[5]

First, judgment was based on the other fruits as well as good works.[6] The others could also validate faith and testify to one's election, so all shared behavioral priority. The other fruits often replaced the use of good works and reduced their importance in some measure. Since the others could substitute, good works were not really indispensable. Weber's not-quite-accurate impression that they were stemmed from his inattention to these alternative fruits.

Besides good works, two important fruits of faith, repentance and sanctification, have been discussed above. Since Puritan salvation anxieties stemmed more from sin than from a paucity of good works (see Baxter 1653:397), these two, by their nature, could provide direct reassurance to the doubtful in addition to confirming faith. Beyond these, faith expressed itself through a number of fruits, including joyful hearing of the word, reverence for ministers, and condemnation of the negligent (Perkins 1970:III, 359; Perkins quoted by Porter 1971:283); love of God (Downame [1604] 1974:II, 288); thankfulness to Christ (ibid.); the spirit of prayer (Preston 1629:18; Downame [1604] 1974:II, 236; Ball 1632:223; Perkins [1606] 1972:I, 76; see also Baxter 1653:446); Christian love, especially of the brethren (Downame [1604] 1974:II, 195; Perkins 1970:III, 371); hatred of sin (Perkins 1970:III, 371; see also Downame [1604] 1974:II, 229, 288, 512); obedience to God (Downame [1604] 1974:II, 282); and "zeale of Gods glorie" (ibid.:II, 195, 229, 288, 512).[7]

Although good works were putatively necessary for assurance of salvation, alternative routes and signs undercut their indispensability in practice. Alternative means were available to confirm faith. This mitigated the need to evince good works, including economic works.

Good works also lost importance because their ability to validate faith was compromised by everyone's human imperfections (Downame [1604] 1974:II, 255, 415, 583; III, 601, 635; Baxter 1653:98, 208, 256 and cited by Keeble 1982:72, 135; Hill [1613] 1975:171–72). All human works were polluted and defiled (Perkins [1606] 1972:I, 24, 72–73; 1970:III, 476; Ball 1632:383; Ames [1639] 1975:III, 82; Downame [1604] 1974:II, 572 and *passim*), so it was impossible to perform *good* works (Perkins [1606] 1972:I, 71; see also Wilcox cited by Mosse 1968:108 and Cartwright 1599:11, 13–14). "As for power to accomplish any good worke," Ball (1632:396–97) declared, "we have it not." The problem was that only *good* works attested to faith, not corrupt works. Lake (1982:162) finds it paradoxical that Puritans' faith was to be validated by imperfect works.

One way out of this paradox was for the works to become good. And, indeed, the works of the faithful could be accepted as perfect because their sinful parts were forgiven through Christ (Downame [1604] 1974:II, 590; III, 630; Perkins [1606] 1972:I, 184; III, 610–11).[8]

Still, one could not know if a person's works were good without knowing if the person had faith. According to Perkins (1970:III, 458; [1606] 1972:I, 70; II, 266; III, 610, 611), a work had to be carried out in faith to be good. Similarly, in Ball's (1632:372, see also pp. 221, 388–89) view, "That act . . . which is not animated by faith . . . is but the naked carkese of a good worke, without life or soule" (see also Baxter 1678:II, 79; Downame [1604] 1974:I, 81; II, 194–95, 200, 320, 589, 590).

Because actions were good works only if the doer had faith, it was virtually impossible to know that good works had been performed unless their perpetrator was known to be saved (see Flavel 1968:V, 522; see also Perkins 1970:III, 464; [1606] 1972:I, 68; Ball 1632:258; Ames [1639] 1975: III, 82; Downame [1604] 1974:II, 589–90). Hence, deeds could not testify for those of unknown regeneracy.[9] Flavel (1968:V, 522, 525; see also Lake 1982:134, 159) taught that the works of the elect and of the unregenerate were usually difficult to tell apart. Both could perform similar actions.

It was difficult to confirm faith through works because a work that was "goodly . . . in the eyes of men" might "bee not the fruites of a lively faith" (Downame [1604] 1974:I, 81). Of course, if it were not, then it could not confirm faith (see Baxter 1653:116 and Coolidge 1970:131). This indeterminacy weakened the value of works for identifying the elect. Works were not infallible signs, but only rough guides (see Lake 1982:134 and Keeble 1982:163).

FAITH VERSUS WORKS

Given that both faith and works could evidence election, it is important to know which one predominated as the chief sign. If faith was paramount, then the quest for certainty would have normally led to an internal search of the heart; but if good works held priority, it would have led to action and had a stronger impact on economic behavior.

Weber ([1904-5] 1958:111) judged that the testimony of faith would prove unsatisfactory, and stressed the "necessity" of proving one's faith through worldly activity (see ibid.:121 and 228 note 41; also pp. 112, 114 and [1922] 1968:575). He ([1922] 1968:570) emphasized works over faith, but faith actually received more weight than good works.

The Important Role of Faith

Faith was important to salvation because of the critical role it played in the salvation process. The covenant was received by faith (Downame [1604] 1974:II, 207; see also Baxter 1653:50 and Peter cited by Stearns 1954:50) and the sins of the faithful were pardoned (Baxter 1653:49 and 1678:II, 144; Hill [1613] 1975:168; Ball 1632:88, 90, 101, 115, 218–19; Downame [1604] 1974:II, 304, 460; Saltmarsh 1649:177; Perkins 1970:III, 380). Christ was won and his benefits as savior applied to a person's case through faith (see Dent [1601] 1974:415; Downame [1604] 1974:II, 201, 478, 564, 571–72; see also Baxter 1678:IV, 273, 1653:49 and [1650] 1962:34). Faith was important because Christ's role as savior was central. Only faith justified the believer (Dering quoted by Emerson 1968:64; Downame [1604] 1974:II, 82, 571, 577, 579). Even when it was accompanied by good works (see above), the works could not cause justification (Downame [1604] 1974:II, 152, 574, 576 and *passim*; Ball 1632:222, 253; Perkins 1970:III, 258; 1601:77, 88; [1606] 1972:II, 362; Baxter [1650] 1962:54).

The Primacy of Faith

Consistent with its greater role in the salvation process, a greater evidentiary weight was placed on faith than on works. In Baxter's (1653:85, 86) view, faith was the "first evidence" and the "main Evidence" of election. Indeed, he (1653:86) considered it "the most Infallible evidence of our salvation, and therefore the fittest mark to try by." Similarly, Downame ([1604] 1974:I, 55) called it the most necessary part of the armor, and Cartwright (1599:12) taught that "without beleefe all other thinges are as nothing."

Lake (1982:167–68) has pointed out the Puritan stress on faith. Consistent with his conclusion, Baxter (1678:IV, 273; see also I, 173) called faith "the Condition sine qua non." Likewise, Hooker (quoted by Emerson

1968:230) said, "No man can be saved but he must believe." Downame ([1604] 1974:II, 319; see also pp. 209, 280, 361, 443 and Ball 1632:267) concurred: "Neither is it possible, that without faith wee should ever attaine unto salvation."

McGee (1976:8) has argued that the Puritans emphasized faith more than "good Christian behavior." Ames (quoted by Sprunger 1972:146), for example, held that "faith holds the first place and spiritual observance the second." He (quoted by Sprunger 1972:146) opposed "too much emphasis on good works." In the new covenant, he (quoted by Mosse 1968:89) taught, "it is man's belief rather than his performance which is important."

Works did not replace the testimony of faith either in the formal doctrine or at the pastoral level (compare Weber [1904–5] 1958:111–12). For example, Downame's ([1604] 1974:II, 196) advice was to acquire faith's "sense and feeling." Typically, works were viewed as just a *supplement* to faith. Tyndale, for example, felt that "assurance was an inseparable part of 'feeling' faith, further witnessed to by good works" (see Breward 1970:III, 94).

The direct testimony of faith diminished the need to demonstrate salvation through works. Good conduct was needed only when faith could not be demonstrated directly. But if faith were apparent, there was no separate need to exhibit works. Since all the marks of election were there together or not at all, then finding any one assured that all were present (see Downame [1604] 1974:II, 270–71). This obviated the need for the faithful to demonstrate works. With faith, works were certain to follow. "Our doctrine," said Preston (quoted by Sprunger 1972:158) was "that faith only is required" and "the rest will follow upon it."

Works were unnecessary in practice because one could pass the trial without them. A person might still be saved despite no "fruites of good workes" (Downame [1604] 1974:II, 481; see also Ames [1639] 1975:II, 16, 17). As Downame ([1604] 1974:II, 573, 575–76, see also p. 150; see also Ball 1632:212 and Dorothy Stockton diary:12) noted, "to him that worketh not, but beleeveth in him that iustifieth the ungodly, his faith is counted for righteousnesse." Thus, works were not required as evidence.

In sum, the centrality of faith as a requirement for salvation made it critical as evidence, at the expense of works. When good works were sought as evidence, it was not primarily for their own sake, but to confirm faith (e.g., Downame [1604] 1974:II, 143, 540). They could not show election without faith. Works supplemented faith as a sign rather than supplanting it. Their role was subordinate to faith. They did not reduce its importance.

Salvation by faith was more important than Weber ([1904–5] 1958:111, 114–17) thought, and good works less important.[10] Although the latter were a sign of salvation, they did not receive the highest priority, but were one among various signs that were stressed. Hence, the pursuit of good works was just one possible path to assurance.

A LIFE OF GOOD WORKS

This section further explores the importance of good works in the quest for assurance. The greater the number of good works needed, the more frequent their performance. Weber ([1904–5] 1958:117) has written that "The God of Calvinism demanded . . . not single good works, but a life of good works combined into a unified system." The state of grace was proved, he (ibid.:118) said, "in the whole meaning of life" as expressed in "every action." Hence, good works had to be performed constantly. If Weber's assessment of Puritanism were accurate, then the performance of good works must have played a very prominent part in the life of the believer. But he exaggerated the requirement for a "life of good works." Evidence follows.

To begin with, it is clear that the unit of judgment was the Puritan life rather than the particular act, just as Weber said. Flavel (1968:V, 562), Baxter (1678:IV, 275; see also I, 384), Perkins (quoted by Reilly 1948:35), Ames (quoted by Mosse 1968:72), and Preston (quoted in ibid.:114) agreed that a person was judged "in the general course and tenor of his life" rather than by "some one deed" or "by that which is unusual or extraordinary."

As Weber ([1904–5] 1958:115–17) claimed, single good works were denied the importance they enjoyed in Roman Catholicism, closing a major loophole. Downame ([1604] 1974:II, 242; see also III, 599) denied that "one or two or many actions" sufficed, nor was it enough to perform "many excellent duties and good workes." Being righteous by fits was not enough (Downame [1604] 1974: II, 242). People were to lead a holy life (Downame [1604] 1974:I, 1; Baxter 1678:II, 123; Hill [1613] 1975:53; Perkins [1606] 1972:I, 87).

Nevertheless, the preachers were ambiguous about just how much good needed to be accomplished to make up a good life. Their pronouncements could be quite imprecise. At one point, for example, Downame ([1604] 1974:II, 479, see also pp. 480, 578) declared good works necessary "in some measure"; and Baxter ([1650] 1962:34) called their omission "not the least evil." In light of this ambiguity, pastoral teachings were uneven about the plenitude of good works required. Some divines fluctuated between demanding continual good works and accepting very few to indicate election.

Sometimes standards were set quite high. Continuous good works were stated as a requirement. People's goodness had to follow a "constant course" (Downame [1604] 1974:I, 42; II, 242, 290, 322; see also Perkins [1606] 1972:I, 63–64, 184). A person's motion had to be strong and constant enough to reach the goal (Baxter [1650] 1962:34, 35, 95).

Perkins ([1606] 1972:III, 615) and Bulkeley (quoted by Coolidge 1970:121–22) pointed to a prescribed "way of life for us to walk in" in order to obtain salvation (see also Sibbes quoted by McGee 1976:60; Downame [1604] 1974:I, 58; Keeble 1982:77). It was a life of holy duties (Baxter 1678:I, 231 and II, 123). People were to serve Christ "all the daies of our life" (Downame [1604] 1974:II, 376–77, see also pp. 240, 416; see also Baxter 1678:I, 106, but also see IV, 265). To be assured, Downame ([1604] 1974:II, 480–81) preached, "we spend our lives in God's service." Baxter (1678:I, 108) told his readers to "do good" as "the Trade and business of your lives." He (1678:II, 115 and IV, 276) urged them to "do all the good you can in the world." They were to ask themselves in the morning what good they could do today and in the evening what good they had done that day (Baxter 1653:337). Each day was provided "for some good work" (Baxter 1678:I, 108); good was not to be performed just "now and then" or "when it fals in your way" (Baxter 1653:336; see also 1678:I, 108 and IV, 261). Charity, for example, was to be performed daily in a constant course rather than occasionally (Baxter 1678:IV, 261). And everyone was to settle into a calling to provide "ordinary and orderly imployment" (Baxter 1678:I, 377, 382). Similarly, Downame ([1604] 1974:II, 540, see also p. 143) stipulated that to confirm faith one had to be "continually conversant in good works."

But despite this rigor, it was also common for the divines to minimize the goodness required (see Breward 1970:III, 95; Perkins 1970:III, 158). In this minimalist view, any fruit was sufficient because it showed the operation of the holy Spirit (Downame [1604] 1974:II, 153, 479, 480; Perkins 1615:10; Ames [1639] 1975:II, 17). Even with "good works few and imperfect," the "worke of Gods spirit" was evident and "effectuall to salvation" (see Downame [1604] 1974:III, 607, 637 and also II, 481, 589, 591; Perkins 1615:31–32; Keeble 1982:71). No greater fullness of good works was necessary. He "doth not require of us a whole harvest of goodnes" but only "the first fruites thereof" (Downame [1604] 1974:II, 591).[11]

As a prime example, not so many works were needed to confirm faith. Indeed, continual good works would be expected as the fruits of a perfect faith; however, since faith was "imperfect in this life, therefore the gifts which we receive thereby, are also imperfect" (see Perkins [1606] 1972:I, 179–80).

Perkins ([1606] 1972:II, 277; 1970:III, 373), Downame ([1604] 1974:III, 607, 624, 626), Ball (1632:288), and Baxter ([1650] 1962:36, 257–58; 1653:148) all commented on the weak grace of the average Christian and even of "the most holy men" (see Perkins 1615:31). This smallness of grace led to a feeble motion (Baxter [1650] 1962:36). Hence, a life entirely composed of good was unrealistic, even for the elect (see Baxter 1678:IV, 276 and also Downame [1604] 1974:III, 629).

Accordingly, people were only required "to do good works, as much as we are able," which was "not so terribly" (Baxter 1678:I, 107; see also Keeble 1982:136). Since high standards created fear, since people were not to fear unnecessarily, and since Satan used excessive fear to discourage Christians, Downame ([1604] 1974:II, 589) branded it a temptation of Satan to believe that God's children "doe continually the workes of righteousnesse."[12] In other words, continual good works were not really needed.

A second form of minimalist reasoning also hinged on the impossibility of perfect performance. Since truly good works were impossible, the new covenant provided for judgment on other grounds, "accepting the will for the deed" (Downame [1604] 1974:II, 241; see also I, 122; II, 516, 591; III, 599; Perkins [1606] 1972:I, 183–85 and cited by Reilly 1948:34; Dent [1601] 1974:427–28; Ball, 1632:175; Ames quoted by Mosse 1968:71; Preston quoted by Mosse 1968:115). According to Downame ([1604] 1974:III, 630), "that which we would performe and cannot, he esteemeth as though it were performed." Baxter's (1678:IV, 275; see also p. 263 and I, 107) view was similar: "what you truly would be, that you are" even if you "fail in the execution." God judged the quality of the "indeavour" rather than of the deed (Perkins [1606] 1972:I, 181–82, 184; II, 286; Perkins quoted by Reilly 1948:34; Downame [1604] 1974:I, 51; II, 127, 240; Preston cited by Mosse 1968:115).

The sufficiency of earnest effort softened the requirement to produce works. Although the Christian ideal was to be "rich in good works" (Baxter 1678:IV, 265), the Puritans could be "Christians rather in our affections and desires than in our workes and abilities" (Downame [1604] 1974:I, 122; see also II, 238 and III, 637). This sufficed because those who "unfainedly indevour" could be "sure we shall be saved" (Dent [1601] 1974:262). Someone who *willed* good would be saved, "though hee finde no meanes to performe that which is good" (Downame [1604] 1974:III, 607). There was "not any achievement" but "a sincere disposition to serve God more truly" (see Keeble 1982:134).

In some pronouncements, endeavor had to lead to lively action. "We must . . . leave bare words, and come to deedes," Dent ([1601] 1974:384, see also p. 385; see also Downame [1604] 1974:I, 61, 83; Baxter [1650] 1962:30; Henry Crosse quoted by Mosse 1968:115) insisted. Preston (quoted by McGee 1976:64) held that election was proved "Not by your desires or good meanings, but by your actions," which were "the things that men see and feel." Similarly, Baxter (1678:IV, 263) felt that "if there be a readiness to will, there will be a performance also"; there was no true resolution, he (1653:273) maintained, that never came to performance. True, hearty willingness would "shew itself in actions" (Baxter 1653:100, see also p. 146). This call to action suggests that some degree of success was necessary to confirm the sincerity of one's endeavors (Baxter 1678:IV, 275 and 1653:100). However, the degree of actual success needed for this purpose was never specified very clearly. And it was sometimes said that those with few good works could still be "accepted of God" (Downame [1604] 1974:III, 637; see also I, 129 and II, 590, 591; Ball 1632:114–15). So, all in all, not much accomplishment was needed; a continuous round of good deeds would be superfluous. This countered the press to accumulate multifold performances.

Insofar as one's fate would not be judged by the number or consistency of accomplishments, there was little incentive to make good works weigh heavily in Puritan lives. Indeed, Baxter reported that many failed to live a life of good works. As indicated in Chapter 4, he (1653:339) wished that good works were practiced "more faithfully"; even the rich, with considerable resources, undertook few good works with their wealth (Baxter 1653:337–39). Likewise, Perkins (1970:III, 84–85) saw no treadmill of good works.

GOOD WORKS AND ECONOMIC CONDUCT

Weber ([1904–5] 1958:115–16) thought that the doctrine of good works intensified capitalist action by tying economic behaviors to supernatural sanctions. He argued that dedication to one's calling and working to grow rich evidenced election because they produced good works, which were necessary characteristics of the elect. Thus, capitalist behavior was reinforced by the quest for certainty. In this view good works were a key link between salvation and economic conduct.

However, that link would have depended, on the one hand, on the strength of the connection between good works and certainty and, on the other, the strength of the connection between good works and economic conduct. As was seen above the connection between works and salvation was weaker than Weber ([1904–5] 1958:115–16) thought.[13] Furthermore, it will be seen below that the connection between works and economic conduct was also weak.

It will be shown that material achievements were just one type of good work. Good works were of many types, and many kinds of good works could serve as signs of election. Furthermore, spiritual works were more important than material achievements. As relatively minor works, economic works were not ideal ways to do good.

The Nature of Good Works

The nature of good works was explained carefully by the preachers. The word "worke" was the same as "action" (Ames [1639] 1975:III, 81). "Good works" were, most generally, "all actions ... that are morally good" (Baxter 1678:I, 106). To be morally good a work had to be an act of obedience to one of God's commands (see Baxter 1678:I, 106; Perkins [1606] 1972:I, 69, 70–71; 1970:III, 458). It was forbidden for individuals to "make choice" of good works; without a commandment, there could be no obedience and, hence, no pleasing of God (Ames [1639] 1975:III, 82).

A "narrower" conception of good works required them to be "also materially good," producing some "advantage" (Baxter 1678:I, 106–7; see also Dent [1601] 1974:385). Good works were "profitable to men," who were "the better for them" (Baxter 1678:IV, 258). A good work "must tend to good effect, for the benefit of man" (ibid.:IV, 259). Ames ([1639] 1975:III, 81) rejected this narrower view, i.e., that good works must "produce something, that is good and profitable unto men"; to the contrary, works "usefull and good unto other men" could be "in many respects evill" (ibid.). His view is seconded by Downame's ([1604] 1974:I, 80–82) sharp distinction between religious works and civic virtues. Yet, in contrast, Perkins ([1606] 1972:I, 69–70) held that "if an action indifferent, comes in the case, of furthering the good of the Commonwealth, or Church, it ceaseth to be indifferent, and comes under commandement." In these cases a material good could become a moral good. In sum, there was disagreement over whether material advantage was necessary and/or sufficient to make a work good.

The Variety of Good Works

For the Puritans "good works" could include a broad range of actions. This served "to confute the doctrine of the Popish church, which teacheth that only almes deedes, and building or maintaining of Churches and religious houses, are the matter of good works" (Perkins [1606] 1972:I, 70). In contrast, according to Keeble (1982:77), "Baxter allows no distinction between our service of God and our workaday lives." Good deeds extended, for example, to the performance of economic and family roles.

In Perkins's ([1606] 1972:I, 69–70) view, it was because of their material advantages that "all kinds of callings and their works, though never so base, may be the matter of good workes." He (1970:III, 458; see also Perkins quoted by George and George 1958:366–67) maintained that "by the right use of every calling the works thereof are made good works, though otherwise they be but mean and base in themselves." Similarly, Baxter (1678:II, 128) taught that "labour ... will be as acceptable to him, as if you had spent all that time in more spiritual exercises." This doctrine allowed every worker "of what condition so ever he be" to perform good works (Perkins [1606] 1972:I, 70). It was unnecessary to be wealthy enough to donate large sums of money.

This evidence supports Weber's tendency to place good works within the calling and undercuts Samuelsson's (1961:46–47) argument that the two types of work were separate. Nevertheless, it is best to distinguish between them. Despite the fact that economic labor could be a good work, it was far from the only or even the chief source of good works in Puritanism.

In fact, the good works most frequently mentioned by Puritan divines were the works of charity (see, for example, Baxter 1678:IV, 259–61 and *passim*; Perkins [1606] 1972:III, 606–8, 610–11, 615; Hieron quoted by Emerson 1968:183; McGee 1976:8, 66). These included feeding the hungry, clothing the naked, taking care of the poor and widowed, giving alms, building almshouses, building and maintaining schools and colleges, maintaining poor students at school, giving religious books and/or religious instruction to the poor, and setting up apprenticeships for poor children (Baxter 1678:I, 109, 233; IV, 225, 260; 1653:338; see also Nuttall 1965:82; Price 1608:20; Hieron quoted by Emerson 1968:183). The sick were to be visited and the sad comforted (Baxter 1678:I, 233); hospitals had to be built (Price 1608:20) and lives saved (Baxter 1678:I, 110; IV, 222, 260, 262). On the lay level, Wallington felt an obligation to relieve the poor (Seaver 1985:128–29, see also p. 124), and his father, John Wallington, Sr., was so charitable that he gave away most of his fortune (see Chapter 2 above).

The works of the calling and of charity were deemed good on account of their material benefits, but in addition there were works with spiritual benefits. Baxter (1678:II, 131; see also I, 233) said, "Do good both to Mens Souls and Bodies." People could benefit souls by aiding the church (Baxter 1653:336–37; [1650] 1962:105; 1678:I, 109, 377; IV, 260). Maintaining a minister was one possibility (Baxter 1678:IV, 260, 262; 1653:337; see also McGee 1976:94), or a scholar studying for the ministry (Baxter 1653:338). One could promote the Gospel, possibly with financial support (Baxter 1653:336–38; 1678:IV, 225); it would help to spread it throughout the world (Baxter 1678:I, 150; IV, 259; see also Nuttall 1965:82). It was also good to help save individual souls (Baxter 1653:100, 337, 339; [1650] 1962:97–101, 104, 105; 1678:I, 109; IV, 260), conferring with them, instructing, persuading, discussing sermons, getting them to give up sins and perform duties, and distributing religious books.

Many other good works stemmed from the fulfillment of religious duties, including praise of God (Baxter 1678:II, 116), giving thanks (Baxter 1678:II, 116; Downame [1604] 1974:I, 50–51), keeping the Sabbath (Baxter 1678:I, 110; see also McGee 1976:94, 177 and Zaret 1985:146–48), taking the sacraments (Baxter 1678:I, 110), meditation (Baxter 1678:I, 231, 233; 1653:96, 436; [1650] 1962:107, 111, 128–29, 184), holy conference (Baxter 1678:I, 233), and prayer (Perkins [1606] 1972: II, 437). In general, worship duties were considered "good works" (see McGee 1976:66).

Puritans were also expected to do good for "the Commonwealth" or state (Baxter 1678: I, 377; IV, 97, 222, 262; 1653:337). These works could involve, for example, the building of bridges (Price 1608:20) or the quenching of fires (Baxter 1678:I, 110 and IV, 222). Other good works were to love "the brethren," i.e., fellow Puritans (Downame [1604] 1974:I, 83; Baxter 1653:245; 1678:I, 149; McGee 1976:207), to love one's neighbor or fellow human (Baxter 1678:I, 110 and IV, 263; Downame [1604] 1974:II, 479), and to love one's enemies (Baxter 1678:I, 149; IV, 260; 1653: 98).

Puritan good works also included works of "Piety" and "Justice" (Baxter 1678:I, 106, 107, 233; 1653:339; Downame [1604] 1974:I, 83; see also McGee 1976:66). There were works of mercy and obedience (Perkins [1606] 1972:III, 614; Downame [1604] 1974:I, 83; see also McGee 1976:66); and suppressing vice was a good (Baxter 1653:339). Finally, there were good works within one's family, including duties to parents, spouse, and children (Baxter 1678:I, 110, 233 and IV, 260, 262), and providing religious instruction (Baxter 1653:339; 1678:II, 131). And good works could be "internal" as well as "external" (Baxter 1678:I, 106; 1653:82).

Good works varied from person to person; each had something different to offer (Baxter 1653:336; 1678:IV, 259). This depended on which talents for doing good had been received from God (Baxter 1653:336; Baxter 1678:I, 108).

In conclusion, besides economic actions, the category of good works included many noneconomic activities. It would be wrong to equate good works with economic tasks and accomplishments. One could perform many other good works without them.[14]

Not only did the broad choice of works make preoccupation with economics less likely, but such a concentration was expressly forbidden. It would have contradicted any claim to be among the saints. Weber ([1904–5] 1958:117) argued that Calvinism required a "life of good works," but a life focused on economic works would have fallen short of this ideal on noneconomic dimensions such as religious practice (see McGee 1976:241). According to Baxter (1653:116), single qualifications were inadequate. Similarly, Flavel (1968:V, 597; see also Perkins quoted by Reilly 1948:34–35 and Downame [1604] 1974:II, 507) warned that "it is a very dangerous sign of hypocrisy, when a man's zeal runs out in one channel of obedience only, and he hath not respect to all Gods commandments." Only the well-rounded Christian could be assured of salvation (see Flavel 1968:V, 598; Perkins quoted by Reilly 1948:34, 35; Perkins [1606] 1972:I, 64; Sibbes quoted by McGee 1976:69). The need for a generally good life undercuts Weber ([1904–5] 1958:178; 1968:630) by denying that economic works could be decisive for gaining assurance.

The Low Priority of Economic Works

Furthermore, economic works were minor works, far from the highest good. For example, Seaver (1985:126, see also p. 125) reports that Wallington considered work a subordinate good. Though admissible as a good work, and as a substitute for charity where funds were lacking, it did not achieve the importance of the more spiritual good works.

In doing good, Baxter (1678:I, 109; IV, 262; see also IV, 260) said to "prefer the souls of men before the body." To convert a sinner and save a soul was "greater than to give a man an alms" (ibid.:I, 109). "A piece of bread is soon eaten, and a penny or a shilling is soon spent," he (1653:337) noted. "But if you could win a Soul to God from sin, that would be a visible everlasting good." Conferring bodily benefits should be "in due subordination," with the ultimate intent of helping the soul (Baxter 1678:II, 131; see also I, 109 and IV, 261–62). Since spiritual matters were much more important than material ones (see ibid.:I, 115), spiritual works were preferable to material achievements. Consistently, spiritual good works were considered the most distinctive marks of the elect. The carnal were inclined toward earthly good, but did little spiritual good (Baxter cited by Keeble 1982:136).

Baxter (1653:336–37 and 1678:I, 231) ranked good works in order of importance. First, promoting the Gospel and the Church helped save "the souls of many" (ibid.). Helping to save individual souls came next (Baxter 1653:337), including "your own souls" and those of "children and servants." Next in priority was the betterment of the Commonwealth (ibid.:337; see also 1678:IV, 262), which provided "Publick benefit" (Baxter 1678:I, 231). Only after these works came provision for people's bodies (Baxter 1653: 337 and 1678:I, 231). This undercuts the notion that labor was "as acceptable" to God as "more spiritual exercises" (see above and Baxter 1678:II, 128; see also Ball 1632:383, 385).

Economic good works, insofar as they served people's bodies, fell into the categories of lowest priority. This implies that doing God's work in this world was not primarily an economic matter. Oftentimes better works could be performed instead. The proper hierarchy of priorities was to be observed (Seaver 1985:124), and Puritans were to learn through study which were the greater works (Baxter 1653:336). Moreover, lesser goods, such as the works of the calling, were limited by their interference with greater goods (Ames [1639] 1975:261).

The status of labor as a good work augmented its importance as a sign of salvation, but as a minor work it could only help assurance in a minor way. Hence, the doctrine of good works did little to connect the calling to the quest for salvation.

The link that works forged between *acquisition* and salvation was even more tenuous because profit-making by itself was not a good work; it was just a means to good works. Accordingly, merchant Elias Pledger (diary:27) limited gain's religious importance: "Riches are no farther useful then as they fit us for the service of God and our generation . . . and therefore they are but means. . . . And therefore the end is to be preferred in our esteem before them." In other words, premia were placed on service directly and on its means, moneymaking, only indirectly. Moreover, since the poor could perform good works just by serving in "base" callings, there was little pressure for them to seek wealth as part of a campaign of works.

In conclusion, judgment through good works produced a mixed economic effect. Since economic diligence and profit could contribute to works, the Puritan salvation drive led in an economic direction. However, noneconomic works might actually have drawn Puritans *away* from their jobs, competing for people's time and energies. Indeed, the higher priority on spiritual actions directed a believer, on balance, *away* from economic life. So, overall, the pursuit of good works did not elevate economic action.

RELIGIOUS PRACTICE AND SALVATION

Additional signs of the elect, and, by the same token, other directional pulls of the salvation doctrine, included the actions of religious participation. Religious practice was required to prove election (McGee 1976:241; see also Downame [1604] 1974:Epistle Dedicatory; I, 81). To follow civic morals would just make people "good natured worldlings" in Downame's ([1604] 1974:I, 80–81) view; it would not show that they were regenerate. Hence, "a lively hope" required an awakening to spiritual matters (Baxter [1650] 1962:184) and the performance of the exercises of piety (Ames [1639] 1975:II, 35; Downame [1604] 1974:I, 81; see also Preston cited by McGee 1976:180).

Religious Practice as a Sign of the Elect

Election could be confirmed, according to Baxter (1678:I, 17; see also Downame [1604] 1974:II, 235 and Zaret 1985:141), by hearing or reading the word of God, public worship of God, private prayer, and confession of sin. Conversely, neglect of "God's worship" was a bad sign (Ames [1639] 1975:II, 5; Downame [1604] 1974:II, 235).

Prayer was a sign of regeneracy (see Preston 1629:18) because it was an effect of sanctification and a testimony of the Spirit (Perkins 1970:III,

257–58). The elect showed a capacity for prayer, which was comforting (Ames [1639] 1975:II, 24; Baxter 1653:101, 446–49; Lake 1982:157; Dent [1601] 1974:34). In contrast, reprobates neglected prayer (Ames [1639] 1975:II, 5; Dent [1601] 1974:34). Ball (1632:182, see also pp. 103, 104) recommended earnest prayer to make people "feele their doubting and feare to vanish."

Likewise, one could gain assurance from hearing the word of God (Downame [1604] 1974:II, 224). The saved attended frequent sermons (Perkins cited by Porter 1971:283; Baxter 1653: 101). Longing after God's word was a sign of grace, and the elect heard it joyfully (Ames [1639] 1975: II, 10; Downame [1604] 1974:II, 235; Dent, [1601] 1974:34; see also McGee 1976:181–82). But the carnal neglected it (Downame [1604] 1974:II, 217, 320), were content to be unaffected by it (Downame [1604] 1974: II, 491; Dent [1601] 1974:34), or were alienated from it (Ames [1639] 1975:II, 5).

Keeping the Sabbath was another indication of election. The truly converted sanctified the Sabbath (Preston cited by McGee 1976:177, 181–82; Dent [1601] 1974:257). To do otherwise was a mark of the condemned (Preston quoted by McGee 1976:180).

Elected Christians had an affinity for religious practice (McGee 1976:241). They enjoyed religious discourse (Downame [1604] 1974:II, 228, 229, 236, 247, 474; Flavel 1968:V, 577). To illustrate, Elias Pledger (diary:8–9, see also pp. 11–12) was confident of his true conversion partly because he delighted in communion with God and felt good in prayer.

The Means of Salvation

Another sign that a person would be saved was that person's use of the means prescribed for salvation (Downame [1604] 1974:II, 182, 471–72, 489, 517; Hill [1613] 1975:53). According to Downame (ibid.:III, 637–38; see also II, 235), people's use of the means tending to eternal life were "forerunners of our salvation." Conversely, anyone not employing the necessary means could not be undergoing the process of salvation and could not be among the saved. These means included prayer, meditation, Bible-reading, taking the Sacraments, hearing God's word preached, conference with the brethren, self-examination, and attempts at self-improvement (ibid.:I, 63; II, 208, 224–25, 316–20, 471; Baxter 1678:I, 386; Wallington Folger diary:261, 263; Pledger diary:27).

Closeness with God

Another important sign was a direct personal focus on God, which involved "living unto God" and rejoicing in the happiness to come with God (Baxter 1678:I, 45; see also [1696] 1931:125). Grace was confirmed for those who enjoyed God, sought him out, and had communion and fellowship with him (Ames [1639] 1975:II, 10; Baxter quoted by Knott 1980:83; Ball 1632:115, 169; Perkins [1606] 1972:I, 79; Downame [1604] 1974:II, 229, 236, 474; Flavel 1968:V, 568, 571, 577, 598) but was doubtful for a stranger to the life of God (Ames [1639] 1975:II, 4, 5). The "truest evidence of saving grace" was said to be a heart centered upon God and heaven (Baxter [1650] 1962:108–9; see also pp. 36, 85, 86 and 1653:88, 95, 229; Downame [1604] 1974:II, 228, 229, 236, 247, 474; Flavel 1968: V, 577–78).[15]

Love

A related sign for identifying the elect was their love of God (Perkins [1606] 1972:I, 84; 1601:67; Downame [1604] 1974:II, 141, 227, 288; Baxter [1696] 1931:118, 125; Baxter 1653:71; Baxter [1650] 1962:86; Ames [1639] 1975:II, 16); but having no love of God led to doubts (Baxter 1653:233–34; Perkins 1970:III, 253–54). Additionally, the saved loved the brethren (Sibbes cited by McGee 1976:172; Dent [1601] 1974:33; Ames [1639] 1975:II, 10–11, 16; Baxter 1653:115, 425; Downame [1604] 1974:II, 141, 192, 202, 243; Ball 1632:256) because the latter were Christians and "visible saints" (Perkins [1606] 1972:I, 79, 82, 83, 100–1 and 1970:III, 257–58, 371).[16] The elect preferred godly company (Preston cited by McGee 1976:183); conversely, the nonelect were uncomfortable in the company of the "saints" (Winthrop cited by McGee 1976:184; see also Ames [1639] 1975:II, 4). God did not save those with "no fellowship in the communion of saints" (Downame [1604] 1974:II, 280; see also Dent [1601] 1974:34, 234).

Worldliness

In contrast to the heavenly minded, whoever delighted in the world more than in God was worldly (see Chapter 2). However, it was necessary to give up the world for heaven, and those who could not would not be saved (Baxter 1678:I, 18, 221; Baxter [1650] 1962:30; Baxter 1653:117; Downame [1604] 1974:I, 95; II, 236, 471; Perkins 1970:III, 465). On the positive side, those who renounced the world were promised eternal life (Ball 1632:262; Downame [1604] 1974:II, 183, 236, 310, 474; Perkins [1606] 1972:I, 84; see also Baxter 1653:88, 115, 117, 172–73). However, predominant worldliness was a "certain sign of death" (Baxter 1678:I, 214, 220; Baxter [1650] 1962:30; 1653:286–87; Downame [1604] 1974:I, 33–34; II, 236). Baxter (1678:I, 222) foretold that the "Love of the world" would damn "millions . . . for ever"; it was "the commonest cause of mans damnation" (ibid.:I, 216, 219).

Although Weber judged Puritanism to be innerworldly in the pull of its salvation doctrine, it was clearly necessary to moderate worldly activities in order to display the signs of salvation. And insofar as economic behavior was considered worldly, it was to be cut back accordingly (see Baxter 1678:I, 5). Typically, concern over riches was considered worldly, and was to be disdained (see, for example, Perkins [1606] 1972:III, 478; Baxter 1678:I, 148, 215). It was a sign of a worldling (Baxter 1678:I, 215). Since the only exception, the quest for wealth to serve God, was just a special case, the pull of the salvation doctrine away from worldliness discouraged profit-seeking.

In comparison to pursuing wealth, work at one's calling was less frequently branded as worldly. Sometimes it was, as when Downame ([1604] 1974:II, 316, 320) referred to "earthly businesses" and "base" commodities and when Wallington viewed the overindustrious as worldly wise (see Seaver 1985:126). Indeed, Baxter (quoted by Keeble 1982:77) acknowledged that some "think . . . it is but worldly business." However, he concurred with Preston (1629:52) that we were "serving God and men in our calling." If work was performed to serve God, it was not worldly and was not condemned (see Baxter 1678:II, 78).

Overall, salvation teachings sometimes pulled behavior in an innerworldly direction as Weber argued but sometimes pulled away from the world. The direction of their pull was much more mixed than Weber implied. And compared to the innerworldly, their pull away from the world seems at least as strong.

THE HOLY SPIRIT

One prominent sign of salvation, as indicated in Chapter 5, was possession of the holy Spirit, which testified to a person's election (Perkins [1606] 1972:I, 75 and 1970:III, 257; Downame [1604] 1974:II, 211–13, 218–21, 479, 519–20, 588; Baxter 1653:68–69, 411; Baxter [1650] 1962:157; Baxter [1696] 1931:110; Baxter 1678:II, 144; Blake quoted by Coolidge 1970:126). According to Baxter (1678:II, 144), it was "Gods mark upon his chosen." On the other hand, the absence of the Spirit led to doubt (Baxter 1653:444; Baxter [1696] 1931:110; Downame [1604] 1974:II, 286).

Weber's analysis ignores the holy Spirit and its importance as a sign, perhaps because its magical nature did not square with his rationalized view of Puritanism.[17] This sign also undercuts the Weber thesis insofar as assurance could be gained by discovering it inside oneself rather than by working at one's calling.

According to Downame ([1604] 1974:II, 212, 219–24, 462, 519, 588; but see also Baxter 1653:68, 69, 70, 158, 444, 448), people could feel the Spirit "powerful in them"; "it crieth alowd in our hearts . . . and witnesseth . . . that we are sonnes of God." Another evidence of the Spirit was to feel inner conflict between spirit and flesh (Downame [1604] 1974:II, 228,

520–22; III, 635; see also I, 125 and Baxter 1653:172–75, 177, 239–40, 435). Then the Spirit was at work inside enacting salvation.

Besides these direct testimonies, the Spirit could also be discovered by its fruits (Downame [1604] 1974:II, 215–16, 220, 479; Perkins [1606] 1972:I, 76; Baxter 1653:68, 141; Blake quoted by Coolidge 1970:126). Perkins (1970:III, 257–58) noted that election could be judged by the holy Ghost's effects. It left its marks through its workings (Baxter 1653:158); and they were the usual graces that Christians sought through self-examination (Baxter 1653:68–69, 79).

THE GRACES

Since the holy Spirit gave the elect their Christian graces, those possessing the graces could know that the Spirit was in them (Downame [1604] 1974:Epistle Dedicator; II, 313; III, 638; Baxter 1653:69, 79, 444–45; Saltmarsh [1647] 1847:177; Blake quoted by Coolidge 1970:126). Hence, one's estate could be judged by one's graces (Baxter 1653:67, 75, 82–84, 177–78 and [1650] 1962:157; Flavel 1968:V, 530, 536; Downame [1604] 1974:II, 141). In fact, the graces were important evidences of election (see Baxter cited by Keeble 1982:135; Dent [1601] 1974:279; Wallington Folger diary:218, 229). These included the virtues of Christ (Downame [1604] 1974:II, 313). Accordingly, faith, hope, obedience, piety, holiness, knowledge, temperance, sobriety, patience, love, godliness, brotherly kindness, mercy, truth, compassion, industry, humility, meekness, peacefulness, chastity, contentedness, keeping the Sabbath, and reverence of God's name were signs of salvation (Baxter 1653:115, 146, 234, 270–77 and cited by Keeble 1982:106, 122; Dent [1601] 1974:257–59; Perkins 1601:67; [1606] 1972:I, 87; III, 614; Perkins cited by Reilly 1948:31, 34; Flavel 1968:V, 572–73; Downame [1604] 1974:II, 141, 192, 240–42, 258, 280, 479, 520, 540; III, 606, 637–39; Hill [1613] 1975:53; see also McGee 1976:94, 117–18, 180).[18]

PERFORMING DUTIES

The performance of duties was another positive sign (Saltmarsh [1647] 1847:177; Downame [1604] 1974:II, 230; Baxter cited by Keeble 1982:135 and 1653:75, 83, 232–33, 281, 314–16, 435). It revealed the grace of obedience, and was part of a holy life. Conversely, the neglect of duty marked the hypocrites (Downame [1604] 1974:II, 222; see also Ball 1632:169 and Baxter [1650] 1962:30, 35, 36, 123), who had no interest in duty (Flavel 1968:567, 595) or no vigor in duties (Baxter 1653:423). It was cause for doubt and a sign of "cursed unbelief" (Baxter [1650] 1962:102; see also Baxter cited by Keeble 1982:87; but see also Baxter 1653:91, 99, 102, 114, 122, 264, 437). Wallington's example shows that the laity connected duty and salvation. He (Folger diary:218) was stirred to duty by thoughts of salvation; and he (ibid.) felt that the performance of "all holy duties" gained eternity.

Not all duties were equally important as signs of salvation. According to Baxter (1653:101) some duties were necessary for salvation because they were "part of the condition of the Covenant." They included "confessing Christ before men when we are called to it; confessing sins; Praying; shewing mercy to the poor; forgiving wrongs; hearing and yielding to Gods Word, & c." (ibid.). But "God hath not laid so great a stress or necessity" on some other duties; performance of the latter signified election only to the extent that they reflected the person's "true Obedience" (ibid.).[19] Of course, true obedience forbade the omission of "any known duty" (ibid.; see also McGee 1976:69, 88; Perkins [1606] 1972:I, 64; Flavel 1968:V, 597), so none could be overlooked entirely.

Since Baxter (1653:101) omitted the work of the calling from this list of essential duties, he apparently considered it low priority for showing oneself to be a dutiful saint. The belief that duties revealed the elect gave only a small boost to the calling's value as a sign. Furthermore, the impetus to prove election through duty pulled away from economics and toward required religious duties which were more central to salvation. All in all, the need to perform duties to assure salvation pulled toward an intermediate work level consistent with both one's calling and religious practice.

LABOR IN ONE'S CALLING

The salvation doctrine provided some reinforcement to the norm of hard work in a calling; and to the extent that it did, there is support for Weber's ([1904–5] 1958:178, see also pp. 121–28) idea that duty in the calling was enforced by supernatural premia. However, the actual degree of reinforcement was weak.[20] It was much more common for diligence in the calling to be mentioned as a duty than as a sign of election in itself.

Although Dent ([1601] 1974:34) listed faithfulness in one's calling as a sign of salvation, it was rarely singled out for mention as a mark of the elect. Likewise, Dent (ibid.:35, 154, 257) was among the minority citing industry as a positive sign and idleness as a negative sign.[21] The majority of divines failed to mention either of these signs. In fact, some, such as Baxter (1678:II, 128), Downame ([1604] 1974:II, 315–16), and Preston (1629:89–91), made it clear that business and salvation were two separate pursuits. Owing to this dissensus, salvation needs could pull to the workplace just the followers of those few divines who stressed industry as a sign.

Economic duties were rarely singled out for special attention in Puritan salvation doctrine. At best, diligence in the calling was but one virtue among the many qualities of an elect Christian (see Keeble 1982:122).

One ambiguity that reduced its value as a sign was that reprobates could work hard at their jobs, too (see ibid.:135). What distinguished them was not their different degrees of industry, but their motives. As Baxter (1678:I, 383; see also Perkins 1970:III, 456–57) taught, it was "the labour and diligence of a believing Saint, and not that of a Covetous Worldling . . . that tends to save the soul." Diligence for worldly motives was "but a making haste to Hell" (Baxter 1678:I, 383). Moreover, too much industry could be a bad sign because those who took "too much businesse" upon them might neglect salvation (Preston 1629:91; see also Downame [1604] 1974:II, 315–16). As noted above, Wallington considered them worldlings, not saints (see Seaver 1985:126).

Those anxious about their state of grace expressed no worries about their economic diligence; sometimes they worried that they were devoting too much time to business, not too little. Although some Puritans may have been drawn to the calling by their quest for certainty, most would not have connected job performance to their state of grace. For these, the pursuit of *noneconomic* evidence of grace pulled away from the workplace.

Clearly, Weber ([1904–5] 1958:178) exaggerated work in the calling as a means for attaining certainty. It played a very secondary role in identifying the elect. Many other signs received more stress from the Puritans. [22]

WEALTH AS A SIGN OF SALVATION

The connection between profit and salvation was as tenuous as that between work and salvation. Only a minority of divines considered wealth and gain to be signs of God's favor and election. Very few mentioned it among the signs to watch for, and some denied its indicative power explicitly (see, for example, Baxter 1678:I, 218, 219 and Downame [1604] 1974:II, 219–20).

On the positive side, Hill ([1613] 1975:46) suspected that riches "may be pledges to mee of heavenly riches," and Perkins (1970:III, 463) taught that only the reborn prospered "at God's hand." However, in opposition, most Puritan preachers discouraged assessment of one's state of grace on the basis of wealth (see, for example, Baxter 1678:II, 126; see also George and George 1958:358; Hudson 1949:9–10; Samuelsson 1961:37, 47). According to Swinnock (1663:111, see also p. 338), "They may be high and have large possessions on earth, whose portions shall be lowest in hell." Similarly,

Ashton (quoted by Lake 1982:136) considered outward prosperity "no proper token of God's child." And Dent and Ball denied that worldly success was a sign of election (see Seaver 1985:134, 137).

Since it was difficult for the wealthy to be saved, and indeed the rich had less chance of salvation than others (see Chapter 4), wealth could even be deemed a *negative* indication. For instance, Baxter (1678:I, 219) warned, "wo unto you who are rich, for you have received your consolation: wo unto you that are full, for ye shall hunger." In many cases, the affluent were suspected of covetousness. According to Ames ([1639] 1975:261–62), Dent (quoted by Seaver 1985: 134), and Baxter (1678:I, 215), those who "made too much ado" about prosperity showed signs of covetousness and were quite possibly condemned. To overlove riches was "a most certain sign of a state of death," especially where the love of riches had the upper hand over God and holiness (Baxter 1678:I, 220, see also pp. 214, 215).

The pursuit of wealth was also a negative sign. Puritans were supposed to be content with what they had. Their "times and calling" were not to be "spent in gathering earthly treasures"; to do so "set bars on heaven's gates" (Perkins 1970:III, 464–65; see also Baxter 1678:I, 220). If one had "set thyself to rise in the world," Baxter ([1650] 1962:123; see also 1653:165) warned, "heaven and thy soul are very great strangers."

Puritan ethics and Puritan salvation doctrine were not always consistent. For instance, though it was a duty to become rich for God, performing that duty did not figure prominently among the marks of election. But Puritan ethics and salvation doctrine *were* mutually consistent in that economic gain was neither the norm for behavior nor grounds for certainty of salvation. Thus, the Puritans did not typically do what Weber (see [1904–5] 1958:155–57) implied, namely, condemn the pursuit of wealth and then make it a sign of election.

Weber thought that its value as a sign of salvation led to the pursuit of wealth; by making it a criterion for salvation, Puritanism could spur the pursuit of gain without actually advocating it. However, it was not widely adopted as a sign. Puritans were not to deal with problems of assurance by rationalizing their economic conduct nor by seeking greater wealth to prove they were saved. When troubled about salvation, they were to think about sin and repentance, not economics.

In general, the connection between economic conduct and salvation premia was weak. It was not absent, but was much more tenuous and uneven than Weber's treatment has indicated. Salvation premia reinforced rational economic behavior quite weakly. Care is required when interpreting Weber's ([1922] 1968:575) statement that Puritanism contributed "to the rational capitalistic temperament" the "idea of the methodical demonstration of vocation in one's economic behavior." Although Puritanism may have introduced the idea, it was not stressed. Systematic economic effort was not considered important for displaying regeneration.

POVERTY

Just as wealth was not widely advocated as a sign of salvation, poverty was not preached as a sign of condemnation (Seaver 1985:134, 137). Ball, for example, talked of poor people who were "in Christ" (see ibid.:137). Certainly, the preachers did not encourage people to view their lack of business success as an omen of damnation. The justified could be poor (Downame [1604] 1974:II, 172; see also Ames [1639] 1975:253 and Baxter 1678:II, 129).

Furthermore, as Samuelsson (1961:38) has argued, it was sometimes held that poverty was a mark of salvation. McGee (1976:191) reports that "the Puritans tended to identify the poor with . . . God's people." For example, Benbrigge (quoted in ibid.) asked rhetorically, "hath not God chosen the poor of this world, rich in faith?" Crowley (see Peel 1937:14) wrote that the poor man's "maister hath yet in store a crowne for him at the last "day," and Swinnock (1663:338) thought that "the poor of the world are the heirs of Heaven."

Since the poor could be among the saved, there was no need to rise above poverty to eliminate fear of condemnation. Consequently, prosperity was neither a positive sign, as argued above, nor a necessity for overcoming doubts arising from poverty.

Consistent with pastoral teachings, neither Elias Pledger nor Nehemiah Wallington interpreted their lack of business success as a sign of damnation. Nor did they hint that greater profits would make them feel more certain of salvation. Neither sought economic success to enhance certainty.

INDIVIDUAL LISTS OF SIGNS

The signs of salvation described above represent a composite list culled from the writings of a number of divines. A Puritan believer exposed to several preachers might have internalized such an eclectic list. On the other hand, a follower influenced primarily by one minister might have used a list of signs developed singly by that one person. In order to capture the flavor of that kind of experience, the individual lists of several divines are presented below.

It can be seen from these individual lists that economic signs were named quite infrequently. Although industry and the duties of the calling were mentioned, their appearance was the exception rather than the rule. Neither wealth nor economic success was listed by any of these prominent ministers.

John Downame ([1604] 1974:II, 235–47) listed ten signs: an earnest desire after the means of salvation, a spirit of supplication, a love of heavenly things rather than the world, sorrow for sin and opposition to it, a hungering for Christ's righteousness, an inward fight between the flesh and the Spirit, new obedience, love of the brethren, love of God's ministers, and an earnest desire of Christ's coming to judgment. Economic conduct was not mentioned.

Arthur Dent is of particular interest because he named some economic signs. He ([1601] 1974:33–34) listed eight "infallible notes and tokens of a regenerate minde, which may well be termed the eight signes of salvation": "a love of the children of God," "a delight in his word," "often and fervent praier," "zeale of Gods glorie," "deniall of our selves," "patient bearing of the crosse, with profit and comfort," "faithfulnesse in our calling," and "honest, iust, and conscionable dealing, in all our actions amongst men." He (ibid.:34, see also p. 35) further noted that the "contraries unto these" were "manifest signes of damnation." Besides these, he (ibid.:257) listed nine additional signs of salvation that were "not certaine: for some of them may be in the reprobates": "Reverence of Gods name. Keeping of his Sabaothes. Truth. Sobriety. Industry. Compassion. Humilitie. Chastitie. Contentation." Besides, he (ibid.:258) noted St. Peter's eight signs: "Faith. Vertue. Knowledge. Temperance. Patience. Godlines. Brotherly Kindness. Love." But he (ibid.:259) considered "the most certaine and infallible evidences of a man's salvation against which no exception can be taken" to be these seven: "Assured faith in the promises. Sinceritie of heart. The spirit of adoption. Sound Regeneration and Sanctification. Inward peace. Groundednesse in the truth. Continuance to the end." Industry and faithfulness in the calling were listed, but alongside dozens of other signs, and with no special emphasis.

Baxter (1653:88) called his signs the five marks of a true Christian:[23] a preference for eternal life with God over the pleasures on earth, willingness to be governed by Christ's laws commanding a holy, spiritual life, willingness to live in holy duties, with sorrow at not performing them better, willingness to follow Christ despite pain, disgrace, unpleasantness, and loss of possessions or life, and the prevalence of this willingness, so that holy duties were ordinarily performed, and sins fought and repented. Note that Baxter (1653:88–91, 101) placed no special emphasis on economic duties here despite Weber's reliance on him to exemplify the Puritan doctrines that bolstered capitalism.

Perkins ([1606] 1972:I, 75–87) compiled a number of signs derived from Scripture. First was the direct testimony of the Spirit, and second was sanctification. The Spirit was also known by its fruits, prayer, and calling out to God. The saved walked "uprightly" and truthfully and had moral virtues such as temperance, patience, godliness, kindness, and love. They had faith in Christ, had fellowship with God, kept the commandments, loved fellow Christians and God, conformed to his holiness, weaned affection from the world, called upon and gave thanks to God, and made "conscience of sinne." If included at all, economic conduct was buried in the general criteria that one perform works and duties.

Ames, too, listed various tests of a person's state (see Sprunger 1972:171). At one point he ([1639] 1975:II, 10–11) listed four signs that confirmed grace: inclination of the will toward God, readiness to listen to God, longing after God's word, and love of the brethren. He (ibid.:II, 24) also listed six signs of the Spirit: prayer to God, a high value placed on adoption by the Spirit, fear and honor of God, obedience to God, conformity to the image of Christ, and hope of "the eternall inheritance." To obtain hope a person was to keep faith lively, keep a good conscience, observe God's love, practice piety, and place hope in God (ibid.:II, 35).

Flavel (1968:V, 598–601) said that the upright: sought the approval of God rather than men, resisted sin, rejoiced to see God's work and glory advanced, desired to comply with all religious duties, resolved to follow Christ in holiness, made conscience of sins and neglected duties, engaged the heart in duties, performed duties without self-interest, retained no secret sin, and abstained from sin even "when there is no danger of discovery."

Clearly, economic conduct received little attention when identifying the elect. Neither wealth nor business success was named in these lists. Work in the calling was mentioned just once by Dent. Other divines referred only to the performance of duties and works; work at one's calling and growing rich to serve God were likely subsumed under those quite general headings. Such treatment undercuts the notion that these economic duties were more significant signs of grace than the myriad of other duties and works. Although capitalist actions could be taken as signs of election, just as Weber ([1922] 1963:252) stated, they were joined and overshadowed by many others. They were by no means central to the quest for salvation.

THE SIGNS IN USE

Despite the large number of signs mentioned, people needed to possess just one or a few to demonstrate grace (Miller 1963:51; Perkins [1606] 1972:I:112–13; see also Baxter 1653:58; [1696] 1931:125). Hence, in practice, Puritans tended to focus on the presence of a few signs, not all. Nor did all necessarily concentrate on the same signs.

It is interesting to note which signs Puritans chose to support their own cases for election. Baxter ([1696] 1931:125; 1653:165; see also Keeble 1982:134) thought that he was saved because he served God; did God's work; gave time and money for the Church and the poor; desired perfect holiness; had a holy, heavenly mind; was content not to rise; and resisted temptations. Perkins (1970:III, 371) expected eternal life because he loved the brethren; wanted to do them good; hated sin and wickedness; longed to see Christ come to judgment; and grieved at being unable to fulfill God's law properly. Finally, Thomas Goodwin (cited by McGee 1976:58) used as support his regrets for his sins and joyful thoughts of "the things of God."

It is instructive that Baxter considered occupational contentment a more positive sign than occupational advancement. He ([1696] 1931:125; 1653:165) did not choose a more lucrative job in order to give more to charitable causes, but valued the spiritual good works he performed as a minister more than additional economic good works.

Most directly pertinent to the Weber thesis are the cases of the merchant diarists, and neither Pledger nor Wallington based assurance on economic signs. Unlike Baxter, whose work was religious, neither mentioned the service of God in their callings.

Elias Pledger (diary:8, see also p. 14) thought that his conversion was true because he was sanctified; he was "not the worst of people"; he loved Christ, and was thankful to Christ; sins troubled and humbled him; he delighted in communion with God and the company of the saints; he tried to perform religious duties with a good heart; he delighted in these duties; he longed for Christ's judgment in order to be freed of all sin; he longed for the Sabbath and tried to keep it holy; he delighted in the Lord's Supper; and he was troubled when he could not think of God in his worldly business. The performance of economic duties was quite peripheral to the assessment of his estate. He (diary:14) suspected his sincerity whenever his thoughts of business became too worldly, but was reassured by the fact that this troubled him (ibid.:8). Clearly, greater dedication to business or profit could not make him more assured of salvation. Nor did his frequent lack of business success reduce his assurance.

Nehemiah Wallington mentioned some signs "where by I know Christ is mine" (Folger diary:233). First, it was God's work to make him want Christ. Second was his love of the saints (ibid.; see also Seaver 1985:189). Third, he (Folger diary:233) was often "with God in prayer." His (ibid.:234) fourth sign was self-denial, "as a sarvant gives up him selfe to the will of his Master." Elsewhere he mentioned additional evidence, "the holy Spirit" (ibid.:308; see also Seaver 1985:7), his "graces" (Folger diary:229), and his love of God in times of adversity (quoted by Seaver 1985:124). He did not mention his economic diligence as a sign; and he gained certainty of salvation with little or no change in economic conduct.

In short, consistent with the relative unimportance placed on economic conduct as a sign of election at the pastoral level, hard work and success received little attention from these individual believers. Relatedly, there was little mention of good works. Baxter was the lone exception; in contrast, Perkins found the desire for good sufficient.

The only indication that the laity departed from pastoral consensus and treated wealth as an important sign of grace comes from an ironic note by Baxter (1653:183) that bodily mercies "though not certain evidence, can more effectively refresh a drooping doubting soul, then the surest Evidence." Although bodily mercies could refer to healing, they could also mean economic prosperity. Baxter gave no indication of the numbers his observation was based on. However, it was probably a minority because none of the individuals in this study used "bodily mercies" to judge their estates. They apparently did not consider wealth a sign of election; Wallington (quoted by Seaver 1985:126), for example, denied that people's riches would "comfort them at their hour of death." So, while some Puritans judged their salvation economically, it does not seem typical. In any event, those who did use wealth as a sign lend no support to Weber because he denied that the lax interpretations of isolated individuals could produce a powerful economic impact (see Chapter 1). But they do provide some credibility for Hill's (1958; 1975) argument that bourgeois Puritans selectively followed their religion's more procapitalist teachings.

THE GENERAL PULL TOWARD WORLDLY ACTIVITY

Although capitalist action was not explicitly required to prove salvation, it has been argued that it was encouraged indirectly because it was a form of innerworldly activity. Weber ([1904–5] 1958:112–13) called worldly activity the best means for achieving certainty.

Activity versus Passivity

There is a measure of truth in Weber's assessment. According to Baxter (1653:84, 232, 233, 244 and [1696] 1931:125), people could take comfort from their actions because they showed the graces in operation. Lively action was both a sign and condition of the everlasting rest in heaven (Baxter [1650] 1962:34; 1653:146; 1678:I, 106; [1696] 1931:125; see also Ball 1632:169, 386).

Nevertheless, Weber's account is misleading in its implications (1) that economic action satisfied that requirement, and (2) that the more active entrepreneur excelled the less active entrepreneur in fulfilling it. First of all, not every form of action led to the eternal rest, Baxter ([1650] 1962:34;

see also Downame [1604] 1974:I, 81) cautioned. Only the proper activities, specified in Christian teachings, led to that end; and they were not, for the most part, business, but, to a great extent, religion. For example, Baxter ([1650] 1962:141–42; see also Knott 1980:70) specified that meditation made for an "active Christian," i.e., active spiritually (see Baxter [1650] 1962:184). Regarding the second point, too much business could lead to the neglect of activities needed for salvation (see above). Economic actions were not worthless in the quest for certainty but got overshadowed by those more directly religious. Puritanism placed a positive value on some external actions as Weber ([1904–5] 1958:113) has stated, but actions considered worldly were devalued. Thus, "worldly activity" was not the "most suitable means" for achieving certainty.

Furthermore, Weber's emphasis on activity exaggerates because it was counterbalanced by a strong dose of passivity. Doubtful Puritans were sometimes advised to be active, but sometimes to be passive. For example, they were directed to be patient if they found no clear evidence of their salvation (Baxter 1678:II, 117; Saltmarsh [1647] 1847:178; Downame [1604] 1974:II, 153–54; Blake cited by Holifield 1974:101). The following examples show the coexistence of active and passive strains in Puritanism.

Puritans were sometimes advised to be content with grace received (Perkins [1606] 1972:I, 57–58; Downame [1604] 1974:II, 154; Ball 1632:189–90). They were told to attend "growth according to the good pleasure of God" (Ball 1632:189–90) and to "waite his leasure" for help (Downame [1604] 1974:II, 529). However, this contradicted other advice to "labour after the increase of grace, using all good means," such as hearing the word (ibid.:II, 153–54, 224–25; Baxter 1653:244). As noted earlier, the elect had to labor to receive God's gift of grace (Perkins [1606] 1972:I, 63–64; Downame [1604] 1974:II, 496), and Baxter ([1650] 1962:34) warned that inactivity would lose it.

Puritans were sometimes told to wait upon the holy Spirit, its testimony, and its gifts (Downame [1604] 1974:II, 496; Scudder 1813:283–85). Since the Spirit, not human beings, performed the work of sanctification (Downame [1604] 1974:I, 126 and III, 638–39; Flavel 1968:V, 572–73; Baxter [1650] 1962:86; Dent 1601:320), people could only wait for God's mercy (Downame [1604] 1974:I, 135; Ball 1632:390; Dent 1601:320). However, this contrasted with other advice that the Spirit needed to be made effectual through sermons, reading, prayer, meditation, and communion (Blake cited by Holifield 1974:101; Scudder 1813:283–85). According to McGee (1976:57–58), the Puritan approach was "anything but patient"; they did not wait passively for the Spirit to make itself known.

In sum, active strains in the quest for assurance were countered by passivity. Some action was produced, but also some inaction. Mixed pastoral advice must have weakened action; conflicting alternatives lead to hesitancy and indecision rather than a strong drive.

External versus Internal Pulls

Likewise, Weber ([1904–5] 1958:112) exaggerated Puritans' emphasis on external acts. The salvation doctrine's strong inward focus diluted its external tendencies.

Outward actions, by themselves, were not infallible signs of regeneration (see Downame [1604] 1974:II, 141; see also Keeble 1982:135 and McGee 1976:240). Since unsound Christians could be assiduous in duties (Baxter 1678:I, 216; Downame [1604] 1974:II, 232; see also Coolidge 1970:131–32), outward observances could give no assurance without internal righteousness (Ball 1632: 114; Downame [1604] 1974:I, 80–82; II, 232, 506–7).

Insofar as it was difficult to gauge one's estate through external acts, Puritans had "to descend into themselves, and to examine how it is with them within" (Coolidge 1970:132; see also Baxter 1653:182 and Ball 1632:175). They needed to scrutinize both external actions (Keeble 1982:142) and "the inclinations, and dispositions, from whence those actions flow" (Ames [1639] 1975:II, 3; see also Baxter 1653:81–82).

Some Puritans gave more weight to internal orientations than to external performances; Downame ([1604] 1974:III, 629 and *passim*) and Perkins (quoted by Reilly 1948:34; see also Seaver 1985:43), for instance, held that Christ "esteemeth much more of our affections than of our actions." However, others were more balanced; for example, Pledger (diary:51) thought that God's judgment weighed a person's work and spirit "in an even balance." All in all, it is clear that salvation required some of both (see Keeble 1982:142–43), and any emphasis on internal attitudes tended to diminish the relative importance of external acts.

One way for external actions to become signs of election was to serve as good works; so when Puritans sought good works to achieve certainty, Weber ([1904–5] 1958:112) assumed that they were pulled toward worldly activity. However, deeds could not become good works on their external merits alone. Hence, the doctrine of good works did not pull in an external direction alone.

Coolidge (1970:151) notes that "good works themselves are only as good as the spiritual 'motions' which they manifest"; hence, "to seek assurance . . . is inevitably to become much concerned with emotional experiences." Neither an act's descriptive content nor its consequence was sufficient to stamp it as a good work (see Downame [1604] 1974:I, 42, 50–51, 82 and also Wilcox cited by Mosse 1968:108). For a work to be good, its motives had to be good (Perkins [1606] 1972:I, 71; Baxter 1653:234;

Ames [1639] 1975:III, 85 and quoted by Mosse 1968:71, 74, 89; see also Seaver 1985:42). Indeed, intentions and affections indicated acceptability better than the acts themselves (Downame [1604] 1974:III, 630; Perkins [1606] 1972:I, 68; Perkins quoted by George and George 1958:367; Baxter 1653:91, 298; 1678:I, 107; II, 116, 144; IV, 275; Ames quoted by Mosse 1968:71). Accordingly, the inner motive for a work was a better sign of salvation than the outer work (see, for example, Downame [1604] 1974:II, 591). For this reason external acts required introspective examination to verify that they were good (see Coolidge 1970:132; but also Baxter 1653:437) .

Beyond this, Puritanism's internal focus derived from more than just the intent of good works. Other important signs and means of salvation were also internal in nature (see, for example, Downame [1604] 1974:Epistle Dedicatory), including certain graces (see Dent 1601:281 and Baxter [1650] 1962:157; see also Zaret 1985:141, 158); "if we would be assured," Downame ([1604] 1974:II, 141) preached, "let us looke into our selves" for "spirituall graces." The internal graces included faith, hope, patience, meekness, love, holiness, and repentance (Downame [1604] 1974:II, 141; see also Perkins [1606] 1972:I, 112 and Holifield 1974:50). The emphasis on faith led to a stress on "the inner man and his condition" (Mosse 1968:71); even when faith was discerned by its fruits, the directional pull was often internal because fruits like purity, love, and repentance (for example) were internal states (Downame [1604] 1974:II, 195, 504).

Another important proof of election, the holy Spirit, could also be discerned inside oneself (see Baxter 1678:II, 144); but even if the Spirit were being discerned by its fruits, the observer could be drawn inward because much of the Spirit's work was "inward" (see Baxter [1650] 1962:54, 85 and Downame [1604] 1974:II, 216). The marks it left inside included hope, joy, trust in God, love, and anguish over sin (Perkins [1606] 1972:I, 76–77; Downame [1604] 1974:II, 215–16, 220, 236, 496, 522; Baxter [1650] 1962:54, 157; Reilly 1948:26–29).

Since much of the evidence of salvation was in themselves, devout Puritans examined themselves frequently (Stannard 1977:75; see also Flavel 1968:V, 581; Seaver 1985:ix, 7, 20). Their search for grace was an introspective one (Stannard 1970:41, 73; Coolidge 1970:132; see also Baxter [1650] 1962:85 and 1653:182).

Evidence of salvation came in part "from the sence and feeling of your owne heart," (Dent 1601:281; see also Flavel 1968:V, 536). In fact, Baxter ([1650] 1962:109; see also 1678:I, 107, 384 and Keeble 1982:135, 136) wrote that the acts "of the heart are the surest evidence." Perkins (quoted by Pettit 1966:14 and Stannard 1977:13), Hodges (quoted by Bridenbaugh 1968:274), Bulkeley (quoted by Coolidge 1970:135), and Baxter (quoted by Keeble 1982:133) recommended searching the heart for signs.

According to Pettit (1966:1), Puritans examined their hearts intensely to find assurance. They looked in their hearts for graces (Ball 1632:85; Ames [1639] 1975:II, 16; Perkins quoted by Porter 1971:269; Perkins [1606] 1972:I, 61; 1970:III, 159) and for imperfections (Downame [1604] 1974:II, 365; see also Pledger diary:63). The search of the heart led inward and away from the world of practical affairs. To illustrate, Hodges (quoted by Briden-baugh 1968:274) said to "carefully space the hours we devote to worldly pursuits to . . . more freely employ ourselves . . . for the examining of our deceitful hearts."

In conclusion, the drive for certainty could pull toward the prayer clos-et, not just the workplace. Prayer, repentance, and self-examination usual-ly took place in private. Although Baxter (quoted by Keeble 1982:77) directed against retirement into solitude, Flavel (1968:V, 592, see also p. 567) said to be "more in your closets" and on your knees. He (ibid.:V, 520) observed that the holy "retire from all the world into their closets, and there . . . pour out their hearts before the Lord." Similarly, Stannard (1977:40) writes that "they closeted themselves in their homes and searched agonizingly for the signs of their own individual deliverance."[24]

Since the salvation quest impelled Puritans toward introspection as well as external works (see Grassby 1995:276), Puritan action alternated with self-examination (Seaver 1985:20). In fact, according to Baxter (1653:244; 1678:I, 111), the doubtful were more likely to engage in self-examination than in good works. The importance of external works was limited in a religion that gave the inner life such heavy weight.

CONCLUSIONS

Two main conclusions may be drawn. First, the quest for salvation pulled in a number of scattered directions, including economic ones. Sec-ond, its pulls away from the workplace were more compelling than its re-quirements for economic action.

The Scattering of Impact

The first point is supported by the sheer variety of signs to pursue, both economic and noneconomic. These gave every Puritan some choice over which to emphasize; hence, for different people the salvation drive led in different directions.

Moreover, different divines differed in emphasis. For example, some stressed actions more, while others stressed intentions. Different preach-ers also listed different signs; for example, some pointed to economic signs of grace while others did not. Hence, the direction of the Puritan salvation drive depended to some extent on whose signs a person was following.

Where preachers disagreed, the laity received conflicting messages; and even the same preacher could communicate two opposing viewpoints. Contradictory statements abounded. Under the circumstances, the direction of a person's response depended on how the teachings were applied. Since applications varied, some Puritans acted in one way while others followed a different path. Some quickened their economic efforts while others became introspective and still others more devoted to the activities of church and conventicle.

Thus, Puritanism produced no single direction for those who sought certainty of salvation. Salvation teachings scattered behaviors rather than focusing them into a single, uniform mass effort as in Weber's ideal type. The diversity of lay responses weakened them all; no particular response was pulled by the full force of the salvation drive. Given the diffusion of religious energies, it is difficult to imagine a forceful boost for economic endeavors stemming from concerns over election. At best the salvation quest, with its scattered pull, created a few economically dedicated pilgrims, but not a whole class of entrepreneurs.

The Weak Economic Impact

This scattering of energies is just one reason for the weak economic impact of the salvation doctrine; equally important, the economic pull itself was relatively weak. Salvation depended mainly on religious, not economic practices. When Puritans doubted their salvation, they turned to religion (see Bridenbaugh 1968:276). They did not strive to excel at work or build grand civilizations.

The salvation drive raised some behaviors' importance at the expense of others. For example, the strong emphasis on faith devalued works. Puritans were rarely unsure of their estate because they sensed an insufficiency of works. Then, when it came time to reform, the inner man or woman needed to improve, not primarily the outer (see, for example, Baxter [1650] 1962:151, 163, 184 and 1653:77). In particular, economic works were not prominent among the features of the elect (see Baxter 1653:101). Good works were mostly charitable or religious, not deeds of economic valor. Furthermore, many good works could be performed without wealth, minimizing the pressure to earn.

Overall, there was little connection of business activity with salvation. Most divines did not think of work or wealth as significant means of assurance. Nor did Puritans worry about salvation because of deficiencies in their economic achievements. Hence, the salvation drive provided no reason to devote oneself first and foremost to business. It may be true, as

Weber ([1904–5] 1958) has argued, that the Roman Catholic doctrine of merit could not direct believers toward the workplace because of its many "escape hatches"; but neither did the Puritan salvation doctrine because it assigned the workplace low priority.

The main priority of the pilgrim was religion, not business. Puritan religion regulated the world, but its quest for salvation directed most energies toward otherworldly matters. One effect of this was to reduce the energy and attention focused on economics. In fact, salvation requirements were incompatible with too strong a focus on economics.

Not only did the signs of salvation pull away from economic action, but the *search* for signs did so as well. Though part of the process for laying hold of salvation, this search competed with attempts to obtain the necessary qualifications. It is critical to the Weber thesis that a sufficient number of Puritans sought certainty by modifying behavior so as to display the signs of grace in themselves. Certainly that was Baxter's (1653:244) advice, to spend most effort in getting and increasing grace by performing "your duty rightly." Without this, the salvation doctrine could have made little impact on conduct. But Baxter (1653:244–45) noted that the laity spent more effort *discerning* their graces than doing anything about them. They were more strongly motivated to know their estates than to change. Thus, the religious pull was more toward self-examination than toward behavioral reform, and that led to the home and closet, not to works or to the world of practical affairs.

NOTES

1. Baxter's advice about becoming rich for God supports Weber's point. Although it was a conduct norm, Baxter advised against it because it endangered salvation.

2. Belief alone was insufficient for salvation if a person continued in sin without repentance (Downame [1604] 1974:II, 288; Dent 1601:279, 296–97). According to Ball (1632:103), "our faith assureth us not of forgivenes of sinnes without prayer, but that God forgiveth us when we pray."

3. Sometimes it was said that faith alone saved (Ball 1632:249, 250, 252, 256; Perkins [1606] 1972:II, 361; 1601:88; Preston quoted by Sprunger 1972:158; Cartwright 1599:12, 13).

4. Despite the predestination doctrine, it was sometimes believed that good works helped to achieve salvation (Perkins [1606] 1972:III, 613–15; Baxter 1678:I, 107, 111; II, 144; IV, 266). Works tended to be most valued as a sign by writers such as Baxter, who also considered them an important means of gaining salvation (see Keeble 1982:69, 77).

5. Weber ([1904–5] 1958:115) noted that works were "occasionally" referred to as necessary; but that implies that they usually were not.

6. In parallel fashion, there were other means of glorifying God besides good works. Any human virtues glorified God (see Downame [1604] 1974:II, 158, 176, 182–83, 528).

7. Still, Downame ([1604] 1974:II, 578) called good works "the fruit of them all." This could mean that they were the most important type of fruit or that they were the final by-products of faith, repentance, and sanctification.

8. Weber ([1904–5] 1958:115) understood that human works were considered too corrupt to be accepted by God; but he did not understand that these works became acceptable through true faith, which secured the aid of Christ in obliterating their impurities (Ball 1632:373; Ames [1639] 1975:III, 82; Downame [1604] 1974:I, 81–82). God did not simply accept the imperfect good works of the faithful; rather Christ's merit was imputed to them (Downame [1604] 1974:II, 581, 583–84, 589).

9. Works could not validate faith unless they themselves were validated, ironically by faith itself. Tautologically, only works known to be fruits of a true faith could prove faith true.

10. Contrary to Weber ([1922] 1968:570), Puritanism was similar to Lutheranism in its stress on salvation through faith. It emphasized both faith and works, so it did not contrast with Lutheranism as much as if its only stress had been on works.

11. This approach made economic good works unnecessary because noneconomic good works could suffice.

12. Declarations by Baxter and Downame championing this lenient standard are at odds with their more rigorous pronouncements elsewhere (see above).

13. Two religions that connect salvation and works much more strongly than Puritanism are Roman Catholicism and Mormonism.

14. The doctrine left open just which good works to perform (see Perkins [1606] 1972:I, 69).

15. Despite the heavy emphasis on heavenly meditation, Baxter ([1650] 1962:107, 140; see also 1653:436) lamented that it was much neglected.

16. It also involved righteousness "toward our brethren" (Downame [1604] 1974:II, 232), forgiving one's neighbors (ibid.:II, 243), and dealing honestly and justly with others (Dent [1601] 1974:34; Perkins [1606] 1972:I, 78–79; Baxter [1650] 1962:123).

17. Although reliance on the testimony of the Spirit was less than in Lutheranism, the Puritan approach should not be strictly contrasted to Lutheranism on this point as Weber ([1904–5] 1958:112–14) did.

18. Weber ([1922] 1968:562–63) associated the need for obedience with Catholic-style institutional grace; but Puritanism required obedience also (see Baxter [1650] 1962:34, 130, 138; Baxter 1653:455; Downame [1604] 1974:I, 61; II, 278–80; Dent [1601] 1974:423; Hill [1613] 1975:II, 53; Dorothy Stockton diary:22).

19. Those with earthly minds performed "common duties" but not "heavenly duty" (Baxter [1650] 1962:124); and when they performed spiritual duties, it was for carnal ends, whereas the elect sought spiritual ends such as the enjoyment of God (Flavel 1968:V, 568, see also pp. 566–67, 598, 600).

20. The salvation doctrine reinforced the work ethic much less than it does in Mormonism, for example.

21. The latter is consistent with Weber's ([1904–5] 1958:178) claim that unwillingness to work was a sign of damnation.

22. One reason why Weber ([1904–5] 1958:172) expected work in the calling to be an important sign of salvation was because it was "the highest means to asceticism." It proved grace, in his (ibid.:111) view, because it was an "exercise in ascetic virtue." Apparently, he (ibid.:161–62) thought that any actions with a "systematic, methodical character" would prove grace. However, this theoretical interpretation of what constituted proof is at odds with the actual signs that Puritans used. For example, a disciplined life was not itself a mark of salvation as Weber (ibid.:118) implied.

23. According to Knappen (1933:13 note 15), Baxter listed twenty-seven signs in all.

24. Wallington practiced introspection (see Seaver 1985:7, 182, 196), but Pledger (diary:51) was negligent in self-examination "for a long time."

7

Premiums and Ethics

Chapters 5 and 6 have assessed to what extent the salvation drive, with its concerns about heaven and hell and its quest for assurance, reinforced the Puritan ethic and especially Puritanism's economic ethic. But that specific issue is merely a special case of the more general question of whether or not *any* religious sanctions reinforced capitalist economic conduct. Chapter 7 addresses that more general question.

Max Weber (1946:321; [1904–5] 1958:97, 178, 197) emphasized the importance of religious sanctions as the force behind Protestantism's economic impact. He (1946:321) insisted that it was "not the ethical doctrine of a religion but that form of ethical conduct upon which premiums are placed that matters." He ([1904–5] 1958:197) pointed out that "an ethic based on religion places certain psychological sanctions on the maintenance of the attitude prescribed by it." These sanctions were said to be "highly effective"; and "Only in so far as these sanctions work . . . does such an ethic gain an independent influence on the conduct of life and thus on the economic order" (ibid.). "This is," he (ibid.) went on, "the point of this whole essay." The aim in this chapter is to examine the applicability of his argument to English Puritanism.

SECT DISCIPLINE

Besides salvation or damnation, treated above, another type of sanction was sect discipline. Weber (1946:307, 321), in his trip to America, not only noted that the Protestant sects carried on "the ancient puritan tradition" of moral asceticism, but also that their enforcement of religious virtues served to propagate and maintain the "Puritan ethic." "The sect controlled and regulated the members' conduct," which had to be righteous and ascetic (ibid.:322).

According to Weber (ibid.:305–6), the Protestant sects maintained a lever for behavioral control through their importance for determining a person's reputation: "sect membership meant a certificate of moral quali-fication," including one's "business morals," but, conversely, "Expulsion from one's sect for moral offenses . . . meant, economically, loss of credit and, socially, being declassed." Furthermore, "persons expelled because of moral offenses were often denied all intercourse with the members of the congregation" (ibid.:317).

Besides "possible excommunication," moral control worked more in-formally through the self-government of lay members using the sanction of "admonition" (ibid.:317, see also pp. 316, 320). Although this form of discipline tended to be "unobtrusive" (ibid.:320), one's "social self-esteem" depended on it (ibid.:321).

Weber (ibid.:320) argued that the conduct demanded was an "inner-worldly form of asceticism"; it was "a certain methodical, rational way of life which—given certain conditions—paved the way for the 'spirit' of modern capitalism." In fact, he (ibid.:322; see also [1923] 1961:270) averred, "the capitalist success of a sect brother, if legally attained, was proof of his worth and of his state of grace." Hence, the ascetic sects, with their methodical way of life, "put a halo around the economic 'individual-ist' impulses of the modern capitalist ethos" (Weber 1946:322).

Despite the cogency of this argument and the undoubted force of group peer pressure, there is some question of how well these mechanisms fit English Puritanism. Weber studied only America, and the English case may not be the same.

One difference is the lesser importance of sects in the latter; most En-glish Puritans were in the Church of England (see Collinson 1982:274–75). They might be less affected by group pressure because, in Weber's (1946:316–17) words, "The discipline of the asceticist sect was, in fact, far more rigorous than the discipline of any church."

But despite their church affiliation, Weber (ibid.:314) argued that the English Puritans "approached the discipline of the sects." What was "de-cisive," in his view, for fostering "church discipline" without sects was the hope of "keeping the Lord's supper pure" by "excluding unsanctified per-sons." Although the purity of sacramental communion has been closely identified with the sects (ibid.) and with New England (ibid.:315), Weber (ibid.) also linked it to "the official church" in seventeenth-century En-gland. He (ibid.) reports that Baxter introduced conventicles in sixteen counties to help "in determining the qualification and exclusion of scan-dalous persons from the Lord's Supper."

The analysis below aims to confirm Weber's report or not. It assesses the typicality and strength of English Puritan discipline, along with its ef-fects on modern capitalism.

The Mechanisms of Discipline

To begin with, there *was* religious discipline. Its basis was the duty to admonish sinners (see McGee 1976:197, 199). Baxter (1653:329; see also Wallington cited by Seaver 1985:103), for example, considered it a Christian duty to reprove and exhort one's neighbors, and Nehemiah Wallington, who strongly favored religious discipline, quoted from Leviticus: "rebuke thy neighbor" (Seaver 1985:146, see also p. 170). These disciplinary restraints were believed to aid offenders' redemption (Marlowe 1956:85; see also Seaver 1985:103) by stimulating their repentance (Ames [1639] 1975:86), by correcting their sinful practices (see McGee 1976:195 and Foster 1991:96), and by enabling them to "goe on . . . in a course of holinesse" (Ames [1639] 1975:86).

Each of the "saints" was duty-bound to counsel and admonish the others (McGee 1976:197, 199). According to Ames ([1639] 1975:86–87), "the correction of a scandall ought to begin with a private admonition." Every believer was to admonish separately, "For all are enjoyned to doe it by Christ" (ibid.:87). If the individual admonitions were rejected, the next step was "to take one or two with us, and to urge the admonition in their presence" (ibid.). The "offending Brother" was "in this manner so long to be admonished, till he doe either manifest his repentance, or impenitencie" (ibid.:88). These lay measures were to precede any official church discipline (ibid.:87–88).

Seaver (1985:8) notes that letters were used to reprove, admonish, and instruct. Wallington, for example, wrote letters of reproof to a cousin, to his sister-in-law, to minister Abraham Colfe, and to a neighbor (see ibid.:68–69, 83, 103, 106, 176). He received letters of moral instruction from his ministerial brother-in-law (ibid.:81). Similarly, Elias Pledger (diary:15, 34–36, 42–45, 53–54) wrote critical letters to his sister, a scandalous minister, a young acquaintance, and an indiscreet person who made "a great profession of religion." A friend of Wallington's wrote a letter urging Wallington's apprentice to be more righteous (Seaver 1985:102), and Lady Harley wrote to her son (ibid.:19, 184).

Lay admonition was supplemented by more formal discipline (see Rowdon 1958:13–16). Weber's (1946:315) report of conventicles is confirmed by those at Chelmsford, Essex, and Boston, Lincolnshire, in the 1620s; these were semiformal companies of godly Christians who "held frequent communion together, used the censure of admonition, yea and of excommunication" (see Foster 1991:96). Baxter's participation in disciplinary activities is confirmed by Nuttall (1965:63); however, rather than conventicles, as described by Weber (1946:315), in this case he set up a conference of ministers who met once a month to confer about cases of discipline. Furthermore, aided by his assistant pastors, he admonished congregants privately, then before two or three others, then at a church board meeting, then before the whole congregation (Nuttall 1965:60, 62). Weber may have had Baxter in mind when he ([1904–5] 1958:155) wrote that Puritan clergymen could use their positions to discipline their congregations.

Nuttall's account places a greater emphasis on ministerial action than lay discipline. Baxter ([1650] 1962:105) and Ames ([1639] 1975:88–89) lent support to his position when they stated that the Church carried out "the discipline of Christ." Baxter (1678:IV, 233–34), for example, argued that lay congregants had to accept as fellow church members anyone admitted by their pastor, and that the call to disciplinary action fell heavily on those whose "Office and place require it, as a Magistrate, Pastor, Parent, Master, Tutor, etc." Similarly, Ames ([1639] 1975:88–89) held that "the administration of the censure pertaineth to the Governours of the Church," since the exercise of discipline was part of their office; and it further belonged to the "Assemblies and Synods."

Disciplinary power was exercised through private admonition, church censure, and excommunication (Rowdon 1958:13–16). Private admonition was used by lay individuals, elders, or groups of the latter against offenders (ibid.:13–14, 15); but, according to Thomas Goodwin and John Owen, if "private admonitions fail, the matter must be brought before the church" to judge (ibid.:14). Ames ([1639] 1975:87–88), agreeing with this sequence of events, specified that "the matter bee brought to those . . . who ordinarily have the direction and administration of publike businesse committed to them."

The next point to examine is the nature of the sanctions used. Cragg (1957:167–77) reports that discipline could be severe. The most extreme punishment was to remove the unholy through excommunication (ibid.; Rowdon 1958:13–16). The excommunicate was cut off from the company of believers, deprived of God's Spirit, and barred from the kingdom of heaven (Perkins [1606] 1972:II, 324–28; Ames [1639] 1975:89–90; Rowdon 1958:16). According to Thomas Goodwin, excommunication was tantamount to delivery into Satan's hands (see Rowdon 1958:15). However, for this reason, Ames ([1639] 1975:88) advised proceeding "with much patience to this last remedie." It was used only against the "stubbornly impenitent" (ibid.; Baxter 1678:III, 150; see also Perkins [1606] 1972:II, 325–28; Holifield 1974:111; Zaret 1985:137). In the reverse direction, excommunicates could not be received back into the favor of the church without signs of "true and serious repentance" (Ames [1639] 1975:90).

Consistent with Weber's (1946:315) thesis, suspension from the Lord's supper was used for disciplinary purposes (Ames [1639] 1975:88; Cartwright quoted by Peel and Carson 1951:169; Baxter 1678:III, 137; see also Nuttall 1965:56 and Holifield 1974:111, 125). Ames ([1639] 1975:88) called it the "lesser Excommunication"; he (ibid.:88) proposed that it "goe before" full excommunication, and that it "bee continued for some time."

Beyond its use as a formal sanction, the practice of sequestration from the Lord's Supper enforced discipline informally by holding would-be communicants to a required level of piety. Only worthy individuals were qualified to receive the sacrament. As Nuttall (1965:56–57) has stated, a certain level of knowledge, faith, and morals was required. According to Downame ([1604] 1974:II, 194) and Perkins (1970:III, 223), only those with true faith were welcome guests at the Lord's table, and repentance and religious knowledge were needed as well (Perkins 1970:III, 223 and [1606] 1972:II, 339–41). Baxter (1678:III, 150; see also Keeble 1982:26 and Nuttall 1965:57) argued that known hypocrites, devoid of "saving faith and repentance, should not come" to the sacrament; and "such Children, Ideots, ignorant persons, or Hereticks, as know not what they are to receive and do" were "not to seek it, or to take it" (Baxter 1678:II, 107; see also III, 137). Wallington (Folger diary:275–76) agreed with the divines that "There is many qualifications in fitting me to Come to the Lords Supper." He listed the knowledge of what it means, faith, longing for Christ, and a disposition to broken-heartedness and a sense of sin.[1]

Puritans were to examine themselves before coming to the Lord's table (Downame [1604] 1974: II, 194; Baxter 1678:II, 108; see also Prynne cited by Holifield 1974:112; see also Pledger diary:13); if unfit, they were to stay away (Baxter 1678:II, 107–8). Unworthy communion, for example by the evil, faithless, or unrepentant, was sinful (Holifield 1974:57; see also Baxter 1678:II, 108 and Hill [1613] 1975:54) and was condemned (Perkins 1970:III, 224 and [1606] 1972:II, 341). However, those unworthy because of human infirmity could take communion; sincerity was required, not perfection (Perkins [1606] 1972:II, 341, 346).

There was considerable Puritan disagreement and debate about whether to permit free admission to communion or to limit it to those presumed regenerate (see Holifield 1974:112–25). Free admission of all church members was favored by Thomas Erastus, George Gillespie, John Humfrey, William Prynne, and Thomas Blake (ibid.:111–14, 117, 124); similarly, Baxter (1678:II, 107) urged that "all that come, and seek it, are to be admitted by the Pastors," with a few exceptions, e.g., heretics, the ignorant, and those without faith or repentance, as noted above. It was argued that the ministers, not being Divine, could not know who to exclude; that communion could improve a person's religious condition; and that since the sacrament had no efficacy for the unregenerate anyway (see Chapter 5), it was unnecessary to sequester the unworthy from its benefits (Holifield 1974:113–14, 118, 120).

In opposition, other preachers demanded more than a minimum standard for admission to the Lord's Supper (ibid.:55); these included Arthur

Hildersam, Ezekiel Culverwell, John Preston, Roger Drake, and John Dod (see ibid.:55–58, 117). For an invitation to receive communion, they required saving faith, or an outward profession thereof; newness of life, or a resolution to discontinue sin; and assurance of salvation, or a reasonable hope thereof (ibid.:55–58). And even divines who were relatively lenient about admission, such as Baxter, Perkins, and Humfrey, sought to exclude scandalous sinners (see Baxter 1678:II, 107; III, 137; Holifield 1974:55–56, 118; see also Collinson 1982:273, 277–78). This restrictive viewpoint apparently prevailed, since the Westminster Assembly voted overwhelmingly to bar the unworthy from communion (Holifield 1974:125).

Nevertheless, according to Holifield (ibid.:56), ministers "took care not to discourage weaker members."[2] For example, even Hildersam permitted "weak Christians" to receive (ibid.). Perkins (1970:III, 223) encouraged those with infirmities as long as they had faith, repentance, and knowledge, and Dod invited everyone willing to put away their sins (Holifield 1974:56–57). Baxter (1678:III, 150) denied that anyone in error about the nature of true faith and repentance, or anyone uncertain of true repentance after their best endeavors, should be kept away from communion. He (ibid.) further noted that examination was unnecessary before each visit to the Lord's table; examination was "fitliest done . . . only once, before their first communicating." This attenuated the social pressure generated by a policy of selective admission. It was by no means a day-to-day or week-to-week pressure.

The Weakness of Church Discipline

Although English Puritanism contained the relevant mechanisms, its discipline did not become very strong. One reason why it was weaker in England than America is that few English Puritans separated, and the Church of England's discipline was weaker than that of the separatist sects.

It is true that some Puritans believed that Christianity should consist of churches of "true beleevers" (Miller 1933:58, 77, 78; Foster 1991:50; Nuttall 1965:56), gathered together from different parishes (see Foster 1991:50), who were "pure in belief and behaviour" (Rowdon 1958:7). Examples include Henry Jacob, William Bradshaw, and William Ames (Miller 1933:77; Stearns 1954:47). However, others in "the Puritan ministry" were loyal to "the ideal of a comprehensive church" (Foster 1991:51). Here they felt they could best serve the unconverted (ibid.:50; Seaver 1985:173; see also Downame [1604] 1974:II, 249). For one thing, they hoped to impose strong religious discipline on everyone (Foster 1991:46; Seaver 1985:189). Baxter (1653:372; see also 1678:IV, 234 and Keeble 1982:27), who exemplified this view, advised his readers not to worry about the fitness of everyone they joined in with at church.

The Puritan preference for a comprehensive church over "gathered" churches affected discipline in more than one way; but one of the most important was that the comprehensive ideal greatly reduced the use of admittance versus exclusion as a sanction. The gathered churches restricted membership to "the proved elect" (Miller 1933:77), but other Puritans did little to exclude "hypocrites and fake professors" (see McGee 1976:178–79).

Among those who objected to gathered churches many believed that "no one . . . should presume to usurp God's place and say who is elect and who is not" (Johnson 1970:29; see also Zaret 1985:140). According to Perkins (1970:III, 258; see also Saltmarsh [1647] 1847:175; but see also Foster 1991:71), "No man may presumptorily set down that . . . any other is a reprobate, for God doth oftentimes prefer those which did seem to be most of all estranged from his favour to be in his kingdom." Similarly, Baxter (1678:IV, 233) noted, "There are many whose faults are secret, and their virtues open: And of such you cannot judge as they are, because you have no proof or evidence to enable you." Conversely, Downame (quoted by Reilly 1948:16–17) warned that some reprobates "may deceive even the church."

Because of the difficulty in judging, Baxter (1678:IV, 233) directed pastors who judged church admittance to consider as "a visible member of the Church . . . every one who maketh a credible profession of true Christianity" by consenting to the covenant. A serious profession was credible if "not disproved by valid evidence of the contrary" (Baxter 1678:IV, 233–34). Baxter (ibid.:IV, 234) declared that "God would have every man the Chooser or Refuser of his own mercies." Each person was the best "Judge or discerner" of his or her own sincerity (Baxter 1678:IV, 246; but see also Foster 1991:71). The pastor was "obliged not to deny him, without disproving him" (Baxter 1678:IV, 246).[3]

In contrast, many separatists and congregationalists believed that "if the churches rigorously examined their candidates and kept a close watch over their members, they might be practically certain that those who took the church covenant had also been received into the covenant of grace with God Himself" (Miller 1933:57; see also pp. 56, 206 and McGee 1976:183, 188–89). Thomas Goodwin (quoted by McGee 1976:178), for example, felt that those whose works were "abominable" demonstrated their reprobation while the saints' profession of strictness "will rise to holiness."

England's gathered churches practiced judgment of a person's state of grace and restricted membership accordingly. Among the Brownists, only those who could prove themselves redeemed could be church members (Miller 1933:55). Similarly, congregationalists excluded from church membership "persons held ungodly and not of the elect" (Stearns 1954:79; see also Miller 1933:77). Moreover, the separatists required a profession of faith to take communion (Holifield 1974:70). Likewise, some Independents such as John Howe "demanded credible evidence of saving faith" from communicants (ibid.:130). Strict maintenance of this standard "often led to the virtual elimination of eucharistic worship," Holifield (ibid.:138) reports.

If most English Puritans had been separatists, their discipline may well have approximated the level that Weber observed in America. But most, as part of the Church of England, were not subject to the strict requirements of the separatists (Zaret 1985:139). Likewise, their disciplinary standards were lower than those in New England (Miller 1933:208).

If church membership had hinged on strict qualifications, nonseparating Puritans would have had to prove faith and sanctification to join and to avoid excommunication. However, Church of England membership entailed no such selection process, and therefore engendered no such religious pressures.

Furthermore, according to Nuttall (1965:60), the episcopal system never disciplined. There were no calls to repentance, no public confessions of sin, and no excommunications (ibid.). There was no moral oversight of parishioners (ibid.).

Many Puritans considered the parishes incapable of discipline (ibid.:56). It was felt that the Church of England had been reformed in doctrine but not in discipline (Lake 1982: 84). Their ideal was religious discipline backed by the power of the magistrates (Seaver 1985: 162, see also pp. 132–33, 189, 194).

It was hoped by reform-minded Puritans that the classis system of the 1640s would institute a full system of discipline (ibid.:147),which would be imposed by Church elders (ibid.).[4] The classis ordered all desiring the sacrament to be examined by conference on their fitness (ibid.:148).

Nehemiah Wallington favored the classis system and served as an elder (ibid.:103, 146–47, 173, 175, 176). However, most in his parish hated godliness, so they reformed very little (ibid.:147). He was mocked and scoffed; it was thankless work (ibid.:150, see also p. 149).[5] Wallington complained that the disciplinary system had no teeth: it could only "investigate, expose, and exhort" (ibid.:176). "Neither the Sword of the Magestry nor Ministrie" were "pulled out" against sin (Wallington letters:169).

England's classes were powerless, a broken reed; "precise rule" and godly reformation never took place (Seaver 1985:163). In fact, according to Seaver (ibid.:148, 194), the classical system was less concerned with discipline than with clerical affairs such as the ordaining, examining, and removing of ministers. Nor were all Puritan ministers interested in discipline or in the classis movement (Zaret 1985:148); few reproved sins (Wallington letters:169). By the mid-1650s half of the classes were defunct; the frame of presbyterian government was dissolving in Wallington's parish (Seaver 1985:148–49). The classis movement failed and died out, leaving no official discipline in the Church of England (Zaret 1985:112–14; Cragg 1957:257). This meant that nonseparating Puritans were not subject to the type of discipline that Weber observed in America.

Some ministers like Baxter imposed parish discipline similar to that of the congregational churches (Nuttall 1965:60–61). But other ministers failed to admonish their wayward parishioners (Seaver 1985:106–8, 176).

Many Puritans fought for Parliament in the Civil War, but Cromwell's lukewarm protectorate did not give the saints the discipline they sought (ibid.:176, 180). They had hoped for a "politics of prayer" in which the leaders would stand firm for God's cause and the people would submit to the ministry (ibid.:181, see also pp. 132–33, 189). But this Puritan revolt failed because Christ's kingdom was never established (ibid.:178). Soon thereafter, the Restoration meant the defeat of Puritan church reform (ibid.:180, 194). Finally, the Act of Uniformity drove Puritans out of the Church as nonconformists (see Baxter [1696] 1931:177–80), ending for good their hope of reforming it with church discipline.

Religious Standing and Economic Reputation

Religious discipline in America, Weber reported, was especially effective for the following reason. One needed to act morally to remain in good church standing; then, in turn, church membership aided business success by enhancing one's reputation for honesty. Businessmen were motivated to conform to religious norms in order to maintain their church membership and along with it their business reputations.

It will be seen below that the English case bore some similarities to Weber's report, but differed in certain respects as well. Because of the differences, this mechanism could not work to strengthen discipline in England as Weber said it did in America.

One feature common to both countries was the pecuniary importance of a merchant's reputation for honesty (see Grassby 1995:298–300). It was impossible in England to get credit without trust, and a merchant's credit was a very important matter (see Grassby 1978:371). Perhaps one reason why Nehemiah Wallington sought a reputation for honesty (see Chapter 3 above) was that he borrowed frequently (Seaver 1985:123).

Another similarity was the connection between religion and honesty.

Baxter (1678:IV, 104) taught that the market should not be a place of deceit; he hoped for mutual trust. Relatedly, clergyman William Crompton counseled businessmen on ethics (Sprunger 1972:162).

It is likely that businessmen practiced religion to enhance their reputations and their businesses; otherwise John Downame ([1604] 1974:I, 91) would not have needed to preach against it. It was wrong, he (ibid.:I, 91) scolded, to "professe religion" and "heare sermons . . . that they may (seeming religious and men of good consciences) have their shoppes the better customed." Although it parallels the situation in America, this practice in England was clearly a sinful aberration rather than the accepted standard of religious and economic conduct. Hence, it probably involved the hypocritical, whose religion had no psychological power to compel adherence to the ascetic Puritan code. Nor, in England, was church discipline strong enough to use businessmen's need for good religious standing as a lever to compel their moral compliance.

Another difference from America was that the Puritans did not necessarily enjoy a good reputation for businessmen to trade on. Many in England avoided Puritan shops, particularly after the Restoration (Marlowe 1956:5, 40). One of Wallington's customers, for example, accused the Puritans of charging too much (British diary:9). Some assumed that a Puritan shopkeeper was more honest than his neighbors, but others considered the Puritans hypocrites (Seaver 1985:190). All in all, it is doubtful that there was any gain in being identified as a Puritan; acceptance in their conventicles did not carry an expectation of heightened trade.

Puritans were very sensitive about their reputation. In response to his customer's complaint about Puritan prices Wallington (British diary:9) quoted a lower price than "otherwise I should." He realized that any charge of sharp practices would reflect on the community of saints (Seaver 1985:131, 132, 187, 190). Customers tried to get the saints to lower the price to avoid giving Puritans a bad name (ibid.:132). In response, the Puritans curbed sharp practices and profiteering (ibid.:131, 132), and tried to act beyond reproach (ibid.:190, see also p. 187). They also disciplined each other. For example, one Puritan with great debts fled London but the reproaches of the godly community pressured him to return (ibid.:96–97). They said that his behavior allowed the wicked to speak evil about the ways of God (ibid.:97). Similarly, John Wallington, Sr., urged another Puritan in a letter not to let others speak evil of his fellow saints by his conduct (see Wallington letters:103).

Unlike Weber's American case, the English Puritans were trying to build a reputation for honesty, not just trading on an established one. Hence, their religious commitment could not so easily be enforced by the reward of a good business reputation.

The Focus of Discipline

Religious discipline in England failed to reinforce rational economic conduct for two reasons. First, as shown above, this discipline was less effective than Weber's American observations suggest. Second, to be shown below, what discipline existed did little to reinforce rational economic practices and economic success. Instead, the causes for disciplinary action were the following:

Religious discipline was a censure for sin (Ames [1639] 1975:86; Cartwright quoted by Peel and Carson 1951:169). It was used against both doctrinal aberrations and moral lapses (Rowdon 1958:20–22).

Only gross sin could lead to excommunication (Zaret 1985:137). According to Ames ([1639] 1975:86), discipline was not used against common infirmities, but against "a scandall." Similarly, Baxter (1678:IV, 234, 246) recommended excommunication only where a person's insincerity was "notorious." Furthermore, Cragg (1957:167–77; see also Ames [1639] 1975:86) specifies that the removal of the unholy was based on their drinking, dancing, sexual immorality, and quarrels. On a more economic note, Perkins (cited by Emerson 1968:157) taught that beggars, rentiers, and their hangers-on should be excluded from the church because they were not productive. Similarly, the Dedham orders took aim not only at premarital fornicators but also proposed to expel those without an honest calling (Foster 1991:35). However, those attacks were leveled against the totally idle rather than the honestly employed or self-employed. Thus, the work habits of laborers and businessmen remained unregulated by church discipline.

As with excommunication, the denial of communion had to rest on "some heinous sin" which is "scandalous in the Church" (Baxter 1678:III, 137). In general, the discipline of the London classis was leveled against smoking, swearing, gaming, slandering and maligning, and tavern haunting on the Sabbath (Seaver 1985:146, 148).

Wallington's moral complaints, the bases for his support of stricter discipline, included covenant breaking, contempt of the Gospel, pride, drunkenness, whoredom, swearing, profaneness, blasphemy and mocking, idolatry and superstition, heresy, errors and schisms, covetousness and greedy pursuit of riches, oppression and economic exploitation, cruelty and unmercifulness to the poor, profaning the Lord's day, long hair, contempt of the ministry, unthankfulness, distrust of God's promises, and idleness (ibid.:107, 132–33, 148, 149, 153, 175–76, 179, 181, see also p. 193). His letter of admonition to his cousin reproved him for drunkenness, profaning the Lord's day, and robbing his father (ibid.:68–69); his letter to his widowed sister-in-law admonished her for her Irish lover, for lying about her pregnancy, and for continuing in sin without repentance (ibid.:83);

and a letter to a neighbor criticized selling wares on the Lord's day, defrauding, deceiving and oppressing others, lying, sleeping in church, and being comfortable in religious duties when guilty of abominations (ibid.:103). Pledger's (diary:15, 34–36, 42–43, 54–55) letters of admonition criticized dancing, gaming, time spent in a public house, irreligious company, churlishness, unmannerliness, undutiful carriage, indecent misbehavior in one's family and as a guest, too little service to God, too little prayer, religious reading, meditating, and hearing the word, and unrepentance. Of all these, only opposition to idleness promoted rational economic conduct; and as above it referred to those who were totally nonproductive. Although diligence at work was a Puritan norm, it was not a focus of religious discipline. Nor was the rationality of an entrepreneur's business operations. Only the most scandalous deviations of economic conduct were disciplined.

Wallington's brother called him incompetent because he needed to borrow (Seaver 1985:124); however, no religious norms were invoked. Wallington once fined himself a farthing for negligence in his calling (ibid.:125); however, no religious body took him to task, and he had fined himself four times as much for looking at a woman with lust.

In short, Puritan religious discipline was but marginally concerned with rational economic conduct. Although it aimed to enforce ethical conduct in general, its effect was to reinforce some norms more than others, and economic ethics to just a very limited extent.[6]

Nor did it function to approve successful businessmen while condemning the unsuccessful. As Seaver (ibid.:134, see also p. 189) has attested (see above), "It was behavior and attitude, not social position and condition, that condemned the wicked and defined the good." Weber's ([1923] 1961:270) identification of ethical fitness with business honor does not apply in seventeenth-century England.

Conclusion

For all these reasons, Puritan discipline did not serve to enforce rational business practices in England as it may have done in America. One must eliminate religious discipline as a mechanism through which English Puritanism helped capitalism. It did not produce the effects Weber described for America.

Religious discipline may have played a greater role in enforcing rational economic conduct in such other Protestant groups as the Baptists and Methodists. Since these faiths were not predestinarian, the Weber thesis would hold that ethical conformity depended less on the reduction of salvation anxiety and relatively more on social pressure.[7] However, that supposition needs to be tested on some nonpredestinarian religions. Clearly in the present study rational economic practices were not strongly enforced by *either* of these two mechanisms.[8]

In Puritanism, Weber (1946:321) stated, "The premiums were placed upon 'proving' oneself before God in the sense of attaining salvation . . . and 'proving' oneself before men in the sense of socially holding one's own within the Puritan sects." However, these two sanctioning mechanisms have been examined above, and scant support has been found for Weber's arguments regarding them. In both cases the sanctions were somewhat weaker in English Puritanism than Weber had inferred, and in neither case were the premiums focused strongly on economic conduct that could aid modern capitalism.[9]

THE ETHICAL IMPACT

Despite Weber's emphasis on religious premia, religious sanctions provide unsatisfactory explanations for any substantial Puritan impact on capitalism. Not only were the effects of salvation anxiety and group discipline weaker than Weber's ideal-typical analysis indicated, but religious sanctions failed to focus enforcement on norms of economic rationality. Furthermore, the religious sanctions approach is largely irrelevant for understanding the later impact of Puritan ideas on the larger culture.[10]

Beyond this, a purely incentive-driven approach to Puritan conduct is inconsistent with the moral nature of the actions themselves, in particular the dutiful nature of work in the calling (Weber [1904–5] 1958:79–92, 162). Even though Weber stressed religious sanctions, he (ibid.:181) noted that the Puritan *wanted* to work at a calling; he or she was a person with a vocation.

Finally, an incentive-driven approach to religious conformity cannot fully explain Weber's hypothesis that the most pious Protestants embraced capitalism most strongly. In an incentive-driven model, those most strongly affected by sanctions would conform the most, not necessarily the most pious.

What is needed to improve upon Weber's approach is the principle that people can conform for the norm's sake as well as for the reward's sake. The Puritan work ethic's impact hinged in no small measure upon its moral force. Accordingly, it is time to put the "ethic" back into the Protestant ethic.

It is clear that diligence in a calling, savings, and their related actions were framed and presented as a code of ethics. They were religious duties. People were to work in their callings to serve the Lord (Ball 1632:391).

The argument that economic norms were backed more by moral force than by sanctions receives indirect support from a review of Puritan religious norms in general. It was common practice to bolster norms ethically.

Puritans were expected to conform for reasons that included (see Coolidge 1970:114) but went beyond rewards and punishments. For example, Downame ([1604] 1974:I, 91, see also p. 81) considered it wrong to perform works chiefly to gain salvation. Nor was repentance true when sorrow was just for one's punishment and condemnation (ibid.:II, 509). Similarly, Baxter (see Keeble 1982:105; see also Baxter 1678:I, 215) taught that religious conformity most appropriately took the form of delightful obedience, not of obedience from fear. Not fear but love should make people want to please God (Downame [1604] 1974:II, 254).

Religious expectations were conveyed in moral terms, not just based on sanctions. Meeting them glorified God and pleased him by fulfilling his will (Baxter 1678:IV, 258; see also Downame [1604] 1974:I, 82). Conversely, sins offended God, and Downame (ibid.:I, 58, see also II, 509) considered that "the greatest evill of all."

Obligations were rationalized through moral reasoning. The believer was bound to "the obedience of the Gospel" (Ball 1632:278) because the covenant "entailed an obligation ... to aspire to moral perfection" (Stearns 1954:50). Baptism was a pledge of obedience, of performing good actions and abstaining from evil (Ball 1632:415), and church membership bound people to perform "duties, both toward God and one toward another" (Ames quoted by Stearns 1954:47). Because of Christ's sacrifice and example, a high standard of conduct "was expected by God from man" (Marlowe 1956:137). According to Perkins (1970:III, 232; see also Ball 1632:391), the faithful were "bounden to obedience" out of "gratitude towards God." Endeavoring to obey showed thankfulness for God's mercy (Perkins [1606] 1972:I, 181–82). Similarly, Downame ([1604] 1974:II, 301, 506; see also III, 610–14) taught that living a holy life showed thanks to God "by glorifying his name," and Baxter (1678:I, 111) concurred that people were "beholden to God."

The two merchant diarists agreed about these moral obligations. Wallington believed that the children of God should reform on account of their special mercies (Seaver 1985:173). He used moral reasoning when he destroyed several false coins (see above), attributing all the glory to God; conversely, to pass a false coin would "be to God's dishonor" (ibid.:141–42). Similarly, Pledger (diary:66) held that "we must be put upon doing in a way of gratitude for what Christ has done on our behalf." A person justified freely by God's grace "cannot but walk in the way of Christ all his days," he (ibid.) maintained. Accordingly, he (ibid.:52) criticized himself when he was negligent and careless in duty towards God. And he (ibid.:35–36) wrote to someone in the godly community that "instead of doing more than others," as expected of the elect, "I think you do less." In sum, there was a clear and accepted code of moral obligation.

Not only was the Puritan code elaborated in moral terms, but the devout responded to it on a moral plane as well. They often followed it for moral reasons. Perkins ([1606] 1972:I, 185) reported that "Gods children have indeede in their hearts a care to please and obey God."

If religious Puritans did not act morally, it is unclear who in all of history could be found to exemplify that type of behavior. The godly community were self-selected and communally accepted devotees, dedicated to religion and to the Puritan politics of prayer as a moral cause.

The obedient were not simply acting to gain premia. To the contrary, there is some evidence that their scruples transcended sanctions.

A prime example is Nehemiah Wallington; there was more to his faith than just concern over his salvation (Seaver 1985:145). Wallington (Folger diary:410–13) thought that keeping conscience avoided displeasing God. Accordingly, he worried constantly about the moral rightness of his actions, motives, and feelings (Seaver 1985:145); these were matters for endless, searching introspection (ibid.). It was not "easy," he (quoted in ibid.) lamented, to practice "conformity of life" to religious teachings. His quest for church discipline and his campaign against long hair were morally inspired: afterwards he (quoted in ibid.: 175, see also p. 176) felt that he had "done my duty." Also, he considered himself an honest tradesman (see ibid.:128). In his shop he (Folger diary:533) had "as grate a care of my Words and Actions that they be just & righteous as I could possibly."

Wallington's father and brother were less scrupulous in business than he was (Seaver 1985:142). However, a number of Puritan merchants were quite concerned about business ethics (see Sprunger 1972:162). According to Seaver (1985:138) artisans' practices closely followed Puritan precepts during this period. As Weber ([1904–5] 1958:180, 181–83) noted, the purely utilitarian approach to business came to dominate only later, after religious fervor had subsided.

The strength of Puritan adherence does not in these instances reflect the reinforcement of moral standards by sanctions. Rather, it shows morality as a force that could influence somewhat independently of sanctions.

In particular, the work ethic was morally influential. For example, Wallington's dedication to his shop stemmed from moral duty (see Chapter 2); he did not think of it as evidence of grace (see Chapter 6). Weber ([1904–5] 1958:178) claimed that the effectiveness of the work ethic depended "alone" on the sanction of attaining certainty through labor, but the work ethic was effective *despite* weak reinforcement from salvation premia or other sanctions. Its "enforcement mechanism" was moral in nature.

The psychological force of Puritan ethics becomes more understandable upon examination of their institutional underpinnings. The practices outlined below contributed to their effectiveness.

First and foremost came the learning and acceptance of Puritan precepts. Wallington's internalization of the divines' teachings is reflected in his own writings (see Seaver 1985:187), and other pious businessmen echoed Puritan morals as well (see ibid.:185). The logic of the precepts was then expressed in action. Wallington, for example, tried to apply these lessons to his life (ibid.).

Puritan morality was instilled through several mechanisms. One likely factor was a strict religious upbringing at home. Winterbottom (see McClelland 1961) has shown that distinctively Protestant child-rearing practices can affect economic behavior.

Another important influence was sermonizing, as Weber (1985:155) recognized. Sermons were very important in Puritanism (Hill 1964:30–78; Cragg 1975:139; Emerson 1968:44; Bridenbaugh 1968:295–97, 302). It was not uncommon to hear several on a Sunday, fast days, or lecture days (Collinson 1982:260–61, 264; Seaver 1985:188); Pledger (diary:30), for example, reported hearing the word preached three times on the Lord's day. Wallington once heard nineteen lectures in a week (Seaver 1985:126) and another time thirty in a month (Wallington Folger diary:203). Afterwards sermons were discussed among the godly (Collinson 1982:264–68) and sold door-to-door in printed form (Bridenbaugh 1968:294). Great crowds came to hear Richard Baxter's sermons (Nuttall 1965:79). Chaderton, Preston, and Cotton lectured all day on Sundays and during the week as well (Bridenbaugh 1968:295–96). Gouge and Sibbes were also popular (ibid.:297).[11]

Preaching was quite effective.[12] Pledger (diary:41) and William Kiffin (quoted by Bridenbaugh 1968:300), an apprentice, both mentioned being affected by the word. And Wallington's outlook was "profoundly shaped" by the divines' "preached and written words, their sermons, guidebooks, and catechisms" (Seaver 1985:viii, see also pp. 185, 187).[13] The work ethic was strongly propagated through preaching; it was emphasized in sermons as it never was in the salvation doctrine or in sect discipline. An effective preacher could reduce idleness and stimulate industry in a community (Hill 1964:137–38).

A further mechanism was community example. Wallington was conscious of his membership in the godly community (Seaver 1985:187) and wanted to "imitate the fashion of the most godly in my calling" (quoted in ibid.:112).

People respond not only to external sanctions but also to self-judgments of pride and shame. Self-esteem could depend on leading a moral life, or one that was "answerable," as Wallington put it (see ibid.:7). When

Wallington did the wrong thing, he felt troubled and guilty (see, for example, British diary:37; see also Folger diary:503). Once he resisted taking extra money from a customer so as not to offend his conscience; but when he finally took the money, his "contience begane a littel to stinge mee" (British diary:9). Similarly, Baxter ([1696] 1931:130) felt guilty for his sins; he was upset "not so much in fear of hell, as in great displeasure against myself."

These mechanisms made industry and saving effective moral virtues, most immediately for Puritans, and later for the broader culture of most of the Occident. Contrary to Weber, Puritanism was able to boost capitalism with little aid from its salvation doctrine. Furthermore, since effective moral influence requires no particular salvation doctrine or premia, other religions were able to reinforce the ethics of working and saving in their own groups and throughout Western culture.

Since one of Weber's ([1922] 1968:587–88, see also p. 575) aims was to explain the historical transformation of greed into economic duty, it seems beside the point for him to understand Protestant conformity in terms of sanctions. If religion made no moral impact, then there was nowhere for the duty component of modern capitalist action to originate.

The cause of this gap in logic is Weber's ambivalence toward the ethical dimension of human behavior. He ([1904–5] 1958:51–54, 71, 196; [1922] 1968:575) attributed a moral dimension to modern capitalist action: this appears both in the work ethic and in his definition of the spirit of capitalism. But then he underestimated the power of religious ethics to shape conduct.

According to Jeffrey Alexander (1982), Weber's overall work was inconsistent in its recognition of the moral dimension in human behavior; he sometimes lapsed into a utilitarian view. It seems that Weber's overemphasis on religious incentives, or "premia," was just such a lapse, which exaggerated self-interest and denied ethics at the expense of a balanced approach. This unidimensionality is poor theory on general principles, as Alexander has charged; in this case it conflicts with the facts of Puritan ethical behavior and makes it impossible to understand Puritanism's ethical influence on modern capitalism.

NOTES

1. Business success was not a criterion, despite Weber's (1946:322; [1923] 1961:270) stress on it in the North American case.

2. Standards for admission to communion were often lower in England than in New England (see Miller 1933:208).

3. Nevertheless, fellow worshippers could judge the probability of a person's

state by signs and evidences, and love each person accordingly (Baxter 1678:IV, 233, 245–46).

4. A classis was a church governing body comprised of minister and elders. It could work to enforce religious discipline.

5. Ministers who reproved sins were despised (Wallington letters:169).

6. Weber's American observations were actually quite similar to the English case. He (1946:305) lists disorderly conduct, frequenting taverns, dancing, theater, card playing, untimely meeting of liabilities, and other frivolities as matters for discipline. While this enforced a general asceticism, it did little to enforce asceticism in the workplace.

7. Weber ([1904–5] 1958:128) argued that because of the exercise of discipline in the processes of member selection and excommunication, sect members had to prove their election even in the absence of predestination. That implied that religion could make an impact even apart from its salvation doctrine. Weber (ibid.:128) saw the sanctions related to predestination as "only one of several possibilities."

8. Even in America, where a Protestant's religious standing was reportedly dependent on economic success, it must be kept in mind that Weber's observations refer to a later time, after the development of capitalism was well under way. It is unknown whether that system of discipline was in place and was stressing the economic dimension soon enough to help modern capitalism spread during its early phase.

9. A third type of religious sanctions, referred to by Weber (1963:1), was neither punishment in the afterlife nor by cobelievers, but God's punishment of sinners "even in this world." However, like the other sanctions, they were invoked for other sins and not a lack of economic rationality; hence, they did not aid rational capitalism.

10. As explained in Chapter 1, Puritanism's long-term cultural influence was based on the voluntary acceptance of certain tenets by the society at large, not on sanctions.

11. Devotees of sermons, including merchants, supported lectureships, many of which were Puritan (Bridenbaugh 1968:295–97). Lectureships were set up in most market towns (Bridenbaugh 1968:302; see also Collinson 1982:258, 260).

12. Weber ([1904–5] 1958:97) affirmed the influence of Puritan preaching but did not stress it. Grassby's (1995:292) view was more qualified since he wrote that wordiness and technicalities reduced sermons' effect.

13. Ministers also influenced through example (Seaver 1985:108) and pastoral counseling (see ibid.:187). Moral lessons were also learned at work as shop masters reproved their apprentices' transgressions (see, for example, Wallington British diary:7).

8
Summary and Conclusions

SUMMARY OF HYPOTHESES

After reviewing the historical data, it is now possible to summarize which of the original study hypotheses outlined in Chapter 1 have been supported, which disconfirmed, which partially supported, and which supported with qualifications. Hypotheses about the work ethic, savings, and legitimation have been verified, albeit with qualifications. On the other hand, those concerning the spirit of capitalism, salvation, religious discipline, sanctions, and the approval of wealth and acquisition were largely disconfirmed.

Hypothesis I. The Work Ethic. This hypothesis is verified in qualified form.

> Hypothesis Ia: Puritanism intensely stressed diligence in the calling. It was a repeated theme in pastoral sermons and writings. Consistently, both merchant diarists worked hard at their businesses, and historical observers have noted the diligence of the Puritans. Still, their norms did not demand as much work as possible.
>
> Hypothesis Ib: Labor was regarded as a duty to God. Wallington, for one, felt obligated to attend his shop despite disliking the work.
>
> Hypothesis Ic: Though it was more innerworldly than many other religions, Puritanism's otherworldly emphasis took precedence. Work in the calling, though important, had to be limited in order to concentrate on religious worship. The religion tended to scale back the business activities of those economically overcommitted like Elias Pledger. The ideal was a balance between the calling and more otherworldly duties.
>
> Hypothesis Id: Puritanism, as part of the Judeo-Christian tradition, helped to introduce the work ethic into Occidental culture. Furthermore, it intensified strands of the work ethic that had developed outside Puritanism. The Puritan work ethic aided

243

capitalism more through its cultural influence than through its influence on Puritans' business practices because the cultural influence lasted much longer, reached more entrepreneurs and workers, and acted outside the economic limitations of the Puritan religious context.

Hypothesis II: Saving and Investment. This hypothesis, too, is confirmed in a qualified form. Puritan savings and investments aided capitalism, but only moderately.

Hypothesis IIa: Frugality was a religious virtue; the stewardship doctrine obligated everyone to use resources wisely (compare Weber [1904–5] 1958:170–71). Later, frugality became a mainstream cultural value. On the other hand, the Puritans forbade miserliness (see Poggi 1983:41); this led to a balanced, moderate approach overall, not extreme asceticism.

Hypothesis IIb: Not all Puritan savings were reinvested economically because the doctrine of stewardship required that charity be given to the poor and to the church. Moreover, though reinvestment was best aided by entrepreneurs who wished to earn but not spend, both Elias Pledger and Nehemiah Wallington sought gain for a better livelihood.

Hypothesis III: The Spirit of Capitalism. This study found no evidence of a "spirit of capitalism" in the form proposed by Weber. Neither Benjamin Franklin, Weber's prime example, nor either Puritan merchant studied here evinced any such spirit. Since there is no known historical example of it, there is no evidence that it has ever existed.

Hypothesis IIIa: Even if entrepreneurs could be found with this spirit, it would have just a *partial* affinity with Puritanism. Although it shared with the Puritan ethic the duty to become rich, Puritanism forbade making wealth an end in itself or making it life's central goal, two components that make up the capitalist spirit. Hence, it is doubtful that the drive to earn for its own sake originated in Puritanism.

Puritanism's suspicion of wealth and profit-seeking put it even further from Weber's "capitalist spirit." Also Puritan business ethics were at odds with the spirit of calculation.

Puritanism failed to instill the spirit of capitalism in the merchants studied here. Wallington found his trade a burden, not the chief end of his life. Pledger (diary:57) sought profit to meet his material needs; this was a traditional view, not the spirit of capitalism.

Nor did the duty to grow rich lead to the spirit of capitalism. Since Baxter reported that few grew rich to perform good works, this duty was too weak in most Puritans to induce the capitalist spirit. Neither did it exert a cultural effect on the spirit of capitalism. The idea of a duty to one's capital (see Weber [1904–5] 1958:170), or to grow rich in order to perform greater works of charity, is quite marginal in Western culture.

Hypothesis IIIb: Since moneymaking was not the key to proving election, and hence not the central aim of those seeking *certitudo salutis*, it could not have evolved into life's central goal when interest in salvation waned. To illustrate, Franklin's orientation, which was strongly influenced by Puritanism, emerged as a secularized version of the work ethic rather than as Weber's spirit of capitalism. It follows that any tendency for modern capitalists to devote life to business achievement must have found its inspiration elsewhere.

Hypothesis IV: The Rationalization of Life.   Although the growth of capitalism called for a shrewd, calculating, and disciplined class, there is no evidence in these data that Puritanism produced them. Though disciplined, these Puritan merchants were not very rational or systematic in their business conduct.[1]

Some Puritans undoubtedly possessed these traits in greater measure; but Puritanism was an inconsistent religion that sent mixed signals and produced mixed results. Too few underwent the dynamics that Weber depicted to produce an entire class with capitalist potential.

Hypothesis IVa: Puritan socialization helped to give capitalism the personality types it needed because its constant struggle against sin increased control over spontaneous impulses and pleasures and led to self-discipline (Seaver 1985:181, 184, 185). While constant vigilance did give life a methodical, systematic character, still it would be an exaggeration to say that the Puritans adopted an overall life plan or a general schema of life.

These effects hinge on asceticism, but Puritanism was less ascetic than Weber's portrayal of it. There was sympathy for the weaknesses of the flesh among the religiously sincere. The will could substitute for the deed, and repentance and pardon were practiced routinely. The rigors of self-discipline could therefore be relaxed somewhat. This produced less rational and disciplined personalities than anticipated.

The final products of a Puritan upbringing were not necessarily well-suited for capitalist enterprise. Nehemiah Wallington, for example, was not well socialized into the capitalist class. He was awkward and uncertain in business matters.[2]

Hypothesis IVb: The struggle for certainty of salvation helped to systematize life insofar as the self-supervision of conduct increased assurance by keeping one's conscience clear (see Seaver

1985:182). However, it did little to rationalize business practice because business discipline was of little importance for proving election.

For different reasons, neither merchant diarist exemplifies the salvation drive leading to world mastery or rational action. Pledger's early conversion experience precluded a struggle for certainty of salvation: the assured felt no anxiety to inspire the systematization of life. In contrast, Wallington struggled for years before he reached assurance. However, typical of the Puritan experience, Wallington's salvation fears led to hysteria and upset rather than rationality or the systematization of life; nor did later assurance make him much more rational.

Hypothesis IVc: Puritanism called for the routine performance of religious duties, regular self-examination, the recording of sins and receipt of Divine mercies (see Wallington British diary:98), the keeping of a spiritual diary, and the leading of a holy life. This increased the rationality of religious life considerably. However, religious discipline did not organize all of life. Beyond devotion to a trade or calling, it required little rationality in economic life. Hence, religious life became more systematized than economic life. Consistent with this pattern, Wallington systematized his religious life but was far from rational in business practice. Religious rationality need not carry over into economic life. Rather, the converse has been true: Puritans' religious method was modeled after preexisting capitalistic rationality.

Hypothesis IVd: Puritanism remained quite traditional rather than trying to break tradition down. Neither of the Puritan merchants studied showed an inclination to break with tradition to transform the economic order. Both approached business traditionally, and neither tried to innovate or conquer the world.

Puritanism, not unlike Catholicism, embraced traditional work motives like supplying life's necessaries and providing useful economic services for the community. Consistently, Wallington and Pledger both illustrate the pursuit of traditional consumption motives in business.

Also, Puritans were to adhere to traditional business ethics. Attempts to follow Christian market ethics brought Wallington and other pious Puritans into moral conflict with the most profitable business strategies. This made it difficult to practice rational calculation (see Seaver 1985:292), maximize profits, or pursue profit for its own sake.

The Puritan ideal of contentment with one's lot also operated as a brake on economic ambition; both Pledger (diary:69) and Wallington (British diary:175–76) tried (with mixed success) to be satisfied with very little. For the most part Puritans were discouraged from rising occupationally. They were to choose the calling that best served God and the community and best avoided sin, rather than the best paying. Each was expected to serve in the place to which he had been called; and that was typically interpreted as one's present job. A low station was considered as good as a high place for serving God.

Puritans were taught to rely on God; this discouraged their active mastery of the world. Reliance on God to provide encouraged passivity (see Wallington British diary:26; Folger diary: 403, 491). As a corollary, Puritans were told to "take no thought for tomorrow" (see Pledger diary:57); this discouraged planning.

One area of reliance on God was in financial matters. Because God codetermined profits, they were not deemed fully amenable to entrepreneurial control. Accordingly, Puritans were directed not to be concerned about profit or the success of their efforts. Wallington (British diary:12, 26, 29) thought of good trading as a mercy of God and prayed for more customers (British diary:26, 144, 170). On the other hand, he (ibid.:5) had made no provision for debts coming due. Neither he nor Pledger had any plans for expansion.

Hypothesis V: Wealth and Profit. The Puritans were mixed about wealth and gain. Although moderate gains could be desired, an immoderate desire for gain was sinful. Teachings were not consistent: wealth was both devalued and made a duty. Overall, the dangers of wealth were stressed more than this duty. The negatives of wealth limited and ultimately outweighed its positives.

Hypothesis Va: Unsought wealth could be accepted as a gift from God. However, wealth was dangerous because it tempted one to pride, worldliness, and irreligion, which made it difficult for a wealthy man to be saved.

Hypothesis Vb: Although wealth could be a blessing of God, it could also be a trap laid by God to expose the wickedness of someone who had lost his favor and whom he intended to condemn. Hence, most Puritans considered it difficult to tell whether or not a person's wealth was blessed by God.

Hypothesis Vc: Puritanism was ambivalent toward acquisition; it was never encouraged in an unqualified manner. Wealth could only be sought for religious purposes; it was sinful to seek it for worldly purposes or as an end in itself. The desire for

gain was regarded with suspicion and often considered covetous. It violated norms of contentment, reliance on God's
providence, and remaining faithful to the station to which one
had been called. Puritans were urged to devote more effort to
their souls than to pursuit of gain. Furthermore, Puritan merchants accepted these teachings rather than selectively reinter-
preting them in a more procapitalist manner.

Hypothesis Vd: Acquisition was a duty when wealth was
sought as a means of serving God, for example through charitable good works, but was sinful when pursued for other motives. Since the duty to seek wealth was a minor one in
Puritanism and since the temptations of wealth made it dangerous to salvation, the pastors recommended against becoming
rich to serve God in most cases; only the most securely pious
could afford the risk.

Hypothesis VI: The Legitimation of Capitalism.   Although capitalism has
been legitimated primarily on secular and utilitarian grounds, based on
its contribution to civic prosperity, Puritanism has helped to strengthen its
legitimacy in several ways.

Hypothesis VIa: The division of labor had been well accepted
long before the Puritan era, and its further expansion required
little justification. Neither Protestantism nor the doctrine of the
calling was really needed to make occupational specialization
acceptable. It was quite expected that people would pursue a
single line of work.

Hypothesis VIb: Successful merchants and industrialists were
prominent, well-respected citizens long before the Reformation.
Neither Puritans nor their contemporaries had moral qualms
about earning their livelihoods through business pursuits. If
anything, Puritanism was more mixed than the general culture
about trades that were idle or sinful.

Hypothesis VIc: In Puritanism the legitimacy of profits did not
depend on how much work went into obtaining them but upon
the motive for seeking them. Profits sought to gain the necessities of life or to do God's work were legitimate, but not profits
sought for worldly purposes or as an end in themselves. Puritanism put the profits it condoned on a firmer moral basis by
making them a duty; thereby it helped to justify some capitalist
action. However, it did not directly legitimate profit-making in
general.

Although sloth and idleness could diminish profits, it was
believed that business success came from God as well as human
effort. Thus, profits were more than the fruit of an ascetic life.[3]

Only later, after English Puritanism had declined, did the Occident believe that hard work created profits directly without God's coaction; so only then could profits be justified by the work that had produced them. When Puritanism strengthened the Occidental work ethic, it also strengthened this justification of profit in the general culture.

Hypothesis VId: Puritanism's legitimation of capitalist inequalities came as a cultural effect. Once the Occident saw wealth and poverty as the outcomes of diligence and sloth, respectively, the work ethic, which had been reinforced by the Puritans and other Judeo-Christian groups, served to justify the rich and condemn the poor.

Hypothesis VIe: Both Puritan divines and merchants were strongly opposed to the oppression of the poor. A charitable approach toward them was urged. Because of the emphasis on mercy and friendly dealing in transactions, businessmen were not to enrich themselves from the labor of the poor (see Seaver 1985:136). Low wages were never justified on grounds that workers were given the opportunity to do good works in their callings or fulfilled their duty through labor.

Hypothesis VIf: Puritans honored market prices, but opposed charging whatever the market would bear. Brotherhood and charity took priority over the dictates of the market.

Hypothesis VIg: The rational actions required to increase profits, even when formally correct, often ran counter to those required of a good Christian. Neither Pledger nor Wallington could please God unless he ran his business traditionally. In actuality, neither had a clear conscience regarding business activity; they often felt guilty about their business pursuits.

Hypothesis VII: Religious Anxiety.   Inconsistently, Puritanism could both breed and reduce anxiety in its followers. Its "norm of assurance" led Puritans toward certainty of salvation, and yet its "norm of anxiety" warned sinners to fear God's wrath. Preachers tried to frighten the "carnally secure" with threats of hell but comfort the fearful with the promise of redemption through Christ.

Hypothesis VIIa: Puritan salvation anxiety did little to drive capitalist activity. Anxieties could not have given capitalism its continuous operation or steady growth because they tended to be weak or sporadic.

Predestination makes salvation no more uncertain than many other Christian beliefs about the afterlife. Furthermore, in Puritanism the secrecy of God's decree had been softened by the Gospel's revelation of the signs and marks of the elect. The regenerate could take comfort as they observed the salvation process working in themselves.

Salvation anxiety was further mitigated by comforting doctrines centering around Christ, the Gospel, the new covenant, faith, and repentance. Rigorous conduct standards had been eased.[4] Also, God was seen as neither icy nor remote, but loving and merciful along with Christ. Loneliness was diminished by pastoral counsel and the support of the godly community. These softer teachings fostered reasonable levels of assurance.

Of the two Puritan merchants, Pledger achieved assurance early in life while Wallington (Folger diary:187) came to believe in his salvation later. They illustrate the feasibility of finding assurance under this doctrine.

There were anxiety-provoking aspects of Puritanism that upset Wallington and others considerably. Nevertheless, the highly anxious were said to be few.

Since the level of anxiety tended to fluctuate, declining between attacks, it could not provide the constant motivation needed for a consistently methodical life. Furthermore, anxiety typically produced withdrawal, melancholy, and/or incapacity rather than greater activity. If anything, it was a hindrance to business.

Hypothesis VIIb: Many Puritans believed in their own election and became self-confident, which was said by contemporaries and historians to spur them to greater economic activity and business success. However, that could not be confirmed here because neither Pledger nor Wallington was bold or confident in business.

Hypothesis VIII: The Quest for Salvation. Puritans seeking assurance could try to acquire the signs of salvation to prove that they were among the elect. The variety of signs and inconsistency of pastoral advice, however, led their conduct in a number of different directions, each taken by just a fraction of all. This dissipated the force of the salvation quest rather than focusing it on one form of conduct. Hence, capitalist action was not energized by the full power of the drive for certainty.

Since Puritans did not normally deal with problems of assurance through their economic behavior, the economic impact of the salvation motive was weak. The chief signs and means of salvation centered around religious activities. Thus, the pursuit of salvation remained largely separate from economic pursuits. Furthermore, concentration on salvation-related religious activities left *less* time for economic action; and too strong a concentration on economic life was at odds with the Puritans' image of the elect.

Since the signs of salvation could be internal as well as external, the quest for certainty led to introspection as well as worldly activity. People concentrated on examining their state of grace but did little to improve it. This implies that it was uncommon for Puritans to modify their economic practices to achieve certainty.

Hypothesis VIIIa: The salvation drive gave little reinforcement to work, which was rarely mentioned as a sign of salvation. Economic labor was a minor good work, and counted as a good work only for the poor. Neither merchant studied here based his assurance upon it (or any other economic behavior).

Hypothesis VIIIb: Wealth was rarely mentioned as a sign of salvation by the Puritan clergy. Although some laity uncertain of their state found reassurance in God's "bodily mercies," the merchants in this study did not think that heaven followed upon capitalist success. The belief that wealth signified election was apparently a minority view in English Puritanism. To the contrary, since wealth lowered one's chance of salvation (see Hypothesis Va), it tended to be a negative indication. Most considered it, or economic gain, unreliable as a sign of the elect. Conversely, poverty was no sign of condemnation.

Since wealth could provide the means for charitable good works, which were signs of salvation, the quest for salvation could encourage acquisition indirectly. However, this effect was weak because good works were a secondary sign of salvation and material works were inferior to more spiritual works. If gain had been motivated by the quest for works, the economically successful would have performed them abundantly; yet Baxter (1653:337–39) saw little inclination toward good works among the rich.

Hypothesis VIIIc: The idea of a life of good works meant to Puritans that they would be judged on the overall tenor of their lives, not on a few atypical actions. Its consequence was not to make standards more rigorous, but to relax them because a few slips could be repented and pardoned under the Gospel. Hence, this doctrine did not encourage the systematization of life as a protection against the occasional error; quite the opposite.

Assurance of salvation, according to some key divines, did not require a constant production of good works; at most, pastoral opinion was divided on this point. The amount required was never clearly specified. Furthermore, evidence is mixed on whether Puritans actually led a life of good works. Although some Puritans could be very charitable, and many served God diligently in their callings, Baxter complained of a paucity of works.

Proof of election required only enough works to confirm faith.[5] Further, since all human works were inadequate, the Gospel accepted earnest effort in their stead, which further reduced the press to perform them. Typically, the doubtful thought they needed fewer sins, not more good works.

Hypothesis IX: Religious Premia. In general, Puritan economic duties were motivated both by ethics and premia. However, religious premia reinforced these duties weakly because, despite their power, they usually led in noneconomic directions.

Hypothesis IXa: Religious discipline was less effective in English Puritanism than among North American Protestants. It affected mainly the few separatists; most Puritans remained in the Church of England, which, with a few exceptions, had weak parish discipline. Furthermore, religious discipline dealt hardly at all with economic conduct or success. It usually involved religious deviance, alcohol, or sexual immorality.

Hypothesis IXb: An English Puritan's religious worth or standing was not a function of business achievement. Economic success was used neither as a criterion for church membership nor for eligibility for communion. Most Puritans belonged to the Church of England, which was relatively open in its admissions; and where communion was denied, the basis was some major sin or scandal, not poverty or poor profits.

Hypothesis IXc: Since little premium was placed on rational economic action, there was little religious incentive to engage in it. Because the work ethic was preached with moral intensity and the devout were sensitive to matters of conscience, Puritans were more likely to work hard out of conviction than for religious rewards.[6]

All in all, some hypotheses were supported, but not every one. This is not surprising given certain logical inconsistencies between them that make it impossible for all to be true at once. Strong religious anxiety, for example, would be incongruent in a self-confident entrepreneur. Also, since much religious anxiety stemmed from guilt over sin, it was incompatible with the clean conscience Weber posited for Puritan businessmen. Conversely, if Puritans had overcome this anxiety, they would have lacked the restless drive to acquire the signs of salvation. As another example, religious influence could not be based completely on sanctions and at the same time contain the moral character necessary to legitimate profits and capitalism.

And with sanctions alone the most pious would not develop the strongest commitment to capitalist action.

THE MECHANISMS OF INFLUENCE

Religious influence on capitalism operated through several different mechanisms.[7] Some, but not all of those were proposed by Weber; and some of the mechanisms that operated did so more weakly than Weber suggested.

The most important of these mechanisms was the work ethic. It exerted its influence both through behavioral and cultural effects. Of these two, the cultural effect was more widespread and longer lasting. On the behavioral side, the duty to work could be quite effective morally. Its strength must be qualified though because Puritanism opposed too great an immersion in economic activity. The cultural effect of the work ethic placed it within the mainstream of Western culture. Industry became both a norm and a value, especially in the middle classes. The culturally transformed work ethic often took the form of professional dedication, as Weber has pointed out.[8] Since many groups worldwide have developed traditions of hard work, the Occident was not culturally unique in that regard. However, within the Occident religion appears to have been a chief source of this value.

The work ethic was also part of another mechanism of influence: it helped to legitimate capitalism through its cultural effect. By John Wesley's time, work justified profits and also inequality. Profits were further legitimized by their connection to charitable good works.

Finally, Puritan norms of saving and stewardship aided capitalism by helping to curtail consumption. By the nineteenth century this effect was broadened when frugality and saving became norms of the dominant culture.

No significant influence was found from mechanisms involving the spirit of capitalism, religious discipline, salvation anxiety, or the demonstration of one's salvation. Similarly, the pursuit of good works did little to further capitalist expansion.

Overall, there were both behavioral and cultural influences at work. Some of the behavioral effects were mixed or limited in their impacts; in comparison, the cultural influences were greater and more lasting. The timing of these two types of mechanism differed. Behavioral effects occurred at the height of Puritan piety; and the pious were the most strongly affected. This coincides with the timing of Puritan prosperity, which was well-established by the seventeenth century (see Marlowe 1956:5).

The cultural effects came later, after a selective borrowing process had taken place, and after dominant capitalism had become institutionalized to the point where it required legitimation.

THE ECONOMIC IMPACT

English Puritanism aided capitalism, but its impact was weaker and less dramatic than Weber claimed. One can assess the effects of each mechanism of influence separately.

The Impact of the Work Ethic

First, the behavioral effect of the work ethic was moderately strong despite its limitations. The industry of Puritan employees and entrepreneurs raised productivity and profits, contributed to business growth (see Marlowe 1956:40, 42), and may have forced non-Puritans to work harder and longer in order to compete. It aided social change indirectly because the expansion of individual firms helped to transform the economy into one dominated by capitalism.

Of course, not just religious morality, but also material needs made Puritans diligent.[9] For example, Wallington (British diary:6 and Folger diary:To the Christian Reader; see also Seaver 1985:126) was moved to diligence by a "grat want of mony." Nor did diligence alone make their businesses successful. Skillful and effective work is needed, not just mindless toil (Grassby 1995:292–93, 296; Rose 1985:134). Wallington was diligent, for example, but was relatively unsuccessful; he barely stayed in business (Seaver 1985:125, see also p. 127). Once he (British diary:148) remarked that "for all my diligence in looking to my shope yet I did not take six pence all yt day." Diligence was just one cause among many of business success and growth.

Hence, the work ethic alone did not make rational capitalism dominant. As Weber indicated, the Occident was unique not in its work ethic but in its total configuration of conditions, which *included* the Protestant ethic.

Although the Puritan work ethic helped modern capitalism expand and dominate the economy, it was not around at the infancy of modern capitalism to give it birth and shape because Puritanism did not develop until the sixteenth century. It was the Catholic form of the work ethic that first bolstered infant capitalism. Kaelber (1998) notes an early Waldensian contribution. Then came Luther's concept of the calling. Puritanism was neither the first Judeo-Christian religion to strengthen the work ethic, nor the last. All major branches of Christianity have endorsed hard work, thrift, and wise use of time. The Methodist work ethic reinforced capitalism in the eighteenth century, after English Puritanism had faded, and the Anglican work ethic pervaded Victorian England and is still strong there today. Overall, the behavioral effects of the Judeo-Christian work ethic came episodically with the flowering of various religious groups.

In sum, a number of religions have encouraged economic action through their work ethics. Cumulatively, they have contributed significantly to economic progress. Puritanism was one of those that contributed.

Although the behavioral effects of the Puritans' work ethic died out with them in the seventeenth century, its influence was extended by centuries though its cultural effect, which helped nineteenth-century capitalism dominate the English economy. This effect produced a stronger work ethic than had been possible earlier when otherworldly values prevailed. Work became many people's spiritual calling in a more secular age. The doctrine of the calling increased dedication to work and gave it a more continuous course. The modern notion of career and the professional's ethic of service owe a lot to this religious concept. The Puritan ethic not only gave modern capitalism a longer workday, which it required, but also gave work a moral component. Those influenced by the work ethic performed economic tasks out of duty and commitment, seeking satisfaction in a job well done.

Weber ([1904–5] 1958:57, 61–63) seems correct that modern economic expansion has been driven by more than pure greed or consumption needs. Material self-interests alone would have remained ineffectual desires without the discipline and persistence necessary to achieve one's interests. The morality of the work ethic disciplined moneymaking and stabilized output through steady application to economic pursuits (see Seaver 1985:194 and Rose 1985:31). Furthermore, contrary to Weber ([1904–5] 1958:182–83), the work ethic did not break down into pure utilitarianism after Puritan piety faded; through its cultural influence it remains a moral force governing modern capitalism.

Impact on the Profit Motive

Besides that from its work ethic, a second economic influence of Puritanism derived from its attitude toward profit. Not just diligence, but attention to profits, is required for commercial success. Hence, the work ethic can foster capitalist success better when combined with the profit motive than it can alone.

But Puritanism *weakened* the profit motive among its devotees. Elias Pledger's avarice was toned down by his religious beliefs and Nehemiah Wallington strove to subdue his economic wants (letters:176; British diary:144). Puritan otherworldliness undermined the profit motive by disparaging consumption and materialist desires; similarly, the doctrine of providence undercut the success drive by demanding contentment with one's lot. Moderate gain was the norm; anything beyond was covetous and sinful. Gains obtained for purposes other than God's service were considered worldly, and the belief that God controlled profits discouraged entrepreneurs from attending to the bottom line.

As long as Puritan piety was strong, these teachings acted as a brake on the economic motives of the devout. This cost capitalism some growth and profits temporarily.

However, over time, English Puritanism died out, and religious opposition to profits faded.[10] Attitudes toward profit have changed from viewing it as deplorable self-interest to seeing it as a moral good and a cultural value. Many business owners have adopted unlimited moneymaking and material success as central life-goals. In many cases their powerful profit drives have combined with the work ethic to propel capitalist expansion.

Impact on Savings and Investment

Puritan thrift aided capitalist firms because in the sixteenth and seventeenth centuries, even more than today, sober living and restraint from spending were needed to accumulate capital, keep debt low, and (contrary to Samuelsson 1961:83–84) achieve growth (Grassby 1978:370; Marlowe 1956:72, 73). Since many new businessmen were undercapitalized, these ascetic virtues were necessary for success (Grassby 1978:370, 378). However, the benefits from this mechanism should not be exaggerated. The divines advocated frugality, but miserliness was to be avoided. Furthermore, there was little reinforcement of thrift by salvation premia; this limited the force of the norm.

Puritans were known for thrift (see Marlowe 1956:45), but neither merchant in this study saved much. Wallington spent too much on news pamphlets, and Pledger lived as comfortably as he could on limited means. The mixed character of this evidence mirrors the mixed Puritan attitude toward frugality. Methodism seems more unqualified than Puritanism in its advocacy of thrift (see Weber [1904–5] 1958:175); its influence came later, in the eighteenth century.

Puritans reinvested less in business growth than the amount saved because of their obligation to give funds to charity. However, Baxter complained of too little of that (see above), and in fact the Puritans gained no great reputation for charity (Grassby 1995:285). Thus, the quantity of Puritan funds diverted from business to charities is indeterminate.

Much later, after religious norms had added a moral component to thrift in the general culture, personal savings could contribute more to capital investment. Freed from Puritan restrictions on how much to save and how to direct savings, the more acquisition-minded nineteenth century could more readily funnel savings into business growth.

Impact on Tradition and Rationality

Contrary to Weber's claim that Puritanism helped capitalism to break through tradition, Puritanism was quite traditional itself, and, like the Asiatic religions, some of its traditional beliefs retarded capitalist growth. For example, work in the calling was similar to Hindu caste *dharma* because both required dutiful obedience, which kept economic actions within traditional limits. This fostered a static, not a dynamic, economy.

Puritans' religious scruples discouraged them from rationally seeking higher profits, attending to profit growth, analyzing profits, and/or making business decisions on grounds of profitability. So their businesses achieved less, especially those of the pious; and "when change came, it was not at the hands of the Puritan artisans and craftsmen" (Seaver 1985:126).

Although Puritan asceticism and impulse control seem likely to give a sense of mastery and embolden the entrepreneur (see Weber [1904–5] 1958:118–19, 166–71), these effects were not found in the data. Puritanism could not take a dismal prospect like Nehemiah Wallington and turn him into a Benjamin Franklin. It could not systematically produce the character types that modern capitalism required.[11]

Nor were the Puritan businesses in this study particularly rational or well-organized. So there is virtually no evidence that Puritanism contributed to the systematization of business enterprise.[12] Many of the rational management practices crucial to modern capitalism had emerged before the Reformation (see Cohen 1980); they were not of Protestant provenance.

Impact on the Capitalist Class

Puritanism helped only indirectly with the formation of the bourgeois class. Again, much of the impact was cultural rather than behavioral.

First of all, as shown above, not all Puritans developed a personality and character suitable for business enterprise. Even some with the work ethic lacked economic rationality.

Second, there were too few Puritans to make up a class. There were few of the godly sort in England (Collinson 1982:258, 276–77; Downame [1604] 1974:II, 246); they were a small minority (Seaver 1958:viii). They formed a self-conscious community (Collinson 1982:268, 276–78), but it was not co-extensive with the business class. Moreover, it was too short-lived to produce large numbers of bourgeoisie. After the Restoration this community diminished (see Stannard 1977:103) as many Puritans moved away to the

New World and English authorities effectively prevented worship in Puritan "conventicles." This community could not have persisted and developed into the English middle class.

More plausible numerically is Weber's ([1904–5] 1958:67–68, 72) idea that only a few rigorous Puritan businessmen were needed to set standards for all, since the others would need to perform equally well in order to compete successfully. Indeed, the work standard for small business owners today is at least a sixty-hour week; somehow, standards have become more rigorous. Yet, the Puritan businessmen studied here were hardly standard-setters. Their religion's otherworldliness and traditional business ethics held them back. Furthermore, it is not clear that, in the seventeenth century, the bulk of English business owners would have had to match a few who were particularly industrious. Although "competition forced them to revise backward techniques" (Grassby 1995:404), the guild system limited the amount of competition that took place. Even so, there would still have been room in the economy for many traditionalists to co-exist. Hence, Weber's question on the origins of the bourgeoisie is better than his answer to it.

Because of the numbers involved, Puritanism's greatest contribution to the middle class came through its cultural effect on Anglicanism (see Marlowe 1956:46). By the nineteenth century the Anglican middle class, following Puritan examples, embraced the values of diligence, thrift, and sobriety (see Chapter 2); and English character came to contain a reserved self-control (see Weber [1904–5] 1958:173).

Impact on Legitimation

Puritanism helped to legitimate capitalism; however, the Puritan contribution was secondary in importance as seen earlier. Since some of capitalism's chief justifications predated the Reformation, Puritanism's support seems largely unnecessary. Contrary to Weber, it is not clear that capitalism really needed religious legitimation. Indeed, young capitalism survived and developed for centuries despite the mixed reception it received from Christianity.

Still, Puritanism, and more generally the Judeo-Christian tradition, played a helpful role in the legitimation of capitalism, primarily through the reinforcement of philanthropy [13] and through contributions to the work ethic. Philanthropy and hard work justified capitalist profits, and hard work also legitimated inequality. Since capitalist inequalities have been a serious problem, this has been important for the stability of the system.

Since much of Puritanism's legitimating effect was cultural rather than behavioral, it came too late to justify infant capitalism or to create the preconditions for capitalist growth. Rather, the beneficiary was mature nineteenth-century capitalism. By that time the procapitalist materials had been extracted from religion, and were being used as part of the dominant secular culture. What resulted was an ideological justification of the capitalist order. It rationalized and stabilized an already dominant system.

Overall Impact of Puritanism on Capitalism

There was clearly some effect, based on the mechanisms just discussed. However, the effect size should not be exaggerated. First of all, the Puritan contributions were not unique. The profit motive provided strong capitalist motivation even without the work ethic and its moral dimension (see Grassby 1995:296; see also Rose 1985:31). And the roles of philanthropy and the work ethic in the legitimation of capitalism were secondary to utilitarian legitimacy. Second, Puritanism's effects were weakened by inconsistencies. Work was a duty but too much of it was worldly. Profit was a duty but dangerous to salvation. One should be thrifty but not miserly. Puritanism bred anxiety but also comforted. Puritans grew confident of election, but had to feel sorrow for their sins. And the quest for certainty led to the prayer closet and the conventicle, not just to the workplace. Thus, Puritanism led in a variety of directions, scattering and diffusing its effects. Third, Puritanism was not the cause of the economic uniqueness of the Occident. It came too late to originate capitalism's most distinctive institutions. Nor did it foster economic rationality, which was not a Puritan norm and was not backed by religious premia. If anything, its traditional business ethics restricted economic rationality. Puritanism called for no unique economic actions. Its work ethic was not unique nor were the religious premia placed on it. It did not enforce economic actions by making them proofs of election; they were minor proofs at best. Rather, it used moral force to secure compliance with economic duties, and that mode of enforcement was far from unique among the world's religions.

The impact of Puritanism was more cultural than behavioral. Behavioral effects were limited because the Puritans were a small minority with few adherents. They formed a godly community, but, aside from a few separatists, lacked their own church organization. This limited their capacity to mount a concerted influence campaign or to discipline believers. Nor did Cromwell's government support their aims despite his Puritan credentials. Moreover, the Puritan period was quite limited in duration. They came too late to have initiated the commercial revolution; commerce was thriving by Elizabethan times. Their movement reached fruition in the seventeenth century but was severely weakened after the Restoration (see Stannard 1977:103), when they lost out to the Anglicans culturally as well as organizationally. Whatever their average contribution in work and

savings had been, their small cadre of seventeenth-century religious entrepreneurs could not have made a decisive contribution to capitalist
growth.

One finds somewhat larger behavioral effects by examining the Judeo-
Christian tradition as a whole. Catholics, Methodists, and others adhered
to the work ethic, and Wesley added to the legitimation of capitalist
profits.

However, the greatest effects were the cultural effects on the nineteenth
century. Puritanism's most procapitalist elements were selectively appropriated by Victorian culture without its contrary elements. The full cultural impact of Puritanism was delayed by more than 150 years, but it
included some broad effects.

It is true that there were some behavioral effects. The combination of industry and frugality spurred capitalist growth, which transformed society
when competing institutions withered. However, the successes of small
shopkeepers do not by any means tell the whole story of capitalist expansion. Contrary to Weber, economic rationality was pioneered by large-
scale capitalists, and expansion was often driven by adventurers who
were willing to take risks. Financiers were often deal-makers rather than
drones, and large-scale industrialists were often driven by powerful crav-
ings for wealth, success, and the defeat of the competition. Adventure
capitalists often provided the impetus and vision for new combinations
(such as mergers, trusts, and acquisitions) and new conquests. Their mentality was often less dutiful, and hence less Puritan, than it was self-
aggrandizing. And their actions were often risky and aggressive rather
than methodical. They must receive much of the credit for increasing the
scale of capitalism.

In sum, the contribution of Puritanism, and of religion in general, was
helpful but not critical. As Mann (1986) has shown, the dynamic of capitalist growth got under way much earlier than the era of the Puritans. Their contribution, as Tawney ([1926] 1961:188) has argued, was to
strengthen this trend later.

ASSESSING THE WEBER THESIS

Testing the Weber thesis is complicated because it consists of a number
of theses. Weber described a number of mechanisms through which
Protestantism might have affected capitalism. Since he named too many
mechanisms of influence, one must sort out which were the correct ones.
Viewed in this way, it is clear that the Weber thesis is partly right and partly wrong. Some mechanisms of influence operated as hypothesized while
others did not.

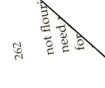

There is <u>something</u> to the proposition that F
<u>modern capitalism, but less than</u> Weber claimed. F
<u>fluence operated than he enumerated; most that</u>
than implied; and their impact was less revolution

The truth or falsity of the Weber thesis depends
At the most general level, it is true that religious id
omy; Protestantism aided modern capitalism. Beyo.
5] 1958:178) correctly specifies the work ethic as a me
However, <u>if the Weber thesis is stated in terms of th</u> ˌpırıt of capitalism,
<u>one is on thin ice.</u> Its existence cannot be verified; and if it did exist, it
would have little affinity to Puritanism since the two would be somewhat
antithetical. Likewise, the <u>Weber thesis is not correct if it hinges on the</u>
way that <u>salvation concerns propelled Puritans</u> toward work and profit,
on the way that religious rationality increased economic rationality, or on
the conquest of tradition by religious individualism.

Many of Weber's supporters know that he made errors, but may be sur-
prised that some of them were so important to the central argument. His
concept of the spirit of capitalism seems to lack validity; and <u>the view that</u>
<u>economic behavior provided the best signs of election stands out as the</u>
<u>most striking inaccuracy in this work.</u> Clearly, his weaker arguments and
overstatements should not be accepted; one must be selective. <u>On the oth-</u>
<u>er hand, Weber's critics and detractors cannot</u> deny that Protestantism
made *some* <u>contribution to modern capitalism.</u> The mechanisms of influence that worked substantially as Weber said represent important insights
and should not be discarded along with the disconfirmed hypotheses.
Perhaps those totally opposed to the Weber thesis have failed to appreciate that it is multifaceted. If one or even several proposed mechanisms of
influence are invalidated, Weber's work offers others that are more consistent with the evidence. <u>Thus, the entire thesis</u> cannot be and has not
been <u>disproven</u> by limited and partial critiques.

Once the Weber thesis is disaggregated into various mechanisms of influence, its truth or falsity need not be viewed as an all-or-none proposition. It is time for Weber's opponents to recognize the impact of the work
ethic, including its cultural effects and its ability to legitimate inequalities.
Conversely, his supporters should fully acknowledge Puritanism's traditional and otherworldly sides, as well as its emphases on faith, worship,
introspection, repentance, and spiritual comfort.

Theoretical Contributions

Weber's great contribution to the Protestantism-and-capitalism question has been theoretical. He argued that religious ideas can have an economic impact. Furthermore, he recognized that modern capitalism could

ish without a supportive culture and institutional structure. One
was for appropriate character types to provide a disciplined labor
ce and to form the bourgeois class. Another was for legitimacy; for one
thing, the central capitalist activity of profit-making had to be made into a
moral good.

His conceptual scheme has provided the starting point for investigating
the effects of religion on modern capitalism. It has generated an abundance of hypotheses for historical testing, and given work on this question theoretical relevance. For proposing various mechanisms through
which Puritanism affected capitalism, the prime source in this study has
been Max Weber. He has provided the conceptual framework used here.

Logical Weakness in Weber's Analysis

Yet, alongside its theoretical strengths, there are weaknesses in Weber's
work. First, there are conceptual difficulties. For example, he left the key
concept "spirit of capitalism" defined only provisionally; and the provisional definition incorporates so many characteristics that it excludes any
business mentality that historians have ever encountered. The idea of
modern capitalism is poorly conceptualized because it is ambiguous. The
rational firm, rational organization of labor, calculable law, and so on may
be *characteristics* of it, but may simply be *preconditions* of it; Weber
([1904–5] 1958:21–27; [1923] 1961:207–9) stated the relationship both ways.
Another problem stems from the inappropriate conflation of differing
concepts. "Asceticism," for example, is so broadly defined as to include
Puritan industry and frugality along with ascetic Asian salvation techniques that achieve Nirvana; this linkage incorrectly suggests that industry and frugality helped Puritans achieve certainty of salvation simply
because of their ascetic character. Similarly, Weber capitalized on the double meaning of the word "calling," which could mean one's occupation or
a call to serve God; since Puritans kept these two meanings quite separate,
and made it clear which was intended, the use of a single word for both
meanings is less significant than it superficially seems. Another "double
meaning" stems from the verbal similarity of the terms "work" and
"works." Although Weber tended to conflate these two, Puritan good
works did not necessarily involve economic work, as seen in Chapter 6.
Likewise, Puritan "action" and "duty" were usually concerned with worship, not economics.

There are also problems of causal logic. Could the spirit of capitalism
have caused modern capitalism if it had been *part* of modern capitalism?
Also, could religious rationality have caused economic rationality when
the latter had developed first? Another time-order problem concerns the
effect of Protestantism on the early growth of capitalism; since the Refor-

mation postdated modern capitalism's infancy, Protestantism could have affected modern capitalism only later in its relative maturity. Finally, there remains the dilemma of which caused which. Weber's method of elective affinities can do nothing to sort out the causal ordering.

Weber's thesis also contains some logical inconsistencies. Because sin caused religious anxiety, it was inconsistent to posit both a clean conscience for the Puritans and, at the same time, religious anxiety. Similarly, Weber asserted both the driving anxiety of the Puritans and their supreme confidence. Another instance concerns the formation of the bourgeois class: religion was said to be important because it systematically produced large numbers of bourgeois, but elsewhere the nucleus of the bourgeoisie was said to be small, just enough to set competitive standards for the economy as a whole. Another flip-flop is found in Weber's criticism of Old Testament rationalism as a small-bourgeois ethic when elsewhere he held that small businessmen had a stronger spirit of capitalism than the great capitalists. Also, it was somewhat contradictory to minimize the capitalistic affinities of Judaism, Catholicism, and Lutheranism in some writings (e.g., [1923] 1961:262) and then to stress the overall contributions of the Judeo-Christian tradition as a whole elsewhere. Weber also reversed himself when, on the one hand, he stressed the importance of legitimacy so the most pious could be entrepreneurs but, on the other hand, argued that Puritanism's greatest impact came after its piety had died down. Similarly, he argued both that Protestantism produced a dutiful approach to economic action and permitted an economic free-for-all. Weber stated that capitalistic business forms and the capitalistic spirit developed independently; but he also claimed that the spirit of capitalism was needed for capitalism to grow. Finally, Weber stressed Puritanism's otherworldly emphasis on salvation but labeled it innerworldly. Some of these inconsistencies are minor, but the sizeable number of them makes for a rather loose logical system.

Empirical Inaccuracies

Weber also ran into problems of factual accuracy. His image of Puritanism contained errors, some minor and others that affect his conclusions. For example, work and economic success were only rarely used as signs of salvation (see Weber [1922] 1968:575); and not every legal pursuit of riches found religious approval (see Weber [1904–5] 1958:176). Also, Puritan businessmen were not always bold, daring, masterful, or economically rational; and they neither opposed tradition nor broke it down.

Almost all of the features that Weber attributes to Puritanism were actually there. However, some were minor doctrines, and Weber overstates their importance. Taken outside their context, they are made to seem central to Puritanism rather than small parts of a larger whole.

His overestimations include the extent of economic effort required by religion, the good works demanded, the extent of frugality and asceticism, the degree of innerworldliness (Weber 1946:289–91, 331–33), the importance of the duty to profit, the orderliness and rationality in Puritans' business life, and the connection of economic behavior to the salvation drive (Weber [1904–5] 1958:178 and [1922] 1968:575). The latter possibility is much more strongly developed in Mormonism, for example, than it was in English Puritanism. Although Puritanism was strongly influenced by John Calvin, its neo-Calvinism should not have been stretched into the whole of its theology. Strict predestinarianism had been softened by the seventeenth century, in part by covenant theology.[14] Since God became less inscrutable, Weber exaggerated the information vacuum in which the Puritan pilgrim worked and the resulting anxiety.

Because of Weber's theoretical stress on religious premia, the impact of ethics was correspondingly diminished. Pious Puritans often conformed for moral reasons and not just for rational benefits.

In general, Weber exaggerated the impact of Puritanism. He overstated the number of mechanisms through which it aided modern capitalism. He overrated its logical consistency and, consequently, the unity of its impact on believers. Yet, the economic effects of Puritanism should not be denied just because Weber made too much of them.

One reason for Weber's inaccuracies was the thinness of his evidence. Although Weber's knowledge and research capacities were amazing, he undertook an encyclopedic worldwide analysis of all the major world religions. This spread his energies, knowledge, and expertise, and made errors more likely. Even in Protestantism he analyzed a number of religions rather than concentrating on one or two.

Hence, even though he considered Puritanism the best example of Protestantism's effect, he had little evidence on it. He relied too heavily on Baxter, who was atypical in some ways, most notably in his rejection of predestination;[15] and his treatment of Baxter was still superficial. Moreover, much of Weber's information was secondhand, based on the opinions of Troeltsch, Schneckenberger, Heppe, and others. Baxter and the other divines had written voluminously, and it would have been impossible to read everything, while at the same time becoming expert on the other main branches of Christianity, and then to publish *The Protestant Ethic* at a relatively early age. Afterwards Weber concentrated on the other world religions. He never finished reworking the evidence on Protestantism.

Weber's analysis of the spirit of capitalism suffered from his overreliance on Franklin. He had no data on Puritan entrepreneurs, and hardly any on medieval businessmen or modern capitalists.

Even when Weber had the appropriate knowledge, he sometimes erred by not letting the information influence his conclusions. For example, he ([1904–5] 1958:155) knew that Baxter could not accept Calvinism, yet went ahead to cite him as a prime example of neo-Calvinism (see MacKinnon 1988b). Similarly, he ([1904–5] 1958:111) knew that "practical pastoral work" came to the aid of suffering Puritans, but did not conclude that it actually mitigated their salvation worries. Weber (ibid.:115) understood that God could not accept Puritans' corrupt works, yet claimed that uncertainty of grace could be dispelled through those works. He also ([1922] 1963:260; [1904–5] 1958:123) knew that the Puritans rejected as "unattainable" the "Talmudic law," but proceeded as if they were judged by strict obedience rather than the mercy of the Gospel with its stress on repentance and forgiveness. Weber (1946:291, 332) knew that Puritanism devalued and rejected the world, but he presented it as primarily innerworldly. He knew that worldliness was a sin, but argued that entrepreneurs could focus their lives on business with a clean conscience. He ([1904–5] 1958:174, see also pp. 156–57) conceded that Puritanism opposed the pursuit of wealth, but still thought that Puritans considered economic success a sign of salvation. That turns out to be truly inconsistent, not just an interesting irony. Similarly, Weber underestimated the logical contradiction between wealth as an impediment to salvation (see ibid.:259–60 note 6) and a sign of it. Finally, though aware (ibid.:172) that the Puritans condemned the pursuit of wealth as an end in itself, he saw an elective affinity to the spirit of capitalism, which included the pursuit of wealth as an end.

Weber sometimes introduces support for his arguments while contradictory elements are neglected. Although Puritanism seems from his account to pull believers powerfully in one direction, in actuality it pulled in a variety of directions with mixed and/or scattered effects.

A prime example is Weber's stress on the economic side of what was a rather spiritual religion. Economic duties were actually second in priority to more spiritual ones. Likewise, though industry and idleness were signs of one's estate, the most important signs were religious, not economic.

Weber sometimes highlighted the procapitalist teachings of Puritanism while downplaying their opposites. Although the Puritans were mixed about work, savings, and wealth, Weber emphasized the positive, focusing, for example, on frugality without the opposition to miserliness. He noted that wealth could be considered a sign of salvation, but did not cite the warnings against relying on it or the ways in which wealth endangered salvation. He also underplayed the concern with traditional business ethics that held back capitalism.

The anxiety-inspiring part of Puritanism is presented but not its anxiety-reducing parts. Short shrift was given to pastoral reassurance, God's love, Christ's mercy, and Christ's efficacy as a savior from sin.

In forging a link between salvation and economics Weber emphasized certain aspects of the quest for certainty while skipping over others. Economic works and worldly activities were overdrawn as means of proof but faith, meditation, and prayer were overlooked as were sin and repentance.[16]

Because of Puritan contradictions and inconsistencies, it is difficult to present all sides; there is a tendency to pull out one part of the religion without the rest. In Weber's case, some conclusions must be qualified, or have been vitiated, because of religious teachings that contradict the ones he stressed.

Problems with Ideal Types

Another reason for Weber's selection of evidence was his use of the ideal-type method (see Weber [1904–5] 1958:98). This method selects elements from theory and reality to use in constructing the type. It is understood that ideal types never exist in pure form, and that the ideal type is not to be confused with the average type (see ibid.:200 note 28 and 1946:292, 294). Nevertheless, any method that permits and even encourages a selection of evidence must be used with extreme caution. Application of the method can lead to a distorted view of reality. The selected features that make up the type may, in reality, be present in different weights, proportions, strengths, or combinations than the ideal type indicates. This not only attenuates the operation of the type, but can alter it qualitatively. Some elements may be attenuated but not others; this alters the balance.

An ideal type simplifies, and this can make presentation and description more efficient. However, complexities sometimes need to be taken into account rather than glossed over, and sometimes the extracted elements of the type need to be put back into context for a full understanding of their meaning and operation.

Some of Weber's inaccuracies in description and conclusion stem from these shortcomings of ideal types. Actually, it is not clear how much of the problem is due to tendencies inherent in the method itself and how much due to its inappropriate application.[17] However, inaccurate conclusions need not be accepted because they are inherent to the method employed.

According to Weber ([1904–5] 1958:98) ideal types put the dogmas into their most logical and consistent form. However, this imposed a false logical consistency on Puritanism, which was inconsistent and even self-contradictory.

Sometimes in Puritanism two incompatible logics were simultaneously in use. For example, the doctrine of predestination declared one's estate immutable; on the other hand the acceptance of God's promises required use of the means of salvation. Similarly, the norm of anxiety demanded fear while the norm of assurance encouraged certainty that one was among the elect. Puritans were to earn money for charitable works; but they had to make their election sure by avoiding the snare of wealth. Similarly, work at one's calling was a duty; yet time was better spent above with God. It was a Puritan's duty to earn profits and do good works; yet only God could make business profitable and impute goodness to human works. Good works were needed to prove one's faith; yet the endeavor could be substituted for the deed.

Weber stated certain Puritan beliefs correctly, but their opposites were also preached. Puritanism could indeed be anxiety-provoking, but could also reassure and reduce anxiety. Puritanism made profit a duty, but also discouraged profit-seeking.

Unlike Weber's ideal type, Puritans could not simply focus on one directive while ignoring its opposite. They were obligated to follow the entire religion. They could not easily wind up with a creed like Weber described.

It would be unnecessarily restrictive to eschew the ideal-type method wherever a religion contains contradictory beliefs. However, if a religion is notoriously inconsistent, its ideal type should include the various inconsistencies and contradictions rather than being the most consistent logical system the investigator can piece together from a selection of its beliefs.

It is ironic that after imposing a false consistency Weber ([1904–5] 1958:128, see also p. 170) concluded that neo-Calvinism was so powerful because it was so consistent.[18] In fact, just the opposite occurred. Because Puritanism was inconsistent, its effects were weak. It could not produce uniformity of action. For example, since it generated both security and anxiety, Puritans were found with various degrees confidence. Moreover, the signs pursued depended partly on which preachers' guidance one was following. Some heightened their levels of activity, works, and performance of duties while others turned inward to search their hearts. This definitely represents a scattering of energies. Puritanism's pull would have been stronger if unidirectional.

Clearly the behavioral outcome of a religious tenet depends on more than its own logic. It must be evaluated in its context. When it coexists with conflicting beliefs, its effect will be the product of people's efforts to reconcile inconsistent directives. Insofar as the ideal-type method ignores inconsistent religious logic, it loses that level of complexity.

A further danger of this method is the combining of elements in the "type" that were never connected in reality. The type implies that these elements worked together when in fact they never did. The most critical example of this is Weber's combination of profit motive, rational calculation, and sense of duty in the "spirit of capitalism." This complex combination has proven elusive in business history. Another example is the combining of predestination with innerworldly activity; by the time it grew more active, Puritanism had become less Calvinistic. Similarly, Weber should not have combined predestination with a focus on works. It is where Puritans sought the means of salvation that works became most relevant.

A final caveat regarding Weber's use of ideal types is that he never followed through completely with the method. Selection of evidence is permissible when constructing a type only if the type is subsequently used in a historical study as a yardstick for measuring reality. Reality is to be assessed through comparison to the type; the type itself is not to be taken as reality (see Weber [1904–5] 1958:183). However, Weber never carried out two distinct analyses (see Chapter 1 above); he telescoped the formulation of the type and the derivation of conclusions into a single step. Consequently, it is difficult to tell which of his historical statements are merely illustrative aids to the presentation of the ideal type and which are to be considered evidence. If Weber's ideal type is seen as preparatory to an investigation, its selective character is no drawback (see Weber [1904–5] 1958:183). However, if his argument is taken as a historical conclusion, the method of ideal types will remain short-circuited and the results misleading.

The Scope of Weber's Analysis

Weber has been criticized for the relatively narrow focus of his early *Protestant Ethic and the Spirit of Capitalism*. However, his later writings broadened and extended his earlier work, overcoming whatever omissions may have limited his scope earlier. For example, *General Economic History* rightly emphasized nonreligious factors in the transformation to capitalism. In this work Weber made it clear that Protestantism must share the credit for capitalist development. Not only did this balance his early attention to the religious factor, but the later writings probably include his best contributions to the understanding of that transformation (see Collins 1980). Similarly, the "Protestant Sects" article, by emphasizing religious discipline, balances his earlier emphasis on salvation premia. It explains why nonpredestinarian Protestants could also contribute significantly to capitalist growth.

Although *The Protestant Ethic and the Spirit of Capitalism* contrasted neo-Calvinism's support for capitalism with the inward piety of Lutheranism and with Roman Catholicism's magical means of salvation, Weber's later work emphasized the differences between Occidental and Oriental religion. The latter's impediments to modern capitalism were outlined, and Occidental religion was treated more as a whole in contributing to societal transformation. This later approach is an improvement because religious effects on modern capitalism, including cultural effects, may be seen as stemming from the Judeo-Christian tradition, not just from neo-Calvinism (see Collins 1996:xx–xxi).

The rationalization of ethics provides a good example. Weber noted the contribution of the Ten Commandments and of the Hebrew prophets to this development in addition to that of Protestantism. Another important example is the work ethic, which can be found to some degree in Christian groups throughout history. Similarly, all of the Judeo-Christian faiths fostered discipline because they required impulse control in order to avoid sin. Also, Catholic businessmen of the Italian Renaissance invented some rational techniques central to modern capitalism. Nor were Puritans the only ones to justify capitalist activity: for example, Italian Renaissance funeral orations glorified merchants' contributions to civic prosperity.

In short, despite some interfaith variations, Weber did well in his later writings to stress the contributions of several different Judeo-Christian religions. Their cumulative effect seems more important than the differences between them.

Of course, this later emphasis is not entirely consistent with what Weber wrote earlier. After minimizing the contributions of Judaism, Lutheranism, and Catholicism early on, it is something of a turnabout to point to their effectiveness later. For example, Weber had specifically denied that Jews bore the capitalist ethos.

Moreover, since much of his comparative religion had adopted the format of a contrast with ascetic Protestantism, one cannot say that neo-Calvinism held no special place in his later works. The Puritans were always at the center of Weber's comparative world-religion.

The Protestant Ethic Debate Now

To resolve some of the disputes between Weber's supporters and critics, new evidence has been garnered and existing evidence applied in new ways. It shows Weber's argument to be neither all right nor all wrong; neither staunch Weber supporters nor extreme critics are correct.

Critiques of Weber's thesis have often been unfair because they have ignored some of his most sophisticated arguments. Among these are the work ethic, the duty to become rich to serve God, innerworldliness, and the unintended fostering of disciplined rationality, some of which are supported by the data. Some critics fail to balance the evidence against Weber with the evidence that supports him, attribute Puritanism's inconsistencies to Weber (MacKinnon 1988b:207), and/or exaggerate the importance of some of his small errors (MacKinnon 1988b:189–94). Still, they have not been able to disprove the valid parts of his work.

On the other hand, Weber's supporters tend not to acknowledge that Puritanism's traditional, otherworldly, and antimaterialistic parts have countered its more positive contributions to modern capitalism. Also, even though Rachfahl and some other early critics did misinterpret Weber, their arguments should not have been completely dismissed. Since Weber did exaggerate both the impact of neo-Calvinism on modern capitalism and the number of mechanisms through which this influence occurred, some criticism has been deserved. Despite Weber's genius and theoretical elegance, and despite the formative role of his work in shaping present knowledge, some parts of his argument must be discarded or modified.

Since the data before us are limited to one Protestant group and a couple of entrepreneurs, the conclusions presented here are by no means final. Nevertheless, this evidence shifts the burden of proof onto Weber's defenders to unearth new diaries and to analyze more Protestant religions if they choose to support his original thesis.

THE ECONOMIC IMPACT OF RELIGION

Weber's original study was important theoretically because it combated economic determinism by showing religion's economic influence. That issue is no longer pressing today but related issues are. The case of Protestantism's impact on capitalism helps theorists assess the relative importance of material and ideational factors in shaping economic institutions. It sheds light on the strength of the religious factor, and shows how it operates. It is a prime example, if not *the* prime example, of religion's economic impact.

It seems clear that a number of religious groups, not all Protestant, have aided capitalism in a variety of ways. They have strengthened the work ethic, encouraged saving, and helped to legitimate capitalism. These positive contributions have countered their anticapitalist devaluation of wealth and worldly pursuits.

Religion's positive economic effects have not been limited to the few examples originally pointed out by Weber. The applicability of his insights on religion and economy does not stop with predestinarianism, Protestantism, or capitalism's early years. Rather, religion has invigorated economic life from time to time and continues to do so. This effect is a repeated sociological pattern, not a unique historical case. Redfield (1950) in Mexico, Willems (1968) in Brazil and Chile, Kanagy (1990) elsewhere in Latin America, and Lenski (1961), Johnson (1961), and Dearman (1974) in the United States have found the work ethic, active participation in trade, and disproportionate economic success in modern-day religious groups.

Furthermore, though Weber ([1904–5] 1958:180–83; [1923] 1961:261–70) expected religion to have positive economic effects only in the Occident, non-Christian Asian religious groups like the Jodo Buddhists (Nakamura 1956; Bellah 1957; Pieris 1968), Santri Muslims (Geertz 1968), Zoroastrian Parsis (McClelland 1961; Kennedy 1963), and the Jains and Vishnavas (McClelland 1961) have dominated trade because their religious ethics have encouraged diligence, thrift, individualism, and profit. It is ironic when a sociologist considers his theory helpful for understanding just a few historical cases, and then to have research prove the theory much more general in its usefulness and applicability.

Religion, when it is effective, has power over the economic behavior of its adherents. It dragged Wallington to his shop despite his weak personal interest in business. Conversely, it made Pledger guilty about his pursuit of business and kept Wallington from pursuing profit strategies that violated traditional market ethics. Not only could it promote capitalist action but it could constrain businessmen to behave contrary to their economic interests. It countered self-interest with religious ethics.

Yet, despite their power to counter material interests among pious Puritans, religious ethics were and are no match in strength for material interests. Weber was wise to emphasize the *economic* causes of modern capitalist development in his later work. Despite its ability to strengthen modern capitalism, religion was not and is not among its prime movers.

The primacy of material forces is apparent at several points in this analysis. First of all, business rationality provided a model for religious rationality rather than the reverse. It was not an outgrowth of religious forces and in fact was quite well developed prior to the precisianism of ascetic Protestantism. Second, the Puritan work ethic, with its opposition to idleness, served bourgeois economic interests both because it raised labor productivity and because it was part of a bourgeois critique of the idle rentier class. The appeal of this ethic to the civic strata encouraged its emphasis by Puritan divines (see Yinger 1957:215–16 and Pope 1942). Finally, as a third example of the primacy of material forces, religious justifications of capitalism developed after it, as if responding to the dominant economic base.

Because much of Puritanism's impact came through cultural effects, it was felt later, after modern capitalism had reached maturity. It came too late to produce the new system's characteristics, so it could only reinforce what had already taken form. Since Puritanism had passed its peak by this time, it lacked the adherents and the moral force to impose its ideas onto modern society. Nor did nonbelievers feel subject to its religious sanctions. It could not simply slam the monastery door behind it and stride into the marketplace of life. Having lost the capacity to initiate, its influence had to be more passive. Its ideas were adopted only when they

were consonant with dominant cultural values, i.e., when they supported
the material interests of the dominant elites. The nineteenth century appropriated the ethics of work and saving while rejecting the Puritans' suspicion of wealth, otherworldliness, and conservative business ethics.

There was no continuous chain of influence through which the Puritan
torch and flame were passed to the nineteenth century. However, the Victorian period was an age of revivals. Their Gothic revival in architecture
and pre-Raphaelitism in art are only two notable examples. In the moral
sphere Victorian puritanism became, in part, a throwback to seventeenth-
century religious asceticism with its emphasis on the particular calling.
Thus, the saints were able to impact the mainstream.

Their influence must be qualified, though, in several ways. First, since
cultural borrowing was selective, many of their most cherished tenets
were overlooked. Second, any cultural revival puts the older ideas into
the context of the new age, so they become part of something new rather
than remaining what they had been before. Third, and of special importance, once Puritanism had lost its initiative in the cultural influence
process, it lost its ability to compel behaviors contrary to material interests. Hence the selection of tenets and the form of the synthesis show a
procapitalist bias, and are best explained through reference to material
rather than religious factors.

From this case study, the economic impact of religion, though not in-
significant, seems less than revolutionary. Its relative weakness can be
seen in comparison to its stronger political impact. The Puritan "revolution of the saints" (see Walzer 1965; Little 1969; Zaret 1985) provides just
one example of religion's political power. Even more powerful are today's
Islamic fundamentalist movements, and in America the influence of the
New Christian Right comes to mind. One reason why religion impacts
politics so strongly is that its moral codes can become political issues, and
are often translated into law. Another is that religious legitimation is more
critical to the survivability of a political regime than to an economic system. By comparison, religion has affected the economy quite moderately.

NOTES

1. The Puritans were not carriers (Träger) of economic rationality.

2. Weber argued that the psychological consequences of Puritanism aided capitalism despite their moral opposition to a number of capitalist practices. In his
view a Puritan socialization produced an ascetic personality suitable for rational
capitalist action. However, the evidence here does not confirm this.

3. Weber ([1922] 1968:588) thought that God legitimated hard work, which in
turn legitimated profits. This logic breaks down because the Puritans did not be-

lieve that human effort created profits; God did, and not everyone who worked hard deserved God's gift of success.

4. For example, sincere efforts usually counted as works. The Puritan doctrine of works was tougher than the Anglican and Lutheran versions but easier than Catholicism's insistence on meritorious good works.

5. Since works could not earn merit as they did in Catholicism, the aim was not to accumulate more and more works. A modest output was sufficient to confirm the imperfect faith most Puritans deemed possible in this life.

6. One suspects that the most pious were most likely to work hard out of the conviction that they were serving God and humankind. The less pious would be more oriented toward religious rewards.

7. Probably including some mechanisms that have not been discussed because they fall outside the scope of this book. These include the contributions of Protestantism toward the rationalization of capitalism's supporting institutions such as science, law, and the modern state.

8. The details of this cultural process need to be tracked down in a further study. It is just sketched out here.

9. When John Wallington, Sr., worked at his shop on the Sabbath, he was obviously not there to do his religious duty.

10. Wesley's attitude toward profit, at least in the passage quoted by Weber ([1904–5] 1958:175), remained mixed rather than wholeheartedly approving. So Christian attitudes still remained mixed about profits as late as the eighteenth century.

11. Rational psychological effects were countered by the Puritan ideal of being meek and lowly (see Baxter [1650] 1962:128).

12. However, Puritanism may have contributed to the organization of time in Occidental culture and business. Puritans sought to redeem time, and the doctrine of the calling appointed set times for work tasks.

13. The flow of charity strengthened the perception that capitalism produced civic benefit.

14. Weber's assessments of the Baptists and Methodists seem more accurate because there is no claim that their impact has hinged on the predestination doctrine.

15. Baxter was also atypical on the doctrines of free grace, perseverance, substitution of the will for the deed, and the gaining of salvation through works.

16. Weber mistakenly relegated salvation by faith to the formal doctrinal level, but it was central to practical pastoral work and to the consciousness of the believer.

17. Kalberg (1994) points out that Weber used ideal types differently in this analysis than in his other works.

18. More accurate was his ([1904–5] 1958:169) observation that "Puritanism included a world of contradictions." Weber (1946:332, see also p. 291) knew that it was a "paradox" that Puritanism considered the calling a means of serving God and yet at the same time devalued the world as "creatural and depraved." He saw some of the inconsistencies in Puritanism despite his emphasis on Puritan consistency.

References

Alexander, Jeffrey C. 1982. *Theoretical Logic in Sociology.* Volume 3, *The Classical Attempt at Theoretical Synthesis: Max Weber.* Berkeley: University of California Press.

Ames, William. [1639] 1975. *Conscience and Cases Thereof.* Amsterdam: Theatrum Orbis Terrarum, Ltd., and Norwood, NJ: Walter J. Johnson.

Ball, John. 1632. *A Treatise of Faith.* London: George Miller.

Baron, Hans. 1969. "A New Attitude Toward Wealth." Pp. 173–82 in *Social and Economic Foundations of the Italian Renaissance,* edited by Anthony Molho. New York: John Wiley and Sons.

Baxter, Richard. 1653. *The Right Method for a Settled Peace of Conscience, and Spiritual Comfort.* T. Underhill.

Baxter, Richard. 1678. *Christian Directory, or a Summ of Practical Theologie.* London: Nevill Simmons.

Baxter, Richard. [1696] 1931. *The Autobiography of Richard Baxter being the Reliquiae Baxterianae* (abridged). New York: E. P. Dutton.

Baxter, Richard. [1650] 1962. *The Saints' Everlasting Rest* (abridged). London: Epworth.

Beetham, David. 1985. *Max Weber and the Theory of Modern Politics,* 2nd ed. New York: Basil Blackwell.

Bellah, Robert. 1957. *Tokugawa Religion: The Values of Pre-Industrial Japan.* Glencoe, IL: Free Press.

Boddington, George. Diary. Manuscript 10823. Guildhall Library, London.

Breward, Ian, ed. 1970. *The Work of William Perkins.* Appleford, England: Sutton Courtenay.

Bridenbaugh, Carl. 1968. *Vexed and Troubled Englishmen 1590–1642.* New York: Oxford University Press.

Burton, William. 1634. *The Rousing of the Sluggard, Delivered in Seven Sermons.* London.

Cartwright, Thomas [1599] 1969. *A Christian Letter of Certaine English Protestants.* Amsterdam: Theatrum Orbis Terrarum, and New York: Da Capo.

Clayre, Alisdair. 1974. *Work and Play: Ideas and Experiences of Work and Leisure.* New York: Harper and Row.

Cohen, Jere. 1980. "Rational Capitalism in Renaissance Italy." *American Journal of Sociology* 85:1340–55.

Collins, Randall. 1980. "Weber's Last Theory of Capitalism: A Schematization." *American Sociological Review* 45:925–42.

Collins, Randall. 1996. "Introduction." Pp. vii–xxxiii in Max Weber, *The Protestant Ethic and the Spirit of Capitalism.* Los Angeles: Roxbury.

Collinson, Patrick. 1967. *The Elizabethan Puritan Movement*. Berkeley: University of California Press.

Collinson, Patrick. 1982. *The Religion of Protestants: The Church in English Society, 1559–1625*. Oxford: Oxford University Press.

Collinson, Patrick. 1988. *The Birthpangs of Protestant England: Religion and Cultural Change in the 16th and 17th Centuries*. New York: St. Martins.

Coolidge, John. 1970. *The Pauline Renaissance in England*. Oxford: Clarendon.

Cragg, Gerald. 1957. *Puritanism in the Period of the Great Persecution 1660–1688*. Cambridge: Cambridge University Press.

Cragg, Gerald. 1975. *Freedom and Authority: A Study of English Thought in the Early Seventeenth Century*. Philadelphia: Westminster.

Davies, Horton. 1975. *Worship and Theology in England: From Andrewes to Baxter and Fox, 1603–1690*. Princeton, NJ: Princeton University Press.

Dearman, Marion. 1974. "Christ and Conformity: A Study of Pentecostal Values." *Journal for the Scientific Study of Religion* 13:437–53.

Dent, Arthur. [1601] 1974. *The Plaine Man's Path-Way to Heaven*. Amsterdam: Theatrum Orbis Terrarum, and Norwood, NJ: Walter J. Johnson.

deRoover, Raymond. 1963. "The Scholastic Attitude Toward Trade and Entrepreneurship." *Explorations in Economic Research* 1:76–87.

Downame, John. [1604] 1974. *The Christian Warfare*. Amsterdam: Theatrum Orbis Terrarum, and Norwood, NJ: Walter J. Johnson.

Eisenstadt, S. N. 1968. *The Protestant Ethic and Modernization: A Comparative View*. New York: Basic Books.

Eisenstadt, S. N. 1973. "The Implications of Weber's Sociology for Understanding Processes of Change in Contemporary Non-European Societies and Civilizations." Pp. 131–55 in *Essays in the Scientific Study of Religion*, edited by Charles Y. Glock and Phillip C. Hammond. New York: Harper Torchbooks.

Elyot, Sir Thomas. [1531] 1937. *The Gouernour*. London: J. M. Dent and Sons, and New York: E. P. Dutton.

Emerson, Everett. 1968. *English Puritanism from John Hooper to John Milton*. Durham, NC: Duke University Press.

Eusden, John. 1958. *Puritans, Lawyers and Politics in Early Seventeenth-Century England*. New Haven, CT: Yale University Press.

Fanfani, Amintore. 1935. *Catholicism, Protestantism, and Capitalism*. London: Sheed and Ward.

Fischoff, Ephraim. 1944. "The Protestant Ethic and the Spirit of Capitalism: The History of a Controversy." *Social Research* 2:61–77.

Flavel, John. 1968. *The Works of John Flavel*, Vol. 5. London: Banner of Truth Trust.

Flynn, John S. 1920. *The Influence of Puritanism on the Political and Religious Thought of the English*. London: John Murray.

Foster, Stephen. 1991. *The Long Argument: English Puritanism and the Shaping of New England Culture; 1570–1700*. Chapel Hill: University of North Carolina Press.

Franklin, Benjamin. 1964. *Autobiography*. Edited and introduced by Leonard Labaree et al. New Haven, CT: Yale University Press.

Franklin, Benjamin. 1795. *The Way to Wealth*. Paris: A. Renouard.

Franklin, Benjamin. 1981. *Autobiography*. Edited by J. Lemay and P. Zall. Knoxville: University of Tennessee Press.

Franklin, Benjamin. 1900. *Poor Richard's Almanac*. New York: Caldwell.

Geertz, Clifford. 1968. "Religious Belief and Economic Behavior in a Central Javanese Town." Pp. 309–42 in *The Protestant Ethic and Modernization: A Comparative View*, edited by S. N. Eisenstadt. New York: Basic Books.

George, Charles, and Katherine George. 1958. "Protestantism and Capitalism in England." *Church History* 27:351–71.

Graham, W. Fred. 1971. *The Constructive Revolutionary; John Calvin and His Socioeconomic Impact*. Richmond, VA: John Knox.

Grassby, Richard. 1978. "Social Mobility and Business Enterprise in Seventeenth Century England." Pp. 355–81 in *Puritans and Revolutionaries*, edited by Donald Pennington and Keith Thomas. Oxford: Clarendon.

Grassby, Richard. 1995. *The Business Community of Seventeenth Century England*. Cambridge: Cambridge University Press.

Greaves, Richard. 1981. *Society and Religion in Elizabethan England*. Minneapolis: University of Minnesota Press.

Green, Robert W., ed. 1965. *Protestantism and Capitalism: The Weber Thesis and Its Critics*. Boston: D. C. Heath.

Haller, William. [1938] 1972. *The Rise of Puritanism*. Philadelphia: University of Pennsylvania Press.

Hamilton, Richard F. 1996. *The Social Misconstruction of Reality: Validity and Verification in the Scholarly Community*. New Haven, CT: Yale University Press.

Herlihy, David. 1969. "Civic Humanitarianism at Pistoia." Pp. 205–13 in *Social and Economic Foundations of the Italian Renaissance*, edited by Anthony Molho. New York: John Wiley and Sons.

Hill, Christopher. 1958. *Puritanism and Revolution: The English Revolution of the Seventeenth Century*. New York: Schocken.

Hill, Christopher. 1964. *Society and Puritanism in Pre-Revolutionary England*. New York: Schocken.

Hill, Christopher. 1970. *God's Englishman: Oliver Cromwell and the English Revolution*. New York: Dial.

Hill, Christopher. 1975. *Change and Continuity in Seventeenth Century England*. Cambridge, MA: Harvard University Press.

Hill, Robert. [1613] 1975. *The Pathway to Prayer and Pietie*. Amsterdam: Theatrum Orbis Terrarum, and Norwood, NJ: Walter J. Johnson.

Holifield, E. Brooks. 1974. *The Covenant Sealed: The Development of Puritan Sacramental Theology in Old and New England 1570–1720*. New Haven, CT: Yale University Press.

Homans, George. 1961. *Social Behavior: Its Elementary Forms*. New York: Harcourt, Brace, and World.

Houghton, Walter. 1957. *The Victorian Frame of Mind 1830–1870*. London: Yale University Press.

Howe, Richard. 1978. "Max Weber's Elective Affinities: Sociology within the Bounds of Pure Reason." *American Journal of Sociology* 84:366–85.

Hudson, Winthrop. 1949. "Puritanism and the Spirit of Capitalism." *Church History* 18:3–17.

Hyma, Albert. 1951. *Renaissance to Reformation*. Grand Rapids, MI: William Erdmans.

Johnson, Benton, 1961. "Do Holiness Sects Socialize in Dominant Values?" *Social Forces* 39:309–16.

Johnson, James. 1970. *A Society Ordained by God*. New York: Abingdon.

Kaelber, Lutz. 1998. *Schools of Asceticism: Ideology and Organization in Medieval Religious Communities*. University Park: Pennsylvania State University Press.

Kalberg, Stephen. 1994. *Max Weber's Comparative-Historical Sociology*. Chicago: University of Chicago Press.

Kanagy, Conrad. 1990. "The Formation and Development of a Protestant Conversion Movement among the Highland Quichua of Ecuador." *Sociological Analysis* 51:205–17.

Keebler, N. H. 1982. *Richard Baxter, Puritan Man of Letters*. Oxford: Clarendon.

Kennedy, Robert. 1963. "The Protestant Ethic and the Parsis." *American Journal of Sociology* 68:11–20.

Knappen, M. M. 1933. *Two Elizabethan Puritan Diaries*. Chicago: American Society of Church History.

Knappen, M. M. 1965. *Tudor Puritanism*. Chicago: University of Chicago Press.

Knott, John. 1980. *The Sword of the Spirit*. Chicago: University of Chicago Press.

Lake, Peter. 1982. *Moderate Puritans and the Elizabethan Church*. New York: Cambridge University Press.

Lehmann, Hartmut and Guenther Roth. 1993. *Weber's Protestant Ethic: Origins, Evidence, Context*. New York: Cambridge University Press.

Lenski, Gerhard. 1961. *The Religious Factor*. Garden City, NY: Anchor-Doubleday.

Little, David. 1969. *Religion, Order and Law*. New York: Harper and Row.

Luthy, Herbert. 1960. *From Calvin to Rousseau*. New York: Basic Books.

MacKinnon, Malcolm. 1988a. "Calvinism and the Infallible Assurance of Grace: The Weber Thesis Reconsidered." *British Journal of Sociology* 39:143–77.

MacKinnon, Malcolm. 1988b. "Weber's Exploration of Calvinism: The Undiscovered Provenance of Capitalism." *British Journal of Sociology* 39:178–210.

Mann, Michael. 1986. *The Sources of Social Power*. Volume 1, *A History of Power from the Beginning to A.D. 1760*. Cambridge: Cambridge University Press.

Marlowe, John. 1956. *The Puritan Tradition in English Life*. London: Cresset.

Marshall, Gordon. 1980. *Presbyteries and Profits: Calvinism and the Development of Capitalism in Scotland, 1560–1707*. Oxford: Clarendon.

Marshall, Gordon. 1982. *In Search of the Spirit of Capitalism: An Essay on Max Weber's Protestant Ethic Thesis*. New York: Columbia University Press.

Martin, Hugh. 1954. *Puritanism and Richard Baxter*. London: SCM.

Mather, Cotton. [1710] 1966. *Bonifacius: An Essay upon the Good*. Cambridge, MA: Harvard University Press.

McClelland, David C. 1961. *The Achieving Society*. Princeton, NJ: Van Nostrand.

McGee, J. Sears. 1976. *The Godly Man in Stuart England*. New Haven, CT: Yale University Press.

Merton, Robert. 1968. *Social Theory and Social Structure*. New York: Free Press.

Michaelsen, Robert. 1953. "Changes in the Puritan Concept of Calling or Vocation." *New England Quarterly* 26:315–36.

Miller, Perry. 1933. *Orthodoxy in Massachusetts*. Cambridge, MA: Harvard University Press.

Miller, Perry. 1963. *The New England Mind—The Seventeenth Century*. Cambridge, MA: Harvard University Press.

Mosse, George L. 1968. *The Holy Pretence*. New York: Howard Fertig.

Nakamura, Hajime. 1956. "The Vitality of Religion in Asia." Pp. 53–66 in *Cultural Freedom in Asia*, edited by Herbert Passin. Rutland, VT: Charles E. Tuttle.

Nelson, Benjamin. 1949. *The Idea of Usury: From Tribal Brotherhood to Universal Otherhood*. Princeton, NJ: Princeton University Press.

New, John. 1964. *Anglican and Puritan*. Stanford, CA: Stanford University Press.

Nuttall, Geoffrey. 1965. *Richard Baxter*. London: Thomas Nelson and Sons, Ltd.

O'Connell, Laura S. 1976. "Anti-Entrepreneurial Attitudes in Elizabethan Sermons and Popular Literature." *Journal of British Studies* 15:1–20.

Peel, Albert. 1937. *Robert Crowley: Puritan, Printer, Poet*. Manchester: R. Aikman and Son.

Peel, Albert and Leland Carson. 1951. *Cartwrightiana: A Catechism by Thomas Cartwright*. London: Allen and Unwin.

Perkins, William. 1601. *The True Gaine: More in Worth then all the Goods in the World*. London: John Legatt.

Perkins, William. [1606] 1972. *A Treatise of Conscience*. Amsterdam: Theatrum Orbis Terrarum, and New York: Da Capo.

Perkins, William. 1615. *A Graine of Musterd Seede: Or, the Least Measure of Grace that is or can be Effectuall to Salvation* and *How to Live and That Well, For All Estates and Times*. London: John Legatt.

Perkins, William. 1970. *The Work of William Perkins*, edited by Ian Breward. Appleford, England: Sutton Courtenay.

Pettit, Norman. 1966. *The Heart Prepared: Grace and Conversion in Puritan Spiritual Life*. New Haven, CT: Yale University Press.

Pieris, Ralph. 1968. "Economic Development and Ultramundaneity." Pp. 252–58 in *The Protestant Ethic and Modernization: A Comparative View*, edited by S. N. Eisenstadt. New York: Basic Books.

Pledger, Elias. Diary. Dr. Williams' Library, London.

Poggi, Gianfranco. 1983. *Calvinism and the Capitalist Spirit*. Amherst: University of Massachusetts Press.

Pope, Liston. 1942. *Millhands and Preachers*. New Haven, CT: Yale University Press.

Porter, Harry C. 1971. *Puritanism in Tudor England*. Columbia: University of South Carolina Press.

Preston, John. [1629] 1976. *The Saints Daily Exercise*. Amsterdam: Theatrum Orbis Terrarum, and Norwood, NJ: Walter J. Johnson.

Price, Daniel. [1608] 1979. *The Marchant*. Amsterdam: Theatrum Orbis Terrarum, and Norwood, NJ: Walter J. Johnson.

Redfield, Robert. 1950. *A Village That Chose Progress*. Chicago: University of Chicago Press.

Reilly, Bartholomew. 1948. *The Elizabethan Puritan's Conception of the Nature and Destiny of Fallen Man*. Dissertation for the degree of Doctor of Sacred Theology, Catholic University of America. Washington, DC: Catholic University of America Press.

Rose, Michael. 1985. *Re-Working the Work Ethic: Economic Values and Socio-Cultural Politics*. New York: Schocken.

Rowdon, Harold H. 1958. *Puritan Church Discipline*. London: London Bible College.

Saltmarsh, John. [1647] 1847. *Sparkles of Glory*. London: William Pickering.

Saltmarsh, John. 1649. *Free Grace: Or, The Flowings of Christs Blood Freely to Sinners*. London: Giles Calvert.

Samuelsson, Kurt. 1961. *Religion and Economic Action*. New York: Harper Torchbooks.

Scott, William. [1635] 1953. *An Essay of Drapery*. Cambridge, MA: Kress Library of Business and Economics.

Scudder, Henry. [1673] 1813. *The Christian's Daily Walk in Holy Security and Peace*. London: J. Banfield.

Seaver, Paul. 1980. "The Puritan Work Ethic Revisited." *Journal of British Studies* 19:35–53.

Seaver, Paul. 1985. *Wallington's World: A Puritan Artisan in Seventeenth-Century London*. Stanford, CA: Stanford University Press.

Seller, Abednego. [1679] 1803. *An Infallible Way to Contentment*. British Library, London.

Simpson, Alan. 1955. *Puritanism in Old and New England*. Chicago: University of Chicago Press.

Smith, Henry. [1599] 1976. *Three Sermons*. Amsterdam: Theatrum Orbis Terrarum, and Norwood, NJ: Walter J. Johnson.

Sommerville, C. John. 1981. "The Anti-Puritan Work Ethic." *Journal of British Studies* 20:70–81.

Sprunger, Keith L. 1972. *The Learned Doctor William Ames*. Urbana: University of Illinois Press.

Stannard, David. 1977. *The Puritan Way of Death*. New York: Oxford University Press.

Stearns, Raymond. 1954. *The Strenuous Puritan*. Urbana: University of Illinois Press.

Stockton, Dorothy. Diary. Dr. Williams' Library, London.

Stockton, Owen. Diary. Dr. Williams' Library, London.

Swinnock, George. 1663. *The Christian-Mans Calling, or a Treatise of Making Religion One's Business*. London: Parkhurst.

Tawney, R. H. [1926] 1961. *Religion and the Rise of Capitalism*. New York: Mentor.

Thrupp, Sylvia. 1953. "Introduction." Pp. 1–13 in William Scott, *An Essay of Drapery*. Cambridge, MA: Kress Library of Business and Economics.

Trevor-Roper, Hugh. 1972. *Religion, the Reformation, and Social Change*. London: MacMillan.

Walker, Eric. 1970. *William Dell, Master Puritan*. Cambridge, England: W. Heffner and Sons.

Wallington, Nehemiah. British diary. "The Growth of a Christian." Additional manuscript 40,883. British Library, London.

Wallington, Nehemiah. Folger diary. "Extract of the Passages of My Life." Manuscript V.a. 436. Folger Library, Washington, DC.

Wallington, Nehemiah. Letters. Sloane manuscript 922. British Library, London.

Walzer, Michael. 1965. *The Revolution of the Saints: A Study in the Origins of Radical Politics*. Cambridge, MA: Harvard University Press.

Watkins, Owen. 1972. *The Puritan Experience*. New York: Schocken.

Weber, Max. [1904–5] 1958. *The Protestant Ethic and the Spirit of Capitalism*. New York: Charles Scribner's Sons.

Weber, Max. [1922] 1963. *The Sociology of Religion*. Boston: Beacon.

Weber, Max. [1922] 1968. *Economy and Society*. New York: Bedminster.

Weber, Max. [1923] 1961. *General Economic History*. New York: Collier.

Weber, Max. 1946. "The Protestant Sects and the Spirit of Capitalism." Pp. 302–22 in *From Max Weber: Essays in Sociology*, edited by H. Gerth and C. W. Mills. New York: Oxford University Press.

Weber, Max. 1951. *The Religion of China*. Glencoe, IL: Free Press.

Willems, Emilio. 1968. "Culture Change and the Rise of Protestantism in Brazil and Chile." Pp. 184–210 in *The Protestant Ethic and Modernization: A Comparative View*, edited by S. N. Eisenstadt. New York: Basic Books.

Wright, Louis, ed. 1958. *Middle-Class Culture in Elizabethan England*. Ithaca, NY: Cornell University Press.

Yinger, Milton. 1957. *Religion, Society, and the Individual*. New York: Macmillan.

Zaret, David. 1985. *The Heavenly Contract: Ideology and Organization in Pre-Revolutionary Puritanism*. Chicago: University of Chicago Press.

Zaret, David. 1992. "Calvin, Covenant Theology, and the Weber Thesis." *British Journal of Sociology* 43:369–91.

Appendix

List of Puritan Divines

Thomas Adams
Isaac Ambrose
Williams Ames
Abdias Ashton
John Ball
Richard Baxter
Paul Baynes
John Beadle
Thomas Bedford
John Benbrigge
Richard Bernard
Thomas Blake
Robert Bolton
John Boyes
William Bradshaw
Thomas Brooks
Peter Bulkeley
Cornelius Burges
William Burton
Thomas Cartwright
Lawrence Chaderton
John Cotton
William Crompton
Henry Crosse
Robert Crowley
Ezekiel Culverwell

John Davenport
Arthur Dent
Edward Dering
John Dod
Thomas Doolittle
John Downame
Roger Drake
Thomas Erastus
George Estye
Simonds d'Ewes
William Fenner
Giles Firmin
John Flavel
John Foxe
George Gillespie
Thomas Goodwin
William Gouge
Richard Greenham
Joseph Hall
Arthur Hildersam
Robert Hill
Richard Hodges
Nathaniel Holmes
Thomas Hooker
John Howe
John Humfrey

Henry Jacob
Francis Johnson
Nicholas Lockyer
Cotton Mather
John Owen
William Perkins
Hugh Peter
John Preston
Daniel Price
William Prynne
Richard Rogers
John Saltmarsh
Henry Scudder
Abednego Seller
Richard Sibbes
Henry Smith
George Swinnock
Thomas Taylor
John Timson
William Tyndale
Samuel Ward
William Whately
William Whitaker
Thomas Wilcox
John Winthrop

Index

285